A   CO

THE SEATTLE &
VANCOUVER BOOK

Sailboats at Vancouver's downtown waterfront Toshi

1ST EDITION

THE SEATTLE & VANCOUVER BOOK

Ray Chatelin

The Countryman Press
Woodstock, Vermont

To the memory of my father, Hugo Chatelin, whose heart was in the Pacific Northwest but for whom circumstance compelled him to remain to the end in the American Midwest. His all-too-infrequent visits were highlighted by the walks we took along the waterfront in the light morning drizzle and by the conversations that always ended with his wish to one day live here. The lingering smell of the cedar trees he liked so much and the joy he got from being with our Newfoundland dog as the animal led him along his own favorite woodland and waterside haunts are forever in my heart and mind.

We welcome your comments and suggestions. Please contact Great Destinations Guide Editor, The Countryman Press, P.O. Box 748, Woodstock, VT 05091, or e-mail countrymanpress@wwnorton.com.

ISBN 1-58157-027-9
ISSN 1552-9959

Maps by Mapping Specialists Ltd., © The Countryman Press
Book design by Bodenweber Design
Text composition by Melinda Belter
Cover photograph by of Canada Place exterior © Gunter Marx Photography/Corbis
Cover photograph of Seattle, Washington © PNC/Getty Images
Interior photographs by Toshi unless otherwise indicated

Published by The Countryman Press, P.O. Box 748, Woodstock, VT 05091

Distributed by W. W. Norton & Company, Inc., 500 Fifth Avenue, New York, NY 10110

Printed in the United States of America

10 9 8 7 6 5 4 3 2 1

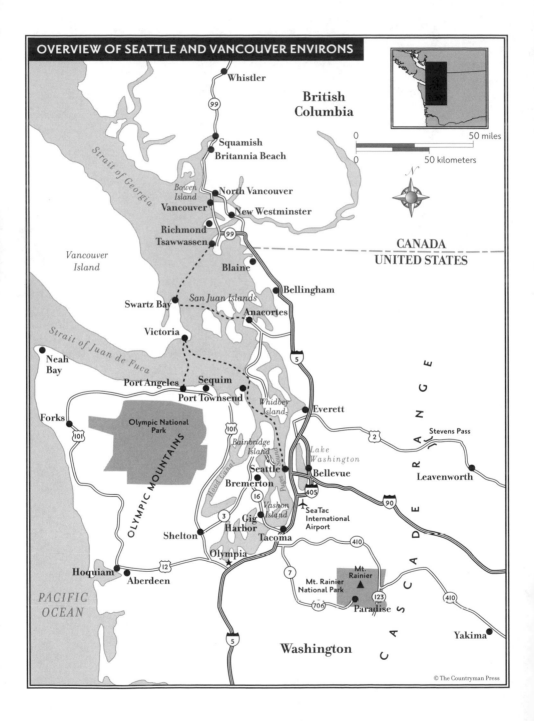

OVERVIEW OF SEATTLE AND VANCOUVER ENVIRONS

Whistler

British Columbia

0   50 miles

0   50 kilometers

N

Strait of Georgia

Squamish
Britannia Beach

Bowen Island
North Vancouver
Vancouver
New Westminster
Richmond
Tsawwassen

CANADA
UNITED STATES

Vancouver Island

Blaine

Bellingham

San Juan Islands
Swartz Bay
Anacortes

Victoria

Strait of Juan de Fuca

Neah Bay

Port Angeles   Sequim
Port Townsend

Whidbey Island

Everett

Forks

Olympic National Park

Bainbridge Island

Lake Washington

Stevens Pass

Puget Sound

O L Y M P I C   M O U N T A I N S

Hood Canal

Seattle
Bremerton

Bellevue

Leavenworth

Vashon Island

SeaTac International Airport

Gig Harbor
Shelton

Tacoma

Olympia

Mt. Rainier

Hoquiam
Aberdeen

Mt. Rainier National Park

Paradise

PACIFIC OCEAN

Washington

Yakima

C A S C A D E   R A N G E

© The Countryman Press

Contents

MAPS

Acknowledgments

The first time I stepped off an aircraft at Vancouver International Airport, back when passengers walked from the aircraft to the terminal along the tarmac, what struck me the most was the sweet, mixed fragrance of the ocean, flowers, and cedar trees. To a young man who had grown up in the less kindly environments of Toronto, Detroit, New York, and other cities in the east, it was like getting a pass into a Nirvana of the senses. My trip out west was to be a short one, to be married and to move back east, where a university degree, a job, and a career awaited my return. It turned out quite differently, and I have been thanking people ever since.

In writing this book, I've drawn on the kindness and expertise of contacts and friends I have accumulated over a long time in both Seattle and Vancouver as well as Whistler, Victoria, the Olympic Peninsula, and Tacoma. On the business side, no matter what changes in personnel have taken place within those areas' convention and visitors bureaus, there has always been a seamless continuation of information and I have never had to catch up.

Special thanks are due to David Blandford of the Seattle Convention and Visitors Bureau, who over the years has always kept me up to date on the rapidly changing face of Seattle. Whenever I've needed updates and information, the bureau has responded quickly and has been more than generous in making sure that I see what I want to see and experience the city in the same way that a tourist would. And just 45 minutes down the road in Tacoma, Julie Gangler of the Tacoma Regional Convention and Visitors Bureau continues to feed me information about that city's changing character as it moves from being an adjunct to Seattle to defining itself in its own terms.

Accommodations and restaurants are always difficult to keep up with in a large city because they are volatile industries in which there are constant turnovers in ownerships, personnel, menus, chefs, and direction. Helping me get through the complex myriad changes and transformations in Seattle were Louis and Lorne Richmond, Lori Meyers, and the staff of Richmond Public Relations, who pointed me not only in the direction of their own clients, but to many others as well. They opened up doors that otherwise might well have been closed. Stephanie Ager of White Dog Press and Gordon Thorne of Thorne Company Communications sent me in research directions I otherwise might not have traveled. A special thanks goes to Alisa Martinez of the Fairmont Olympic Hotel, who kindly put her concierge staff to work in searching for out-of-the-way places that might otherwise have been overlooked.

Kristine George of Tourism Victoria continues to overwhelm me with the goings-on of that little piece of Britain-in-Canada; and Kate Colley Lo of Tourism Vancouver keeps her finger on that rapidly evolving city. Laura Serena and Heather Kirk of Immedia PR make sure that I miss absolutely nothing that their clients are doing.

To my friends who travel a lot between the two cities and who make regular and detailed reports on restaurants, hotels, and attractions: many thanks. You are too numerous to name, but you know that I value your input. And thank you to the countless numbers of entrepreneurs who make spending time in these places so enjoyable and whose professionalism and hospitality you'll enjoy when you visit. My editor, Kris Fulsaas, edited this manuscript with care and attention well beyond the call of duty and in the process fre-quently saved me from myself.

Most of all, I've been fortunate in having a wife who was born in this region and who has guided me over the years in making the transition from eastern attitudes to western values about life, work, and play. Many of Toshi's photos are in this guide, but her input goes well beyond her talents behind the lens. She has put up with vacations that always, somehow, turn into work; with photo requests that are vague and whose parameters are explicit only in my mind's eye; and with the not-always-necessary hours spent on my computer when I should have been helping around the house. Thank you.

Introduction

A Tale of Two Cities

On the surface, no two cities in North America are so similar as Seattle, Washington, and Vancouver, British Columbia. Both spring from common roots and share a common tongue, both generate their respective area's economic energy, and both are the cultural and spiritual hearts of their regions. And because both cities are located in spectacular surroundings of mountains and ocean, they define themselves through their outdoors activities and their adventurous personalities, even though these are sometimes obscured by winter rains.

Despite their outdoorsy identity, both cities are sophisticated places where the arts thrive, local cuisine is inventive, and citizens live in distinct neighborhoods that have unique qualities, even though they are within easy walking distance of one another. You will also see familiar outlets for merchandising, chain restaurants and hotels, and many icons of North American industry and fast foods advertised on television on both sides of the Canada–United States border. In that way, you'll feel comfortable enjoying the outward familiarity. There will always be a bit of home in both Seattle and Vancouver.

Over the years, both cities have also preserved the heart of their cultural and historical roots: in Seattle, the Pioneer Square Historic District is the city's birthplace; in Vancouver, Gastown is where the city first began. And both of these historical neighborhoods today are among the most exciting areas of each city, with galleries, restaurants, boutiques, and attractions that reflect their richly varied past.

Statue of an orca (killer whale) near Vancouver's convention center Toshi

The land on which Seattle and Vancouver rest was originally territory of the Pacific Northwest's indigenous peoples, the Coast Salish. These people, who boated and traveled along the coast from Oregon to Alaska, are part of a vast Native American community that once depended on fishing and hunting for survival. Spanish, Russian, and British explorers came to the region in the 1500s and 1600s in search of the rumored Northwest Passage, a hoped-for body of water that would connect the Pacific and Atlantic oceans. Unfortunately for the native peoples, Europeans brought with them disease and imperial ambitions. Explorers such as George Vancouver, Juan de Fuca, and Charles Barkley sailed, mapped the region, and left their names permanently a part of the area. The Strait of Juan de Fuca,

Barkley Sound, and the city of Vancouver are permanent legacies of those early explorations.

The explorers didn't find the Northwest Passage, but they did lay claim to the Pacific Northwest, not always without conflict. Capt. George Vancouver claimed the San Juan Islands for England in 1791, and Capt. Charles Wilkes did the same for America in 1841. The British built a stockade and encampment on the west side of San Juan Island on a gorgeous cove; the Americans built their camp on the exposed, windy southern tip. Thus the islands were occupied by both nations' citizens and military—a prescription, even today, for calamity. Although the international border was peaceful for most of its history, one nasty spat almost led to war between the two countries. It was, of all things, caused by a wandering pig.

In June 1859, one of the 25 American settlers on San Juan Island shot a British-owned pig rooting in his garden. The Englishman demanded payment, the American refused, and the Englishman then demanded that the Yank be brought to trial in Victoria, British Columbia. The Americans refused to participate; the soldiers of both nations stood at arms' length until the matter was settled by arbitration 13 years later by Kaiser Wilhelm I of Germany, who gave the San Juan Islands to America. The pig, as it turned out, was the only casualty. Both camps are now part of the San Juan Islands National Historical Park.

At the main international border crossing at Blaine, Washington, south of Vancouver and north of Bellingham, today the Peace Arch monument bears the inscription "Children of a Common Mother," signifying the shared heritage that the United States and Canada have in their British origins. In reality, these two "children" have grown to have distinct differences, politically and socially. America eventually revolted against its "mother" and became its own nation in 1776, while Canada retained its colony status until 1931. It wasn't until 1982 that Canada adopted its own constitution, replacing the ancient British North America Act that had its origins in London, England, and had been the nation's guiding force.

A significant political difference is that the United States has a presidential system of government, whereas Canada has a parliamentary system. Culturally, Seattle is part of America's melting pot; Vancouver reflects the Canadian belief in multiculturalism even though Canada is officially bilingual—French and English. The United States revels in its merging of cultures into a well-defined national character; Canada prides itself in its distinct cultural differences.

Even the sporting activities are different, though they have the same names. Football in Canada may look the same as in the United States, but the rules are different and the game is played differently. Seattle is a town of baseball, football, and basketball; Vancouver is primarily a hockey town, although it does have other professional sports. And though you won't see cricket played much in Seattle, a walk through Vancouver's Stanley Park on a summer weekend takes you to a giant field where white-clad cricket players passionately engage in their sport.

So, though there are many similarities between Seattle and Vancouver, the fact that one is American and the other is Canadian makes each city unique, each having its own cultural, political, and social histories and ethnic makeup. This guide is a tale of two very different cities—and each imparts a distinct experience to visitors. Each city will take you into its heart, of course, but you will also delve into two varied worlds. The arts are different, culinary experiences are diverse, and side trips are a unique part of each city's region. And all are imbued with the peculiar history and background of each city.

Yet despite their many pleasant differences, Seattle and Vancouver have one overwhelming similarity: Each city is part of the Pacific Northwest, a place where myth and reality exist side by side, where ancient traditions and contemporary lifestyles have blended into a new culture. You simply cannot separate the two cities from their physical environment. In many ways, the cultures of both cities have been defined by where they are, and it is impossible to write about either without reflecting the physical reality of their respective locations.

The entire Pacific Northwest, stretching from northern California to the Alaskan panhandle and including both sides of the Canada–United States border, is a magical harmony of contrasts: towering mountains, inland ocean channels, cosmopolitan cities, rustic and fast-lane resorts, giant fir forests, rolling hills in the wine country, and high bluffs of the Pacific Coast. It is a place of deserts and rain forests, roaring surf and gentle streams, apple blossoms and cactus flowers, powerful volcanoes and icy snowfields.

On the edge of this spectacular region, Seattle and Vancouver stand as two great cities that just 150 years ago were trading posts on the edge of an enormous wilderness. Today, both cities have distinguished orchestras, vibrant opera companies, great museums, and a variety of dance, ballet, and theater ensembles.

Just an hour's drive south of Seattle is Tacoma, once the forgotten and ugly-duckling neighbor of Seattle. The city has carved out its own niche of late, embracing the world of glass art and preserving the state's historical artifacts. Another hour's drive south is lofty Mount Rainier, whose snowy presence links Tacoma and Seattle. To the west of Seattle are the Kitsap and Olympic peninsulas, beckoning the populous Puget Sound region to explore by circuitous highways and bridges or by ferry. Bainbridge Island, the rugged Olympic Mountains, vast West Coast shorelines, and quaint towns and villages scattered along both sides of the peninsulas give you the sensation of being alone with nature.

On the Canadian side of the 49th parallel, which separates the two nations, Vancouver Island and its main city, Victoria, offer a British experience found nowhere else on the continent. It's a place where afternoon tea is still a tradition and where double-decker buses cruise the city. Getting there is half the fun, as a 90-minute car-ferry ride from Vancouver takes you across the Strait of Georgia through the spectacular Gulf Islands (a geologic extension of the U.S. San Juan Islands) to Vancouver Island. And a 90-minute drive north of Vancouver is Whistler, one of the finest winter and summer recreational destinations in the Pacific Northwest. It has been selected as the site for the 2010 Winter Olympics.

You'll find, as you explore Seattle and Vancouver, a world of little things that bring joy to those who live here and those who visit. You'll find it in the perfectly groomed golf courses in their magnificent settings; in microbreweries and intimate restaurants; in bookstores where coffee-sipping book lovers discuss the merits of yet-unknown authors; in art galleries that feature the works of native peoples and Pacific Northwest artists; and in the unusual museums that contain memorabilia and the histories of the region.

These two cities stand at the edge of a geographical masterpiece. Enjoy them for their uniqueness and their distinct flavors. They are gentle, safe places that will beckon you back repeatedly.

The Way This Book Works

Organization

The two main chapters cover the cities of Seattle and Vancouver. Each is followed by a chapter describing side trips in that city's vicinity. All the chapters give a brief overview of the area and directions for getting there. Sections describe amenities you'll find, under the headings of accommodations, restaurants, attractions, entertainment and the arts, recreation, shopping, and events.

A series of indexes at the back of the book provides easy access to information. The first, a standard index, lists entries and subjects in alphabetical order. Next, hotels, motels, bed-and-breakfasts, and hostels are categorized by price. Restaurants are organized in two separate indexes: one by price, one by type of cuisine.

Because this guide covers two different countries over a wide geographical area, information on customs and immigration, currency, telephone area codes, national holidays, and useful contact numbers is given in each chapter.

Prices

This guide rates accommodations and restaurants within a price range, rather than providing specific prices that are subject to frequent changes.

Accommodations prices are normally based on per person/double occupancy for hotel rooms and per unit for motels, bed-and-breakfasts, and hostels. Price ranges reflect the difference between off-season and high season rates (usually Christmas through Easter); some establishments offer off-season packages at special rates. Pricing does not include local taxes or gratuities.

Restaurant price ranges are based on the range of dinner entrée prices or, if dinner is not served, lunch entrée prices. Again, pricing does not include local taxes or gratuities.

Rates

	Accommodations	*Restaurants*
Inexpensive	Up to $100	Up to $15
Moderate	$101 to $150	$15 to $25
Expensive	$151 to $249	$25 to $35
Very Expensive	Over $250	Over $35

Abbreviations and Codes

Credit card information is listed as follows:

AE	American Express
DC	Diners Club
Disc	Discovery Card
MC	MasterCard
V	Visa

Meals served are abbreviated as follows:

B	Breakfast
L	Lunch
D	Dinner

Days open are abbreviated as follows:

M	Monday
Tu	Tuesday
W	Wednesday
Th	Thursday
F	Friday
Sa	Saturday
Su	Sunday

The Space Needle at Seattle Center, the city's most familiar landmark Toshi

1

SEATTLE

Metropolitan Puget Sound

The tourism people have given Seattle the name of Emerald City—which, of course, virtually everyone ignores. You'll never hear the name used by anyone who works outside the convention and tourism bureau office. If there's one thing Seattle people dislike, it's being pigeonholed and being told what they are.

In Seattle, residents brag about their bookstores. It's said that's because it rains a lot and during the winter there's nothing else to do but read. That's only partly true, of course, but reputations and perceptions are often difficult to change. Seattle is actually a place of intense activity, both physical and artistic, at all times of the year. Opera, books, sailing, and baseball blend easily into a style of living that's both unique and the envy of anyone who has visited.

But let's be frank about it: it does rain here, as it does along the entire Pacific Northwest coast. However, it does not rain nearly as much as Seattle's reputation suggests, though it might help to explain Seattle's love affair with coffee shops, bookstores, and movie theaters. In fact, more sunglasses per capita are purchased here than in any other city in America, even though the winters are defined by low-hanging, water-saturated clouds. And Seattle has the country's highest percentage rate of residents with a college degree and one of the highest rates of home Internet access.

The city is continually reinventing itself. If you've been to Seattle before but not in the past five years, you may not even recognize the place. Not only has there been construction of new buildings in the downtown area, the city has also rehabilitated previously run-down sections, transforming them into prime living and visiting areas.

It has also given new life to its arts community. In recent years, a new art museum has been constructed downtown near a new performance hall for the Seattle Symphony. At Seattle Center, site of the 1962 World's Fair, a new performing arts center has been constructed for theater and Seattle Opera performances, and a music museum unlike any in the country enthralls and entertains anyone who visits.

Everywhere you walk in the city and its neighborhoods, you find people just sitting around, reading newspapers, talking, staying out of the rain or sitting outdoors in the sunshine. Seventy percent of the coffee that is sold in Seattle is specialty coffees, about 10 times the amount sold in other cities. If all of this makes it sound as though the locals are a bit schizophrenic, trying to decide between indoor pursuits and outdoor activities, you are right. When it rains, they complain. When it doesn't, they miss it—and complain. That's also part of the Seattle character.

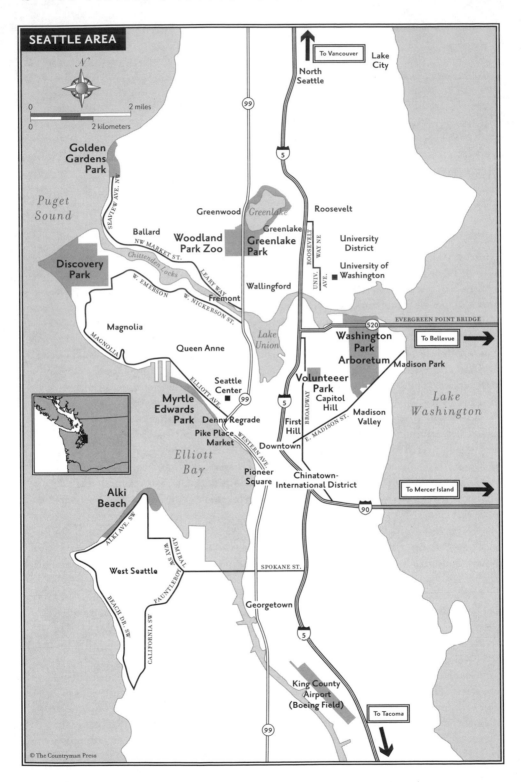

SEATTLE AREA

To Vancouver

North Seattle

Lake City

Golden Gardens Park

Puget Sound

Greenwood

Greenlake

Roosevelt

Ballard

Woodland Park Zoo

Greenlake

Greenlake Park

University District

Discovery Park

Chittenden Locks

Wallingford

University of Washington

Fremont

Magnolia

Lake Union

Washington Park Arboretum

EVERGREEN POINT BRIDGE

To Bellevue

Queen Anne

Madison Park

Seattle Center

Volunteeer Park

Capitol Hill

Lake Washington

Myrtle Edwards Park

Denny Regrade

First Hill

Madison Valley

Pike Place Market

Downtown

Elliott Bay

Pioneer Square

Chinatown-International District

To Mercer Island

Alki Beach

West Seattle

SPOKANE ST.

Georgetown

King County Airport (Boeing Field)

To Tacoma

© The Countryman Press

Seattle has been chosen America's best in many categories—including best bicycling city, most livable, best city to locate a business, best hotels, and best place to visit—by a variety of magazines, books, and even America's mayors. It is certainly a place where its citizens partake in its good fortune. It is ranked fourth in America in sales at eating and drinking establishments, fourth in frequency of opera performances, and fourth in spending money for its libraries, plus it has more theater performances annually than any other city except New York. And Seattle gorges on its sea culture at restaurants beside Puget Sound, Lake Union, or Lake Washington.

People here just do things differently. Maybe it's from living in a larger-than-life environment where the mountains and the ocean seem to put things in a different perspective. But as soon as you arrive, everything seems more relaxed. To begin with, people seem to talk more, and then you realize that Seattle is a place where tourism and daily living are integrated, where nothing has been imposed, and where virtually every interesting place is there for a reason. In fact, there just may be fewer tourist traps per square foot in Seattle than anywhere in North America.

First-time visitors are usually astonished at the wealth of natural beauty in and around Seattle, the 23rd largest city in the United States. Literally touching the city's boundaries are thousands of square miles of evergreen forest and salt- and freshwater shorelines. Bracketed east and west by freshwater Lake Washington and salt water Puget Sound, the city occupies a north–south corridor that is slender at the "waist" and embraces several hills.

Fishing and lumber were the prime industries in early Seattle, and that cultural and economic past is today's fashion. The city grew up around and outward from downtown's Pioneer Square, centered on its former "skid road," which today is a chic gathering place for artists and artisans and where many of the city's most current restaurants are located. The city's strong maritime traditions are still in working order at Fisherman's Terminal, near the Hiram M. Chittenden Locks; home to the U.S. North Pacific fishing fleet, Fisherman's Terminal has moorage facilities for 700 boats. The Lake Washington Ship Canal connects Puget Sound with Lakes Union and Washington, and the locks, near the western entrance to the canal, offer a fine vantage point from which to watch the bobbing procession of tugs, fishing boats, pleasure craft, barges, and research vessels as they are raised and lowered 21 feet (6.4 m) between freshwater and salt water.

An architectural transformation in the past decade has been both physical and cultural, especially in the downtown core. The downtown commercial core is about 15 blocks north to south and eight blocks east to west. Dominated by the 76-story Columbia Seafirst Center, it's the financial hub of the Pacific Northwest. Seattle hosts large conventions at the downtown Washington Trade and Convention Center. You can easily travel around the financial district free on city buses marked for that service. Major hotels such as the Hilton, Fairmont Olympic, Alexis, Westin, Mayflower Park, Holiday Inn Crowne Plaza, Stouffer Madison, Seattle Sheraton, and Vintage Park are within a six-block area here.

Although this is obviously a city rejuvenating itself with contemporary towers, Seattle has also refurbished many old buildings, converting them into shopping malls. It gives the downtown core a sense of continuance. As a result, large areas that just a decade ago were unattractive and even dangerous are now desirable for living and visiting. Along First Avenue in Belltown, just north of Pike Place Market, a series of new construction has resulted in a vast change. And in the lower downtown area near Pioneer Square, where before broken-down buildings and derelicts once dominated, new stores, restaurants, a clothing district, and small hotels have sprung up in recent years.

Seattle proper has about the same population as Vancouver, about 564,000, but the population of the greater Seattle area of King, Snohomish, and Island Counties is almost 2.1 million. Oddly, you never feel that the city and its environs are ever impersonal or even big, as the regional population suggests it might. Instead, it's a city and a regional district of small enclaves that have distinct identities and unique character. There's a face and style to Seattle that is new, bright, young, innovative, and service oriented. Adjacent to downtown Seattle department stores such as the Bon-Macy's and Nordstrom's, Westlake Center shops are a magnet for shoppers and visitors alike. The plaza is a central draw for outdoor concerts, for meeting people, for brown-bag lunches, and for people watching.

HISTORY

In prehistoric times, the area now known as Washington State was home to several dissimilar Indian cultures from at least four different linguistic groups. Among the coastal tribes were the Makah, Quinault, Salish, Puyallup, Nisqually, and Skykomish, who lived in the Puget Sound area and after whom many of today's towns and regions are named. For the coastal tribes, the main source of food was the salmon that spawned in Washington's many rivers. The predictability of the spawning seasons produced permanent villages within short distances of each other. Some tribes were highly proficient whalers, using large canoes made from the plentiful softwood cedar trees, which held up well to water. In that aspect of their lives, they were similar to the Kwakiutl people to the north in Canada.

Many of the region's native peoples were skilled artists, producing ceremonial masks, decorated boxes, and other objects that today can be found in virtually every regional museum, at the University of Washington in Seattle, and at the Museum of Anthropology

The Seattle skyline today, as seen from Elliott Bay Toshi

located on the University of British Columbia campus in Vancouver. The tribes of the south concentrated more on trade than on hunting and fishing. They used the Columbia River as a water highway to reach tribes located east of the high Cascade Mountains in a region made up of high desert and rolling hills extending east to the Rockies. These interior tribes—including the Sanpoil, Yakima, Wenatchee, Spokane, Palouse, and Walla Walla—lived in settlements that were less permanent than those of their coastal counterparts. Instead, they established camps where they found food, much like the Plains tribes farther east.

Seattle's history of European settlement is like that of a child who developed late: explorers were in and around what is now the Seattle area in the late 1700s, but it was another century before the first settlers arrived. No one really was in a hurry to settle the region because it contained poor farmland; there were only trees and ocean. The native peoples knew the value of both these resources, but white explorers couldn't see past the immense trees.

When Capt. George Vancouver explored Puget Sound in 1793, he was probably surprised to discover that the region had thousands of years of native culture. He honored his crew and members of the British admiralty by naming just about everything in sight after them. In fact, the sound got its name from Vancouver's second lieutenant, Peter Puget. It wasn't until 1872 that Britain agreed to cede lands south of the 49th parallel, which had been controlled by the Hudson Bay Company, to American control.

On November 13, 1851, a group of 23, led by Seattle founder Arthur Denny, arrived at Alki Point, in what is now West Seattle, aboard the ship *Exact*. One of the original settlers to the region, Charles Terry of New York, wanted to call the new settlement New York, but fellow residents rejected his efforts, and instead it was called New York Alki, (Salish for "New York by and by"). A year later, the settlers moved away from Alki Point, which was exposed to vicious storms, and across Elliott Bay to where Pioneer Square is now located. The settlers named the new settlement Seattle, Chief Sealth, a local Native American chief who befriended the whites.

But the Europeans' relationship with the native peoples was hardly congenial. Early white settlers, believing they were entering a world of rampaging red men having a single cultural identity, were initially confused by the peaceful nature of the native peoples and by their widely differing cultures and languages. In extending his good will to the settlers, Chief Sealth could not have envisioned that they would, in turn, exile his people to a reservation, which is what eventually happened. After the Treaty of Port Elliott, signed in 1855, Chief Sealth eloquently summed up his people's plight by saying, "The Indian's night promises to be dark. Not a single star of hope hovers above the horizon."

Unfortunately, he was right. In January 1856, a band of Yakima and Klickitat Indians attempted to destroy the fledgling town. The settlers took refuge in a blockhouse as a naval vessel bombarded the attackers, forcing them away. This defeat extinguished the hopes of the culturally sophisticated native peoples of Puget Sound to get back their land. Instead, the town grew up around them.

As the Great Northern Railroad moved north and west, Seattle hoped to be the terminus. In 1873 the city offered the company $250,000 in cash and bonds, 7,500 town lots, 3,000 acres of undeveloped land, and half the waterfront in exchange for that privilege. In one of the worst business decisions of the time—or since, for that matter—the railroad rebuffed the offer and chose Tacoma instead. Nevertheless, Seattle's population continued to grow.

The mid-1880s were rough. The city was hard hit by the national depression, and local fishermen, lumber workers, and miners found themselves competing for jobs with out-of-work city employees and Chinese laborers, who had been recently fired after completing the area's railroad. It was not a pretty time in Seattle's racial history; resentment exploded in anti-Chinese violence in February 1886. Five men were shot, Chinese homes and stores were demolished, and 200 Chinese were forced aboard a San Francisco–bound steamship. Eventually, 500 Chinese were removed from Seattle; it would be another decade before the Chinese community rebuilt itself to its former numbers.

Seattle's population grew from 3,553 to 42,837 in the 1880s, and the railroad finally linked the city to the east in 1893. The city grew rapidly as it cut lumber and sent it south to California, becoming a rat-infested, grungy place that by all descriptions was festering with disease and poverty. The great fire of 1889 culminated a decade of violence and economic ruin, burning to the ground virtually every building in Seattle's core. It was a blessing in disguise.

The Yukon gold rush pulled Seattle out of its economic slump during the late 1890s and the city became a boomtown, a transportation gateway and chief supplier to the northward-bound prospectors. In a twist of irony, Seattle's equipment suppliers made more money from the gold rush than most prospectors ever did. By the time many gold seekers reached Alaska and the Canadian Klondike, most land claims had already been made and the gold was spoken for.

Seattle citizens celebrated their own good fortune by staging the Alaska-Yukon-Pacific Exhibition in 1909; some of the structures built for that fair still exist on the University of Washington campus. Seattle became the jumping-off point for later prospectors. And by the time the northern gold rushes lost their vitality, Seattle's population had exploded, reaching 200,000 by 1914, so that the city now challenged Portland as the region's biggest metropolis.

But it was in 1916 that the city was forever transformed. It was then that William Boeing and Clyde Estervelt launched their first airplane, a floatplane from Lake Union. The enterprise, designed to carry mail to and from Canada, became the Boeing Company, which grew to be one of the biggest employers in the region. Between 1940 and the early 1980s, as Boeing went, so went Seattle. In those days, when Boeing suffered, the whole city felt the pain.

By the end of the '60s, the big Apollo project wound down and the company hoped to increase sales of commercial aircraft to make up for the decrease of space-related business. Unfortunately, due to the recession in the aviation industry, Boeing went 18 months without a single new domestic order. The 747 jumbo jet had not yet established itself in the market and also had unexpectedly high startup costs and initial delivery problems. The SST (Super Sonic Transport) was a faster-than-sound aircraft meant to compete with the French and British Concorde that had been heralded as the aircraft of the future. But, its expensive operating costs and low passenger loads—the Concorde flew with only 150 passengers, environmental concerns, and rising fuel costs—made Boeing back away from its Boeing SST project. At about the same time, the Russians also cancelled their plans to launch an SST. The end of the SST program dealt another blow. Congress pulled the plug on SST funding in March 1971, forcing Boeing to cancel the program. Seattle discovered in 1970–71 how much an economic downturn could change a city. In less than two years, Boeing shrank its workforce from 80,400 to 37,200, and thousands of families picked up and moved out. At the height of the 1970s economic downturn, a local billboard urged the last person leaving Seattle to turn out the lights.

Needless to say, the lights weren't turned out. Seattle had stopped being a sleepy little town in the eyes of the world when it hosted the 1962 World's Fair and constructed the Space Needle. That structure captured both the city's then present and its future, bringing promise of an outward-looking, high-technology place that combined leading-edge industry and a livable environment.

When Bill Gates and Paul Allen, then living in Albuquerque, New Mexico, invented and licensed a computer program called Basic in 1975, they changed the world. It was the world's first language written for the personal computer. When the two men moved their fledgling company to the Seattle suburb of Bellevue in 1979, the information and computer revolution came to Seattle with the advent of Microsoft, the world's dominant software company. In 1979, Seattle University was the first school in the nation to offer a master's degree in software engineering. Microsoft continued its series of hits with MS-DOS, Microsoft Word, and the Microsoft Windows operating system.

Microsoft was a comfortable fit in an area that had already been the scene of technological innovations because of Boeing, whose contracts with the U.S. Department of Defense had brought Seattle thousands of technologically knowledgeable and highly educated aerospace workers. Most important, Microsoft attracted other high-tech industries to the area, such as RealNetworks, Adobe, and Amazon.com. With Microsoft, Adobe, and Amazon all headquartered in the area, Seattle was hit hard when the dot-com bubble burst in the late 1990s. But even the resulting unemployment from these companies didn't dampen the vibrant spirit of the city.

Today, with earnings of around $35 billion, Microsoft is still the world's dominant software company. The Eastside area that embraces Microsoft's offices is called the Microsoft Campus because of its spread-out facilities and research and office buildings. No, there are no tours.

In Seattle you can't ignore Microsoft or Bill Gates, the company's cofounder and the world's richest man. Nor is Microsoft cofounder Paul Allen an economic wallflower. Both have contributed enormously to Seattle's arts and medical research fields. The Gates Foundation is the largest charitable organization in the world, contributing millions to health, education, and computer literacy programs. The contributions of the high-tech boom can be seen at the symphony hall, the football and baseball stadiums, and the Experience Music Project. Seattle has learned to enjoy its blessings regardless of any temporary setback. The city has since become much more diversified and less reliant on Boeing, though thousands of residents still owe their living to the giant aircraft manufacturer.

The battle to keep the Boeing Company above the economic waterline is an ongoing one. And in recent years, the company has spread its economic wings with mergers and acquisitions. In December 1996, Boeing merged with Rockwell International Corporation's aerospace and defense units. Rockwell's space systems, aircraft division, Rocketdyne, Autonetics, missile systems, and aircraft modification divisions were renamed Boeing North American Inc. and operated as a Boeing subsidiary. In 1997, Boeing merged with McDonnell Douglas Corporation. In January 2000, Boeing bought Hughes Electronics Corporation's space and communications business and, in quick succession, purchased Jeppesen Sanderson Inc., a leading provider of aeronautical charts, and Hawker de Havilland, a designer and manufacturer of commercial and military aero structure components.

There's no doubt that the dot-com bubble bursting had an enormous impact on the local economy, and some say the good old days of the 1990s are not likely to return.

Although no one expects Microsoft to return to the wildly profitable days of the 1990s, it will nonetheless remain one of the city's two dominating business cultures. The company is expected to dominate in many areas of computer software for the next while, though it is facing increased competition, especially from Apple, with its OS X operating system, and from Linux.

Thanks to Microsoft and Boeing, Seattle has two of the most powerful economic engines in the 21st century. Few cities have the basis for growth that Seattle does, especially in a world that will be driven for the foreseeable future by aerospace and high tech. Today's Seattle is a city in transformation and profound change. It's a fairly youthful city. Restaurants, shopping boutiques, small coffee shops, and bookstores permeate every segment of the city. Regardless of what the economic future brings, Seattle has been left with an enormous wealth of facilities as a result of the high-tech boom of the '90s: a new symphony hall, two great stadiums, museums, parks, and a lifestyle that a visitor to the city will remember long after the trip back home.

WEATHER

Does it rain in Seattle? Do Seattle residents drink coffee? Of course it rains, but the rainy season is predictable. In Seattle, it doesn't officially begin until October 1, and winter is the wettest season. As for snow, the white stuff does fall from time to time, usually in December and early January. However, it doesn't stay long, and locals find the stuff somewhat amusing, as though it has appeared as an unexpected guest. Spring in Seattle is mild and green, but it can be very wet at times, too.

The average yearly rainfall is 36.2 inches (92 cm), which, locals agree, is a lot more than the 19.5 inches (50 cm) that fall in San Francisco. But it's less than the 39 inches (99 cm) that fall on Washington, D.C., or the 40.3 inches (102 cm) New York has to endure.

So you can see that many large cities on the East Coast receive more annual precipitation than Seattle. However, when it stops raining in these East Coast cities, the sky clears. In Seattle, when it stops raining, the sky often stays overcast. So even when it's not raining, it seems as though it is—thus the misperception that it rains all the time. The rain in Seattle is usually a light or fine misty rain rather than a drenching downpour, though those can happen too, usually in November.

There are two sides to Washington State: wet and dry. Those living east of the Cascades are dry siders; those living west of the Cascades are—you guessed it—wet siders. Seattle's climate, like much of the Pacific Northwest's, is mild throughout the year. The average high in July—its hottest month—is 62 degrees F (16.6 degrees C), though it can, on occasion, reach 90 degrees F (31 degrees C). By comparison, in Walla Walla, in the southeastern region of Washington State, the average July temperature is 76 degrees F (24.5 degrees C), though it is often 95 degrees F (35 degrees C) and higher. In January, Seattle averages 38 degrees F (3 degrees C), while in Spokane, on the central eastern border with Idaho, the average is 25 degrees F (-4 degrees C) and often colder. The mountains, like those elsewhere, are unpredictable and sometimes have snow in June at higher elevations.

Summers in Seattle are usually warm, dry, and sunny, with long days and cool nights. The driest time of year in Seattle is the last half of July and the first half of August. During this time, Seattle will often go 10, 20, or 30 days without any measurable precipitation. The warm, mild weather often continues into fall, with cooler temperatures at night.

The Pacific Science Center's arches grace Seattle Center. Toshi

To dress for Seattle, in the summer bring a light sweater for evening wear because it tends to cool off once the sun dips below the horizon. Any time of year, bring a good rain jacket; locals tend to sneer at umbrellas because high winds invert them. Wise travelers touring the state after spending time in Seattle bring a range of clothing to adapt to the varying conditions.

GETTING THERE

By Car
I-5, a solid strip of pavement that runs from San Diego in the south to the Canadian border in the north, bisects the heart of Seattle north to south. From the east, I-90 travels from Spokane (and farther east) through Eastside and Mercer Island to cross Lake Washington on the floating bridge and connect with I-5 south of downtown. From the east, you can also take US 2 from Spokane through the rolling farmlands of central Washington, through Leavenworth, a scenic Bavarian-themed town, and over the Cascades through Stevens Pass at 4,061 feet (1,238 m) before merging with I-5 north of Seattle at Everett. Countless smaller roads off these main arteries go through the heart of Washington State. From eastern Oregon, you can take I-84 through the Columbia River Gorge to connect with I-5 near Vancouver, Washington.

By Air
If you arrive by airplane, you'll most likely land at **Seattle-Tacoma International Airport** (www.portseattle.org/seatac), otherwise known as Sea-Tac, a sprawling complex 14 miles (22.5 km) south of the city. Sea-Tac is the largest and busiest airport in the Pacific Northwest, with 26.8 million passengers passing through its gates each year. It has a standard airport layout with a main terminal and six concourses. Two satellite terminals, mainly for international flights, are connected to the main terminal by an easy-to-use subway.

The customs and immigration process for incoming international passengers can be lengthy, so prepare yourself for considerable waits, especially if several flights arrive at the same time. Nonetheless, once you're past the paperwork or leaving the airport rather than arriving, you'll find it's an agreeable and sometimes uplifting place to be.

A general information booth is located in the baggage claim area, close to Carousel Eight; language translators are available. In the baggage claim area near Carousel One can be found the Japanese center, designed specifically for Seattle's many Japanese-speaking visitors. Before or after visitors gather their luggage, they can go to the booth and collect a wide variety of brochures and maps and have their questions answered by Japanese speakers familiar with the needs of Japanese visitors.

A garage connected to the main terminal by sky bridges on the fourth floor offers short-term and general parking. Valet parking is also available. Five car-rental companies offer on-site car rentals; counters are located in the baggage claim area. Other ground transportation includes shuttle, bus, and taxi companies.

But Sea-Tac is more than just a place to drop off passengers coming or going. The design of the airport is like that of a small village, with shops and dining areas in a central plaza and additional shopping at the entranceway to individual concourses. Recently remodeled Concourse A has the airport's first true food court, with Manchu Wok, Great American Bagel Bakery, Africa Lounge, Starbucks Coffee, and The Grove Natural Snacks.

Farther down the concourse are Tully's Coffee, Red Hook Mountain Room, and La Pisa Café. The new concessions all offer street pricing. Hudson Group has three news/gift stores as well as a bookstore along the concourse. Despite the concourse's almost half-mile length, passengers are never more than 300 feet from services and amenities, and there's a view of Mount Rainier.

As you make your way through the airport, you'll see artwork mounted, installed, and encased throughout the rooms and corridors. To help you locate current exhibits, five free-standing directional signs, complete with maps, are located on the esplanade behind the ticket counters in the main terminal. The art collection features some of the finest contemporary work in glass, sculpture, photography, painting, and sound. The region's diversity is well represented through European, all-American, Asian, Northwest Native American, and folk-art influences. Some of the works are by 20th-century artists of great renown, such as Frank Stella, Louise Nevelson, and Robert Rauschenberg. Others are by regional and emerging artists who vitalize the collection with wit, charm, beauty, and occasional irreverence.

The airport was developed as a direct response to the Japanese attack on Pearl Harbor on December 7, 1941. Military needs limited civilian access to existing airports such as Seattle's Boeing Field and Tacoma's McChord Field, and the federal Civilian Aviation Authority sought a local government to undertake development of a new regional airport. Initial construction was completed in October 1944, but full civilian operation did not commence until dedication of a modern terminal building on July 9, 1949.

Sea-Tac Airport opened its first new terminal facility in 30 years on June 15, 2004. The architecture of the new south end adds nearly a million square feet of space for departing and arriving passengers. The 2,102-foot Concourse A includes 14 airline gates, a dozen new restaurants and shops, several pieces of new artwork, and the airport's first moving sidewalks. From the airfield side, passengers and employees have expansive views of the Olympic Mountains.

The adjacent Arrivals Hall, with its soaring, exposed structural steel ceiling and 300-foot-long curved wall of glass, provides a spacious, light-drenched place for people to meet arriving passengers. Both inside and outside the window wall is a unique rock and water feature designed by landscape architect Robert Murase. Nearly $2 million worth of public art was integrated into the public areas and concourse for both practical and aesthetic reasons. A stunning art glass wall, for example, helps guide passengers to the escalator going to the satellite train station.

By Train

Amtrak (800-872-7245 or 206-382-4125; www.amtrak.com) serves Seattle in a spectacular way along the West Coast, both south from Vancouver, British Columbia, and north from Los Angeles, San Francisco, and Portland (the Coast Starlight). Service also extends to the east (the Empire Builder) through Spokane and on to Chicago. Trains arrive and depart from **King Street Station** (303 S. Jackson St.), near the International District, a few blocks south of the heart of downtown.

By Bus

Greyhound (800-229-9424 or 206-628-5526; www.greyhound.com) provides intercity bus service from its station in the Denny Regrade (811 Stewart St.), not far from Lake Union and the Seattle Center. Numerous budget chain motels are within walking distance of the terminal.

CUSTOMS AND IMMIGRATION

With the advent of the Department of Homeland Security and increased border security regulations in the past couple of years, getting into the United States takes more time and demands more identification than in previous years. Although residents of Canada are generally admitted with a birth certificate, the best identification is a passport. Non-Canadians who are nonimmigrants to the United States must have a valid nonimmigrant visa and a passport valid for a minimum of six months beyond the initial period of stay in the United States. U.S. citizens returning from Canada or from overseas are required to bring proof of citizenship and can bring back only up to $800 worth of goods. Due to heightened security, it is strongly recommended that U.S. citizens also present their passports even when returning from travel only to Canada or Mexico. Check out the **U.S. Customs and Border Protection** Web site (www.customs.ustreas.gov/xp/cgov/home.xml) for more information.

CURRENCY AND TAXES

American currency is the means of exchange, although most areas close to the Canadian border will accept Canadian dollars at their current exchange rate. Foreign exchange is available at Seattle banks and at major hotels.

Local taxes include a sales tax of 8.8 percent in Seattle, with varying rates in other parts of the state.

INFORMATION

Before you go, scour the **Seattle Convention and Visitors Bureau** Web site (www.see seattle.org). In town, the bureau (1 Convention Place, 701 Pike St., Ste. 800, Seattle, WA 98101; 206-461-5840) offers several convenient services, such as the **Citywide Concierge Center** (206-461-5888) at the Washington State Convention and Trade Center, Galleria Level, at Seventh Avenue and Pike Street in the heart of downtown. It's a public concierge service for travelers, convention delegates, residents, and business professionals. The center features state-of-the-art electronic information about what's happening in town and can provide hotel and other bookings. It's open year-round, weekdays, 9–6.

For the Seattle Super Saver Package for hotel deals, see the Accommodations section later in this chapter. To find out what's happening in town, for frequent reviews on restaurants, the performing arts, and galleries, and for updates on attractions, pick up a copy of *Seattle Weekly*, a free publication that comes out every Thursday. Seattle also has two daily newspapers, the *Seattle Times* and *Seattle Post-Intelligencer*. Listings in both papers are most extensive on weekends.

Holidays
New Year's Day (January 1)
Martin Luther King Day (third Monday in January)
Presidents' Day (third Monday in February)
Memorial Day (last Monday in May)
Independence Day (July 4)

Labor Day (first Monday in September)
Columbus Day (second Monday in October)
Remembrance Day (November 11)
Thanksgiving Day (third Thursday in November)
Christmas Day (December 25)

Area Codes

In Seattle and greater Puget Sound, the area code is 206; on the Eastside it's 425; south of Seattle the area code is 253; and the rest of western Washington is 360. Eastern Washington's area code is 509.

GETTING AROUND

North–south highways through the city are I-5 and US 99 (the Alaska Way Viaduct), both of which connect the south end with downtown and the north end. The West Seattle "freeway" and bridge connect both I-5 and US 99 to that neighborhood. I-90 and WA 520 cross Lake Washington on bridges to connect the city with the Eastside. On the Eastside, I-405 runs north–south between South Center and Bothell.

Because of Seattle's hilly and water-surrounded terrain, the street system outside the downtown area is somewhat confusing. It isn't helped by streets that often change names several times along a route. Nonetheless, distances between points are relatively short and there is a system to street names; once you figure it out, it's not too hard to get around. Even if you get lost, it only leads to discovery—and there's plenty to discover.

Streets run east–west, avenues run north–south, and outside of the downtown area, the names of both streets and avenues bear compass directions that indicate the location of the neighborhood, as follows: Ballard, NW; Fremont/Wallingford, N; University District, NE; Capitol Hill, E; West Seattle, SW; Beacon Hill, S; Rainier Valley, SE. Neighborhoods are linked by bridges, including the First Avenue South bridge into downtown, the University Bridge and Montlake Bridge between Capitol Hill and the University District, the Aurora Bridge and Fremont Bridge between Queen Anne and Fremont, and the Ballard Bridge between Interbay and Ballard.

Driving in the City

Seattle suffers from horrendous traffic jams, especially during the usual rush-hour periods. You can make a right-hand turn at a red light and a turn from a one-way street onto another after coming to a complete stop.

If you're downtown, park the car and save it for trips to outlying neighborhoods such as the University District or for side trips to places such as Tacoma. Use public transportation (see below). Parking lots downtown cost anywhere from $12 to $20 a day; street parking is extremely limited, though you'll find the occasional spot in the off hours. The best parking rates are at Seattle Center, where you can park for $3 to $6 a day. Sometimes there is free street parking available near the Space Needle. When attending events at the Seattle Center, you're best off taking the Monorail from Westlake Center (see Public Transportation).

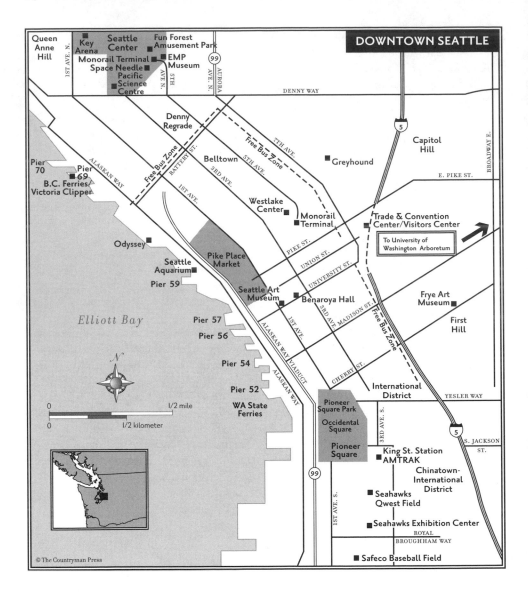

DOWNTOWN SEATTLE

Public Transportation

Exploring the city by public transportation is both inexpensive and adventurous. Exploring downtown is easy by Metro Transit's Ride Free Zone. For those who want to explore outside the downtown area in off-peak hours, the fare is $1.25 for adults and 50 cents for children 5–17 years of age; during peak hours fares are $1.50 for adults and 50 cents for children. All-day passes are also available on weekends. Seattle's **Metro Bus System** (206-553-3000, www.transit.metrokc.gov) offers free service in the downtown area between 6 am and 7 pm, with the free ride area between Alaskan Way in the west, Sixth Avenue and I-5 in the east, Battery Street in the north, and South Jackson Street in the south. Some of the city's most popular attractions, including Pike Place Market, the waterfront piers, the art museum, the symphony hall, all of the major downtown hotels, and the two stadiums, are in that area; at Battery Street, you are only six blocks away from Seattle Center.

In 1989 four 1927 trams from Melbourne, Australia, were put into service, extending the city's trolley route along the Seattle waterfront through Pioneer Square to the International District. Now the city's entire transit system is linked, and the Seattle waterfront is easily accessed by a public streetcar with character and charm. The waterfront streetcar operates every 20 minutes daily, 6:30 am–7 pm, and costs the same as the Metro buses. The streetcars run through from Pier 48 to Pier 70 along Alaskan Way, past the bottom of Pike Place Market, and past the Edgewater Hotel, ending at Myrtle Edwards Park at the end of Alaskan Way. It's a "must" experience, a great way to sightsee, and a pleasant, slow way to spend your time. While some locals use the old-fashioned trolley buses, they are mostly for visitors who want a leisurely look at the city. Various stops along the waterfront make it easy to get off and explore; just ask for a transfer when you pay your fare.

Seattle's Monorail is a zippy ride from Westlake Center downtown to Seattle Center. Toshi

The **Monorail** (206-905-2620; www.seattlemonorail.com) is a short, elevated ride between downtown, from the Westlake Center shopping mall at Fifth and Pine, and Seattle Center, passing through the middle of the Experience Music Project. The trip takes about two minutes and costs $3 for adults and $1.50 for seniors, the disabled, persons with Medicare cards, and children ages 5–12. It operates weekdays 7:30 am–11 pm, and on weekends 9 am–11 pm. It opened to the public on March 24, 1962, a month before the opening of the World's Fair. The full $3.5 million cost of the system was recovered during the first six months of the fair, as more than eight million passengers rode the train. Today, the train carries 2.5 million riders yearly and is the nation's only fully self-sufficient public transit system. It leaves every 10 minutes from the station at Seattle Center and from the Westlake Center Mall.

Taxis are hard to come by, but they can be flagged down sometimes. Your best bet is to stop at a hotel entrance and ask for one. The flag drop charge is $1.80 and fares are $1.80 a mile afterward. You can also call any cab company's dispatcher.

NEIGHBORHOODS

Seattle's neighborhoods are a direct result of its history. Built on seven hills, Seattle is virtually a city in the middle of water. Puget Sound, Lake Union, and Lake Washington bound the area west and east, and the city is split south and north by the Lake Washington Ship Canal, which connects to Puget Sound. Seattle's neighborhoods are not split into distinct cultural and ethnic districts, each with a specific ethnic makeup, though there are some exceptions: the International District is Asian, and Beacon Hill is Asian and Hispanic. Nonetheless, each neighborhood has its own identity.

The north end includes North Seattle, Greenwood, Ballard, Green Lake, Roosevelt, Fremont, Wallingford, and the University District. South of the ship canal are Magnolia, Interbay, Queen Anne, Eastlake, South Lake Union, Capitol Hill, Madison Valley, First

Hill, Belltown, Denny Regrade, Downtown, Pioneer Square, International District, Sodo and Georgetown.

Ballard
North of Magnolia and the Lake Washington Ship Canal, this neighborhood reflects its Scandinavian origins. Golden Gardens Park adjoins a large marina on the sound. The Nordic Heritage Museum graphically describes the legacy of every Nordic country. The Owl Cafe is the area's oldest bar, established in 1902. The Ballard Historic District along NW Market Street features wonderful music clubs, antique shops, and Scandinavian specialty stores. Lately this area has been rediscovered by investors, and new developments are booming.

Belltown and Denny Regrade
A historic neighborhood north of downtown that takes its name from one of Seattle's founding families, Belltown became a focus for Seattle's young avant-garde musicians and theater people during the mid- and late 1980s. With the increased activity, developers began tearing down and rehabilitating the area's boarded-up, sleazy buildings, turning the neighborhood into high-rise housing, upscale restaurants, and fashionable boutiques.

When Denny Hill was razed at the turn of the 20th century, the neighborhood was renamed the Regrade. Today it links I-5 and Capitol Hill with the waterfront and downtown. It too has seen recent redevelopment, with office towers and apartment buildings replacing surface parking lots. You'll still find lively clubs here, though.

Capitol Hill and First Hill
No, you won't find a state capitol on Capitol Hill, which lies just east of downtown. It may have been the dream of the original settlers, but it never came to pass. However, no neighborhood in the city has a more active sidewalk scene, day or night, than Broadway, Capitol Hill's version of Main Street, even where the sign over the Safeway has an art-deco style. Stretching north–south along the western crest of Capitol Hill, Broadway is a collage of lights and noise, a parade of people, restaurants, and boutiques where casual walkers are out as late as midnight in a nonthreatening environment. It's the hangout of punk fashion. Broadway's collection of restaurants, nightspots, neighborhood stores, and boutiques seems never-ending.

Few neighborhoods in the city have a more diverse population. Seattle's gay community, grunge rockers, and twentysomethings of many backgrounds share the area with longtime residents ensconced in the historic mansions of Millionaire's Row on 14th Avenue East, elegant old homes, and classic apartment houses. And it's a place in which educational institutions enliven daily life, with Seattle University, Seattle Central Community College, and Cornish College of the Arts all located in the area.

The Egyptian and Harvard Exit movie theaters are leftovers from the golden age of 1920s theater architecture. The new multilevel Broadway Market, with its vegetarian restaurants, is worth a stop as one of the city's great people-watching places. There are clubs, taverns, and a variety of shops and restaurants from around the world.

Known locally as Pill Hill because of its concentration of major hospitals, First Hill is just south of Capitol Hill. Largely a neighborhood of apartment buildings on the eastern fringe of downtown, First Hill is home to the Frye Art Museum, which houses permanent exhibits of 19th- and 20th-century painters. The Frye, which offers free admission, also hosts exhibits from local photograhers as well as traveling exhibits such as works from Russian painters.

Downtown

Your first experience with Seattle will likely be downtown. It's a large, walkable region that stretches from Belltown in the north to Pioneer Square in the south, from Elliott Bay in the west to I-5 in the east. Downtown includes some of the city's most famous sites. And, frankly, most tourists never get beyond this area. It is rich in things to see and do, and it is the cultural heart of the city. If you're staying in any of the downtown hotels, you'll be close to the Westlake Center, Pike Place Market, the waterfront, the Seattle Art Museum, Benaroya Hall, Seattle Center, and Pioneer Square—all places in which you can spend hours, if not days.

The skyscrapers downtown date primarily from the 1980s, though there has been massive renovation of pre-1980s structures, some being converted into shopping malls and others simply being brought into the 21st century. The 76-story Columbia Seafirst Center, 44-story Pacific First Center, 62-story AT&T Tower, and other core buildings have been a boon to local and international sculptors. That's because in 1973, the city passed an ordinance outlining art requirements for new structures. Henry Moore's sculpture *Three Piece Vertebrae*, outside the Seafirst Center, predated the law, but the bank has more than 1,200 pieces of art in its collection.

The $27 million Seattle Art Museum at University Street and First Avenue is a fairly recent addition to the downtown. It's currently being expanded in the block to its north. And around the corner, up University Street, is Benaroya Hall, where performances of the Seattle Symphony Orchestra are heard.

The Sheraton Hotel is flanked by the Washington State Trade and Convention Center, whose architecture resembles a series of green glass tubes. Built astride I-5, it is flanked by Freeway Park, a shady green space in the heart of the city. Stop off to visit the ground-floor tourist office and then visit the structure's second floor to see bells from each of the state's 39 counties. The bells, controlled by a computer system, are programmed to play on the hour.

Eastlake/South Lake Union

The Eastlake area is separated from the rest of Capitol Hill by I-5, and it sits, as you might suppose, on the east shore of Lake Union. William Boeing had his start in a hangar at the foot of Roanoke Street, building seaplanes that he tested on the lake. Lake Union, which is connected to Seattle's working waterfront by the Lake Washington Ship Canal, itself is host to a variety of boating outlets and two small but historical shipping museums. A colorful houseboat community is moored at the northern end near the University District, and the lake's north end is also where you'll find Gas Works Park.

The Residence Inn-Marriott's $25 million hotel complex is on the lake's south shore. The Center for Wooden Boats at the south end has a wonderful collection of 75 rowboats and sailboats, many of which can be rented. Several restaurants front the South Lake Union area, which is currently being revitalized as part of Seattle's bid for the biotech industry.

The Eastside

East of downtown, on the shores of Lake Washington, you'll find the communities of Mercer Island, Bellevue, Kirkland, and Redmond, areas that are growing but that few tourists take the time to explore. Both I-90 and WA 520 cross bridges to the Eastside, where I-405 links communities north to south. Lake Washington, which separates the main city from the Eastside communities, has a series of parks and recreational areas along its shore.

The Meydenbauer Center, a convention and performing arts center, is in downtown Bellevue, 9 miles (14.5 km) east of Seattle and 17 miles (27 km) from Sea-Tac Airport. Facilities include a 410-seat theater and a 36,000-square-foot (3,344 square-meter) exhibit hall. The performing arts theater showcases performances by the Bellevue Philharmonic Chamber Orchestra and Issaquah's Village Theater. Nearby attractions include the shops at Bellevue Mall and the Chateau Ste. Michelle and Columbia Wineries.

Fremont and Wallingford

Fremont is just north of the ship canal across the Fremont Bridge, with Ballard to the west, the Woodland Park Zoo to the north, and Wallingford to the east. The last

A large new apartment building in Fremont sports an eye-catching facade. Toshi

stand for 1960s and '70s hippies—and wannabes—Fremont is a unique place of small shops and funky restaurants that calls itself "the Center of the Universe." In its retail district you'll find such curiosities as an actual rocket, a huge statue of Lenin brought in from Russia (which generated long and angry debate when it was placed here), and a huge sculpture of a troll who rests under the Aurora Bridge feasting on a Volkswagen Beetle. The Lenin statue was originally erected in 1988 Czechoslovakia, but it was torn down by angry Slovaks during Czechoslovakia's 1989 liberation from communism and left in a junkyard. Lewis Carpenter, a Seattle resident and art connoisseur who happened to be teaching in the area, bought it and had it shipped to Seattle, where it now stands on the corner of North 36th Street and Fremont Avenue.

Wallingford, nestled between Fremont and the University District (U District), has a comfortable family feel with its tree-lined streets, its grand homes more than 100 years old and 1920s bungalows, and a lively commercial district along its main street, North 45th. A collection of international-themed restaurants, interspersed with bookstores and gift shops, and a variety of about 1,600 storefronts line both sides of North 45th Street. Wallingford has a distinctly different style from Fremont or the U District, certainly more residential and middle class, with an assortment of restaurants, bars, antique stores, vintage clothing dealers, and movie theaters. The district's biggest attractions are the attractive and spacious Woodland Park Zoo and Gas Works Park. But, unlike the top sights in Fremont, these attractions are spread out and more suited to reach by car than on foot.

Madison Valley

Madison Street extends from the waterfront east through downtown, dividing Capitol Hill and First Hill, and where it drops from the hills toward Lake Washington, it gives the Madison Valley neighborhood its name. Seattle's first black resident, William Grose, settled on this street, and until recently the area was predominantly a black neighborhood. More family-oriented than Capitol Hill, Madison Valley is now a neighborhood in transition; many homes are being remodeled, and the shops along Madison Street reflect a young, diverse neighborhood. Here you'll find small parks, two greenbelts, a pea patch, three schools, craftsman-style houses, and a cozy, upgraded business district boasting several of Seattle's best neighborhood restaurants, including **Rover's** (2808 E. Madison St.; www.rovers-seattle.com), acknowledged as one of Seattle's finest neighborhood eateries. North of Madison Street is the Washington Park Arboretum, with its winding streets and footpaths amid lofty forests.

Magnolia and Interbay

Magnolia sits on a series of hills and bluffs above Puget Sound, between the ship canal and Elliott Bay; some of Seattle's most desirable residential areas overlook the sound. Discovery Park covers 400 acres of beaches and wooded areas in this neighborhood immediately west of Queen Anne. Between Queen Anne and Magnolia is the Interbay area, a commercial district along 15th Avenue West that funnels traffic from Denny Regrade across the Ballard Bridge to the north end.

North Seattle and Greenwood

Between Ballard and Green Lake lie Phinney Ridge and the Greenwood neighborhood, with US 99/Aurora Avenue North to its east. The heart of this neighborhood north of Fremont is the intersection of North 85th Street and Greenwood Avenue. Here you'll see banners that highlight special events, such as the Greenwood/Phinney Art Walk in May or the Greenwood Classic Car & Rod Show in June. Many of the brick storefronts look as they did in the 1920s, but now they're occupied by a mix of merchants who sell everything from antiques and collectibles to comic books and clothes. The upper floors of the buildings are often leased out as apartments, giving the neighborhood a lived-in feeling at all times.

Pioneer Square and International District

Pioneer Square anchors the south end of downtown, with the waterfront to the west, the International District to the east, and Sodo and its two stadiums to the south. The birthplace of Seattle, Pioneer Square is now a historic district where handsome buildings from the 1890s have been rehabilitated for use as offices, art galleries, bookstores, sidewalk cafés, upscale condos, and carpet stores. The area's historic buildings stand on an irregular 20-block grid that begins at triangular Pioneer Square (First Avenue and Yesler Way). Long an area for working men, today Pioneer Square's Occidental Park, with its Alaskan totem poles, is where many of the city's homeless congregate. The 42-story Smith Tower, constructed in 1914 at the corner of Second Avenue and Yesler, was once the tallest building west of the Mississippi. Many historic buildings were damaged in the 6.8-magnitude Nisqually earthquake of 2001, in which damage was estimated at more than $2 billion.

The International District lies northeast of the two stadiums and borders the Pioneer Square district. It's not called Chinatown, though much of the original Chinatown motif still dots the neighborhood. Its name reflects its population: about one-third Chinese,

International District Square, with the Smith Tower in the background Toshi

one-third Filipino, and the balance from all over Asia—plus a dusting of whites, blacks, and Native Americans. The International District has none of those bright, neon-lit streets that characterize large North American Chinatowns in San Francisco, Vancouver, and New York; it's not a mini–Hong Kong, nor is it meant for tourists. That makes it refreshingly honest if somewhat bland. But you'll find great restaurants, dim sum shops, the Uwajimaya department/grocery store, Hing Hay Park, and the Wing Luke Asian Museum.

Queen Anne and Seattle Center

Queen Anne occupies one of the city's largest hills, between the ship canal and downtown, with Interbay to the west and Lake Union to the east. Originally known as Queen Anne Town, this area once separated Seattle's wealthy residents from the rest of the city. Historic revival mansions towered above the city, and the only neighborhood access, other than walking, was riding streetcars tugged by counterweights up a steep incline. The name was shortened to Queen Anne at about 1900, but the mansions and grand homes continued to be built. It didn't become the accessible area it is today until the World's Fair of 1962 opened the neighborhood to exploring visitors. Today's Queen Anne doesn't have museums or official "must-see" sites, but it is still a wonderful place for simply walking and looking out over Puget Sound. The traffic corridors bordering Queen Anne to the east (Aurora Avenue) and west (Elliott Avenue) provide almost no access to the district. But if you take the steeply sloped Queen Anne Avenue heading north, you'll find small restaurants, clothing shops, and boutiques. The area between Harrison and Roy Streets is known as Lower Queen Anne, a commercially oriented stretch with little connection to the well-heeled residents and their estates above it. The many bars and nightspots handle the crowds after sporting events at Key Arena and Memorial Stadium. Seattle Center, however, is more than just a collection of theaters, arenas and museums. It's really a mini-district and locals consider it the cultural heart soul of the city, representing the city's collective imagination and creativity.

Seattle Center dates from 1962, when it was the site of the Seattle World's Fair, and it still is the core of many of the city's cultural events, including the Northwest Folklife Festival and Bumbershoot. The former Seattle Opera House was gutted in 2002–03 and was rebuilt as the Marion Oliver McCaw Hall in a $125 million renovation. The symphony, which used to perform there, now has its own facility downtown. But McCaw Hall is still home to the Seattle Opera, Pacific Northwest Ballet, and other performers, and the nearby Bagley Wright Theater houses the Seattle Repertory Theater.

But perhaps most notably, Seattle Center is home to the Space Needle, the most visible symbol of Seattle. The center, a large urban green space well loved by its citizens, is also where the NBA Seattle SuperSonics play their games, in KeyArena, and where you'll find the Pacific Science Center (which includes a laserium) and IMAX Theater, the Fun Forest Amusement Park, arts and crafts centers, the International Fountain, the Mural Amphitheater (an outdoor stage), the Seattle Children's Museum, and the spectacular Experience Music Project. The latter is a dramatic interactive music museum that celebrates creativity and the history of rock 'n' roll and other American music forms. Seattle Center, however, is more than just a collection of theaters, arenas, and museums. It's really a mini-district and locals consider it the cultural heart and soul of the city.

Roosevelt and Green Lake

Located north of the University District, Roosevelt is largely residential, with homes dating from the early decades of the 20th century. It has a lively retail district centered on Roosevelt Avenue NE near NE 65th Street. The Kirsten Gallery has cutting-edge exhibits exploring newage aesthetics.

A view of downtown Seattle from the Queen Anne neighborhood Toshi

A few blocks northwest of Roosevelt, Green Lake is one of Seattle's best-loved recreational areas. Feed the ducks at the Waldo Waterfowl Sanctuary, play nine holes at the Pitch 'n' Putt Golf Course, catch a play at the Bathhouse Theater, or stroll the 3-mile promenade around the lake. The neighborhood has shops and restaurants, a Carnegie branch library, and a community center.

Sodo and Georgetown

On the way to and from Sea-Tac International Airport via I-5, you pass Southcenter, at the southern confluence of I-5 and I-405, one of Seattle's largest covered shopping malls, sitting on 92 acres and housing 125 stores. As you continue north toward downtown, you pass through the city's commercial and industrial area. The region around the two new stadiums is called Sodo—originally for "south of the King Dome" but now for "south of downtown." It's becoming an extension of the downtown's retail sector, merging with the industrial core.

The industrial section south of downtown and Sodo is Georgetown, an old residential neighborhood recently discovered by artists who consider it a haven from development. Nearby Boeing Field is the location of the Museum of Flight and its world-class Great Gallery.

University District

The area northeast of Lake Union, centered around the University of Washington campus, also encompasses residential areas and a retail district that has several blocks of what once would have been called Bohemian character, with small ice cream shops and coffeehouses on streets filled out by small shops catering to exotic tastes in clothing and art. Among the campus highlights are the Drumheller Fountain, with its glorious view of Mount Rainier; Red Square; Husky Stadium; the Thomas Burke Memorial Museum, with its excellent North Coast Native American collections; and the Henry Art Museum, with its 19th- and 20th-century art. Nearby are the Museum of History and Industry and the University Book Store, billed as the continent's largest university bookstore. University Way NE is the main drag, but locals just call it "the Ave." They queue up at the Varsity or Neptune Theater for the latest Hollywood flicks and then go to the College Inn Pub or the Big Time Brewery and Alehouse afterward.

Waterfront

Seattle's western waterfront, once known as "the Gold Rush Strip" from the time when boats headed for the Yukon, stretches from Pier 51 on the south to Pier 70 on the north; it is a popular spot for strolling, dining, and exploring. The Washington State Ferry terminal

Looking south down Seattle's waterfront, with Qwest Stadium in the background Toshi

is at Colman Dock on Pier 52, with its Joshua Green Fountain outside the entrance. This is where you catch ferries to Bainbridge Island and Tillicum Village on Blake Island. Sightseeing boats to Alaska and Seattle Harbor Tours boats depart from Piers 56 and 57 for narrated cruises of Elliott Bay's working waterfront and the Lake Washington Ship Canal.

Most of the piers have been transformed into shopping centers, especially Piers 55 and 56. Pier 54 is the home of Ye Olde Curiosity Shop and Museum, which specializes in souvenirs and oddities, and Ivar's Acres of Clams, the business of colorful local businessman Ivar Haglund, who made a fortune selling clams at several regional restaurants. The area is a tourist attraction for a number of reasons, including the Seattle Aquarium at Pier 59, the IMAXDome Theater, and the Maritime Discovery Center, to say nothing of several eateries along the waterfront.

ACCOMMODATIONS

Seattle hotels offer disability access, whereas small inns and B&B facilities may not. If you arrive in the summer, book well in advance, especially if you'll be in town at the same time that a major event is taking place. Most hotels have a variety of packages that include cultural events such as theater, the symphony, the opera, or the art museum as well as sporting or special events. Be sure you ask about them to get the best out of your visit. Quite a few moderate and inexpensive hotels are within walking distance of the city's major attractions and sights, and depending on when you visit, often you can stay at a major downtown hotel for a large discount.

In recent years, Seattle has become one of the most pet-friendly cities in America, and few accommodations refuse to have them, though some do. The listings in this guide indicate whether a hotel allows pets. However, policies do change, so be sure to check beforehand whether the property does indeed allow them.

Hotels and Motels

As in most cities, the closer you get to downtown Seattle, the higher the hotel rates. Also, summer is when the rates are the highest because bookings are close to 95 percent. Some establishments, like the Fairmont Olympic Hotel, have long and complex histories, while others, like the Seattle Marriott Waterfront, are brand-new. By far the biggest concentrations of hotels are in the downtown and airport areas; the University District and the Eastside suburbs of Bellevue and Kirkland also have a few. Hotel construction in the downtown area is expected to continue for several years. In the summer of 2006, for example, Pan Pacific Hotels and Resorts will be opening a high-end 160-room boutique hotel that will be the focal point of a major project in Seattle's South Lake Union neighborhood.

AIRPORT AREA

The hotels and motels in the area of Sea-Tac Airport are essentially places to bed if you have an early morning flight out or a place to recover if you've had a long flight in and don't want to drive right away. None are places where you would want to stay for any length of time if you're in town to see things. Not to be confused with Sea-Tac Airport is the nearby town of Seatac, which uses no capital T or hyphen in its name. All the hotel properties take major credit cards, most are in the inexpensive or moderate range, and all are within five minutes of the airport and about 30–45 minutes from downtown. They all have airport pickups and drop-offs. If you're driving to Sea-Tac and want to leave your car during your trip, some hotels allow you to leave your car with them for a few days. You can also use long-term parking at the airport, though **Doug Fox Parking** (206-248-2956 or 1-800-562-5027; www.dougfoxparking. com) is cheaper, secure, and just a few minutes away with drop-offs and pick-ups at the terminal.

Expensive
Seattle Marriott Hotel Sea-Tac, 3201 S. 176th St., Seattle, WA 98188; 206-241-2000, 1-800-314-0925; www.marriott.com/seawa

Moderate
Holiday Inn Seattle Sea-Tac, 17338 International Blvd., Seattle, WA 98188; 206-248-1000, 1-877-573-2823; www.holiday-inn.com

La Quinta Inn Sea-Tac, 2824 S. 188th St., Seattle, WA 98188; 206-241-5211, 1-800-531-5900, www.laquinta.com

Radisson Hotel Seattle Airport, 17001 Pacific Hwy. S., Seattle, WA 98188; 206-244-6000, 1-800-333-3333; www.radisson.com/seattlewa

Red Lion Hotel at Seattle Airport, 18220 International Blvd., Seattle, WA 98188; 206-246-5535, 1-800-426-0670; www.westcoasthotels.com/seatac

Prime Hotel Sea-Tac, 18118 Pacific Hwy. S., Seattle, WA 98188; 206-244-6666, 1-800-870-2889; www.primehotelsandresorts.com

Inexpensive
Quality Inn Sea-Tac, 2900 S. 192nd St., SeaTac, WA 98188; 206-241-9292, 1-800-393-1856; www.choicehotels.com

Best Western Airport Executel, 20717 International Blvd., Seattle, WA 98198; 206-878-3300, 1-800-648-3311; www.bestwestern.com/airportexecutel

Clarion Hotel Sea-Tac Airport, 3000 S. 176th St., Seattle, WA 98188; 206-242-0200, 1-877-424-6423; www.clarioninn.com

Motel 6—Sea-Tac South, 18900 47th Ave. S., Seattle, WA 98188; 206-241-1648, 1-800-466-8356; www.motel6.com

Quality Inn and Suites, 1400 S. 348th St., Federal Way, WA 98003; 253-835-4141, 1-800-424-6423; www.choicehotels.com

Red Roof Inn, 16838 International Blvd,. Seattle, WA 98188; 206-248-0901, 1-800-733-7663; www.redroof.com

Rodeway Inn Sea-Tac, 930 S. 176th, Seatac, WA 98188; 206-246-9300, 1-800-347-9301; www.rodeway.com

Sea-Tac Inn, 17108 International Blvd., Seattle, WA 98188; 206-244-1230, 1-800-500-1230; www.seatacinn.com

Sleep Inn Sea-Tac Airport, 20406 International Blvd. S., Seattle, WA 98198; 206-878-3600; www.sleepinn.com

Travelodge Sea-Tac Airport North, 14845 Pacific Hwy. S., Seattle, WA 98168; 206-242-1777, 1-800-578-7878; www.travelodge.com

CAPITOL HILL/FIRST HILL
First Hill Executive Suites
400 10th Ave.,
Seattle, WA 98122
206-621-9229, 1-800-571-0848
Price: Inexpensive to moderate
Credit cards: AE
Special features: Long-stay apartments
Pets: No

The First Hill Apartments are located blocks from downtown Seattle within walking distance of the Swedish Medical Center and Harborview Hospital across from Seattle University. Therefore these long-stay apartments that provide a bit of home are probably more suited to those in the medical profession, though the suites are available to anyone. The fully furnished studios and one- and two-bedroom suites come with in-room coffeemakers, a hair dryer, a private phone line, cable TV, a microwave, a full-size refrigerator, a stove, linens, pots and pans, dishes, an iron and ironing board, and high-speed Internet access. There is a free shuttle to nearby hospitals in the First Hill area.

Inn at Virginia Mason
1006 Spring St.
Seattle, WA 98104
206-583-6453, 1-800-283-6453
Price: Moderate
Credit cards: AE, Disc, MC, V
Special features: Adjacent to hospital
Pets: No

This 1920s apartment building originally built for "single women of privilege" was converted into a cozy inn, and since it's next to Virginia Mason Hospital, many of the guests are visiting patients or out-of-towners in for treatment. Still, this charming hotel is welcoming to leisure travelers. It is a good option for those who want to be near downtown yet prefer a quieter locale. The 79 rooms are comfortable and spacious; standard rooms have a queen or two double beds and a small sitting area. Select suites feature fireplaces, jetted tubs, and city views. The library suit includes a large separate sitting area, a desk, an extra-large bath area, and a library filled with medical books. Some rooms have views of downtown or First Hill, but many look out at the hospital. The inn's rooftop patio provides a breathtaking view of downtown Seattle and a relaxing getaway. It is in a quiet location within a block of the Sorrento Hotel, which has a great bar. And it's an easy walk to shopping and the convention center.

Sorrento Hotel
900 Madison St.
Seattle, WA 98104
206-622-6400, 1-800-426-1265
www.hotelsorrento.com
Price: Very expensive
Credit cards: AE, DC, Disc, MC, V
Special features: Old-world luxury
Pets: OK

The Sorrento first opened in 1909 and has remained a classical touch of old-world elegance, even with a complete renovation in 2002. Its iron gates, palm trees at the entrance, and richly appointed lobby give this 76-room boutique hotel the look and feel of unabashed luxury. Its rooms are all different, with most set up for business travelers; the standard rooms are almost the same size as the suites. The hotel is located high on First Hill, just above the downtown core on the east side of I-5, and so rooms on the west side of the hotel have commanding views of the city and Puget Sound. Limosines provide shuttle service downtown if you choose not to walk the steep few blocks to the downtown core. In the summer, tables are set up for eating in the courtyard. The dining room is a cozy, warmly decorated place that's perfect for a rainy-season escape. In the lounge, where there's live jazz, you can get a light meal with your entertainment.

DOWNTOWN/BELLTOWN
Ace Hotel
2423 First Ave.
Seattle, WA 98121
206-448-4721
www.acehotel.com
Price: Inexpensive to moderate
Credit cards: AE, DC, Disc, MC, V
Special features: Euro-chic
Pets: OK

The Ace is a new approach to downtown lodging in a historic building. Next to Pike Place Market, shopping, and the waterfront, it is Seattle's most-talked-about new hotel. Why? Ace is a kind of superaesthetic barracks, with an economy of style featuring vintage French army blankets that cover the low beds and institutional stainless-steel sinks bolted to the wall. Floor-to-ceiling photo murals and graffiti art offer the only

The lobby of the Alexis Hotel Courtesy of Kimpton Group Hotels

adornments, while a glowing white cube on the floor helps illuminate. The Ace's 28 rooms feature loftlike ceilings, white-on-white decor, hardwood floors, and a single sink and vanity in each room. Half the hotel has custom private bathrooms; for the budget-minded traveler, European rooms have shared bathrooms. It's a brightly decorated place for travelers wanting a unique hotel experience with high-speed Internet access. A young clientele means a touch more noise than some might want.

Alexis Hotel
1007 First Ave.
Seattle, WA 98104
206-624-4844, 1-866-356-8894
www.alexishotel.com
Price: Expensive to very expensive
Credit cards: AE, DC, Disc, MC, V
Special features: Fine-art decor
Pets: OK

The Alexis Hotel is a luxury boutique hotel located between Pike Place Market and Pioneer Square. The building in which it is located was originally an office building, built in 1901. In 1980 the building was converted to a hotel and was then renovated in 1996 by Kimpton Hotels, its current owner. Listed on the National Register of Historic Places, the Alexis has a rotating collection of art from a variety of Northwest artists on display throughout its public spaces, with some rooms displaying original works by the likes of John Lennon and Miles Davis. The foyer of the hotel houses the "Circle of Friends" piece by renowned glass artist Dale Chihuly. The colorful lobby nightly has complimentary evening wine receptions. All rooms feature large windows, high ceilings, and a richly colored environment in a warm maize yellow with an eclectic mix of traditional fabrics. Some of the 109 rooms and suites have wood-burning fireplaces. Others have two-person jetted tubs and spacious sitting and dining rooms, all done in impeccable decor. The Alexis is home to the Library Bistro and the Bookstore Bar and Cafe. Reminiscent of the 1940s and 1950s, the Library Bistro is a cozy neighborhood restaurant serving local and seasonally inspired cuisine.

Commodore Motor Hotel
2013 Second Ave.
Seattle, WA 98121
206-448-8868, 1-800-714-8868
www.commodorehotel.com
Price: Inexpensive
Credit cards: AE, MC, V
Special features: Great value
Pets: No

This is one of Seattle's best hotel values. The family-owned and family-operated European-style hotel is centrally located to all downtown attractions, and the 100 comfortable rooms are an exceptional value for budget-conscious travelers. It is two blocks from Pike Place Market and four blocks from Westlake Center and the Monorail. It has cable TV and early morning coffee and newspapers in the lobby.

Crowne Plaza Hotel Seattle
1113 Sixth Ave.
Seattle, WA 98101-3048
206-464-1980, 1-800-521-2762
www.crowneplazaseattle.com
Price: Expensive
Credit cards: AE, DC, Disc, MC, V
Special features: Business oriented
Pets: OK

Located just off 1-5 in downtown Seattle, the Crowne Plaza is close to the convention center, so it is perfect for convention delegates and businesspeople. Although it's generally geared to business traffic, with all of the usual electronics and Internet access in every room, the hotel is also a comfortable refuge for tourists because its location makes it handy to all of downtown's major

sights and activities. The warmly appointed guest rooms have large, panoramic windows that afford excellent views of the city, mountain ranges, or the sound, depending on which side of the building you're located on. The best deals are on weekends, when you will get a 15 percent discount.

Executive Pacific Plaza Hotel
400 Spring St.
Seattle, WA 98104
206-623-3900, 1-800-426-1165
www.pacificplazahotel.com
Price: Inexpensive to moderate
Credit cards: AE, DC, Disc, MC, V
Special features: Nonsmoking
Pets: OK

This European style hotel was renovated in 2001, and it is a terrific bargain, considering its location in midtown Seattle. Built in 1928, this hotel is one of the few bargain hotels in the downtown area. There is no air conditioning, so the west-facing rooms can get a bit warm in the summer. Rooms are small, but if you do not expect to spend a lot of time in them, they're fine. The hotel has 24-hour bell service and a concierge, and a continental breakfast is included in the room price. Parking is available.

Fairmont Olympic Hotel
411 University St.
Seattle, WA 98101
www.fairmont.com/seattle
206-621-1700, 1-800-441-1414
Price: Very expensive
Credit cards: AE, DC, Disc, MC, V
Special features: Old-world luxury
Pets: OK

If you want the very best, stay here. That has been this hotel's history even when it was owned and/or run by other chains, and it continues today. The hotel sits on a 10-acre city-center tract deeded to the University of Washington by Seattle pioneer Arthur A. Denny; the university's first building was

The Fairmont Olympic Hotel's Spanish staircase dates from 1924. Courtesy of Fairmont Hotels

constructed where the hotel now stands. Listed on the National Register of Historic Places in 1979, it still retains the Italian Renaissance style of architecture popular in the 1920s, accented with high, arched Palladian windows. When it opened on October 31, 1924, the hotel was decorated with hundreds of antique mirrors, Italian and Spanish oil jars, bronze statuary, and terrazzo floors installed by Italian workers who came to Seattle specifically for the project. Many of these items have remained even though the hotel underwent a two-year, $62.5 million restoration and infrastructure modernization, including $5 million in seismic upgrades. When it reopened in 1982, the original oak-paneled walls were refinished, the crystal chandeliers were brought out of storage (where they had been for decades), and 756 rooms were redesigned and reduced to 450. Even if you don't stay here, do come in, walk around, have a meal or a casual drink in the hotel lobby area, and just look around. Few hotels have this kind of old-world quality. Package deals make the hotel affordable to many, especially the Seattle Super Saver package, which starts at $179. Schuckers, located at the hotel, is one of Seattle's original oyster bars. The Garden at the Fairmont is a bright atrium with lush tropical foliage where you can have a light meal. The hotel's premium restaurant, the Georgian, has a classic continental and Pacific Northwest menu. The hotel has all imaginable amenities.

Grand Hyatt Seattle
721 Pine St.
Seattle, WA 98101
206-774-1234, 1-800-233-1234
www.seattlegrand.hyatt.com
Price: Expensive to very expensive
Credit cards: AE, DC, Disc, MC, V
Special features: Business oriented
Pets: OK

Business travelers like the high-speed Internet connections and power outlets at each of the 151 seats in the meetings theater, which allow you to download material from presentations and log on to the Internet. Even the guest rooms have Internet connections. Beyond the business toys, the hotel is simply high quality, beginning with the Willem de Kooning sculpture outside the front door and the regional glass art that permeates the lobby. There is no swimming pool, but the health club has everything you need to get rid of the calories you'll consume at the Wine Cellar dining room, located one floor below the main restaurant, 727 Pine, which features Northwest cuisine. The 312 stylish rooms and 113 luxury suites are exquisitely decorated; oversize bathrooms feature a glass-enclosed shower and separate tub. The least-expensive rooms are somewhat small and more suitable for single travelers.

Hilton Seattle

1301 Sixth Ave. (at University St.)
Seattle, WA 98101
206-624-0500, 1-800-426-0535
www.seattlehilton.com
Price: Moderate to expensive
Credit cards: AE, DC, Disc, MC, V
Special features: Views from every room
Pets: OK

It's a Hilton. But it's a Hilton with a difference. All of the 237 deluxe guest rooms are above the ninth floor, where you'll find the lobby. So every room, including the 45 executive-floor rooms, features window views of the Seattle skyline, Puget Sound, and, on a clear day, the Olympic Mountains. The bottom portion of the hotel is devoted primarily to parking space. All of the tastefully appointed guest rooms are decorated in soft tones and have cable TV. There's 24-hour room service, a concierge, a gift shop, a restaurant, a lounge, a lobby lounge, valet laundry service, a senior citizen discount, and a family plan. The hotel is located one block away from the Fairmont Olympic in the heart of downtown Seattle, so it's a short walk to Nordstrom's, Nike Town, Pacific Place, Pike Place Market, the waterfront, and theaters. It is also connected by an underground concourse to the Washington State Convention and Trade Center, 5th Avenue Theatre, and Rainier Square retail shops.

Homewood Suites by Hilton Downtown Seattle

206 Western Ave. W.
Seattle, WA 98119
206-281-9393, 1-800-225-4663
www.homewoodsuites.com
Price: Expensive to very expensive
Credit cards: AE, DC, Disc, MC, V
Special features: Apartment-style suites
Pets: OK

On the edge of Belltown, the hotel offers spectacular views of Elliott Bay and the Olympic Mountains. The rooms will make you feel at home because each has the comforts you'd expect from a well designed apartment with kitchens that have all of the usual appliances and with a layout that separates the living room and bedroom, including a pull-out sofa to accommodate children or another guest. The location is within walking distance of the Key Arena, the Space Needle, and performance venues located within Seattle Center. You're not far from the waterfront or from the Queen Anne neighborhoods with its restaurants and nightlife. The hotel offers a complimentary hot breakfast and, as with several other hotels in the Seattle area, there are designated evenings that offer small wine and snack receptions for guests.

Hotel Ändra

2000 Fourth Ave.
Seattle, WA 98121
206-448-8600, 1-800-715-6513
www.hotelandra.com
Price: Expensive to very expensive
Credit cards: AE, DC, Disc, MC, V
Special features: Cutting-edge
Pets: OK

This used to be the Claremont Hotel, which was originally built in 1926. But the classic

Hotel Monaco's lobby hosts an evening wine reception for guests. Courtesy of Kimpton Group Hotels

brick and terra-cotta building was thoroughly renovated in 2004 to become the Hotel Andra, with 119 rooms averaging more than 400 square feet each. The largest of the rooms is the Monarch Suite, at 1,500 square feet. Rooms and suites are decorated with khaki walls, alpaca headboards, and a charcoal blue chenille bedspread, accented with warm, minimalist, dark wood furniture and sparked with brushed stainless-steel accents. Business travelers like the oversize walnut-stained desk equipped with a comfortable working chair, ample lighting, two-line cordless speaker phones, and wireless Internet connections. The hotel also offers 4,000 square feet of meeting space. Located on the edge of Seattle's trendy Belltown neighborhood, it is close to Pike Place Market and to major department stores and shopping centers. The lobby fireplace, built of local split-grain granite, is surrounded by floor-to-ceiling golden maple bookcases and topped with a floating steel-wrapped plasma screen projecting an ever-changing collection of electronic fine art. On-site Assaggio Ristorante's menu is continental Italian, winner of several awards.

Hotel Monaco

1101 Fourth Ave.
Seattle, WA 98101
206-621-1770, 1-800-945-2240
www.monaco-seattle.com
Price: Very expensive
Credit cards: AE, DC, Disc, MC, V
Special features: Hip business hotel
Pets: Encouraged

Have you ever been greeted at the front desk with a goldfish in a monogrammed bowl? Now, that's a hotel with a special focus. There is nothing subtle about the Monaco. Its decor is bold, with striped wallpaper in some of the rooms and hues of raspberry, crimson, and bright yellow; reproductions of ancient Greek murals in the lobby go with the hotel's retro-contemporary overall design. Its clientele is young and affluent, and the hotel is pet friendly—dogs even get a monogrammed raincoat. If you don't have a pet, you'll be offered the goldfish in a bowl to keep you company. In the evenings, the hotel has a complimentary wine reception. A 24-hour business center is available, and all rooms are wired for the business traveler. If you happen to be in Seattle during the rainy

season, you won't find a cheerier place to stay. The hotel's restaurant, Sazerac, features Pacific Northwest cuisine. The nearby Allstar Fitness, a fully equipped fitness center with classes and a swimming pool, is available to guests for $10 a day.

Hotel Seattle

315 Seneca St.
Seattle, WA 98101
206-623-5110, 1-888-265-9330
www.thehotelseattle.com
Price: Inexpensive to moderate
Credit cards: AE, DC, Disc, MC, V
Pets: OK

Situated in the heart of downtown Seattle, the Hotel Seattle is just steps away from the financial, federal, and business districts, and Seattle's finest shops and theaters, the waterfront, historic Pioneer Square, and the convention center are all within walking distance. All of the guest rooms have been recently remodeled, with bath and shower combinations, direct-dial telephones, and color TVs equipped with AM/FM radios. Bernard's on Seneca Restaurant is open daily with a menu of Bavarian, Continental, and American cuisine.

Hotel Vintage Park

1100 Fifth Ave.
Seattle, WA 98101
206-624-8000, 1-800-624-4433
www.hotelvintagepark.com
Price: Expensive to very expensive
Credit cards: AE, DC, Disc, MC, V
Special features: Wine focused
Pets: OK

This elegant hotel was designed with wine lovers in mind. Everywhere you go, walls detail the wine industry and winemakers and their products. In the afternoon, the lobby has a complimentary wine tasting for guests, with soft music and a knowledgeable concierge who gives you background without being snobbish. The hotel is on the

Hotel Vintage Park's intimate lobby Courtesy of Kimpton Group Hotels

National Register of Historic Places and had a complete renovation in 2000; each room is decorated in the wine schemes of the five Washington State appellations (official wine regions). It has the feel of a European boutique hotel without the class distinctions that Europe often brings to its hotels. The lobby is a statement of quiet elegance with a large fireplace, antiques, rich leather, and a feeling of intimacy and romance. The 126 guest rooms all have the usual high-speed Internet access that businesspeople need. If you can, try to get the Chateau Ste. Michelle Suite, which features a draped canopy bed, a wood-burning fireplace, a tiled spa bath, a granite vanity, and surround-sound stereo system in a suite decorated in shades of gold, persimmon, and sapphire blue. The hotel is also home to Tulio Ristorante, one of the finest restaurants in Seattle, featuring northern Italian cuisine.

Inn at Harbor Steps

1221 First Ave.
Seattle, WA 98101
206-748-0973, 1-888-728-8910
www.innatharborsteps.com
Price: Expensive
Credit cards: AE, DC, Disc, MC, V
Special features: Large rooms
Pets: No

Located on the lower part of one of the most elegant high-rise apartment buildings in Seattle, this B&B-style property does not fit any of the usual B&B definitions. It's across the street from the Seattle Art Museum and is well located for exploring the downtown area. The inn is an easy walk from Pike Place Market. The rooms are large, all have a gas fireplace, and the largest rooms have a whirlpool tub. Most have beautiful garden views. Each room has one or two queen beds or a king bed, a sitting area, a wet bar and refrigerator, data ports, and voice mail.

Rates include full breakfast and afternoon tea and appetizers. Sharing the building is the Wolfgang Puck Café that has waterfront views and contemporary decor to complement its Pacific Northwest menu.

Inn at the Market
86 Pine St.
Seattle, WA 98101
206-443-3600, 1-800-446-4484
www.innatthemarket.com
Price: Expensive
Credit cards: AE, Disc, MC, V
Special features: In Pike Place Market
Pets: No

This 70-room boutique hotel, built in 1996 overlooking Elliott Bay and Pike Place Market, feels more like a Parisian property than an American one. Movie buffs might recognize it from the film *Sleepless in Seattle*, in which it was featured. You enter the hotel through a small, European-like plaza just off Pine Street. The lobby displays an art collection by such Northwest masters as Guy Anderson, Richard Gilkey, and Jay Steensma. Splendid sculpture, antique objets d'art, and a magnificent slate wall fountain add to the sense of serenity and invite guests into a French-like boutique experience. Rooms are trimmed in silk and chenille. The inn's private rooftop garden provides spectacular views of the Olympic Range and the bay. From this vantage point, you can also follow the lively scene down in the market. But try to get one of the water-view rooms that have bay windows for great panoramas. Two fine restaurants, Campagne (the hotel's formal main dining room) and Café Campagne, serve French fare.

Marriott SpringHill Suites
Seattle Downtown
1800 Yale Ave.
Seattle, WA 98101
206-254-0500, 1-888-287-9400
www.springhillsuites.com
Price: Expensive to very expensive
Credit cards: AE, Disc, MC, V
Special features: Business oriented
Pets: No

These large suites are more like apartments than hotel suites. And they have everything that business a traveler could yearn for: data ports, two-line telephones with voice mail, minirefrigerators, microwave ovens, coffeemakers, daily continental breakfast buffets, a business center, a restaurant, and a lounge. Not only that, it's located near the convention center.

Mayflower Park Hotel
405 Olive Way
Seattle, WA 98101
206-623-8700, 1-800-426-5100
www.mayflowerpark.com
Price: Moderate to very expensive
Credit cards: AE, DC, Disc, MC, V
Special features: Hip business hotel
Pets: OK

The historic, elegantly appointed Mayflower Park Hotel occupies one of Seattle's finest shopping and business locations in a building that dates from 1927. It opens directly into Westlake Center, from where you can ride the Monorail to Seattle Center, the

A luxury suite in the 1927 Mayflower Park Hotel
Courtesy of Mayflower Park Hotel

Space Needle, and the Experience Music Project. Pike Place Market, the waterfront, and the Seattle Art Museum are just a short walk away, as are the major shopping malls and department stores. Independently owned, the Mayflower Park Hotel offers 171 classically styled guest rooms, including 19 luxury suites a Mediterranean restaurant, Andaluca, in the basement and Oliver's Lounge, a popular bar offering what many claim are the best martinis in town, on the lobby level. The best nonsuite rooms are on the corners. Meeting rooms for up to 200 people also offer wireless Internet connection. This means guests attending a meeting can sit in meeting rooms, public spaces, or their guest room and still wirelessly access the Internet through their laptops. For guests carrying laptops that do not provide for wireless connectivity, the hotel provides an instant Ethernet wireless bridge. The hotel's 5th Avenue Theatre Package includes two theater tickets, a classic or deluxe room, and valet parking. The theater is conveniently located within walking distance of the hotel along Fifth Avenue.

Moore Hotel
1926 Second Ave.
Seattle, WA 98101
206-448-4851, 1-800-421-5508
www.moorehotel.com
Price: Inexpensive
Credit cards: MC, V
Special features: Contains a theater
Pets: OK

It's a basic hotel with clean rooms and it's in a historic building in the heart of Seattle next to Pike Place Market, downtown shopping, and the waterfront. If you're not expecting too much in the way of amenities, you can't beat the location or the price. This hotel is perfect for budget travelers. The rooms are comfortable, with antique lighting and historical charm. The Nitelite Restaurant and Lounge offers a varied menu

and drinks. Attached to the hotel is the Moore Theater, home to a wide range of live theater and touring Broadway shows. Some of the rooms have views of Puget Sound.

The Paramount Hotel
724 Pine St.
Seattle, WA 98101
206-292-9500, 1-800-663-1144
www.paramounthotelseattle.com
Price: Inexpensive
Credit cards: MC, V
Special features: Elegance and style
Pets: No

Built in 1996, the Paramount leaves the initial impression of being an English gentleman's country lodge with a lobby complete with a fireplace, dark wood furnishings, and warm lighting. Yet the restaurant, Dragonfish, has an Asian motif and a menu to match. You'll be greeted by parking valets who will take your vehicle to covered parking. The 146 guest rooms have one king or two queen-size beds and state-of-the-art features such as high-speed Internet access and two separate phone lines. Each room has soft, neutral tones and is elegantly appointed. The grand suites on the top floor offer a bird's-eye view of the surrounding city and feature a separate king bedroom, dining/conference room, wet bar, and sitting area with a double-sided gas fireplace and a queen-size sofa bed. A large bathroom features an oversize jetted tub, a separate shower, and a double vanity. An optional connecting room has two queen beds. This hotel is one block from the convention center, the Paramount Theatre, and Pacific Place and two or three blocks from Westlake Center and the monorail to the Space Needle and Seattle Center.

Red Lion Hotel on Fifth Avenue
1415 Fifth Ave.
Seattle, WA 98101
206-971-8000, 1-800-325-4000

www.westcoasthotels.com
Price: Moderate to expensive
Credit cards: AE, DC, Disc, MC, V
Special features: In the heart of downtown
Pets: OK

You can't be more in the heart of downtown than this. Sitting across the street from the 5th Avenue Theatre, this high-rise hotel has spectacular views from its 297 rooms, fitness center, and terrace garden restaurant and lounge. If you want the action, you'll get plenty of it here, since the city's best shopping, theaters, and attractions are just a few steps from the door. The hotel is near the convention center, so the rooms are wired for businesspeople. Secured parking costs $21 nightly, which seems to be the area standard. A departure fee of $50 applies if you depart prior to your scheduled departure date.

Renaissance Madison Hotel
515 Madison St.
Seattle, WA 98104
206-583-0300, 1-800-546-9184 (US);
1-800-468-3571 (Canada)
www.renaissancehotels.com
Price: Expensive
Credit cards: AE, DC, Disc, MC, V
Special features: Great view from restaurant
Pets: Service animals only

This recently renovated hotel is on the edge of the downtown core, next to the new dramatic Seattle Public Library and the freeway but isolated from I-5's noise and traffic. Freeway access is easy, and you are within easy walking distance of the stadiums, shopping, and sightseeing. The high-ceilinged lobby has bright and colorful furnishings, and its walls are lined with paintings from a local artist depicting colorful city scenes. Rooms are Renaissance standard, with high-speed Internet access and complimentary coffee and tea. Grayline Airport Express offers shuttle service to and from Sea-Tac International Airport, 20

minutes away, for a fee. The restaurant, Prego, offers some of the best views in the city from its 28th-floor location.

Roosevelt Hotel
1531 Seventh Ave.
Seattle, WA 98101
206-621-1200, 1-800-325-4000
www.roosevelthotel.com
Price: Moderate
Credit cards: AE, DC, Disc, MC, V
Special features: Great view from restaurant
Pets: Service animals only

The rooms are small, but the decor in this newly renovated 1929 hotel is tasteful and the atmosphere is sophisticated. The lobby is a jewel, decorated to resemble an old mansion with bookshelves around the fireplace and a nearby grand piano. The cheapest rooms are small and have only a shower, no bathtub. Try to upgrade to a larger room for more space. The hotel restaurant, Von's Grand City Café, more than 80 years old, specializes in applewood-grilled fish and meat. The hotel is located one block from the convention center. Amenities include in-room movies, valet parking, room service, a fitness center, same-day dry cleaning, a 24-hour concierge, and a senior citizen discount.

Seattle Suites
1400 Hubbell Pl., Ste. 1103
Seattle, WA 98101
206-232-2799
www.seattlesuite.com
Price: Moderate to expensive
Credit cards: AE, MC, V
Special features: Homey atmosphere; nonsmoking
Pets: No

If you're going to stay for a minimum of three days, these upscale, one-bedroom executive condo suites located in the heart of downtown Seattle are perfect either for business travel or for a vacation. Located one block east of the Washington State Convention and Trade Center and in the heart of the shopping district, each apartment is fully furnished with all the amenities of home, many with fabulous city views. This hotel is one of the best values downtown since you'll have a king or queen bed in the bedroom, a sofa bed in the living room, a 25-inch color TV with 80 channels of cable, a VCR and DVD player, a full kitchen complete with dishwasher, microwave, and coffeemaker, and a phone with voice mail and free local calls. Starbucks coffee and a variety of teas are provided, as are all dishware, linens, and household items. There's a game room with a regulation-size pool table and a big-screen TV. Laundry facilities and a business center with a fax machine and copier are available. Weekly and monthly rates are also available.

Sheraton Seattle Hotel and Towers

1400 Sixth Ave.
Seattle, WA 98101
206-621-9000, 1-800-325-3535
www.sheraton.com/seattle
Price: Expensive to very expensive
Credit cards: AE, DC, Disc, MC, V
Special features: Conventions
Pets: OK

The second-highest hotel in Seattle, at 35 stories, the Sheraton proves that looks can be deceiving. Although the lobby resembles the arrivals area at Sea-Tac Airport, with conventioneers and groups arriving en masse, there are surprisingly intimate places in the area. A wonderful little wine bar in the lobby area serves only estate wines from the Pacific Northwest in a quiet, intimate setting. The guest rooms are large and have been recently renovated. Try to get a room on one of the upper floors for a great view of the city. The hotel has just about everything you can ask for in a full-service property: 24-hour room service, a concierge, a coffee shop, a gift shop, three restaurants, a business center, a lounge, entertainment, senior citizen discounts, a valet, a Jacuzzi, an indoor pool, and a sauna. The Towers/Club section includes private check-in, a lounge, and complimentary continental breakfast.

Sixth Avenue Inn

2000 Sixth Ave.
Seattle, WA 98121
206-441-8300, 1-800-648-6440
www.sixthavenueinn.com
Price: Inexpensive to moderate
Credit cards: AE, DC, Disc, MC, V
Special features: Good value
Pets: OK

You won't get better value in the downtown area than the Sixth Avenue Inn. It's near Pike Place Market and the downtown shopping area and within walking distance of the major sights and waterfront. The rooms, all of which were renovated in 2001, are large and brightly decorated. The Sixth Avenue Bar and Grill has a garden view and serves all meals, in addition to having a firelit lounge. A sports bar is also on the premises. Parking is complimentary. Guest-room amenities include all that you could want.

Summerfield Suites by Wyndham

1011 Pike St.
Seattle, WA 98101
206-682-8282, 1-800-996-3416
www.wyndham.com
Price: Inexpensive to very expensive
Credit cards: AE, DC, Disc, MC, V
Special features: Homelike
Pets: No

Located downtown on Pike Street next to the Washington State Convention and Trade Center, this is downtown Seattle's only suite hotel with separate living and dining rooms and a full kitchen. Obviously, it's where you'd spend more than just a night or two, and it is focused on business travelers attending conventions next door. But it is also great for families. Many of the rooms have views of the Space Needle. You have the choice of cooking your own meals or making use of local restaurant delivery service. Of the 193 units, 174 are nonsmoking; some have a fireplace, whirlpool tub, and balcony. Amenities include complimentary continental breakfast, downtown shuttle service, an outdoor heated pool, a Jacuzzi, a steam sauna, and an exercise room.

Travelodge Seattle City Center
2213 Eighth Ave.
Seattle, WA 98121
206-624-6300, 1-800-578-7878
www.seattlecitycenter.com
Price: Inexpensive to moderate
Credit cards: AE, DC, Disc, MC, V
Special features: Two blocks from free bus zone
Pets: OK

This hotel is almost the spitting image of the Travelodge by the Space Needle except that it's closer to the central downtown core. A Quick Coach Shuttle stop to and from Vancouver, British Columbia, for a fee, is nearby. Your doggy or kitty will cost you an extra $10 a night and will place you in smoking rooms only.

Vance Hotel
620 Stewart St.
Seattle, WA 98101
206-956-8500, 1-800-956-8500
www.vancehotel.com
Price: Moderate
Credit cards: AE, DC, Disc, MC, V
Special features: Seattle landmark
Pets: No

The first thing you notice about the Vance is its neon sign, high above on the roof. Located in the heart of downtown, the hotel was built in the 1920s by lumber magnate Joseph Vance and still carries his name.

The historic hotel lobby is accented with rich wood, stained-glass windows, and marble details. The 165 guest rooms all have European-boutique-style furnishings and soft colors of cream and gold that accent the overall vintage appeal. Rooms come with the usual amenities, such as a hair dryer, an iron and ironing board, cable TV including pay-per-view movies, and Nintendo. The Yakima Grill has Latin cuisine.

Warwick Hotel Seattle
401 Lenora St.
Seattle, WA 98121
206-443-4300, 1-800-426-9280
www.warwickhotel.com
Price: Moderate to expensive
Credit cards: AE, DC, Disc, MC, V
Special features: Near Cinerama
Pets: OK

The Warwick Hotel is on the corner of Fourth Avenue and Lenora Street, across from the newly renovated Cinerama and within easy walking distance of Pike Place Market, the convention center, and the theater district. This is a lovely, often overlooked hotel. Its rooms are tastefully appointed with Italian marble, fine woods, textiles, and soft, rich carpeting. All rooms feature a king-size bed or two double beds, a wet bar, and a personal beverage refrigerator or minibar; many have city or Space Needle views. There are 12 rooms designed for disabled guests, each featuring one king bed and the regular amenities plus a refrigerator instead of a minibar and no wet bar; the bathroom features safety bars around the toilet and inside the bathtub, and three of these rooms feature a roll-in shower. Four luxury suites have a parlor and separate bedroom, a Jacuzzi tub, a separate shower, and a king bed.

WestCoast Grand Hotel
1415 Fifth Ave.
Seattle, WA 98101
206-971-8000, 1-800-325-4000

www.westcoasthotels.com
Price: Moderate
Credit cards: AE, DC, Disc, MC, V
Special features: Great view from restaurant
Pets: OK

It's a high-rise with 297 guest rooms located one block away from Pike Place Market, and the entrance is set back on a pleasant square. Like many of the downtown hotels, it is ideal for both businesspeople and vacationers, with rooms that are fully wired and brightly decorated. Children 18 and younger are not charged if they share the room with parents or guardians. The Terrace Garden is a restful spot among the busy streets of Seattle, featuring Northwest cuisine, full-service dining, room service, and the largest outdoor terrace in the downtown, with spectacular sunset views of Puget Sound. For a casual lunch or late-night dinner, the Elephant and Castle Pub is perfectly situated at the lower level of the hotel.

Westin Seattle

1900 Fifth Ave.
Seattle, WA 98101
206-728-1000, 1-800-937-8461
www.westin.com/seattle
Price: Expensive to very expensive
Credit cards: AE, DC, Disc, MC, V
Special features: Tallest Seattle hotel
Pets: Small OK

Former president Bill Clinton stayed here during an APEC conference in December 1993, if that's important to you. The hotel, designed as two cylindrical towers with nearly 900 rooms, is one of Seattle's finest convention hotels. It has everything you can imagine in a megahotel owned by Starwood Resorts, one of the country's most visible high-end chains. The rooms provide the finest views in all of Seattle, as you'd expect from the tallest location in town. The unusual curved windows allow a wider angle for looking out over the city. In the

Lobby Bar, the atmosphere is as warm as in your room, with sunken couches and gorgeously high ceilings. A late-night menu served until 1 am features ribs, crab cakes, and brie with fruit. Try the chocolate pyramid, a combination of mousse, caramel, chocolate icing, and cookie crust. The hot apple pie (served with spiced cider, Tuaca, and whipped cream) is the second choice on a menu that's wonderfully decadent.

W Seattle

1112 Fourth Ave.
Seattle, WA 98101
206-264-6000, 1-877-946-8357
www.whotels.com
Price: Very expensive
Credit cards: AE, DC, Disc, MC, V
Special features: Business oriented
Pets: OK

The hotel was conceived by Starwood Hotels and Resorts with one purpose in mind: to accommodate the business traveler who needs refuge from a hectic world. Certainly, the atmosphere is almost Hollywood-like: the lobby looks as though it came out of a film director's mind, with dramatic lighting and ultracontemporary furniture and accents. In the evening it becomes a trendy lounge. Among the 417 guest rooms are nine spacious suites designed to give you smart style and the ultimate in comfort. All come with framed black-and-white photos of Seattle, a glass water carafe by the bed, and an upholstered banquette for gazing out over the city. The bed consists of a pillow-top mattress with soft, 250-thread-count linens, a fluffy goose-down comforter, and pillows. The CD player comes with a large CD collection, and the 27-inch TV has Internet access and first-run movies on demand. And, because it's a business hotel, rooms have two dual-line telephones with conference and modem capabilities, high-speed Ethernet laptop access, an oversize desk, plus a printer, fax, or scanner on request.

EASTLAKE/SOUTH LAKE UNION
Courtyard by Marriott
925 Westlake Ave. N.
Seattle, WA 98109
206-213-0100, 1-800-321-2211
www.courtyardlakeunion.com
Price: Moderate to expensive
Credit cards: AE, DC, Disc, MC, V
Special features: Music package
Pets: OK

Located on the west shore of historic Lake Union north of downtown Seattle, this hotel is minutes from the Seattle Center, Space Needle, and Key Arena and about 2 miles from the downtown financial district and Pike Place Market. If you are planning a trip to the San Juan Islands or Victoria, the hotel is located directly across the street from the Kenmore Air terminal. Across the street are several waterfront restaurants. Depending on your point of view, the seaplanes can be either a noisy intrusion or an exciting addition to your trip as you watch them from your room. The hotel has a package arrangement with the Experience Music Project, which provides tickets to the facility and a music package. The rooms are standard Marriott; the lobby area has a cozy fireside lounge and the Courtyard Café. Business travelers will appreciate the free high-speed Internet access. An indoor swimming pool and hot tub, a fully equipped fitness center, and 2,300 square feet of meeting space round out the amenities.

MV Challenger
1001 Fairview Ave. N., Ste. 1600
Seattle, WA 98109
206-340-1201, 1-800-288-7521
Price: Inexpensive to expensive
Credit cards: AE, Disc, MC, V
Special features: It's a tugboat(!); not
  wheel-chair accessible
Pets: No

This 1944 renovated army tug just might be the most unusual bed-and-breakfast in the entire Pacific Northwest. Once inside, you won't find a tugboat but a modern-day cruising vessel providing yachtlike comfort while maintaining the nautical charm of its era. The *MV Challenger* is located just 10 blocks from the heart of downtown Seattle on Lake Union, with Seattle Center a walk or quick drive away. Nearby, the Center for Wooden Boats, a hands-on museum, has a collection of historic boats available to rent. The tug actually goes out on cruises; where it goes depends on the wishes of the guests. The main salon has a fireplace, solarium, and wall-to-wall carpeting, and the stay includes an extensive buffet breakfast. The staterooms are small, but they're filled with character and amenities. Try to get the Admiral's Cabin, which has a queen four-poster bed, phone, color TV, VCR, stereo, refrigerator, private bath with raised soaking tub and shower, and views of the city, lake, and marina. The Captain's Cabin has a private bathroom, refrigerator, and in-your-face lake and downtown views. Guests in smaller rooms have to share bathrooms, but all spaces have their own TVs and VCRs. Some tugboat!

Silver Cloud Inn—Lake Union
1150 Fairview Ave. N.
Seattle, WA 98109
206-447-9500, 1-800-330-5812
www.silvercloud.com
Price: Moderate to expensive
Credit cards: AE, DC, Disc, MC, V
Special features: Family friendly
Pets: OK

The rooms are large, and the place offers some good views of the Space Needle and Lake Union. It is near restaurants along the South Lake Union waterfront, and complimentary shuttles make it easy to get downtown. The two swimming pools, indoor and outdoor, are great for families. And the floatplane terminal is across the street if you want air tours of the city. In-room amenities include a coffeemaker, an iron and ironing board, a microwave, and a refrigerator. Breakfast, which is included, consists of three types of cereal, instant oatmeal, fruit, fresh waffles, pastries, bagels, a variety of yummy muffins, English muffins, hard-boiled eggs, cheese, juices, yogurt, coffee, tea, milk, hot chocolate, etc. It is served in a room with a fireplace, two televisions, and seating inside and out overlooking Lake Union. There is no restaurant, but there's a weekly reception for guests.

THE EASTSIDE
Woodmark Hotel
1200 Carillon Point
Kirkland, WA 98033
425-822-3700, 1-800-822-3700
www.thewoodmark.com
Price: Expensive to very expensive
Credit cards: AE, DC, Disc, MC, V
Special features: On-site spa
Pets: No

It's located in Kirkland, one of the wealthier suburbs east of Seattle, 45 minutes east of downtown and 3 miles from the high-tech corridor of Redmond, Bellevue, and Bothell. But as the only hotel on the eastern shores of Lake Washington, it's an alternative for those who don't mind being off the beaten path to experience a unique part of the area. It's an integral part of Carillon Point's 31-acre waterfront community, which offers a variety of specialty shops, restaurants, a fitness facility, a travel agency, a scenic marina, and the Spa at the Woodmark, a full-service destination spa. Because the hotel is on the lakeshore, activities such as kayaking make use of the location. (From Seattle, take WA 520 heading east over the Evergreen Point floating bridge. Take the Lake Washington Boulevard NE/Kirkland exit. Continue

north on Lake Washington Boulevard NE to the light at Lakeview Drive; turn left into Carillon Point. From Sea-Tac Airport, follow signs to I-405 North/Renton, then continue north for about 18 miles and take exit 17, NE 70th Place. Turn left at the first light and then left at the next light, NE 70th. Continue southwest for 1.5 miles to the intersection of Lake Washington Boulevard NE and the entrance to Carillon Point.)

PIONEER SQUARE AND INTERNATIONAL DISTRICT
Best Western Pioneer Square Hotel
77 Yesler Way
Seattle, WA 98104
206-340-1234, 1-800-800-5514
www.pioneersquare.com
Price: Expensive to very expensive
Credit cards: AE, DC, Disc, MC, V
Special features: Historic building
Pets: No

This elegantly restored turn-of-the-20th-century boutique hotel is located in the heart of historic downtown Seattle and is the only hotel in Pioneer Square. It is the closest hotel to Safeco Field and the Stadium Exhibition Center. It has 75 European-style rooms/suites equipped with individual climate control, data/fax port telephones, hair dryers, irons, and coffeemakers. It is a thoroughly restored Romanesque-Victorian hotel with small but comfortable rooms. All the city's major attractions are within walking distance or a free bus or trolley ride away. The square can get a bit noisy/seedy late at night, but the hotel is a good bargain and is well monitored.

Panama Hotel
605½ S. Main St.
Seattle, WA 98104
206-223-9242
www.panamahotelseattle.com
Price: Inexpensive
Credit cards: MC, V
Special features: A touch of history
Pets: No

Although it may not be for everyone, this is probably the most vibrant of Seattle's historic hotels. It is a collection point for all things Japanese, and if you don't mind sharing washroom facilities, you can experience a major piece of Seattle history. Built in 1910 as a working-man's hotel, it catered to Alaskan fishermen and other itinerate workers. Located in the heart of the International District, the hotel makes up in charm what it might not have in amenities. It was saved in 1986 from the wrecker's ball primarily through a groundswell of support for current owner Jan Johnson, a local artist who had bought the property and then started a "save the Panama" movement that succeeded. One of the reasons for visiting the hotel is to see the perfectly preserved Japanese bathhouse in the basement. It's the only one left in the US and it was used by Japanese clients until it was closed in 1950. You'll find that the rooms are small, comfortable and clean, but be prepared to use common toilets—men's and women's—that are located on each floor. There is daily maid service and a central lounge. The basement parking nearby is not covered in the hotel's rate. A multilingual staff can direct guests to museums, galleries, stadiums, and local events. The hotel teahouse serves teas from around the world. Free wireless Internet access is available.

QUEEN ANNE AND SEATTLE CENTER
Best Western Loyal Inn
2301 Eighth Ave.
Seattle, WA 98121
206-682-0200, 1-800-528-1234
www.bestwestern.com
Price: Inexpensive to moderate
Credit cards: AE, DC, Disc, MC, V
Special features: Good value
Pets: OK

The Loyal Inn has 91 nicely decorated, oversize rooms four blocks from the Space Needle at the north end of downtown, eight blocks from the convention center, nine blocks from the waterfront, 12 blocks from Pike Place Market, and about 1 mile north of Safeco Field. Amenities include a 24-hour Jacuzzi and sauna, a sundeck, guest laundry service, free parking, free newspapers, and an exceptional complimentary deluxe continental breakfast. If you are looking for good value for your money, you will not be disappointed here. All rooms have satellite and HBO, voice mail, data ports, and individual climate control.

Comfort Seattle Center
601 Roy St.
Seattle, WA 98109
206-282-2600, 1-800-517-4000
www.comfortsuites.seattle.com
Price: Inexpensive to moderate
Credit cards: AE, Disc, MC, V
Special features: Newer hotel
Pets: No

If you intend to spend much of your time in or near Seattle Center, the Comfort Inn is a great location. It is within walking distance of the Space Needle, Experience Music Project, and Pacific Science Center. It is also just a few blocks away from the Seattle Monorail, which takes you downtown in two minutes. The hotel, which opened in 1999, offers a wide range of amenities, including continental breakfast, free covered underground parking, a 1,200-square-foot meeting facility, and two-line phones in each room with high-speed Internet access and voice mail. You can leave your car at the hotel parking lot the whole time you are in town. That alone will save you a lot of cash. There's a courtyard and exercise room and in-room coffee, microwave, and refrigerator.

Days Inn Town Center
2205 Seventh Ave.
Seattle, WA 98121
206-448-3434, 1-800-648-6440
www.daysinntowncenter.com

Price: Inexpensive
Credit cards: AE, DC, Disc, MC, V
Special features: Good value
Pets: OK

No surprises here. It is clean, comfortable, and within walking distance of Seattle Center, Pike Place Market, and shopping. The free downtown bus is nearby, and there's a combination restaurant/bar if you don't feel like going out. A senior citizen discount applies year-round.

Hampton Inn and Suites—Downtown
700 Fifth Ave. N.
Seattle, WA 98109
206-282-7700, 1-800-426-7866
www.hamptoninn-seattle.com
Price: Moderate
Credit cards: AE, DC, Disc, MC, V
Special features: Newer hotel
Pets: OK

Located in the heart of Queen Anne, this property is within a short walk of the Space Needle, Experience Music Project, and Pacific Science Center. It's a good location if you're in town to attend the the Seattle Opera, the Pacific Northwest Ballet, the Seattle Repertory Theater, or a SuperSonics basketball game. And it is just a few short blocks from the Seattle Mono-rail to downtown. Opened in 1996, the rooms are bright and up-to-date, offering choices from king deluxe to double beds. Two-room suites with kitchen, balcony, and fireplace are well suited for extended stays. There's free parking, voice mail, and high-speed Internet access.

Holiday Inn Seattle Center
211 Dexter Ave. N.
Seattle, WA 98109
206-728-8123, 1-800-465-4329
www.holiday-inn.com/seattlewa
Price: Moderate
Credit cards: AE, DC, Disc, MC, V
Special features: Newer hotel
Pets: OK

This is one of Seattle's newer hotels, opened in the fall of 2001. It's a Holiday Inn that goes beyond the usual impression that older Holiday Inns give. It is an elegant, full-service hotel with bright, comfortable rooms having a microwave, fridge, coffeemaker, and two-line phone. This hotel is far superior to other budget hotels and motels in the area. And though the rooms are a bit more expensive than at competing hotels, they are roomier and a lot more comfortable. Amenities include covered parking, a fitness room, a restaurant serving Asian and Northwest cuisine, a lounge, and room service.

Inn at Queen Anne
505 First Ave. N.
Seattle, WA 98109
206-282-7357, 1-800-952-5043
www.innatqueenanne.com
Price: Moderate
Credit cards: AE, DC, Disc, MC, V
Special features: B&B style
Pets: No

A pleasant garden surrounds this hotel built in 1929 that offers a high level of personalized service, comfortable rooms, and plenty of charm. Complimentary deluxe continental breakfast, featuring a variety of breads, muffins, croissants, fruit, fruit juices, and fine coffees and teas, makes this seem like an English B&B rather than a hotel. The 68-room inn has rooms rich in tones of olive, sage, cinnamon, and burgundy. Tiffany lamps, boldly textured walls, and tasteful furnishings accent the inn's lobby and hallways. It is conveniently situated adjacent to Seattle Center and the Key Arena. There is also a wine reception on selected evenings.

La Quinta Inn and Suites
2224 Eighth Ave.
Seattle, WA 98121
206-624-6820, 1-800-437-4867

www.laquinta.com
Price: Moderate
Credit cards: AE, Disc, MC, V
Special features: Good value
Pets: No

This is one of seven La Quinta properties in the Seattle area and, like the others, it is clean and offers good value. This seven-story high-rise is within walking distance of most downtown attractions, including Seattle Center, the Space Needle, the Elliott Bay waterfront, and Pike Place Market. The hotel offers free guest parking, a complimentary continental breakfast, a fitness center with dry sauna and Jacuzzi hot tub, and a 24-hour sundries shop.

MarQueen Hotel
600 Queen Anne Ave. N.
Seattle, WA 98109
206-282-7407, 1-888-445-3076
www.marqueen.com
Price: Moderate
Credit cards: AE, Disc, MC, V
Special features: Historical character
Pets: No

When you arrive, a uniformed door attendant greets you at the door, and how many times does that happen in a value-priced property? The hotel, with 56 rooms, is in a renovated 1918 brick building three blocks away from Seattle Center; from there it's an easy ride via the Monorail to downtown. Each of the spacious rooms includes a coffeemaker with Torrefazione coffee, a hair dryer, and an iron and ironing board; many have a separate seating area and full kitchen, which is great for families staying for a while. The dark wood trim and hardwood floors give the rooms an old-fashioned feel, but they are not stuffy. There's no room service or restaurant here, but plenty of restaurants are within a two-block area, and some offer hotel guests the option of charging meals to their room at the hotel.

The Mediterranean Inn
425 Queen Anne Ave. N.
Seattle, WA 98109
206-428-4700, 1-866-525-4700
www.mediterranean-inn.com
Price: Inexpensive to moderate
Credit cards: AE, Disc, MC, V
Special features: New hotel
Pets: OK

One of Seattle's newest hotels, it's located near Seattle Center in the vibrant Queen Anne neighborhood adjacent to Key Arena. All 180 rooms are designed as furnished studio apartments and are appointed to embrace the feel of the Mediterranean. Warm cherry-wood furniture and complementing granite countertops and rich carpeting welcome you with a comfortable, relaxing feeling. The hotel isn't opulent but it is comfortable, with each room having a small area for a microwave. It is on Queen Anne Avenue across the street from a movie theater and within a 10 minute walk of many restaurants. Rooms come with high-speed Internet access, voice mail, free local phone calls, plenty of parking, a business center, meeting rooms, an exercise room, and guest laundry. Weekly and monthly rates are quite reasonable.

Travelodge by the Space Needle
200 Sixth Ave.
Seattle, WA 98109
206-441-7878, 1-800-578-7878
www.travelodge.com
Price: Moderate
Credit cards: AE, DC, Disc, MC, V
Special features: Family friendly
Pets: OK

This is an 88-room midpriced motor hotel just two blocks from Seattle Center, the Experience Music Project, and the Monorail terminal. The rooms are clean and were upgraded in 1997. With each room comes a continental breakfast and *USA Today* newspaper; a coffeemaker with complimentary coffee and tea, a data port telephone, and remote-control cable TV with ShowTime. Families with children get the Sleepy Bear's Den, a two-bed room, and there's a seasonal outdoor pool.

UNIVERSITY DISTRICT
The area around the university, as you might expect, is generally occupied by younger people of university age, and several hotels fall into the budget or moderate range. However, ignore the clichés, for there are plenty of reasons why people choose accommodations in the area. It's only 15 minutes or so from downtown, and some of Seattle's major attractions are in the vicinity, such as the Burke Museum, the Museum of History and Industry, the Henry Art Gallery, Woodland Park Zoo, and activities that are part of everyday University of Washington life. Plenty of inexpensive, hearty restaurants in the area make this a good budget option.

Best Western University Tower Hotel
4507 Brooklyn Ave. NE
Seattle, WA 98105
206-634-2000, 1-800-899-0251
www.universitytowerhotel.com
Price: Inexpensive to very expensive
Credit cards: AE, DC, Disc, MC, V
Special features: Historical character
Pets: No

You won't see many hotels with a price spread like this one's, but prices in this elegant art-deco gem next to the University of Washington range from $99 to $750. Located 2½ miles from downtown Seattle, the 16-story Best Western University Tower is a boutique hotel featuring panoramic views and 155 newly redesigned guest rooms that average a generous 300–500 square feet. The hotel was completed in 1931 during the Depression and the penthouse suites were to have been the hotel's crowning glory, but they were never completed until recently. The three new suites that occupy the 16th

floor are surrounded by more than 2,000 square feet of decking, with a virtually unobstructed 360-degree view of water, mountains, and cityscape. In May 2003, the restaurant and lounge on the ground floor were totally renovated, reopened, and renamed the District. All rooms have complimentary continental breakfast, complimentary parking, and use of a fitness center.

Silver Cloud Inn—University Village
5036 25th Ave. NE
Seattle, WA 98105
206-526-5200, 1-800-205-6940
www.silvercloud.com
Price: Moderate
Credit cards: AE, DC, Disc, MC, V
Special features: Good value
Pets: OK

This is a clean, standard motel with 180 rooms, some with kitchen and Jacuzzi. The Silver Cloud chain is well known in the Pacific Northwest, with 12 properties between Seattle and Portland and another under construction near the stadiums in downtown Seattle. Rooms are spacious and bright, and the motel has an indoor swimming pool and fitness facility, and a continental breakfast is included. Business travelers will find all they need, including conference rooms.

University Inn
4140 Roosevelt Way NE
Seattle, WA 98105
206-632-5055, 1-800-733-3855
www.universityinnseattle.com
Price: Moderate
Credit cards: AE, DC, Disc, MC, V
Special features: ADA compliant
Pets: OK

The west-side deluxe rooms offer views of Lake Union. And though they are somewhat more pricey, they're a lot more comfortable than the standard rooms. Either way, this is an attractive place to stay. The 100 percent nonsmoking hotel is three blocks from the University of Washington. The best views are from the roomy junior suites, all of which have large windows, microwaves, and coffeemakers. One of the rooms, No. 331, has a view of Mount Rainier, as long as it's not raining. Free parking, a seasonal heated pool, a spa, and a fitness room round out the amenities.

University Motel

4731 12th Ave. NE
Seattle, WA 98105
206-522-4724, 1-800-522-4720
www.university-hotel.com
Price: Inexpensive
Credit cards: AE, DC, Disc, MC, V
Special features: ADA compliant
Pets: OK

If you're looking for a long stay residence in the university area, you be pleased with this place. It has 21 suites that are large (651 sq. ft.) and with all of the amenities you'd expect from your own apartment back home including cable TV and data ports. There are laundry facilities on site and the building is located in a quiet area, five blocks from the university and a short drive to the U of W Medical Center and Children's Hospital.

Watertown

4242 Roosevelt Way NE
Seattle, WA 98105
206-826-4242, 1-866-944-4242
www.watertownseattle.com
Price: Moderate
Credit cards: AE, DC, Disc, MC, V
Special features: New hotel
Pets: No

Owned by the same people who run the University Inn, Watertown features 100 nonsmoking rooms that include free high-speed Internet access. The room decor reflects Seattle's "water" aspect, with colors and character inspired by a nautical theme. The bathrooms are large, with gran-

ite counters, frosted portals on the doors, luxury Aveda products, and an abundance of natural lighting. Televisions are on swivels, so you can watch from any part of the room, and closets are cleverly designed with double doors that are accessible from both the bedroom and the bathroom. Platform beds, ergonomic desk chairs, and full-length mirrors round out a contemporary look and feel.

WATERFRONT

Edgewater Hotel

2411 Alaskan Way, Pier 67
Seattle, WA 98121
206-728-7000, 1-800- 624-0670
www.edgewaterhotel.com
Price: Expensive to very expensive
Credit cards: AE, DC, Disc, MC, V
Special features: Spectacular bay views
Pets: OK

Even with the construction of the new Marriott nearby, the Edgewater remains the only hotel directly on the waterfront, since the Marriott is on the other side of Alaskan Way. Moreover, if you have a waterfront room, you have a spectacular view of Elliott Bay and the Olympic Mountains. The hotel was built for the 1962 World's Fair. The Beatles fished out of the windows of Room 272 while staying during their first American tour in 1964. In 2001, the hotel completed a comprehensive $7 million renovation, including guest rooms, lobby, hallways, reception, grand entrance, and the new Six Seven Restaurant and Lounge. Oddly, the renovations are not in a seaside motif but, rather, in a mountain chalet design. A woven-antler chandelier juxtaposed with rustic crystal candelabras, artwork depicting local wildlife (much of it by local artists), plush overstuffed furniture, and a two-story stone fireplace studded with fabricated salmon are focal points of the lobby living room. Columns dressed in bark to resemble trees, with branches from pruned Washington apple trees, connected by stainless-steel hinges, complete the overall look. The less-expensive rooms look out on only the city. The restaurant has garnered rave reviews for its seafood and West Coast cuisine and for the centerpiece, the sushi bar, that is backed by a wall of holographic fireplaces.

Seattle Marriott Waterfront

2100 Alaskan Way
Seattle, WA 98121
206-443-5000, 1-800-455-8254 (US);
1-800-228-9290 (Canada)
www.marriott.com
Price: Expensive
Credit cards: AE, DC, Disc, MC, V
Special features: Spectacular views
Pets: No

This newest hotel in Seattle helps make up for a lack of waterfront accommodations. Although it doesn't have the spectacular views found at the nearby Edgewater, it nonetheless offers enough to make the location worth considering. The majority of the 358 rooms feature views ranging from the cityscape to Mount Rainier, Elliott Bay, and the Olympic Mountain range. Many rooms have private balconies. A lot of guests stay here before embarking on a cruise at the nearby cruise-ship terminal, and the location is just steps away from Pike Place Market, shopping, and the major downtown attractions. The hotel is designed with the business traveler in mind; each room features dual-line phones (one cordless), high-speed Internet access, and in-room Starbucks coffee. As you'd expect from a brand new Marriott, the lobby is bright, fresh, and inviting.

Bed & Breakfasts

Because Seattle has diverse neighborhoods, you'll discover many fine B&Bs throughout the city. Contact the Seattle Bed & Breakfast Association (800-348-5630, 206-547-1020, www.lodginginseattle.com). The Pacific Reservation Service (800 684-2932, 206-439-7677; www.seattlebedand breakfast.com) represents dozens of accommodations, mostly B&Bs, in the Seattle area.

Chambered Nautilus Bed and Breakfast Inn

5005 22nd Ave. NE
Seattle, WA 98105
206-522-2536, 1-800-545-8459
www.chamberednautilus.com
Price: Moderate
Credit cards: AE, MC, V
Special features: Georgian Colonial home; no wheelchair access
Pets: No

This is a large, three-storied house that has been converted into an elaborate and comfortable bed and breakfast with six guest rooms that have private baths and phones with modem access. It is located with a few minutes walk of the U of W campus and near bus routes into the downtown area. Owners Joyce Schulte and Steve Poole have created an atmosphere of luxurious comfort. Four of the rooms have porches that look out to gardens at to distant mountains.

Gaslight Inn Bed & Breakfast

1727 15th Ave.
Seattle, WA 98122-2614
206-325-3654
www.gaslight-inn.com
Price: Inexpensive to moderate
Credit cards: AE, MC, V
Special features: Art collection; no wheelchair access; no smoking
Pets: No

This 1906 home located on Capitol Hill was restored and remodeled in 1981, and in 1983 it opened for business as the Gaslight Inn. Owned and run by Steve Bennett and Trevor Logan, it is a combination of original turn-of-the-20th-century ambience, charm, and warmth, and the conveniences and contemporary style needed by today's travelers. With an enormous entryway and staircase, museum-quality arts-and-crafts period furniture, and authentic Northwestern Indian artifacts, the house is a miniature gallery. The 15 rooms and suites (12 with private baths) are each furnished with a quality double or queen-size bed, a refrigerator, and a television. The studios have shared washrooms, while the larger rooms have private baths, and some have decks with fabulous views or fireplaces. The entire house is decorated in rich, dark colors and oak paneling. The living room, with its large oak fireplace, is an exceptionally warm and inviting place to read a book or just relax. Continental breakfast is included. Parking is limited, though suites have off-street parking.

Budget Options

For those on a limited budget, a string of inexpensive, budget motels can be found along Aurora Avenue North, beginning at the northern end of Fremont. In addition, there are several choices just off the freeway in the University District. Although the ambience of the Aurora Avenue motels is unexciting, they make a good base for exploration downtown, which is only about 10 minutes away.

Many hotels drop their prices in mid-October. Not all are part of the Seattle Super Saver Program that is valid November-March. While general hotel discounts usually begin in mid- to late October by hotels not included in the **Seattle Super Saver** program (800-535-7071; 206-461-5882 (Canada); www.seattlesupersaver .com), Super Saver rates are effective November to March. Its online bookings, give Web-based hotel bookers a run for their money with huge discounts to leading hotels. The program offers discounts of up to 70 percent at 48 Seattle hotels and several expanded features such as room upgrades and deep discounts on suites. Program coupons offer savings for Seattle shopping, dining, cultural events, and sightseeing.

Book a hotel through the Seattle Super Saver program and you'll get the lowest available rate at the time of the reservation. The Seattle Convention and Visitors Bureau offers benefits and services that include prepayment, no cancellation fees (up to 24 hours prior to check-in), and no hidden fees. Hotel loyalty programs still apply. Seattle Super Saver rates are effective November to March. To receive the discounted rate, you have to stay at least one night at a participating hotel with reservations made through the Seattle Super Saver Web site or toll-free telephone reservation line. Reservation lines are open 8:30–5 (Pacific Time) Monday through Friday and 10–2 Saturday and Sunday.

Hostelling International—Seattle
84 Union St.
Seattle, WA 98101
206-622-5443
www.hiseattle.org
Price: Inexpensive
Credit cards: AE, MC, V
Special features: Near Pike Place Market
Pets: No

Like most hostels, whether in Seattle, Vancouver, or elsewhere, this is essentially a young-people's facility, but it welcomes everyone. Built in 1915, the building originally served as a longshoreman's hall and is just a few blocks from the waterfront. Its main clientele are young European and Asian travelers. It's perfectly located next to Pike Place Market, making it easy for visitors to explore downtown and Pioneer Square. It has a general kitchen and luggage storage area, and some of the rooms have a view of Puget Sound. Dorm rooms sleep 10, semiprivate rooms sleep four and share a bath, and private rooms are perfect for couples and families. (To find the hostel, walk through Post Alley to the corner of Union Street.)

RV Parks

Bellevue Park

15531 SE 37th St.
Bellevue, WA 98006
425-747-9181, 1-800-659-4684
www.trailerinnsrv.com
Price: $17–$29 per day, $126–$174 per
week, $400–$590 per month; $100 refund-
able deposit required for stays of one
month or more
Credit cards: MC, V
Special features: Just off I-90
Pets: OK

From Seattle, drive east on I-90 and take
exit 11A. The RV park is located south of
the freeway near the main interchange. It's
easy to drive from here to all areas of the
Seattle region. With a sauna, therapy pools,
a swimming pool, laundry, phones, a clubhouse, cable television, 100 percent hook-
ups, and other amenities, it is one of the
area's premier RV parks.

RESTAURANTS

There's no shortage of places to eat in
Seattle, no matter where you are in town:
there are some 760 restaurants in the city,
not including the suburbs. Obviously, the
selections are enormous, from steak houses
and seafood restaurants to burger joints,
greasy spoons, and general eateries, from
low to high-end price ranges. You'll find
them in hotels, as stand-alones, on nearly
every street, and along the waterfront.

So where do you begin? That depends on
what you want to eat and where you happen
to be. Lunch is easy. Just pop into whatever
catches your eye in whichever district you
might be. For instance, in the International
District, one of the best dim sum places in
town is the **House of Hong** (409 Eighth
Ave. S.; 206-622-7997), with its purely
Cantonese cuisine and choice of 75 dim
sum items. Even simple classics such as
ginger beef dumplings and *ha gow* are fla-

vorful and brought in piping hot. At the
Viet My restaurant (129 Prefontaine Pl. S.;
206-382-9923), the owner, Chau Tran,
serves authentic Vietnamese dishes and an
incredible seafood soup.

In Seattle, you have to work hard at
finding a restaurant that will give you less
than fine food. Downtown, there's an
almost unlimited choice of restaurants
serving a variety of styles, and in Pike Place
Market area, you'll find a delightful combination of ethnic and seafood restaurants
that range from French to Bolivian to
Pacific Northwest and Asian. They are not
just along the nearby side streets but also
within the market itself.

On Broadway, in the Capitol Hill area,
literally rows of eateries can be found, and
on South Lake Union you'll find seafood
and Japanese restaurants with magnificent
views of the water. Try a restaurant that
overlooks the locks in Fremont or one of
the latest "in" places featured in the *Seattle
Weekly* listings.

Nowhere will you find a newer batch of
wonderfully decorated restaurants than in
the Belltown area. As the high-tech people
raked in money over the past five years and
moved into the neighborhood's chic, high-
end condos and townhouses, so too did
restaurants spring up to accommodate their
free-spending lifestyles. These restaurants
all went overboard in creating upscale and
contemporary-fashionable interiors for
their eating clientele, and the high cost of
doing so was reflected in the food prices.
But that changed with the high-tech crash.
Today, you can find superb meals at moderate prices in restaurants that many could
never have afforded before.

Obviously, listing every eatery in town
would take up this entire book. But this
section features a sampling that reflects
the city's unique West Coast culinary experience. The listing focuses on areas that
you're most likely to visit. The suggestions
here are by no means the only places where

you can find superb cuisine; they represent only the tip of Seattle's huge culinary iceberg.

Seafood

No place in the Pacific Northwest has a passion for seafood like Seattle does. In this city, sea cuisine is not a simple matter of cooking a fish. In a world defined by water and what lives in it, Seattleites have a wide-ranging appetite for what lies below the water surface. Not all sea life, of course, is eaten. Whales are not, for example, though they were a staple for the coastal Makah Indians from the Neah Bay area. Nor are seals and most other mammals that come from the sea. But, generally speaking, if it swims or crawls, it's a potential meal. So you should know what you're eating.

The common salmon has a pedigree. The king, or chinook, is the largest and most prized. Spring chinook is the tastiest, the firmest, and the most expensive. The silver, or coho, is coveted by Europeans for smoking; to some, coho is the tastiest and has a firm texture. Sockeye, or red salmon, is prized because of its fighting abilities and its richness; sockeye is most frequently seen as canned fish. Chum is a mild, delicate fish that in its canned form is sometimes called keta; it is often used for feed, such as for dogs—hence its nickname, dog salmon. Pink salmon, the smallest of the five Northwest species, is light in color and the least expensive.

Salmon can be prepared in a myriad of ways. The native peoples often wrapped the fish in leaves and baked them over hot coals, steaming them in their own juices. Salmon is still made that way in many restaurants around Seattle. The influence of Asians has introduced other procedures and techniques, ranging from drying the fish to smoking it or eating the meat raw.

If the king salmon is the Rolls Royce of the Pacific Northwest, bottom fish are the

In a city that loves seafood, salmon is a Seattle passion. Toshi

compact cars. Actually, *bottom fish* is a generic, catchall term encompassing all edible fish that live near the ocean floor. Caught either commercially or for sport, Northwest bottom fish include rockfish, flatfish, lingcod, sculpin, and bass. The rockfish family is the most prolific, with more than 60 species in sizes ranging from 6 inches (15.2 cm) to 3 feet (91.4 cm). They aren't the prettiest fish around, though often they are quite colorful. They can be pinkish red, orange red, black and blue, orange and gray, or yellow and black, and they have compressed bodies, large mouths, and spiny heads.

Flatfish are given that name because both of their eyes are on the same side of their body; they lie around on the bottom of the ocean and often bury themselves in the bottom with just their eyes exposed. Flatfish include halibut, sole, flounder, and turbot. Halibut caught off the Oregon coast can weigh more than 100 pounds (45 kg), causing more than one person to compare catching a halibut to pulling a refrigerator off the ocean floor. Culinary classics in the group are petrale and Dover sole.

The lingcod, though very scarce these days, is highly prized not only because it cooks up tastily white and firm, but also because it can be fried, baked, sautéed, broiled, or poached and works well with many seasonings.

Compared to the lingcod, the basslike snapper doesn't adapt as easily to all recipes. But the darker-fleshed red snapper is a favorite among cooks, especially cost-conscious ones. It works well with heartier seasonings.

Among trendy diners, the cabazone, a member of the sculpin family, is becoming a favorite. The flesh can be greenish but turns white when cooked. You won't be served the eggs because they're poisonous.

Crawfish, sidestripe shrimp, Dungeness crab, and gooseneck barnacles have their supporters, and seafood restaurants throughout the Puget Sound area have them on their menus. Shellfish such as clams, oysters, and mussels are other local delicacies. Mussels have only recently gained popularity in the region, although they have always been prominent in Europe. In the past, travelers coming back from Europe were the ones seen plucking them off rocks and dock piers at low tide. Cooking them in their own juice is popular, as is placing the meat in a chowder mix.

Getting some of these items is becoming difficult. Clamming is restricted in many parts of Puget Sound, and diving for geoduck, the prime ingredient of great chowder, is strictly regulated—as are all fisheries. The razor clam, once a mainstay of the Pacific coastal beaches, is infected with a disease that does not affect humans but that will, in time, likely wipe out the creatures. The rare and tiny Olympia oyster lives only in some reaches of Puget Sound: Big Skookum, Little Skookum, Oyster Bay, and Mud Bay. It's population was almost wiped out by pollution and the importation of Japanese Pacific oysters, that brought their own disease. Today, only a few hundred bushels of Olympia oysters are harvested yearly, and finding them on a menu is rare indeed.

Seafood remains the obsession of Seattle diners, and nearly every eatery and bar features a variety of salmon on the menu. In late spring, when wild salmon appears on menus, the city is awash in salmon celebrations. The rest of the year, the salmon you get might be farmed varieties from British Columbia. They lack the deep taste that you'll find with wild varieties, but they are nonetheless a part of the Seattle seafood experience. Ask whether the salmon is farmed or wild before you order.

Wine

At some time during your stay in Seattle, you may need to make a decision on what wine to drink, either on its own or with your meal. You are in for a pleasant surprise. In Washington State, wine is a growth industry in more ways than one. Although the state long had the potential to be a major grape-growing region, it wasn't until the mid-1970s that the industry expanded from a minor one to its current formidable status. Its best products are now recognized as competitive with the best on the continent. Together, Washington and Oregon are the second-largest producers of wine in the United States, behind only California.

The premium European varieties— including cabernet sauvignon, pinot noir, chardonnay, and Riesling—make up the bulk of the Pacific Northwest grape harvest. Washington State has some 80 wineries, and if just one-third of the potential premium grape acreage (which experts estimate at 150,000 acres [60,000 hectares]) were to be developed, Washington's wine industry would equal that of California's Napa/Sonoma wine region.

Washington also supplies wine grapes to wineries in northern California, southern British Columbia, and eastern Canada. Most of the vineyards are in eastern Washington, which is on the same latitude—just north of 46 degrees latitude—as some of France's great grape-growing regions, such as Bordeaux and Burgundy.

There are three viticultural areas: the Columbia Valley, the Yakima Valley, and the Walla Walla Valley. But it's the Yakima region that's the state's wine center, with 40 wineries between Yakima and Walla Walla. And, like the Napa and Sonoma regions in California, these appellations have helped create a tourism industry that has encouraged the growth of country inns and B&Bs. If you want to taste the very best of Washington State, Oregon, and British Columbia wines, stop off at the wine bar in the Seattle Sheraton Hotel lobby and order from the extensive wine list. The wines are not inexpensive, but they are the best quality.

The wine-growing valleys have hot days and cool nights, with frost toward autumn, and the growing season usually produces well-ripened grapes with an acceptable balance of sugar and acidity. These conditions make Washington State vineyards particularly suitable to the best of classic European varieties. Some of the best vineyards in eastern Washington are on south-facing slopes above the Columbia, Yakima, and Snake rivers, where they get as much as 16 hours of sun daily. Kiona Vineyards (Benton City and Mattawa), Hogue Cellars (Prosser), L'Ecole No. 41 (Lowden), and Hunter Hill Vineyards (Othello) are all small, family operations that produce well-known proprietor labels.

The Columbia Winery, the oldest in the state, is located just east of Seattle in Woodinville. And just across the street from the Columbia Winery is the Northwest's largest winery, Chateau Ste. Michelle. In a clever replica of a French chateau, the winery offers daily tours and concerts during the summer. Also in the Woodinville area are the French Creek Cellars and Tegaris Winery. Located in Seattle's south end is the small, family-operated E. B. Foote Winery; a newcomer to the area is Salmon Bay Winery, also in the south end. Covey Run, which makes wine in eastern

Washington, has a tasting room in Kirk-land. Around Puget Sound are Snoqualmie Winery (Snoqualmie Falls), Quilceda Creek Winery (Quilceda), Bainbridge Island Winery (Bainbridge), and Neuharth Winery (Sequim) on the Olympic Peninsula.

BELLTOWN AND PIKE PLACE MARKET
Campagne/Café Campagne
1600 Post Alley
206-728-2233
Cuisine: French
Meals served: L, D
Open: Daily
Price: Expensive; café, moderate to
  expensive
Credit cards: AE, DC, MC, V
Reservations: Necessary for dinner at both;
  jacket required for dinner in main
  restaurant
Wheelchair accessible: Yes

This is actually two restaurants in one, with a main dining room opposite the Inn at the Market and the more relaxed Café Campagne, complete with an outdoor patio, located on the Post Alley side of the building. The interior of the main restaurant is richly appointed with Oriental rugs and the kind of tasteful art you'd expect at a high-end French restaurant. The menu has traditional dishes flavored with cream and butter instead of vegetable essences, oils, or light stocks; favorites include lavender-fried quail and duck salads, panfried scallops with green peppercorn–tarragon sauce, and cinnamon-roasted quail served with carrot and orange essence. Café Campagne serves a bistro cuisine such as cassoulet, garlic mashed potatoes, and poulet roti. Its casual design includes wooden banquettes, custom-made tables, rush-bottom chairs, and hand-etched glass partitions. Vintage posters, traditional enamel signage, and antique light fixtures add to the ambience.

The Copacabana Café has an enticing balcony overlooking Pike Place Market. Toshi

Copacabana Café
1520 Pike Pl.
206-622-6359
Cuisine: Bolivian
Meals served: L, D
Open: Daily
Price: Inexpensive to moderate
Credit cards: AE, MC, V
Reservations: Not necessary
Wheelchair accessible: No

As you walk along Pike Place Market, look up and you'll see this café right across the street on the second floor. And when you get tired of walking the market, sit on the Copacabana balcony and watch all the action down below. The restaurant dates from 1963, when it was opened by Ramon Pelaez, a former owner of Bolivia's largest radio station and longtime political activist. Pelaez died in 1979, but his daughter and son-in-law continue to run this, the city's only Bolivian restaurant, and the original family recipes are still used. The traditional dishes offer a wide variety of flavors such as in the Bolivian Sopa de Camarones, a spicy shrimp soup, or the flavorful paella. Spanish flan and Tres Leches, a Nicaraguan white cake, are great desserts and another reason to linger on the balcony.

Cutters Bayhouse
2001 Western Ave.
206-448-4884
Cuisine: Seafood, international
Meals served: B (Sat–Sun only), L, D
Open: Daily
Price: Moderate
Credit cards: AE, DC, Disc, MC, V
Reservations: Not necessary
Wheelchair accessible: Yes

Cutters is next to Victor Steinbrueck Park and right across the street from Etta's. Occupying a high point just above the waterfront, the window tables offer a grand view of the docks, the waterfront, and much of Elliott Bay. It's pleasant for casual dining and lunch. The menu offers a wide range of seafood, ranging from enormous salads to specialty items such as the roasted garlic prawns. The menu is all over the international map, with Chinese, Cajun, and Italian, but the food is prepared with care. The sushi bar produces some offbeat items such as cajun hot sushi.

El Gaucho

2505 First Ave.
206-728-1337
Cuisine: Steaks
Meals served: D
Open: Daily
Price: Moderate to very expensive
Credit cards: AE, DC, MC, V
Reservations: Recommended
Wheelchair accessible: Yes

If you are looking for a late-night steak in a restaurant with unique style, go no farther than here. The only thing missing from this movie set–style restaurant, with character that would be at home in a 1930s–40s film noir, is Humphrey Bogart and Ingrid Bergman. It even has a cigar lounge with overstuffed furniture, eclectic wall hangings, and perfect attendants who know their craft. The long bar conjures up a nightclub style that was lost several decades ago. The 28-day dry-aged Angus beef steaks are the star of a menu that features steak and potato classics such as a Caesar salad tossed tableside and chateaubriand carved in front of you. There are also nonsteak items, of course, such as venison chops, ostrich filet, and Australian lobster tail.

Etta's

2020 Western Ave.
206-443-6000
Cuisine: Seafood, Northwest
Meals served: L, D
Open: Daily
Price: Moderate to expensive
Credit cards: AE, DC, MC, V
Reservations: Recommended for dinner
Wheelchair accessible: Yes

This is one of four restaurants owned by local chef Tom Douglas, and it's certainly his showcase eatery. Located a block west of Pike Place Market and named after Douglas's daughter, the restaurant was formerly a sports bar, and there still is a relaxed atmosphere to the place, with green-backed booths, a long counter and bar, and plenty of conversation. Douglas has a menu that can be described as Northwest/Asian fusion with seafood as the common link. You'll find everything from fish-and-chips to pit-smoked salmon and, of course, his famous crab cakes. Entrées include oysters on the half shell and Maine lobster and local Dungeness crab steamed or wok-seared in a hot black-bean sauce. If it's on the menu, try the crab bisque.

Pink Door

1919 Post Alley
206-443-3241
Cuisine: Italian
Meals served: L, D
Open: Tu–Sat
Price: Moderate
Credit cards: AE, DC, MC, V
Reservations: Recommended for dinner
Wheelchair accessible: Yes

Don't look for a sign. The only thing here to indicate the restaurant is the pink door. When you open it, stairs lead to a cellarlike space that in the summer is usually empty because customers are on the deck, which offers a view of Elliott Bay. The restaurant has terrific character, with informal dining that is relaxed and purposefully downplayed. You'll sit at tables with oilcloth coverings, drink water from plastic glasses, and generally feel that you've been transported to a local eatery in Tuscany. The menu, with Italian standards such as rigatoni with sausage and gnocchi, is standard Italian fare, but with an exquisite offbeat atmosphere.

Place Pigalle
81 Pike St.
206-624-1756
Cuisine: Continental, Northwest
Meals served: L, D
Open: M–Sat
Price: Moderate to expensive
Credit cards: AE, DC, MC, V
Reservations: Recommended
Wheelchair accessible: Yes

In the early 20th century, this was a bar frequented by patrons of a nearby bordello. Now it's one of the most agreeable restaurants in Pike Place Market, a cozy bistro that's romantic, relaxing, and fun. The black-and-white tiled floor, walls with original art, and fresh flowers everywhere create an intimate Gallic charm. In addition, you have an unobstructed view of Puget Sound. The menu constantly changes and includes whatever is seasonally fresh, leaning heavily toward such seafood as Dungeness crab, hazelnut-covered red snapper, and a delicious item called Steamed Mussels Pigalle that is dressed with bacon, celery, shallots, and balsamic vinaigrette. Appetizers include Montrachet Soufflé, yearling oysters, steamed mussels, and Twice-Baked Goat Cheese Soufflé. Tempting entrées include Roasted Rabbit Roulade, Duck Aromatique, Seared Alaska Weathervane Scallops, and Lamb with Curried Eggplant.

DOWNTOWN
Andaluca
405 Olive Way
206-382-6999
Cuisine: Mediterranean
Meals served: B, L, D
Open: Daily
Price: Moderate
Credit cards: AE, DC, Disc, MC, V
Reservations: Recommended
Wheelchair accessible: Yes

Like many of the downtown hotel restaurants, this adjunct to the Mayflower Park Hotel stands on its own, with a menu that has a niche market. For years the restaurant has been drawing a loyal clientele to its dimly lit, rosewood-walled room with wooden floors, a place that evokes a romantic sense of southern Spain. The Mediterranean menu features tapas, or shareables. Appetizers range from ground lamb in grape leaves dressed in a fiery lemon cream to Indian-inspired deep-fried duck croquettes with cucumber raita and apricot chutney to a tomato-based Tuscan bread soup. The house paella is an excellent version of the classic dish and can be ordered in small individual portions. The Zarzuela Shellfish Stew, which shouldn't be missed, is a cumin-scented tomato broth with prawns, clams, mussels, fish, and fingerling potatoes, swirled with saffron aioli.

The Georgian
411 University St.
206-621-7889
Cuisine: Seafood, Continental
Meals served: B, L, D
Open: Daily
Price: Expensive to very expensive
Credit cards: AE, DC, Disc, MC, V
Reservations: Always
Wheelchair accessible: Yes

The entrance to Andaluca is elegant and inviting.
Courtesy of Mayflower Hotel

Traditional and formal, the Georgian serves serious haute cuisine. Courtesy of Fairmont Hotels

The place reeks of class and position. That's its charm. For a short period—unless you really do have position and class—you can pretend to be among the elite of old money in surroundings of elegant and ornate grandeur. The Palladian windows and spectacular chandeliers, the warm oak paneling, and the minute attention to detail create an aura of sophistication. Located in the upper lobby of the Fairmont Olympic Hotel, this is by far the most traditional and formal restaurant in the city, with meals that are serious haute cuisine. The conscientious service by an upbeat and friendly staff easily has you convinced that yours is the only table in the restaurant. The Georgian features Northwest cuisine prepared by chef Gavin Stephenson, with a menu that includes such classic starters as Smoked Black Cod with Spinach and Garlic Agnolotti, Grilled Knob Onions, Crispy Squid, and King Crab with

Spicy, Sweet, and Salty Dipping Sauces. Try one of the signature Northwest dishes, such as Dungeness crab bisque ladled from a tureen tableside and garnished with thickened cream and caviar. There's always thick-cut, cold-smoked, poached salmon bathed in apple brandy sauce.

McCormick and Schmick's

1103 First Ave.
206-623-5500
Cuisine: Seafood
Meals served: L, D
Open: Daily
Price: Inexpensive to moderate
Credit cards: AE, DC, Disc, MC, V
Reservations: Recommended
Wheelchair accessible: Yes

Sometimes looks really can be deceiving. When you first walk into this warmly appointed restaurant in the heart of the city's business district, the first impression is that this must be a steak house. It just looks like one, with polished brass, leaded glass, wood paneling, and an air of opulence. Yes, you can get a steak if you want, but this is essentially a seafood house, with 30 or so seafood entrées that include grilled Quinault River steelhead. The pan-roasted pork tenderloin with grain mustard–tarragon cream is a good choice for meat eaters; end with a three-berry cobbler for dessert. If, in the evening, the restaurant is crowded, don't leave. Instead, sit at the counter, watch the chefs working with fire, and order some of the tasty bar appetizers.

Metropolitan Grill
820 Second Ave.
206-624-3287
Cuisine: Steaks
Meals served: L, D
Open: Daily
Price: Moderate to expensive
Credit cards: AE, DC, Disc, MC, V
Reservations: Recommended
Wheelchair accessible: Yes

It's a classic steak house located in a historic building built in 1903, where guests enter past massive granite columns and through tall mahogany doors, under a bright green awning, to be greeted by a tuxedo-clad maître d'. Inside the door is a glass case full of meats ranging from filets mignon to lamb chops. Twenty-foot columns trimmed with original moldings reach to the ceiling. Mahogany tables, brass railings, and plush oversize booths add a sense of opulence. Framed photographs of the celebrities, sports heroes, and local politicians who have eaten at the Metropolitan line the walls. The menu is headlined by 28-day aged steaks. You'll see many suits here since it's one of the favorite eateries of the business crowd.

The Oceanaire
1700 Seventh Ave.
206-267-6277
Cuisine: Seafood
Meals served: L (M–F), D
Open: Daily
Price: Expensive to very expensive
Credit cards: AE, DC, Disc, MC, V
Reservations: Necessary for dinner
Wheelchair accessible: Yes

Designed to resemble an ocean-liner dining room from the 1930s, this is where you can spend a moderate amount or the entire bank account. Either way, you'll have a culinary experience that's a bit like going to a Disney theme park. The Oceanaire has quickly become Seattle's premier seafood house, and once you've experienced the menu, you'll understand why. You'll like the red-leather booths and chef Kevin Davis's menu, which elevates sea life to haute cuisine. Expect a lengthy tableside dissertation regarding the menu; questions are encouraged. A specific wine will be recommended with each selection on a menu of items ranging from Oysters Rockefeller and Clams Casino, broiled with butter under diced peppers and bacon, to lobster and local specialties. If cost is no barrier, ask Davis to make you his own selections. He'll confer with you, determine what you might like, and then disappear until the selections begin to appear at your table.

Rock Bottom Restaurant and Brewery
1333 Fifth Ave.
206-623-3070
Cuisine: American casual
Meals served: L, D
Open: Daily
Price: Inexpensive
Credit cards: AE, DC, Disc, MC, V
Reservations: Not necessary
Wheelchair accessible: Yes

Is it a brewery with food or a restaurant with beer? Rock Bottom has 29 locations across the United States, and each is built the same way: rich in brass, warm woods, and earth tones with gleaming brewing vessels. This one is next to Rainier Square and across the street from the 5th Avenue Theatre, and it attracts locals on their work breaks, theatergoers, and tourists. In addition to the variety of home brews is a menu of familiar American food that ranges from Brown Ale Chicken and Alder-Smoked Salmon, Fish-and-Chips to Texas Fire Steak and Barbecue Ribs and Chicken. There is also a variety of salads, sandwiches, and burgers. And if you want to try the home brews, you can get a six-glass sampler before you make your decision. Good value.

Shiro's

2401 Second Ave.
206-443-9844
Cuisine: Japanese
Meals served: L, D
Open: M–Sat
Price: Moderate to expensive
Credit cards: AE, MC, V
Reservations: Recommended for dinner
Wheelchair accessible: Yes

Seattle has surprisingly few Japanese restaurants, though in Pike Place Market area there are several. This is one of the finest. This little corner restaurant, under the guidance of chef/owner Shiro Kashiba, covers the basics in Japanese cuisine but also serves the finest sushi in town. A way to know how a Japanese restaurant ranks is to check out the number of visiting Japanese businesspeople at the sushi bar. Here, there are always a few every day of the week. Kashiba owned the Nikko restaurant for more than 20 years before selling and moving it to the Westin Hotel, where he continued to preside for another year before "retiring." He then opened this place. The chef's-choice Sushi Dinner covers the basics, but be adventurous and sample individual items from the sushi list.

13 Coins

125 Boren Ave. N.
206-682-2513
Cuisine: American casual
Meals served: L, D
Open: 24 hours daily
Price: Moderate
Credit cards: AE, DC, Disc, MC, V
Reservations: Not necessary
Wheelchair accessible: Yes

A Seattle culinary institution, this is the city's favorite 24-hour restaurant, and if you don't think it draws a late-night crowd, drop in on a Saturday morning at about 4 am The restaurant has been in a variety of locations since 1967, and its present incarnation is in the Seattle Times Building, ensuring that it has a constant clientele of late working newspaper types. It has a huge menu of meats, seafood, salads, sandwiches, and pastas. Classic 13 Coins dishes include Steak David (an 8-ounce filet mignon served on a bed of sautéed spinach and topped with Dunge-ness crab and hollandaise sauce) and Hazelnut Cappelletti Pasta (stuffed hat-shaped pasta in hazelnut-garlic cream sauce with julienne breast of chicken).

Tulio Ristorante

1100 Fifth Ave.
206-624-5500
Cuisine: Italian
Meals served: B, L, D
Open: Daily
Price: Moderate to expensive
Credit cards: AE, DC, Disc, MC, V
Reservations: Necessary for dinner
Wheelchair accessible: Yes

Sitting in the cozy confines of Tulio, it's hard to imagine that the restaurant is attached to the Vintage Park Hotel in the heart of high-rise downtown. Unlike at a busy high-end restaurant, eating here is much like having a pleasant gathering of neighbors in an Italian neighborhood. It has the ambience of a Mediterranean villa, with cream-colored walls, wood paneling, and white tablecloths. The menu includes a wide, fresh range of Italian/Mediterranean items. The kitchen staff cures its own meats, makes its own bread and pasta, and even stretches its own mozzarella. Appetizers such as the sweet potato gnocchi with sage butter and wood-roasted asparagus wrapped in prosciutto or main dishes such as linguini with clams or roasted chicken with lemon risotto make your meal a celebration. The smoked-salmon ravioli in lemon cream sauce is a winner, and many regulars favor the roasted lemon chicken risotto.

EASTLAKE/SOUTH LAKE UNION
BluWater Bistro
1001 Fairview Ave.
206-447-0769
Cuisine: Seafood
Meals served: L, D
Open: Daily
Price: Moderate
Credit cards: AE, MC, V
Reservations: Recommended
Wheelchair accessible: Yes

Restaurants in the South Lake Union area include BluWater Bistro and I Love Sushi. Toshi

Try to pick a sunny day, because the view from this place is expansive. On the water's edge, located next to the Electric Boat Company in the same complex as the I Love Sushi restaurant, this waterfront spot on Lake Union combines upscale fare with an upbeat, bright ambience. It's a small, cozy café with a lively bar that attracts a singles crowd. The outdoor patio is one of Seattle's "in" spots. The BluWater serves fish, pasta, steaks, chicken, burgers, sandwiches, and salads. Start with the Parmesan-baked artichoke dip and move on to a salad of blue cheese, sliced pears, and smoked almonds. Another option is grilled mahi mahi served with sautéed spinach.

Chandler's Crab House
901 Fairview Ave. N.
206-223-2722
Cuisine: Seafood
Meals served: L, D
Open: Daily
Price: Moderate
Credit cards: AE, MC, V
Reservations: Recommended
Wheelchair accessible: Yes

The picture-book setting on the dock has views through a glass-encased eating area or from a large outdoor deck, and the kitchen features a wide selection of seafood. The new bar area takes advantage of the incredible view of Lake Union. There is even a huge new fireplace for chilly Seattle evenings. Although most diners will opt to eat in the main dining area, the bar menu has an impressive selection of sushi, oysters, scallop ceviche, seared ahi tuna, tempura prawns and asparagus, lobster spring rolls, and many of the main menu's selections. Steaks, chicken, and pasta dishes are also available if you're not a seafood lover.

I Love Sushi

1001 Fairview Ave.
206-625-9604
Cuisine: Japanese
Meals served: L, D
Open: Daily
Price: Moderate
Credit cards: AE, DC, MC, V
Reservations: Recommended
Wheelchair accessible: Yes

This small, intimate Japanese restaurant is as discreet as its menu. Located on the water level west of the same complex that houses the BluWater Bistro, it offers a gentle escape from the outgoing nature of its neighboring competition. Locals regard this sushi restaurant as one of the best in the city, so prepare yourself for an occasional wait if you don't have a reservation. If you prefer tempura dishes, in preparing the deep-fried items the chef uses rice bran oil, which apparently has triple the amount of vitamin B as does olive oil. Regardless, the views dockside are tranquil and the food is fresh.

Ivar's Salmon House

401 NE Northlake Way
206-632-0767
Cuisine: Seafood
Meals served: L, D
Open: Daily
Price: Moderate to expensive
Credit cards: AE, DC, Disc, MC, V
Reservations: Recommended
Wheelchair accessible: Yes

No visit to Seattle is complete without a visit to at least one Ivar's restaurant. You'll find them all over Seattle, including one down on the waterfront at Pier 54, which has been a popular destination since 1938. The chain now has some 25 quick-serve seafood bars in the Pacific Northwest and three full-service restaurants. Ivar Haglund, who started the chain, has since departed this world, but the restaurants live on; this one is a gorgeous cedar replica of a Northwest Indian longhouse, complete with an open-pit Indian-style barbecue for preparing alder-smoked entrées. The room is filled with Northwest native artifacts and historical photographs, and when you're not looking at them there are views of boats cruising on Lake Union with the city skyline in the background. Try the alder-smoked salmon, prawns, or alder-smoked chicken.

Serafina

2043 Eastlake Ave. E.
206-323-0807
Cuisine: Italian
Meals served: L, D
Open: Daily
Price: Moderate to expensive
Credit cards: AE, DC, Disc, MC, V
Reservations: Recommended
Wheelchair accessible: Yes

Treat your date, spouse, or lover to this one. It's a romantic, special place located off the water but in the Lake Union area. Soft piano music and a torch singer in an ambience that is oh-so-Italian make this a must for a romantic Seattle adventure. The menu is northern country Italian, and the prices are remarkably moderate, considering that you're getting some of the finest Italian fare the city offers. Try to get a table on the garden patio. The service is casual but consistently warm and knowledgeable. Be sure to try the house-made misto di salsiccia, a generous plate of sausages over creamy grilled polenta topped with a pile of caramelized onions and tiny, sweet grapes. The pasta selections are served with heavy spicing and robust flavors.

FREMONT

Ponti Seafood Grill

3014 Third Ave. N.
206-284-3000
Cuisine: Regional, seafood
Meals served: L, D
Open: Daily

Price: Moderate to expensive
Credit cards: AE, DC, Disc, MC, V
Reservations: Advised
Wheelchair accessible: Yes

Not officially in Fremont, it's nonetheless close enough to be part of the Fremont action. It's located at the south end of the Fremont Bridge and overlooks the Lake Washington Ship Canal. Weather permitting, try to get a table on the terrace overlooking the canal. Ponti is one of Seattle's most elegant restaurants. Seafood is the specialty here, and you'll find it in many Italian and Asian dishes such as penne with grilled prawns; tomato-saffron risotto with salmon; mussels, and prawns; ahi tuna with soy-sake ginger sauce, and grilled mahi mahi which is served with plum wine and a spicy soba noodle salad. The signature dish is the Thai penne curry with scallops and crab in a spicy blend of tomato-ginger chutney and coconut milk. Start with the large, round scallops in lemon butter. The restaurant was among the first in Seattle to introduce the fusion of Asian and European classical cooking, and most of the entrees are Pacific Rim seafoods. Even if you're not on the terrace, the views of the bridge and the ship canal with its boat traffic are good enough to entertain you.

MADISON VALLEY
Rovers
2808 E. Madison St.
206-325-7442
Cuisine: Vegetarian, Northwest
Meals served: L, D
Open: Daily
Price: Expensive to very expensive
Credit cards: AE, DC, Disc, MC, V
Reservations: Recommended
Wheelchair accessible: Yes

How many times does a vegetarian restaurant garner rave reviews from just about every source? Actually, the restaurant hedges its bets by also having a seafood menu that's next to none in the city. Nonetheless, Rover's head chef, Thierry Rautureau, uses imagination and flair in designing his side-by-side menus. The restaurant is tucked away in a small house east of Capitol Hill, but it's easy to get to and worth the 10-minute drive from downtown. The menu is ever changing and, given the character of the place, quite eclectic. The vegetarian menu might include vine-ripe tomato with vegetable medley; micro greens, and balsamic infusion; wild mushrooms and goat cheese tart with almonds and sherry vinaigrette; and glazed honshimeji mushrooms in phyllo with matsutake mushroom ragout. The seafood menu could include steamed Maine Lobster with baby white asparagus; Perigord truffle, and lobster sauce, or Columbia River sturgeon and guinea fowl mousseline with braised red cabbage and apple-smoked bacon. You can bring in your own wine for a $40 corking fee, provided it's not on the restaurant's wine list, which might be difficult since there are some 300 listings. (Take Madison St. east from downtown and it's just past 28th on the left side of the street.)

MAGNOLIA AND INTERBAY
Chinook's at Salmon Bay
1900 Nickerson St.
206-283-4665
Cuisine: Seafood
Meals served: B (Sat–Sun), L, D
Open: Daily
Price: Moderate
Credit cards: AE, DC, MC, V
Reservations: Not accepted
Wheelchair accessible: Yes

At some time during your Seattle sojourn, you'll likely find yourself at Fisherman's Terminal, where the Alaskan salmon-fishing fleet ties up during the winter and becomes a camera buff's dream. Above the moored boats is Chinook's, a large place with many windows through which to view the fleet. The large menu contains many of the selections generally found in any major seafood restaurant. A favorite among Seattleites is the alder-plank-roasted salmon. (Getting there is easy. Take Elliott Avenue north, which turns into 15th Avenue West, and continue north, taking the last exit before crossing the Ballard Bridge. Then just follow the signs to Fisherman's Terminal.)

Pioneer Square and International District

Al Boccalino
1 Yesler Way
206-622-7688
Cuisine: Italian
Meals served: L (M–F), D (Sat–Sun)
Open: Daily
Price: Moderate
Credit cards: AE, MC, V
Reservations: Recommended for dinner
Wheelchair accessible: Yes

Located on the corner of Yesler and Alaskan Way, the interior has a warm and *very* Italian atmosphere, with stained glass, dark wood, and brick. If you want romance with your ravioli, you won't find a better place. The traditional Italian menu does offer much more than just pasta. Try creamy risotto, moist vitello (veal), perfectly sautéed gamberoni (prawns), seared scallops, or the saddle of lamb marinated in olive oil with fresh rosemary and served with a sweet vermouth sauce.

Elliott Bay Café
101 S. Main St.
206-682-6664
Cuisine: American casual
Meals served: L, D
Open: Daily
Price: Inexpensive
Credit cards: AE, MC, V
Reservations: Not necessary
Wheelchair accessible: No

Obviously, the idea is to sell books in this place, since it's in the basement of one of Seattle's leading bookstores. There's no elevator—just stairs lead down from the middle of the store. Many tourists dismiss the place as a dining option, but there's no better place in the Pioneer Square area for a quick bite in a bookish atmosphere. The café is a lot more upscale than it was a couple of years ago, but it remains a place of sandwiches, salads, soups, and baked goods. Try the smoked turkey and havarti on chewy sourdough or a pastrami sandwich grilled on rye with sauerkraut, Swiss, and spicy mustard. The wild-greens house salad has a tart character with a lemon-rosemary vinaigrette. You can also get beer and wine to help in your digestion.

F. X. McRory's Steak, Chop and Oyster House
419 Occidental Ave. S.
206 623 4800
Cuisine: American
Meals served: L, D
Open: Daily
Price: Inexpensive to moderate
Credit cards: AE, DC, MC, V
Reservations: Recommended for dinner
Wheelchair accessible: Yes

Located directly across the plaza and parking lot from Qwest Stadium, F. X. McRory's Steak, Chop and Oyster House is as much a part of Seattle's sporting life as football and baseball. It's a wonderful combination of sports bar, restaurant, and neighborhood hangout, with an interior of dark walnut chairs, hardwood floors, linen tablecloths, and nonstop art provided by LeRoy Neiman. Be sure to sit in the high-ceilinged bar section of this multiroomed restaurant and feast your eyes on the massive, spectacular wall of mirrors and bottles behind the bar. The formidable menu has six varieties of raw oysters daily from the stand-up oyster bar, plus aged steaks and chops and slow-roasted prime rib. Salmon, live Dungeness crab, and local chicken add a Northwest flavor.

House of Hong
409 Eighth Ave. S.
206-622-7997
Cuisine: Chinese
Meals served: L, D
Open: Daily
Price: Inexpensive
Credit cards: AE, DC, MC, V
Reservations: Recommended for dinner
Wheelchair accessible: Yes

This is the place to go for dim sum when you're in the International District. The tiny dishes of dumplings, pot stickers, and stuffed wontons that compose dim sum are not too greasy or starchy, and there's plenty of meat in the fillings. However, there's more to the menu in this big yellow building than the 10-to-5 dim sum. House of Hong also has a standard Chinese menu, and the price is right and the atmosphere welcoming.

Merchant's Café
109 Yesler Way
206-624-1515
Cuisine: American
Meals served: L, D
Open: Daily
Price: Inexpensive
Credit cards: AE, DC, Disc, MC, V
Reservations: Not necessary
Wheelchair accessible: With difficulty

Seattle's oldest restaurant has a great story behind it. Originally it was a drugstore with an upstairs area displaying photography by E. M. Sammis, Seattle's first resident photographer. In the late 1890s, it became a tavern selling five-cent beers to Klondike gold miners, who also patronized the high-class brothel upstairs. In fact, this may be the original Skid Row saloon. Although the brothel is gone and the beer costs more, the café has retained a certain character. A well-worn tile floor surrounds the bar, which came around Cape Horn in the 1800s, and an old safe and gold scales are reminders of when Seattle was a bit of civilization for Yukon prospectors. It remains a great place to soak up some Seattle history and to have a burger, a sandwich, or soup and to chill out. With its decorative glass and blinking neon sign out front, this is a living museum of Seattle history and style. It caters to a business clientele during the day and the nightlife crowd in the evening.

Trattoria Michelli
84 Yesler Way
206-623-3883
Cuisine: Italian
Meals served: B, L, D
Open: Daily
Price: Inexpensive
Credit cards: AE, DC, MC, V
Reservations: Not necessary
Wheelchair accessible: Yes

In this place, it's hard to tell when dinner ends and breakfast begins. Night owls love it because it's open for meals until about 4 am Tuesday to Saturday and until 11 pm on Sunday and Monday. It attracts the late-movie crowds and Pioneer Square's after-theater clientele as well as a variety of revelers who don't get started before midnight. Where else can you get a huge plate of ravioli in butter and garlic at 2 am or a pizza an hour later? If you're not into the late times, don't worry. There's a full Italian menu available through the day with prices that are *bella, bella.*

QUEEN ANNE AND SEATTLE CENTER
Canlis
2576 Aurora Ave. N.
206-283-3313
Cuisine: Seafood, Continental
Meals served: B, L, D
Open: Daily

Price: Expensive to very expensive
Credit cards: AE, DC, Disc, MC, V
Reservations: Always
Wheelchair accessible: Yes

How many years has Canlis been at the top of many people's "best" list? It seems like forever, certainly, and, with the average life span of a restaurant being just a few years, the 55 years it has been in business does seem like forever. Peter Canlis started the restaurant in 1950, and today a third generation of the Canlis family is running the operation. From its first days, the restaurant has garnered awards, something it is still doing. It's the only restaurant in the northwestern United States to win the Grand Award from *Wine Spectator Magazine* eight years in a row. With more than 1,500 wines from which to select, it's no wonder. The decor has changed over the years and now reflects its current menu, Asian and Continental. Original Canlis classics such as famous broiled steaks from the copper grill, Dungeness crab legs, and the Canlis Salad are still favorites, while new offerings include Pacific king salmon grilled with rhubarb and ginger chutney. Steaks are still a featured menu item. The restaurant has a spectacular view of Lake Union.

UNIVERSITY DISTRICT
Bombay Café
4737 Roosevelt Way NE
206-632-5072
Cuisine: East Indian
Meals served: L, D
Open: Daily
Price: Inexpensive to moderate
Credit cards: AE, MC, V
Reservations: Recommended
Wheelchair accessible: Yes

This used to be the India House, but it changed its name and direction in November 2002, when it became the Bombay Café. How does an Indian restaurant change direction? Well, it now emphasizes seafood, and that makes it unique among Seattle's Indian restaurants. You can still get traditional foods such as vegetable pakoras, tandoori chicken, and kebabs, but there are now seafood specialties that include Burmese salmon grilled with crushed cilantro seeds and tamarind and served on a tamarind-coconut curry sauce with saffron rice pilaf. You might like the tandoori prawns in a pepper yogurt masala or tandoor-grilled trout marinated in tandoori spices and lemon juice.

WATERFRONT
Anthony's Pier 66
2201 Alaskan Way
206-448-6688
Cuisine: Seafood
Meals served: D
Open: Daily
Price: Moderate
Credit cards: AE, DC, Disc, MC, V
Reservations: Recommended
Wheelchair accessible: Yes

The Anthony's restaurant chain is a mini-waterfront empire in the Puget Sound region, with some 18 waterfront establishments in 13 locations. This one is on the downtown Seattle waterfront in the same building as Anthony's Bell Street Diner and Anthony's Fish Bar. There's nothing pretentious about this place. You have panoramic views of the downtown Seattle skyline, Mount Rainier, and Elliott Bay's boating activity, and the seafood is simply prepared in a contemporary yet sophisticated waterfront setting. An abundance of art glass sets this place apart from most of the area's waterfront restaurants. Upstairs, which is more upscale, you'll find Asian-inspired seafood dishes. Downstairs, at the Bell Street Diner, meals are less expensive though far less creative. For the higher prices, you get better views. In summer, the decks are the place to be.

Elliott's
1201 Alaskan Way, Pier 56
206-623-4340
Cuisine: Seafood
Meals served: L, D
Open: Daily
Price: Moderate
Credit cards: AE, Disc, MC, V
Reservations: Recommended for dinner
Wheelchair accessible: Yes

You like oysters? This is the place to get them. A word of warning: Elliott's has been around for more than 30 years and is well known to locals, so you may have a tough time getting a table unless you're there early. The restaurant is on the waterfront. Though the view is somewhat limited, you're there for the food: the fresh local Dungeness crab, wild Northwest salmon, Alaskan halibut, fresh Pacific fin fish, and Northwest shellfish, along with it's specialty, fresh oysters. The oyster bar can have as many as 20 varieties available, so be prepared to experience all types of this Northwest bivalve. It also has a reputation for having the widest selection of white wines in Seattle.

Six Seven
2411 Alaskan Way, Pier 67
206-728-7000
Cuisine: Continental, Northwest
Meals served: B, L, D
Open: Daily
Price: Moderate to expensive
Credit cards: AE, DC, MC, V
Reservations: Recommended for dinner
Wheelchair accessible: Yes

Located in the Edgewater Hotel, the dining room has the area's best view of Puget Sound and the Olympic Peninsula—as it should, since it sits out over the water. As with the rest of the hotel, it is decorated in a Pacific Northwest mountain-lodge motif with a river-rock fireplace that adds a casual and comfortable style, especially on a rainy Seattle night. The contemporary look of the room, with timber, stone, and steel, reflects a 21st-century city. The menu includes everything from pasta to veal to seafood. salmon filet, Alaskan halibut fillet, tuna steak, and Canadian sea scallops are constant daily features.

ATTRACTIONS

Unlike the case in many cities, Seattle's attractions are simply part of its everyday life. Walking through the old town of Pioneer Square is itself an attraction, with the square's hundreds of small stores, unique restaurants, and plazas. And being entertained by the colorful fellows selling fish at Pike Place Market is both an attraction and a way of life in urban Seattle. The same is true with Seattle Center, Seattle's major gathering place for a host of cultural and simply fun things to do. Even the Space Needle, the symbol of the 1962 World's Fair and of Seattle's future, is both a tourist attraction and a place where you can identify scores of activities within the Seattle area through some 60 exhibits. And what better place to have an aquarium than along the waterfront, an area that also is one of the main transportation hubs of the city, with ferries fanning out to near and distant islands in Puget Sound?

If you're in town for a short period and you want to get the full Seattle experience, be sure to buy a **CityPass** (www.citypass.com) to get the most for your money. Included are admission tickets to many of Seattle's most popular attractions, including the Space Needle, the Museum of Flight, the Pacific Science Center, the Seattle Aquarium, and an Argosy Cruises Harbor Tour. The combined value of the tickets in each CityPass is $84.50, but passes cost just $42 apiece and are sold at any of the attractions mentioned above.

The International Fountain at Seattle Center is a popular cooling-off spot in the middle of the city. Toshi

Many of the city's attractions are unique to the Seattle area—and free to boot. In fact, you can get a feel for the city and the people by focusing on tours and entrances to attractions that will cost you nothing or very little.

Gardens and Parks

Seattle boasts many parks that offer stunning views of the city, Elliott Bay, Mount Rainier, and the Olympic Mountains or just a quiet, shady retreat from the fast-paced city. Pack a picnic lunch of fresh fruits, meats, and cheese from Pike Place Market and enjoy Seattle from off the beaten path.

Ballard: Hiram M. Chittenden Locks (see below) are one of the city's most popular visitor attractions But the locks aren't the only reason for going there. It is also the location for the **Carl S. English Jr. Botanical Garden** (3015 NW 54th St.; 206-783-7059), a city park that's filled with shrubs and trees, many of which are rare and unusual. The gift shop has a wonderful garden pamphlet that can help you find many of the rare and exotic plants waiting to be discovered. Every trip to the locks should include a walk in the garden, watching the boats, visiting the fish ladder, and exploring the exhibits and gift shop in the visitor center.

Capitol Hill: At **Volunteer Park** (1247 15th Ave. E.), look down upon the city from this prime hilltop location. Be sure to climb the water tower for "the best free view in Seattle," as voted by readers of the *Seattle Weekly*. At Volunteer Park, you have one of the finest views of the Space Needle, Puget Sound, and the Olympic Mountains. Volunteer Park, originally a cemetery for the city's first European residents (it was moved in 1887), was renamed from the original City Park, in 1901, to honor the volunteers who served in the Spanish-American War. On the grounds are the 1932 art deco building that houses the Seattle Asian Art Museum, home of the Seattle Art Museum's Asian collection, and the Volunteer Park Conservatory's three greenhouses, with its collection of tropical, desert, and seasonal floral exhibits; admission is free. An outdoor Shakespearean festival is held on the grounds in August.

Downtown: At the north end of Pike Place Market is **Victor Steinbrueck Park** (Western Ave. and Virginia St.), from where you can watch the ferries that link Seattle with Bainbridge Island and Bremerton on the far side of Puget Sound. **Waterfront Park** (Pier 57) has a public fishing pier, fish-and-chip bars, and import houses with merchandise from around the world.

Greenwood: The Woodland Park Zoo (see Kids' Favorites) is surrounded by nearly 200 acres of **Woodland Park** (South Gate: N. 50th St. and Fremont Ave. N.; West Gate: N. 55th St. and Phinney Ave. N.), a natural preserve and popular escape from city life located near Fremont, Wallingford, and Green Lake. Be sure to visit the **Rose Garden,** where you'll find thousands of species of flowers.

Madison Valley: The **Washington Park Arboretum** (east on Madison St. to Lake Washington Blvd. E. and north into the arboretum, or from I-5 take exit 168/Bellevue–Kirkland onto WA 520, and take the first exit to Lake Washington Blvd. E. and follow it south into the arboretum; 206-543-8800; http://depts.washington.edu/wpa) collects, conserves, and teaches about Northwestern plants. Its 230 acres are filled with 10,000 native plants, and it's an excellent setting for hands-on learning and recreation. Its

The Conservatory at Volunteer Park houses tropical and desert flora. Toshi

diverse collection has trees, shrubs, and plants in bloom no matter what season you visit. It's a spectacular urban green space on the shores of Lake Washington just east of downtown Seattle and south of the University of Washing-ton. The University of Washington, in association with the Center for Urban Horticulture, manages the arboretum and its plant collections.

Located at the south end of Washington Park Arboretum, the **Japanese Garden** contains native Japanese flowers, shrubs, and trees in a tranquil setting. It is open March 1 –November 30. Chado, a traditional Japanese tea ceremony, is presented free with admission on the third Saturday of the month, April–October, at 1:30 pm Admission is $2.50 for adults and $1.50 for children, students, and seniors.

Magnolia: Discovery Park (3801 W. Government Way) is the perfect urban retreat. Spend the day exploring 534 acres of wooded trails where small animals hide among native plants. Open meadows and bluffs overlook Puget Sound and the Olympic Mountains; trails lead to a narrow beach along the sound. Stop by the Daybreak Star Indian Center to view original Native American arts and crafts; entry is free.

Queen Anne: Kerry Park (211 W. Highland Dr.) is a small grassy strip on upper Queen Anne that offers a picture-perfect view of Seattle Center, downtown Seattle, and Elliott Bay. On clear days, Mount Rainier looms above, providing a stunning backdrop. Kerry Park is out of the way but worth the trip for camera buffs. (From I-5 take exit 167/Mercer St.; veer right off the ramp and make a left at the first light, Valley St., which becomes Broad St. Turn right onto Denny Way. Continue down Denny to First Ave. N.; turn right onto First. Turn left onto Roy St. At the next light, Queen Anne Ave. N., turn right. Proceed uphill to the flashing yellow lights at Valley St. Turn left onto W. Highland Dr.; Kerry Park is on the left two blocks down.)

Hiram M. Chittenden Locks
3015 NW 54th St.
Ballard
206-783-7059
Open: 10–6 daily May 1–Sep 30; 10–4 Th–M Oct 1–Apr 30; free guided tours Mar 1–Nov 30
Admission: Free
Wheelchair accessible: Yes

The Hiram M. Chittenden Locks are one of Seattle's most popular destinations. Construction of the Lake Washington Ship Canal and Hiram M. Chittenden Locks was completed in 1917 by the U.S. Army Corps of Engineers to connect the waters of Lake Washington and Lake Union to the tidal waters of Puget Sound at Salmon Bay. The locks (just like the Panama Canal, only smaller) raise and lower boats between 6 and 26 feet between salt and freshwater. Hang around and no matter what time of year, you'll see a vessel of some kind going through the locks. Once home to the project's blacksmith and carpenter shop, the visitor center is where you should stop first on your exploration of the locks to see displays about the history and operation of the canal and locks and the role of the Corps of Engineers in the Pacific Northwest. Watch salmon make their way up the fish ladder from the viewing window (sometimes you might see a sea lion hunting for a meal) or just watch pleasure boats go through the locks.

Historic Buildings and Sites

Few cities in America are more conscious of their history and the impact it has on everyday life than Seattle. It's a city fiercely proud of its neighborhoods, its historic buildings, and the lifestyle that comes with living in a city that preserves the best of its past. No matter what part of town you explore, you'll find something of interest that reflects some part of the city's past. Yet the past has been so seamlessly woven into today's Seattle that it's often difficult to separate what was from what is.

Boeing
3003 W. Casino Rd.
Everett
206-544-1264, 1-800-464-1476
www.boeing.com/companyoffices/aboutus/tours
Open (tours): 9–3 M–F; no bags, backpacks, beepers, cameras, cell phones,
infants in carriers, or notepads are allowed on the tour
Admission: $5 adults, $3 seniors and children under 16; kids have to be at least
4 feet 2 inches tall
Wheelchair accessible: Yes

As you drive from Seattle southward on I-5, you'll pass an airfield with new jets lined up alongside. It's Boeing Field, where the company prepares its aircraft for delivery to clients, and it's also the site of the Museum of Flight. The company headquarters, which used to be on the other side of the airfield in a small, low building, is now located in Chicago, closer to the head offices of the airlines that buy its products. When the move to Chicago became known in 2001 and finally took place in September 2002, it caused only a ripple. It says a lot about the city's declining dependency on Boeing, even though the company still employs 40,000 people in the Puget Sound area.

The 747 is built in the largest single building under one roof in the world, in Everett north of Seattle, with the hangars measuring 200 million cubic feet (5.66 million cubic meters). Visitors to the facility sometimes see workers assembling parts that were manufactured elsewhere. During 2002, the company started to build two new longer-range jetliners, the 747-400ER and the 777-300ER. You can take a tour of the huge Everett plant that assembles the 747 and other aircraft. It's an hour drive from downtown Seattle and tours are on a first-come, first-served basis. (Take I-5 north from downtown and drive west on WA 526; the road is well marked.)

Chinatown/International District Historic District

Yesler to S. Dearborn St.,
Fourth Ave. S. to I-5
International District
206-382-1197

The Benevolent Association Building in the International District Toshi

The area east of Pioneer Square became home to Chinese after they had completed work on the transcontinental railroad, and the neighborhood has remained fairly intact despite anti-Chinese riots during the 1880s and even after the internment of Japanese-Americans during the Second World War. It's a place of small stores, Southeast Asian and Chinese restaurants, herbalists, massage parlors, acupuncturists, and scores of private clubs where residents gather for gambling and socializing. The **Wah Mee Club** (on Canton Ave.) gained notoriety in 1983 as the site of a multiple murder that was linked to gangs and gambling interests.

The **Nippon Kan Theater** (628 S. Washington St.; 206-467-6807) was once the focal point for Japanese-American activities, including Kabuki, and was renovated and reopened in 1981 as a national historic site. In mid-July, Pacific Island dancers, Thai musicians, dragon dancers from China, Taiko drummers, and others celebrate the district's diversity at **Hing Hay Park** (Maynard Ave. S. and S. King St.).

King Street between Fifth Avenue and I-5 is where most of the Chinese activity takes place, and it's where you can buy shark fins, trussed poultry, herbs, and ingredients known only to residents of the area. **Jackson Street** between I-5 and 14th Avenue has been referred to as "Little Saigon" because it houses many of the 450 Vietnamese-owned businesses in Seattle, including many Vietnamese restaurants, where you can get that wonderful blend of Vietnamese/French cuisine at reasonable prices. For information, contact the Chinatown– International District Business Improvement Area (409 Maynard Ave. S., Ste. P-1, Seattle, WA 98104; 206-382-1197).

Lakeview Cemetery
15th Ave. between Highland Dr. and Howe St.
Capitol Hill
206-322-1582

If graveyards give you a more personal relationship with history and with the people who shaped their own worlds and left behind what would become ours, visit Lakeview Cemetery, adjacent to Volunteer Park. With sweeping views embracing North Seattle, Lake Union, and Lake Washington, Lakeview is a spectacular place in which to get close to the people who formed Seattle's history. Many of Seattle's pioneers rest there, including Princess Angeline, the daughter of Chief Sealth; Dexter Horton; and Doc Maynard and his wife, Catherine.

If you find a crowd here, it's probably kung fu fans flocking to the graves of movie actors Bruce Lee and his son, Brandon Lee. Though neither of the Lees gained international notoriety until after their deaths, their relationship to Seattle is long and focused. The elder Lee was born in San Francisco in 1940, grew up in Hong Kong, and moved back to the US in the late 1950s, enrolling at the University of Washington in the early 1960s. Lee's career took off when he was in Hong Kong, where he made several action films, including *Enter the Dragon*. Prophetically, in early 1973, just before the U.S. release of that film, he told his sister that he expected to die soon. Months later, he died in his sleep of a cerebral aneurysm. When *Enter the Dragon* premiered in the US, Lee became an icon. His son, Brandon, born in 1965, was working on the film *The Crow* in 1993 when he was shot to death in an accident while filming a scene involving a gun that was supposed to be empty. He died the same day he was shot.

Pike Place Market National Historic District
85 Pike St.; bound by Pike St., Virginia Ave., and Western Ave.
Downtown
206-682-7453

If the Space Needle is the symbol of Seattle's economic outlook and its most obvious landmark and Seattle Center is the city's cultural heart, then Pike Place Market is Seattle's soul and its sense of smell and taste. Just outside the front entrance, Pike Place Market Foundation placed a giant piggy bank. In the almost 20 years since, the bronze pig Rachel, created by local artist Georgia Gerber and modeled after her neighbor's late pig, has collected more than $100,000 for neighborhood charity.

Rachel the Pig is a well-known meeting spot in Pike Place Market. Toshi

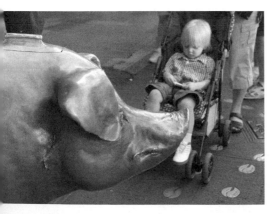

The market began in 1907 as a place where farmers gathered to sell their produce to city dwellers, but it has expanded over the years to become the oldest continuing working market in the United States. It is a nine-acre National Historic District that is home to more than 100 farmers, 300 commercial businesses, 500 residents, and 50 street performers. It is filled with delightful characters hawking their fresh fish and produce in a dozen accents. The world's first Starbuck's opened in the market in 1971 and is still brewing its beans at the site. The cultural mix of foods and peoples is a menagerie of competing sensual pleasures, a social statement defining the region and its people. As at London's Covent Garden, Paris's Les Halles, and Jerusalem's Triple Bazaar, come prepared to partake in a feast. For information, contact the Pike Place Market Development Association (85 Pike St., Rm. 500, Seattle, WA 98101; 206-682-7453).

Pioneer Square Historic District
20-block grid between Second Ave. and the Alaskan Way Viaduct, from
   Columbia St. to King St.
Pioneer Square

Long before European settlement, what is now Pioneer Square Historic District used to be an Indian village. This is where Seattle began back in 1852 after the original settlers abandoned Alki Point—where they had landed a year before—because of the hard, cold, windy winters and poor moorage for sailing vessels. Today, the only reminder of the original Duwamish Indian village that preceded Pioneer Square is a 60-foot totem pole and a bronze bust of Chief Sealth at **Pioneer Place Park** (First Ave. and Yesler Way).

Pioneer Square is between downtown proper to the north and the sports stadiums and International District to the south. The Pioneer Square area is where loggers built the original Skid Road (now Yesler Way) to skid logs downhill to the waterfront. Constructed by Henry Yesler, the skid was designed to transport logs from the steep surrounding hills down to his waterfront sawmill. It became known as Skid Road, a term that was eventually absorbed into American lexicon as "skid row" to denote a city's run-down area, the home of derelicts and winos. Locals are as sensitive to the use of "skid row" as San Franciscans are to their city being called "Frisco."

The vast majority of buildings in what was then downtown Seattle were wooden, and both the streets and buildings were built on stilts to keep them above high tide because the area was a huge tidal flat. The great fire of 1889 occurred when a carpenter accidentally ignited glue that he was boiling on his woodstove. The fire quickly spread and ignited 50 tons of ammunition being stored in nearby hardware stores. Goodbye, Seattle.

After the fire consumed the flimsy buildings that had occupied the region, new buildings were constructed to a literally higher standard, several feet above the previous foundation lines. The new building code included a sewer system, which meant that new buildings had to be built one story above the previous level. However, since it took 30 years to complete, it meant a somewhat slow transition in which customers sometimes had to descend from the new street level by ladder to the old street level where a few stores still operated. The first story of some commercial buildings ended up below the street level, accessible by stairs. The shops that remained belowground were eventually condemned in 1907, but that didn't stop their economic activity; the boulevard-below-ground had already become Seattle's brothel and gambling center.

The fire actually created stability because of the resulting street improvements, and many handsome stone and red brick buildings were constructed around Pioneer Square. The historic district is an irregular 20-block grid that begins at triangular **Pioneer Square** (First Ave. and Yesler Way). The odd angles of street intersections here are the result of the city's founders, Arthur Denny and David "Doc" Maynard, not agreeing on whether the streets should parallel the shore of Elliott Bay or run north and south by the compass. In the end, they each designed their own street grid the way they wanted on their own land claim, and the meeting of the two grids resulted in the odd angles that are still apparent.

A more recent event also had an impact on Pioneer Square when, on February 28, 2001, the 6.8-magnitude earthquake hit the Seattle area. Though the quake was centered 35 miles (56k) southwest of Seattle, the impact to the area was substantial. Many of the Pioneer Square buildings, made of brick and mortar, were damaged and some sections of the Pioneer Square area were cordoned off for several months while damage was assessed and buildings repaired. But no buildings had to be demolished and all are safely back in use. Just south of Pioneer Square are two new stadiums, Qwest Stadium and Safeco Field, host to NFL football and American League baseball, respectively.

Smith Tower Observation Deck
506 Second Ave.
Pioneer Square
206-622-4004
www.smithtower.com
Open: Daily; seasonal hours (call ahead)
Admission: $6 adults, $5 seniors and students, $4 children, free under 6 years
Wheelchair accessible: Yes

When the gleaming white, 42-floor Smith Tower opened on July 4, 1914, it was the fourth tallest building in the world, and it remained the tallest building west of the Mississippi River for almost 50 years. It was originally constructed to be what it is today: an office building. The elevators were provided by the Otis Elevator Company of New York, and six of the seven elevators remaining in the building are still powered by their original DC motors. The building's 2,314 windows are encased in bronze frames, most containing their original 1914 safety glass. Unlike the case in modern skyscrapers, Smith Tower windows can be opened and closed. A $28 million renovation in the late 1990s brought the building into the 21st century and gave it a complete seismic upgrade. The Nisqually earthquake of 2001 didn't affect the building at all. Access to the Observation Deck and Chinese Room is via the last manually operated elevators on the West Coast. These brass and copper, caged, original 1914 elevators depart from a ground floor recently returned to its original design, as part of the restoration. The 35th-floor, open-air Observation Deck wraps completely around all four sides of the tower, providing panoramic views of Mount Rainier and the Olympic and Cascade mountain ranges.

Space Needle
Seattle Center
Queen Anne
206-905-2100
www.spaceneedle.com
Open: 9 am–11 pm M–F, 9 am–midnight Sat–Sun
Admission (elevator to Observation Deck): $13 adults, $11 seniors, $10 youth 4–13
Wheelchair accessible: Yes

Located at Seattle Center a short walk from the Monorail stop and across from the Experience Music Project, the Space Needle opened April 21, 1962, as the World's Fair's centerpiece. The theme of the fair was Century 21. In a real sense, the 1962 Seattle World's Fair and the construction of the Space Needle heralded the end of the image America held of the Pacific Northwest as merely a provider of wood, fish, and other such natural resources. It announced that the area was the future cornerstone of a new economy. And that's exactly what it has become. In keeping with that original theme, the Needle, with its view of Mount Rainier 75 miles (121 km) away, has come to symbolize Seattle's powerful aerospace and high-tech economy. The 605-foot (184 m) Space Needle is both a symbol and a landmark. It demands attention, not just for itself, but for a city that has transformed itself from a center of basic Northwest industries to a leading-edge, high-tech force.

Originally constructed for a cost of $4.5 million, the privately owned structure is basically an elegant tripod with a pod atop it. Weighing 3,700 tons, including 146,000 pounds (66,225 kg) of steel weld, it sits on a foundation that is 30 feet (9.1 m) deep and that contains 2,800 yards (467 truckloads) of concrete and 250 tons of reinforcing steel. During the 1962 World's Fair, nearly 20,000 people a day went up in the elevators. The 20,000 mark was never quite attained, however, missing by fewer than 50 one day. The Space Needle hosted more than 2.3 million visitors during the fair. It now has 1.2 million visitors annually.

The Space Needle features an observation deck, a revolving restaurant, and retail gift shops and banquet facilities on the Skyline level at 100 feet (30.5 m), which accommodates up to 350 people. As tourist traps go, this is one of the better ones you'll encounter. There are no hucksters competing for your buck, and at the end you feel you've had something for your money.

It takes 43 seconds aboard any of the three glass-enclosed, 25-passenger elevators to reach the top level. From there—at the 518-foot (158 m) level—you find a 360-degree view of the surrounding scenery, including the Olympic and Cascade mountain ranges, Mount Rainier, downtown Seattle, Lake Union, and Puget Sound.

Eighteen feet (5.5 m) below the observation deck—at the 500-foot (152 m) level— is the revolving restaurant called Sky City which turns on a 14-foot-wide turntable, making one complete revolution each hour. The family-oriented restaurant offers Northwest cuisine in an informal setting, emphasizing fresh seafood and produce from Pike Street Market and lamb from Ellensburg in eastern Washington.

The heaviest visitor to the Needle was the king of Tonga, who weighed in at 400 pounds (181.4 kg) and had to have a special chair carried up the service elevator. In the summer of 1974, a "streaker" circled the Needle nude in a private plane; restaurant patrons applauded his arm-flapping and leg-waving as he appeared in the plane's open door. The Needle has also been the site of numerous marriages, one birth, three suicides, and a 1975 jump by two parachutists. Although built to withstand a wind velocity of 150 miles (241 km) per hour, the Space Needle closed in 1962 when wind gusts of 83 miles per hour (133.5 km) were recorded and again in 1973 for winds of 75 miles per hour (120.6 km). Should the great Pacific Northwest earthquake that everyone is worried about ever arrive (it has been anticipated for several centuries), the Space Needle just might be the place to be. It has withstood earthquakes without damage, including the 2001 tremor that measured 6.8 on the Richter scale.

Theaters and Classic Movie Houses
Seattle has always had good theaters in which to hold concerts and present films. Part of the reason is because Alexander Pantages founded his vaudeville empire here at the turn of the 20th century. At one time his theaters graced every West Coast city, though much of

what he built has been torn down. One of the grandest of his buildings was in Vancouver, British Columbia, but it was removed for a parking lot in the 1960s. In their day, the the-ater palace architects were faced with a building program almost unrivaled in its complexity, requiring a vast collection of rooms under one roof. Frequently the theaters were situated on odd-shaped pieces of land. Built decades before Hollywood created the moving picture extravaganza, the theaters were spectacles in their own right. They were built not as romantic extremes, but to draw people to the box office.

Capitol Hill: Built in 1915, the **Egyptian Theatre** (801 E. Pine St.) was originally built as a large Masonic temple, with offices, a main auditorium, and a smaller auditorium. In the 1970s, the Masons used the large auditorium as a wrestling arena to earn extra money. In the early 1980s it became the home of the Seattle International Film Festival (SIFF), at which point the founders of the festival moved in. The theater's Egyptian decor is part of its original design. The Egyptian continues to host the SIFF, the largest film festival in North America, and also features a wide array of independent film, foreign-language cinema, documentaries, and restored classics.

The **Harvard Exit Theatre** (807 E. Roy St.), can be found on a quaint, tree-lined street at the north end of Broadway and, like the Egyptian, is run by Landmark Theaters. Built in 1925, the Harvard Exit originally was constructed as a clubhouse for the Woman's Century Club, which continues to hold meetings in the lobby. The building was sold in 1968 for conversion to a movie theater, but its large, glorious lobby retains a cozy 1920s atmos-phere, adorned with a fireplace, a grand piano, and a chandelier. It now plays independent and foreign-language films. Annually, the Harvard Exit is also host to the SIFF and the Lesbian and Gay Film Festival.

Downtown: B. Marcus Priteca, a Seattle native, was a master theater designer who was kept busy in his hometown building theaters that were both functional and attractive. Perhaps his most famous theater was the opulent Hollywood Pantages at the famed corner of Hollywood and Vine in Los Angeles. In Seattle there are still examples of his work. The **Coliseum Theater** (Fifth Ave. and Pike St.) is a Priteca-designed house that was one of the first giant movie theaters in the country. Built in 1915, it was the largest theater in the West—including Los Angeles—for years. The **Paramount Theater** (907 Pine St.) is another Priteca design. It opened in 1927 and is still considered one of the most acoustically per-fect theaters on the coast. Now used as a live theater and musical venue, it has a wonderful Wurlitzer pipe organ that has been restored to original condition.

The **5th Avenue Theatre** (1308 Fifth Ave.) is one of the most favored buildings in Seattle, and its gaudy old hall, used today primarily for long-stay Broadway shows, is prob-ably the finest example left of the old theater tradition. It's also the most faithful to its ori-gins. Built in 1926, the highly ornate auditorium is a near-perfect duplication—at twice the original scale—of the Imperial Palace in Beijing's Forbidden City. The only detail designer R. C. Reamer changed was the color scheme, giving the carved "wooden" beams (actually plaster) a green hue for a Northwest flavor.

Aside from the skyscraper, no building type is more clearly representative of 20th-century architecture than the movie palace, the heyday of which is still a part of Seattle's makeup. In the age of multiplex theaters in shopping malls and downtowns, Seattle's classic movie houses are gorgeous survivors from the era of individual movie theaters. Few cities have retained and have cared for them as has Seattle.

Drumheller Fountain on the University of Washington campus Toshi

University of Washington Campus

NE 45th St. to ship canal, 15th Ave. NE to Mary Gates Memorial Dr. and Lake Washington
University District
206-543-2100
www.washington.edu

The history of the University of Washington is almost as diverse as its academic programs.
Early in 1861 Arthur and Mary Denny, Charles and Mary Terry, and Edward Lander donated
land on a forested 10-acre knoll overlooking Elliott Bay, where the university was established on the site of what is now the Fairmont Olympic Hotel on University Street in downtown Seattle. The Territorial University of Washington opened November 4, 1861, but was
little more than a backwoods school that closed for lack of funds several times during its
earliest years. The first faculty consisted of one professor who taught a curriculum that
included Latin, Greek, English, history, algebra, and physiology. When Washington became a state in 1889, the university was firmly established. Growing enrollment and the
lack of available land in what was becoming downtown Seattle soon made a larger campus
necessary, and in 1895 classes opened in Denny Hall, the first building on the present
Seattle campus. In 1909 the University of Washington was the site of a world's fair called
the Alaska-Yukon-Pacific Exposition. The University of Washington, now with 694 acres
and 34,000 students in 16 schools and colleges, is one of the largest universities on the
West Coast, and it takes up almost half the University District neighborhood.

Cutting through the heart of the University District is 15th Avenue, which provides
the easiest entry to both the campus and its surroundings. Neighborhood streets reflect
the university character, with bookstores, clothing shops, coffeehouses, and a variety of
inexpensive cafés and restaurants. This region is why Seattle consistently ranks high in per-
capita movie attendance and coffee sales, as students frequent every part of the neighborhood. The main street is **University Way NE**, which, among other things, is the focal point

for the annual **University Street Fair** held every May. This popular arts and crafts fest brings vendors and street musicians, most of whom look like 1960s retreads.

The main entrance to the campus is at the intersection of NE 45th Street and 17th Avenue NE, which leads you south past the **Burke Museum** (see Museums). When you walk around the upper campus, you'll find yourself in a picture-book atmosphere of ivy-covered Gothic buildings grouped with maple and oak trees, accented by curved walkways that wind through landscaped grounds. The central plaza is referred to as Red Square because of its dominating red brick paving. Guitar-playing and Frisbee-throwing students lounge here, eating their lunches. The **Henry Art Gallery, Meany Hall** (see Entertainment and the Arts), and the **Suzzallo/Allen Library**, an ornate Tudor Gothic building dating from the 1920s, are located here. The Suzzallo Library architect, Carl Gould, was founder of the university's architecture department, and he also designed 18 other campus buildings. Look at the west façade of the library for the 18 terra-cotta figures, including Shakespeare, Beethoven, and Plato.

The lower campus is newer and has striking architecture, including the **Drumheller Fountain**, one of the focal points for student lounging about. **Husky Stadium**, home of the Washington Huskies football team, is located at the southeast corner of the campus and seats 72,500 people. It was here that the wave cheer was invented in 1981 by the marching band's director and cheerleader, Robb Weller.

Kids' Favorites

Odyssey: The Maritime Discovery Center
2205 Alaskan Way, Pier 66
Waterfront
206-374-4001
www.ody.org
Open: Daily; seasonal hours
Admission: $7 adults, $5 seniors and students 5–18, $2 children 2–4, free under 2
Wheelchair accessible: Yes

Odyssey is a regional showcase where people can discover Seattle's links to Puget Sound and the north Pacific, including commercial fishing, shipping, trade, transportation, recreation, and marine protection. It's a combination interactive promotion and educational tool highlighting Seattle's working waterfront, and it complements the stories of marine wildlife told at the Seattle Aquarium, of science and technology at the Pacific Science Center, and of air transportation at the Museum of Flight. Through lively, hands-on experiences, you'll discover the nuts and bolts of a working waterfront, the basics of nautical operations, and the latest in commercial fishing technology. You can pilot a container ship, step into a replica modern naval bridge, take a virtual kayak tour, and load containers.

Walk among tropical butterflies in the Pacific Science Center's special exhibit. Toshi

The Seattle Aquarium includes a waterfront deck on Elliott Bay. Toshi

Pacific Science Center and IMAX Theater
Seattle Center
Queen Anne
206-443-2001
www.pacsci.org
Open: 10–6 daily
Admission: science center $9 adults, $6.50 children; IMAX $7.50; combination
center/IMAX $14.50 adults, $12 kids
Wheelchair accessible: Yes

The Pacific Science Center, located under the five white arches near the Space Needle,
is composed of five large interconnected buildings. The displays are aimed mainly at
children. The permanent exhibits allow you to travel back in time to the Mesozoic Era and
to meet seven moving, roaring, robotic dinosaurs in a lifelike environment. Among the
most gorgeous of the exhibits is a lush, indoor tropical environment for free-flying butterflies. Beautiful species arrive biweekly as chrysalises that were raised on tropical butterfly
farms. The Insect Village has giant robotic insects, interactive exhibits, and live displays
that give you a close-up look at the world of insects and other arthropods. The Puget Sound
Model and Saltwater Tide Pool have real tides and currents in action in a 100-square-foot
scale model of Puget Sound. You can see yourself on TV, meet a ferret face to face, scope
out a snake, test your reaction time, and see how much energy you produce on the Calorie
Bicycle and other neat indoor things. Giant-screen, IMAX nature films bring an intimate
relationship between creatures and the audience. In the museum's Smith Planetarium,
brilliant colors, intense imagery, and breathtaking aerial beams are projected throughout
the larger-than-life Adobe Laser Dome. Choreographed to your favorite music, the shows
feature state-of-the-art lasers.

Seattle Aquarium
1483 Alaskan Way, Pier 59
Waterfront
206-386-4300
www.seattleaquarium.org
Open: 10–5 daily Labor Day–Memorial Day, 10–8 daily Memorial Day–Labor Day
Admission: $11.50 adult, $7.50 youth 6–12, $5.25 children 3–5, free 2 and under
Wheelchair accessible: Yes

Seattle's aquarium is not as large as some of the other marine exhibits along the West
Coast—in Vancouver, British Columbia, or Monterey, California, for example—but it features a wide range of marine life, much of which is native to the Pacific Northwest. There
are no large mammals here, but you'll have a lot of fun watching the aquarium's stars:
the river otters and the giant octopus. Don't miss the underwater viewing dome, from
which you'll get a fish-eye view of sea life below the surface. Daily feedings and lectures
are scheduled every 20–30 minutes. There are several different permanent displays, but
the most interesting to locals is "Life on the Edge," which opened May 31, 2002, as the
Seattle Aquarium's 25th anniversary present to the community. This exhibit allows visitors
to experience the tide-pool life of Washington's outer coast and Seattle's inland sea, showing such creatures as aggregating anemones and sunflower sea stars. Large video screens
help demonstrate the unique lifestyles of the amazing creatures that thrive in the harsh
conditions of Washington's tidal zones. (You can see the other two waterfront attractions,
the IMAXDome Theater and the Maritime Discovery Center, with combination tickets at
greatly reduced prices.)

Seattle Children's Museum/Seattle Children's Theatre
Seattle Center
Queen Anne
206-441-1768 (museum), 206-441-4488 (theater)
www.thechildrensmuseum.org, www.sct.org
Open: 10–5 M–F, 10–6 Sat–Sun
Admission: $7.50 adults and children, $6 grandparents, free under 1
Wheelchair accessible: Yes

When you walk into the Seattle Children's Museum, you'll feel like Gulliver walking among
the tiny people. Kids can put on a play at the Bijou Theatre, explore kid-size houses from
around the world, or hike in the Pacific Northwest woods and slide down a glacier. It's a
place where you and your kids can manipulate objects, role-play, problem solve, and
develop eye-hand coordination with a variety of unique exhibits and programs. You'll
discover other cultures in the Global Village and Time Trek, learn about the Pacific Northwest forests on the Mountain Forest, and rush to a fire on a child-size fire engine in the
Neighborhood. The Imagination Station is where kids can explore different art media;
other areas are designed for toddlers and kids of varying ages. An artist in residence guides
kids through art projects using varied media and techniques.
   The Seattle Children's Theatre celebrated its 30th season in 2004–05 and has a program that has become a part of the overall Seattle theater scene, attracting adults as well as
children. The program strikes a delicate balance in which childlike sensibilities are piqued
and adult sensibilities are respected. The sets and costumes are bright and imaginative,

and every play concludes with a cast discussion, in which the audience can ask questions of cast members. Before or after the show, families can visit an in-theater gift shop that sells toys and books related to that season's plays. Each of the two auditoriums features a cry room at the back for restless babies and toddlers and their parents. Drama classes are offered year-round, and day camps are offered during the summer.

Soundbridge Seattle Symphony Music Discovery Center

200 University St.
Downtown
206-336-6600
www.seattlesymphony.org/soundbridge
Open: 10–4 Tu–Sun
Admission: $7 adults, $5 children 5–18, free under 5
Wheelchair accessible: Yes

This is every music lover's dream: a chance to realize a lifelong ambition to conduct a symphony orchestra. In 1998, when construction of Benaroya Hall was approaching completion, the Seattle Symphony received a donation of $5 million, of which $1 million was earmarked to jump-start a learning center—Soundbridge Seattle Symphony Music Discovery Center—within the concert hall. The result is a hands-on learning center that allows you to feel what it's like to be in front of an orchestra or to sit in the first chair of one of the orchestra's sections. There's a listening bar of some 500 CDs and interactive activities for playing the piano like Horowitz or conducting like Gerard Schwarz.

The African Village at Woodland Park Zoo Dennis Conner

Woodland Park Zoo
5500 Phinney Ave., North
Greenwood
206-684-4892
www.zoo.org
Open: Daily; seasonal hours
Admission: $10 adults, $7 children 3–12, free under 3; discounts for seniors and disabled
Wheelchair accessible: Yes

This is one of America's best zoos, famed for revolutionizing the world of zoos by immers-ing visitors in naturalistic exhibits. Over its 105-plus-year history, Woodland Park has set an international standard for animal care and realistic landscape exhibits that allow ani-mals to thrive and be seen in naturalistic environments. In 1979, it opened the first naturalistic gorilla exhibit in the world, establishing a prototype that has been copied throughout North America. The zoo has a spacious layout, with large plots of open green space, that allows the zoo to have theme areas such as Northern Trail, Tropical Asia, Tropical and Temperate Forests, plus more. It can be covered in three to four hours with-out difficulty. Some of the animals can be seen only at a distance because they're allowed to roam free. (From downtown, take I-5 north to exit 169/NE 50th St. Go west 1.3 miles to the South Gate at N. 50th St. and Fremont Ave. N. Or take Metro bus #5 north from Third Ave. and Pine St. to the West Gate at N. 55th St. and Phinney Ave. N.)

Museums

Many of Seattle's museums have days in which you can attend free of charge (see listings below). And at the **Coast Guard Museum** (Seattle waterfront at Pier 36; free), you'll see a collection of Coast Guard memorabilia, uniforms, and guns. The Arctic icebreakers are usually moored nearby.

Burke Museum of Natural History and Culture
45th Ave. NE and NE 15th St.
University District
206-543-5590
www.washington.edu/burkemuseum
Open: 10–5 daily; 10–8 first Th each month
Admission: $8 adults, $6.50 seniors, $5 students and youth, free 4 and under
Wheelchair accessible: Yes

Located on the campus of the University of Washington, the Burke Museum is a major national resource for information on 500 million years of the natural and cultural history of the Pacific Northwest. Here you can get a taste of the Pacific Northwest and the Pacific Rim's treasure trove of natural and artistic wonders, including towering totem poles and huge, hand-carved cedar canoes; the region's only dinosaur skeleton; beautiful gems and minerals; fascinating fossils; and birds, beetles, and butterflies. There are more than five million specimens in the museum. Its best-known collection is of the human remains of "Kennewick Man," found on federal lands in eastern Washington in 1996. The 9,300-year-old skeleton, one of the oldest found in North America, has been the object of law-suits among scientists, the federal government, and Native Americans over whether the skeleton can be used for research. The Burke Museum has been chosen by the court, with the agreement of the litigants, as the most suitable repository for the safekeeping of these human remains.

The Center for Wooden Boats
1010 Valley St.
South Lake Union
206-382-2628
www.cwb.org
Open: Daily; seasonal hours
Admission: Free
Wheelchair accessible: No

This is a wooden-boat buff's dream. Located on the southern shore of Lake Union and adjacent to the Northwest Seaport and Maritime Heritage Center, this is both a museum and a boat rental business. But you don't have to rent a boat or take lessons to see the museum. Most of the boats are dockside, and some are in drydock storage on the dock itself. Many of the boats on display can actually be rented and taken out onto the lake. Rentals, workshops, and lessons are available year-around; the cost for rentals varies according to the size and type of boat you want. There are free classic boat rides on Sundays, 2–3 pm.

Experience Music Project
Seattle Center
Queen Anne
206-770-2702
www.emplive.com
Open: 10–5 M–F, 10–9 Sat–Sun
Admission: $20 adults, $16 seniors and children 13–17, $15 children 7–12, free under 7
Wheelchair accessible: Yes

The guitar tower at the Experience Music Project Toshi

The only popular-music collection that comes close to this place's is Cleveland's Rock and Roll Hall of Fame. The Experience Music Project started out as the brainchild of Microsoft cofounder Paul Allen, who originally wanted to create a tribute to Seattle native Jimi Hendrix. But the idea expanded until it embraced all of the Pacific Northwest music scene and history as well as the overall accounting of popular music in America.

The project space is huge, with some 80,000 interactive displays and studios. So to do justice to the admission cost and possibilities for exploration in the museum, leave the better part of the day to play in it. You'll be handed a prerecorded guide at the entrance. Each exhibit has a number; press that number, and an explanation comes on in your earphones. It is essential that you have this device, or you'll miss much of what the exhibits, especially the old posters and artifacts, have to offer.

The building was designed by architect Frank O. Geary and has an aluminum exterior purposely designed to fade with time. Each of the facade's 21,000 shingles, in purple, silver, gold, red, and blue, has a different shape and size. Inside, concerts are held in the main hall, known as the Sky Church. The Hendrix Gallery is filled with rare artifacts that illustrate both the personal and the superstar aspects of the guitar hero, from his childhood growing up in Seattle to his time on the world stage. You'll follow his career from his time as sideman with the Isley Brothers to his funk group Band of Gypsies.

Costumes from the Vault is a whimsical journey into the wardrobes of the wild, featuring costumes and clothing from a selection of musicians, superheroes, and science-fiction stars. You'll view costumes from Elton John, Notorious B.I.G., Batman and Robin, and a variety of pop artists. Songcraft plunges you into the art and craft of professional songwriting, exploring the key aspects of songwriting: melody, rhythm, tempo, lyrics, instrumentation, harmony, and production. It illustrates how successful songwriters are able to create popular tunes. The most popular of the exhibits is the large Sound Lab, in which you can play electric guitar, bass, keyboards, drums, and DJ turntables, with help from the staff and with interactive computer terminals. You'll be able to mix on a professional console and play with effects pedals.

Frye Art Museum
704 Terry Ave.
First Hill
206-622-9250
www.fryeart.org
Open: 10–5 Tu–Sat, noon–5 Sun, 10–8 Thu
Admission: Free
Wheelchair accessible: Yes

Charles and Emma Frye were Seattle pioneers who purchased their first European painting at the Chicago World's Fair in 1893. Their collection grew to more than 230 works, eventually covering the walls of their home from floor to ceiling. After Emma's death, Charles provided money in his will for the creation of a free public art museum to house and display the art collection. He died in 1940 at age 81, and the museum opened to the public in 1952. Among the artists on display are Andrew Wyeth, Pablo Picasso, and Edward Hopper. Special exhibits are held throughout the year. The museum's rotunda leads into an elegant, naturally lit lobby; enhancing the ambience are an outdoor reflecting pool, waterfall, and courtyard garden.

Henry Art Gallery
15th Ave. NE and NE 41st St.
University District
206-543-2280
www.henryart.org.
Open: 11–5 Tu–W and F–Sun, 11–8 Th
Admission: $8 adults, $6 seniors, free students and children under 14
Wheelchair accessible: Yes

The art museum of the University of Washington, located on the west side of the campus, houses permanent collections of artists and photographers such as Stuart Davis, Robert Motherwell, Morris Graves, Diane Arbus, Ansel Adams, Imogen Cunningham, Man Ray, and Garry Winogrand. It also routinely offers exhibitions of contemporary and modern art. Founded in 1927, the Henry was the first public art museum in the state of Washington and has since become the Pacific Northwest's premier modern and contemporary art museum. The permanent collection of more than 20,500 objects includes late 19th- and 20th-century paintings, the extensive Monsen Collection of Photography, and a textile and costume collection, along with a collection of cutting-edge works in new media. It's the new media that sets this museum apart from others in the area, as it explores the technological potential in contemporary art. It's a place where you'll find yourself thinking differently about what art is. The building itself is a collage of glass, textured stainless steel, and cast stone.

Klondike Gold Rush National Historic Park
117 S. Main St.
Pioneer Square
206-553-7220
www.nps.gov/klse
Open: 9–5 daily
Admission: Free
Wheelchair accessible: Yes

Seattle was transformed in 1897 when news of a gold strike in the Canadian Yukon reached the city. The result was a rush north to the Klondike goldfields. From 1897 to 1898, tens of thousands of people from across the United States and around the world descended on Seattle's commercial district, creating instant wealth for a city that was trying to recover from its devastating fire. While in Seattle, the hopeful miners purchased millions of dollars worth of food, clothing, equipment, pack animals, and steamship tickets. The outcome of the gold rush was to bolster the city's reputation as the Pacific Northwest's most important city, a fact that wasn't made clear for several generations. Thousands of prospectors passed through San Francisco, Portland, Tacoma, Seattle, Victoria, and Vancouver, British Columbia. Of the approximately 100,000 miners who started for the goldfields, 70,000 used Seattle as their point of departure. As was the case with other gold rushes in the western United States, it was the merchants who profited from the Klondike gold rush, and Seattle provides an excellent example of how this event encouraged population growth and the development of businesses that outfitted and transported the miners.

The Klondike Gold Rush National Historical Park is half of a two-part park; the other half is in Skagway, Alaska, and admission to both is free. Both museums are run by the National Park Service (NPS), and in the Seattle museum you'll find a fine mix of history and NPS services. Audiovisual programs varying in length from 15 to 30 minutes are available throughout the year. Gold-panning demonstrations, ranger programs, and a walking tour of the Pioneer Square Historic District are given daily from the middle of June to Labor Day. From September to the end of May, the park offers formal education programs.

Original Boeing aircraft hang from the ceiling of the Museum of Flight. Toshi

Museum of Flight

9404 E. Marginal Way S.
Georgetown
206-764-5720
www.museumofflight.org
Open: 10–5 daily; 10–9 first Th each month
Admission: $12 adults, $11 seniors, $7.50 youth 5–17, free 4 and under
Wheelchair accessible: Yes

This is the most wonderful toy factory for airplane buffs west of Washington, D.C.'s
Smithsonian Institution. As you would expect in a city that virtually invented the passenger
aircraft, you'll experience flight here as you never have before. The museum is on the
grounds of one of Boeing's main plants at the eastern edge of Boeing Field, from where
new aircraft are flown out to customers complete with their corporate logos. You'll see
54 of the world's coolest airplanes, authentic and in mint condition. Original Boeing
aircraft—including a B-29—hang from the ceiling or stand on the grounds. In the Personal
Courage Wing of the museum is a collection of 28 fighter aircraft in a spectacular setting.
In the steel and glass Great Gallery, dozens of full-size aircraft fly in formation six stories
above. You can sit in the cockpit of a real SR-71 Blackbird or F/A-18 Hornet; outside, you
can board America's first presidential jet, Air Force One, and you can climb aboard the
sleek Concorde SST. Seattle's tribute to its aviation history is experienced in a replica of
the original Boeing airplane factory. Allow at least a half day for this exciting and thoroughly inventive, interactive museum. (From I-5 take exit 158 and go west; turn right at

the first light onto E. Marginal Way S.; the museum is on the right in ½ mile. Or take Metro bus #174 from downtown Seattle.)

Museum of History and Industry
2700 24th Ave. E.
University District
206-324-1126
www.seattlehistory.org
Open: 10–5 daily; 10–8 first Th each month
Admission: $7 adults, $5 seniors and youth 5–17
Wheelchair accessible: Yes

In McCurdy Park near Lake Washington, at the north end of the Washington Park Arboretum, this museum is dedicated to preserving the history of Seattle and King County. Its collection of artifacts tells the stories of early pioneers, and if you're interested in what life was really like before the great fire of 1889, this is where to go. The re-created storefronts of early Seattle let you peek into the business world at that time. There are exhibits of virtually every aspect of Seattle's history, from prehistory to the first Boeing mail plane of the 1920s. The museum even documents the first attempts to create a monorail, in 1892, when a full-scale demonstration monorail was built in the area, decades before the 1962 World's Fair.

Northwest Seaport and Maritime Heritage Center
1002 Valley St.
South Lake Union
206-447-9800
www.nwseaport.org
Open: Varies; call for hours
Admission: By donation
Wheelchair accessible: No

There really isn't much of a building to differentiate this maritime heritage center at the south end of Lake Union. It is more like a work in progress, just as you'll find with the ships the center is restoring. The center is dedicated to the preservation and interpretation of the maritime heritage of Puget Sound and the Northwest Coast. The shipyard features four newly restored historic ships, for which there are guided tours. Tall-ship buffs will enjoy exploring the *Wawona*, the largest three-masted schooner ever built in North America and dating from 1897. On site are also a 1904 lightship called *Swiftsure*; an 1889 tugboat, the *Arthur Fuss*; and a 1933 salmon troller, *Twilight*. Sea chanty sings are held on the second Friday of every month.

Russian Cobra
101 Alaskan Way, Pier 48
Waterfront
206-223-1767
www.russiansubseattle.com
Open: Daily
Admission: $10 adults, $8 seniors and children 8–14, $7 active or retired military
Wheelchair accessible: No

Yes, this is a real Soviet-era submarine. This style of Soviet submarine, known to NATO as the Foxtrot Class, was the most successful class of submarine ever in service to the Soviet Navy, and one built in 1972 is now moored at the south end of the waterfront. More Foxtrots were constructed by the Soviet Union than any other type of submarine, and this type, code-named "Cobra," was one of the best. After going on board and viewing a video that gives you information about Soviet subs, you can take a tour of the sub. In addition to the self-guided tour of the innards, complete with an audio recording explaining what you're seeing, there's a retired U.S. Navy submariner to explain general questions about the sub and its uses in the Cold War.

Seattle Art Museum
100 University St.
Downtown
206-654-3100
www.seattleartmuseum.org
Open: 10–5 Tu–W, 9–9 Th–Su; 9 am–midnight first Th each month
Admission: $15 adults; $12 seniors 62 and over and children 7–17 and students with ID; free 6 and under and first Th each month
Wheelchair accessible: Yes

If it seems that the Seattle Art Museum (SAM) is taking over the local arts scene, it's only because it continues to grow. The downtown location is undergoing expansion to accommodate a growing and diversified artistic program as well as to create new spaces for further exhibits. Demolition of the building north of SAM began in January 2004, and though the museum is open, the changes will have an effect on parking and bus stops. Major construction will last until 2006, and the expanded SAM is expected to open in spring of 2007.

In addition, the gallery is involved in the creation of the new Olympic Sculpture Park, an 8.5-acre green space along the north end of the waterfront, a place for people to experience art outdoors with sculptures that reflect the Pacific Northwest. In addition to classic, modern, and contemporary permanent sculptures, the park will host temporary installations and draw people together for art-related musical and theater performances, as well as year-round educational programs. The opening is planned for spring of 2006, and the dirt from the downtown expansion is being used for the Olympic Sculpture Park landfill. As well, the museum has the Seattle Asian Art Museum in Volunteer Park on Capitol Hill.

SAM's permanent collections number about 23,000 objects, representing a wide range of art from ancient Egyptian reliefs to contemporary American installations using photography and video. The collections are particularly strong in five areas: Asian, African, Northwest Coast Native American, modern and European painting and decorative arts. As well, major touring art exhibits are a mainstay throughout the year. In addition to the permanent and touring collections, the museum includes classrooms for several disciplines, hands-on activities, a café, and an expanded museum store with one of the best selections of art books on the West Coast. An admission ticket includes an audio tour; the ticket can also be used within one week for a free visit to the Seattle Asian Art Museum on Capitol Hill.

The Seattle Asian Art Museum is in Volunteer Park on Capitol Hill. Toshi

Seattle Asian Art Museum
1400 E. Prospect St.
Capitol Hill
206-654-3100
www.seattleartmuseum.org/visit/visitsaam.asp
Open: 10–5 Tu-Su, 10–9 Th
Admission: $3 suggested donation, free on first Th and Sat each month
Wheelchair accessible: Yes

This museum is exactly what its name says—a place for Asian art—and it's the biggest draw at Volunteer Park, having one of the largest collections of Asian art objects outside of Asia. On a single level, the exhibits chronicle the various epochs and dynasties of Chinese, Japanese, Vietnamese, Korean, and Southeast Asian art. The Japanese collection, among the most distinguished outside of Japan, has significant examples of ink painting, calligraphy, Buddhist sculpture, metalwork, and folk textiles. The Chinese collection spans the Neolithic period through the 19th century and includes tomb figures, ceramics, ritual bronzes, sculpture, painting, lacquers, textiles, jade carvings, snuff bottles, and more than 350 Chinese puppets. Be sure to attend one of the informative discussions about the collections. The museum's large-scale Chinese Buddhist sculpture is particularly noteworthy. (From downtown, take Olive Way east across I-5 and turn left onto Broadway; turn right onto E. Prospect St. From I-5, take exit 166 onto Denny St. or Olive Way, then take Broadway to E. Prospect.)

Wing Luke Asian Museum
407 Seventh Ave. S.
International District
206-623-5124
www.wingluke.org
Open: 11–4:30 Tu–F, noon–4 Sa–Su
Admission: $4 adults, $3 students and seniors, $2 children 5–12
Wheelchair accessible: Yes

Named for the first Asian ever elected to office in Seattle—as a City Council member—Wing
Luke Asian Museum features exhibits emphasizing Asian history and culture. An acupunc-
ture exhibit shows how needles are inserted at various body points to generate energy, to
eliminate pain, and to heal. The permanent exhibits include costumes, fabrics, crafts, and
traditional medicines.

Nightlife and Other Pleasures

Seattle's nightclub and action scene is complex and varied. The best way to find out what's
new is to consult the *Seattle Weekly* sections because acts and venues change with the seasons. The major areas for pub-crawling, nightclubs, and general after-dark revelry are
Pioneer Square, Belltown, Ballard, and Capitol Hill.

Ballard: The **Tractor Tavern** (5213 Ballard Ave. NW; 206-789-3599), in an otherwise quiet
neighborhood, programs a wide variety of music, from rockabilly bands to swing ensembles to Irish groups. The **Ballard Firehouse** (5429 Russell Ave. NW; 206-784-3516)
attracts a young crowd into its converted firehall to mostly reggae bands and a smattering
of R&B-based rock.

With baseball and soccer-ball awnings, F. X. McRory's is a favorite watering hole of sports fans. Toshi

Belltown: The **Crocodile Cafe** (2200 Second Ave.; 206-441-5611) is a combination restaurant, bar, and nightclub where rock-and-roll is played late into the night. Musicians jam there after their gigs at large concert venues such as Key Arena or Memorial Stadium. The **Virginia Inn** (1937 First Ave.; 206-728-1937) is a nonsmoking bar/restaurant that has an old Seattle feel and French food. Few jazz spots can compare with **Dimitriou's Jazz Alley** (Sixth and Lenora; 206-441-9729), that features name performers.

Downtown: The **Showbox** (1426 First Ave.; 206-628-3151), across from Pike Place Market, is a huge space that attracts lots of big-name national acts and is *the* place for performers with a national following. If you're in the Pike Place area and you want a break, stop in at the **Alibi Room**, down the alley under the market clock (85 Pike St.; 206-623-3180). It has a setting that will remind you of a 1920s speakeasy, and it is frequented by artist types.

Pioneer Square: Plenty of bars offer a loud atmosphere, if that is what you seek. Old-time drinking places include **Doc Maynard's Public House** (610 First Ave. S.; 206-682-4646) and the **J&M Cafe and Cardroom** (201 First Ave. S.; 206-292-0663). Some of the clubs and bars in Pioneer Square have a joint cover-charge promotion that lets you access any and all participating places for $8 to $10. **Marcus** (88 Yesler Way; 206-624-33223) is Seattle's only underground martini and cigar bar. It's a great place to hear music (provided by a DJ) without being over the top. After a Mariners or Seahawks game, **F. X. McRory's Steak, Chop and Oyster House** (419 Occidental Ave. S.; 206-623-4800; www.fxmcrorys. com) is the watering hole of choice. **New Orleans' Creole Restaurant** (114 First Ave. S.; 206-622 2563) features name jazz performers. Comedy clubs have sprung up in recent years, including the ever-popular **Comedy Underground** (622 S. Main St.; 206-628-0303), an underground nightspot where local and nationally known comics hone their talents.

Seattle Center: The **Experience Music Project** (206-770-2702; www.emplive.com) isn't just a music museum; the main hall, Sky Church, plays host to major bands and acts. The Liquid Lounge is EMP's bar, where live and recorded music make for a lively scene.

Quieter Pursuits
If you want to get away from the hustle of sightseeing and picture taking at the end of a long day, Seattle has cozy, out-of-the-way places that are refuges against chaotic city life, where you'll simply want to nurse your drink, eat slowly, and talk, read, or simply unwind.

Downtown: At **Oliver's** (in the Mayflower Hotel, 405 Olive Way; 206-382-6995), in the heart of downtown, you can find nine different martinis, all with fanciful names and made with your choice of Tanqueray gin or Stolichnaya vodka and a touch of vermouth. For eight consecutive years, Oliver's has won Seattle's Martini Classic Challenge. The recipe for Oliver's classic martini (shaken, not stirred, of course) is found in the drink.

Deep in the heart of Pike Place Market, **Place Pigalle** (81 Pike St.; 206-624-1756) is an elegant and cool contrast to the hustle and high energy of the market. It's the perfect little bar, overlooking Elliott Bay and specializing in premium and unusual spirits, a choice of French and Swiss wines, and assorted beers from many countries. Most of all, it has a relaxed, Continental feel and a romantic atmosphere. So bring a date and watch the sun set over the bay.

The **Bookstore** (in the Alexis Hotel, 1007 First Ave.; 206-382-1506) is aptly named. It's a favorite stopping-off spot for office workers in the neighborhood who like to drink, talk, and look at the titles on the floor-to-ceiling bookshelves and the racks of international newspapers and magazines. An added bonus is the pub fare prepared in the same four-star kitchen that produces the food for the Painted Table, the restaurant at the other end of the lobby that yearly makes somebody's "best" list.

Adjacent to the Fairmont Olympic Hotel lobby, the **Terrace** (411 University St.; 206-621-1700) is a cosmopolitan place that has whispers of chic. A sophisticated piano bar is located in the heart of the main lobby, where you can sip exotic martinis, champagnes, ports, indulgent coffees, and cocktails of every description while savoring hors d'oeuvres and other tempting bites. And there's live piano music daily during cocktail hour. Each month spotlights different specialty beverages, and a broad selection of wines are available by the glass.

If you're a wine aficionado, be sure to hit the **Gallery Wine Bar Sheraton** (1400 Sixth Ave.; 206-621-9000), where you'll find the finest wines from the Pacific Northwest. It's doubtful that you'll find any other place in Seattle that serves such a variety of wines, some from well-known and others from mostly obscure wineries in Washington State, British Columbia, and Oregon.

First Hill: The Sorrento Hotel's **Fireside Room** (900 Madison St.; 206-622-6400) has a roaring fireplace to keep both the body and the romance warm. It has soft, cushiony chairs that you sink into and an elegance that's reflected in the drawing-room atmosphere. Light entrées and an international menu vary in style and texture from simple to sublime, from seared rare tuna to burgers. With a wide selection of cognacs and coffee extravaganzas, the Fireside is especially good as a late evening place.

Red Square at the University of Washington has a statue of George Washington, with Suzzallo Library behind him. Toshi

The waterfront streetcar is a popular way to see downtown Seattle. Toshi

Tours and Sightseeing

Beer and wine tasting: Beer, of course, is a Seattle industry. Even before the microbrew revolution in the 1980s, Seattle was ranked as having America's largest per capita consumption of beer. Today you'll find microbreweries throughout the Puget Sound area, many of which are in Seattle and some of which offer tours. Convenient to downtown is **Pyramid Brewery** (1201 First Ave. S.; 206-682-3377), located across from Safeco Field, offering free tours and tastings at 2 and 4 pm Monday through Friday and on Saturday and Sunday at 1, 2, and 4 pm. **Redhook Brewery** (14300 NE 145th St., Woodinville; 425-483-3232; www .redhook.com) is Puget Sound's largest microbrewery; it offers tours and tastings for $1. The tour includes a tasting of four beers and a complimentary beer glass. Also in Wood-inville, an Eastside suburb northwest of Seattle, you can take a free wine tour and tasting of the nearby wineries, including **Chateau Ste. Michelle** (425-488-1133), **Columbia Winery** (425-488-2776), **Hedges Cellars** (425-391-6056), and **Silver Lake Sparkling Cellars** (425-486-1900).

Downtown: If you want to really learn about Pike Place Market's secret passages and neat places, contact the Pike Place Merchants Association and **Market Heritage Tours** (1531 Western Ave.; 206-774-5249) for a tour Wednesday through Sunday, 11 am and 2 pm. The one-hour tours meet at the Market Heritage Center.

South Lake Union: Kenmore Air (425-486-1257 or 1-800-543-9595; www.kenmore air.com) began operation in Seattle in 1946 and is one of the oldest and largest floatplane operators in the world, with a fleet of 22 aircraft logging some two million miles and carrying 60,000 passengers a year. It has regularly scheduled flights between Seattle and Victoria, British Columbia (45 minutes one-way), as well as to Friday Harbor and other points in the San Juan Islands, Whidbey Island, and British Columbia's Gulf Islands. Charter fishing and other packages, plus short Seattle "flightseeing" excursions, are also offered.

University District: You don't have to be a student to take a free tour of the **University of Washington campus** (Visitors Information Center, 206-543-9198). The 90-minute walking tour allows visitors a glimpse of Red Square with its Gothic-style buildings, Drumheller Fountain, Husky Stadium, and other notable sights. Spring, when the cherry trees on campus are in bloom, is an especially gorgeous time to visit. Two tours are offered Monday through Friday, at 10:30 am and 2:30 pm; no reservations are necessary.

Waterfront: As well as the many bus tours by **Gray Line** (206-626-5208 or 1-800-426-7505; www.graylineofseattle.com), you might want to try the **Argosy Cruise** (1101 Alaskan Way, Pier 55; 206-623-1445) tour along the waterfront, leaving from Pier 56. You can take a one-hour tour of Seattle's harbor and Elliott Bay or a two-hour cruise of Lake Washington and Lake Union. Argosy also has a dinner and/or lunch cruise featuring wild chinook salmon and other Northwest seafood delicacies.

Bill Speidel's Underground Tours
608 First Ave.
Pioneer Square
206-682-4646
www.undergroundtour.com
Open: Daily; seasonal hours
Admission (cash only): $10 adults, $8 seniors and students, $5 children
Wheelchair accessible: No

It was after the great fire that destroyed Seattle in 1889 that reconstruction of the city created an underground and aboveground Seattle. The city's new building regulations demanded that new buildings be elevated, so the former city was covered with dirt. This tour takes you into some of the now-underground remnants of 1889. Roaming the subterranean passages that once were the main roadways and first-floor storefronts of old downtown, you'll get humorous stories about what old Seattle was like. The tour begins with an introduction inside Doc Maynard's Public House, a restored 1890s saloon. Then you walk outside through historic Pioneer Square to three different sections of the underground—about three blocks in all.

Above-ground you'll find the ornate ironwork, brick sidewalks, small side streets, and charming and intimate buildings that define the area. Yet in the early 1960s, Pioneer Square was a human dump, occupied by degenerates and drunks. It was saved from being turned into parking lots and high-rises when locals defeated an urban renewal plan.

Be prepared for the underground landscape to be moderately rugged; you'll encounter six flights of stairs, uneven terrain, and spotty lighting. The tour ends at Rogue's Gallery, where you'll find portraits of Seattle's colorful characters and other displays depicting Seattle's past and you'll have a chance to purchase work by local artisans or a memento of your visit. While the underground portion covers just three blocks of the original 33, it nonetheless is an entertaining way to spend a few hours.

Tillicum Village and Tours
2992 SW Avalon Way
West Seattle
206-933-8600, 1-800-426-1205
www.tillicumvillage.com
Open: Daily

Admission (including ferry to/from Blake Island): $59.74 adults, $54.23 seniors, $22.98 children 5–12
Wheelchair accessible: Yes

Tillicum Village and Tours has a cruise from Pier 55 to Blake Island State Park for a salmon bake dinner and a Northwest Coast Native American dancing presentation. Located 8 miles off the coast of downtown Seattle's central waterfront, Blake Island is believed to be the birthplace of Chief Sealth; the island was made a state park in 1959. If you have a boat, the park has four boat-in-only camping areas with a total of 54 sites, protected moorage with a jetty and 12 floats, 21 buoys, a pier, 12 miles of trails, and 5 miles of beach with magnificent views of the Olympic Mountains, Mount Rainier, Mount Baker, and the Seattle skyline.

Most tourists, however, visit the island for a taste of Northwest Native American culture with the Tillicum Village tour. It's a dinner cruise that leaves daily from Pier 55 on the Seattle waterfront, bound for Tillicum Village on tiny Blake Island, which is opposite West Seattle and just north of Vashon Island. Once on the island, you'll experience a narration about the native people's history, a Northwest salmon dinner served in a decorated longhouse, and Native American dances and entertainment. Yes, it's showbiz combined with history and culture, but it is both entertaining and informative. You'll get a traditional Native American potlatch with baked fresh coho or chinook salmon prepared for one hour on cedar stakes over alder fires, along with new potatoes, warm bread, beverages, and a chocolate salmon for dessert. After dinner, a 30-minute show depicting Northwest Coast Native American culture is acted out on a stage. There's also time to explore the island.

ENTERTAINMENT AND THE ARTS

It wasn't so long ago that the cultural identity of Seattle was in question. While the 1962 Seattle World's Fair is an acknowledged landmark for the region's economy and move into a technological universe, it was also a major point of reference for cultural activity. Until the fair, the Seattle Symphony's only competition for artistic endeavors was the Seattle Art Museum. There was no professional opera, theater, or dance, very few art galleries, only a part-time orchestra, and three museums with limited exhibitions. Seattle was, in short, a cultural wasteland, perfectly representing what eastern Americans thought of the Pacific Northwest: all trees, no brains.

Then, almost overnight, the arts began an explosion that has carried over to today. Simultaneously with the closing of the fair, the Seattle Opera and the Seattle Repertory Theater were established, and within the next decade, the Pacific Northwest Ballet and many smaller groups made the city culturally livable. In Seattle, there are fewer sacred cows and the major organizations are relatively young, with histories that pale when compared to those of the giant cultural industries of New York, Chicago, or Philadelphia. This lack of cultural baggage allows for flexibility. The Seattle Symphony's music director, Gerard Schwarz, for example, convinced his board of directors that the orchestra should embrace the music of certain 20th-century American composers. So the Seattle Symphony is acknowledged nationwide for its brilliant interpretations of neoromantic American music from David Diamond, Howard Hanson, and others.

Performing arts, however, are not the only cultural expression in Seattle; culture also sometimes comes in small, unheralded, and downright unusual packages. A two-level shop in Seattle's Pioneer Square area, the popular and eclectic **Elliott Bay Book Company** (101 S. Main St.; 206-624-6600), is the nerve center of the city's literary life. To someone coming from the large metropolitan regions of the Midwest or East Coast, the idea of a bookstore being the focal point for a city's writers and thinkers must seem odd, indeed. However, the literary world is a working one in Seattle, unlike in New York, where major publishing parties involve the media and cultural figures meeting in a common purpose, rubbing elbows and clinking wine glasses. While authors abound here, they generally fade into the background, bound to their word processors. In fact, there is yet no large collection of work that can be identified as "Pacific Northwest" as there is "Southern" or "New York." Tickets for readings at the Elliott Bay Book Company are free but quickly snapped up. The Elliott Bay Café downstairs provides strong coffee, and its annex serves as the literary cradle where readings take place. Outside, in Pioneer Square, large crowds mingle on nights when famous authors come to read.

Seattle Arts and Lectures (105 S. Main St.; 206-621-2230) also brings distinguished writers and artists to town to give lectures about their work and issues in contemporary culture. Participants have included Edward Albee, Margaret Atwood, Saul Bellow, Billy Collins, Robertson Davies, Frank O. Gehry, Seamus Heaney, Maxine Hong Kingston, David Mamet, Anchee Min, Toni Morrison, Salman Rushdie, John Updike, August Wilson, and Jeanette Winterson.

Seattle Center used to be the locus of all major cultural activity, most of it occurring at the old Seattle Opera House. However, in very recent times, the symphony moved downtown, to Benaroya Hall, across from the Seattle Art Museum. The old Seattle Opera House has been gutted and rebuilt and is now the home of various theater groups and the Pacific Northwest Ballet Company and Seattle Opera. Seattle Center is also the site of numerous festivals, including the **Bumbershoot Arts Festival** (206-281-7788; www.bumbershoot. com) in September, the most popular of the city's gatherings, when theater, art exhibits, music of all kinds, and crafts take it over.

On the Boards (see below) and the **Center of Contemporary Art (COCA)** are the city's leading new cultural centers, while the Seattle Repertory Theater stages mainstream works. The COCA brings shock therapy to the city's art traditionalists a couple times a year with exhibitions that try to break new ground; On the Board's stages contemporary dance, music, and a multimedia mix of expression. Seattle's live performance world is exciting, innovative, and perfectly suited to a city that believes it has a major role in defining America's new arts culture.

Main Venues

The Seattle Center continues to be a prime gathering place for Seattle's performing arts, although in recent years there have been major changes in the venues themselves. The Seattle Symphony performs in downtown's Benaroya Hall, but at Seattle Center you'll find Marion Oliver McCaw Hall, the **Bagley Wright Theater**, the **Intiman Playhouse**, the **Seattle Center Coliseum**, **Memorial Stadium**, and in the Experience Music Project the **Sky Church** performance hall. In addition, the **5th Avenue Theatre** and the **Paramount Theater** (see Historic Buildings and Sites) are grand old ladies of Seattle's performance world and are still wonderful venues. And Meany Hall on the University of Washington campus is the site where most of the university's classical music, world dance, opera, and world music events are staged. All these performance venues are wheelchair accessible.

McCaw Hall at Seattle Center, new home of the Seattle Opera Toshi

Downtown: Benaroya Hall (Third Ave. between Union St. and University St.; 206-215-4747) in downtown Seattle is the Seattle Symphony's home. With 2,500 seats in the main hall, it is acoustically superb and visually breathtaking, and it sets the standard for concert venues in the Pacific Northwest. The rectangular form of the S. Mark Taper Foundation Auditorium and the circular Samuel and Althea Stroum Grand Lobby that surrounds it are at the center of the site. The lobby is enclosed in a series of subtly articulated bay windows; you get outstanding views from its several levels, including views of Puget Sound, the Seattle Art Museum, and the city's skyline. At night, its surfaces of clear and frosted glass give the effect of a giant lantern illuminating the streetscape.

Benaroya Hall is more than a performance space. Along Third Avenue, a block-long, glass-enclosed arcade, the Boeing Company Gallery, which has entrances from three streets, links the building's various components, offering access to the concert hall and recital hall lobbies, the ticket office, shops, a café, a coffee shop, an underground garage, and the tunnel connecting to the transit system adjacent to the site. The Boeing Company Gallery is open on weekdays regardless of whether there is a performance, so that the space not only serves as the outer lobby on concert nights but also becomes a part of the city's streetscape and retail activity during the day. The main concert hall is home to a magnificent pipe organ and a pair of Dale Chihuly chandeliers.

Since orchestral performances require long reverberation times, the wood paneling on Benaroya's walls is divided into smaller panels, each one a different size so that each resonates with a different frequency of sound. Acoustics is a complex science that seems to have been perfectly applied in the hall. The 540-seat Illsley Ball Nordstrom Recital Hall provides an elegant venue for performances by smaller ensembles and solo artists, and with equally superb sound delivery. The stage house and stage floor are of cherry wood, providing a visually and acoustically warm environment for the performers. Tours of the hall are available.

International District: Nippon Kan (628 S. Washington St.; 206-467-6807) is a performance hall for Asian productions and the site of the Japanese Performing Arts series October through May.

Seattle Center: Marion Oliver McCaw Hall (305 Harrison St.; 206-684-7200) is the home of the Pacific Northwest Ballet and the Seattle Opera. It is at the northeast corner of Seattle Center. This opera and ballet hall is the envy of every city west of Chicago and north of San Francisco. The new hall reopened in June 2003 after renovations that saw the outer shells of the original 1962 and 1927 buildings stripped away and replaced with a gleaming glass curtain wall. More than 70 percent of the old building was replaced by new construction, which included a new auditorium, lobby, backstage, orchestra pit, and café. A new lecture hall was added, as were additional restrooms, a coat check, and a gift shop called Amusements. So if you haven't been to an opera performance in Seattle in some time, you're in for a very pleasant experience.

University District: Meany Hall for the Performing Arts (4001 University Way NE; 206-543-4880) on the University of Washington campus is the focal point for dance, music, and theatrical performance. It includes the 1,206-seat Meany Theater and the 238-seat Meany Studio Theatre. Meany Hall hosts performances offered by the academic performing arts units: the School of Drama, the School of Music, the Dance Program, and the Digital Arts and Experimental Media Program, as well as the University of Washington World Series.

Tickets

Full-price advance-purchase tickets to many performing arts events are handled by **Ticket-master** (206-292-2787; www.ticketmaster.com) and through the box offices of the individual organizations. But there are ticket bargains as well. For half-price, day-of-show tickets to a wide variety of performances all over the city, stop by **Ticket/Ticket** (206-324-2744), which has booths in Pike Place Market (information booth; noon–6 Tu–Sun), on Capitol Hill (Broadway Market, 401 Broadway Ave. E.; noon–7 Tu–Sat, noon–6 Sun), and in Bellevue (Meydenbauer Center, NE Sixth St. and 112th Ave.; noon–6 Tu–Sun).

Dance

Seattle has a fairly active dance scene, and the major organization, the Pacific Northwest Ballet Company, is highly regarded throughout the country. Yet although ballet in Seattle is not as active or as popular as theater and classical music, there is always something going on, including performances by touring companies, University of Washington Dance Department faculty and student performances, and the Northwest New Works Festival. The best way to find out what's on is to pick up a copy of the *Seattle Weekly* for comprehensive listings. **Seattle Early Dance** (206-935-6908) is a dance company devoted to the reconstruction, performance, and teaching of baroque dance, in particular the dances from the court of Louis XIV, and the company performs at a variety of venues.

On the Boards

100 W. Roy St. (Behnke Center for Contemporary Performance)
Queen Anne
206-217-9888
www.ontheboards.org

On the Boards is a 26-year-old contemporary performing arts organization staging 200 performances a year in two theaters: the 350- to 500-seat Mainstage Theater and the intimate 100 seat Studio Theater. The company has premiered breakthrough mixed-media performances by Laurie Anderson, Bill T. Jones, David Dorfman, Wim Vandekeybus, Pat Graney, 33 Fainting Spells, Norman Durkee, Meredith Monk, the Kronos Quartet, Spalding Gray, Mabou Mines, Sankai Juku, Ping Chong, Wooster Group, Diamanda Galas, Min Tanaka, Urban Bush Women, Bobby Baker, and many others. As the list indicates, there's a no-holds-barred attitude in designing season programs. In addition to dance performances by Northwest artists, there are a variety of productions each year by internationally known performers.

Pacific Northwest Ballet

321 Mercer St. (Marion Oliver McCaw Hall)
Seattle Center
206-441-2424
www.pnb.org

Seattle's premier dance company's season runs from September to June, staging a wide range of classics, new works, and works choreographed by George Balanchine. If you're in town during the Christmas season, be sure to catch a performance of Tchaikovsky's *The Nutcracker*, with outstanding dancing and sets and costumes by children's-book author Maurice Sendak. It is the highlight, in terms of sellouts, every season.

Spectrum Dance Theater

800 Lake Washington Blvd. (Madrona Dance Studio)
Capitol Hill
206-325-4161
www.spectrumdance.org

Spectrum, one of America's most prominent jazz dance companies, has been in Seattle since 1982, founded by a group of dancers who wanted to create works of ballet, jazz, modern, and tap dance collaboratively. It has blossomed into a company that tours internationally and still manages a solid Seattle schedule. Its home stage is at the Madrona Dance Studio, in Madrona Park on the edges of Lake Washington. But the company gets into the downtown area during the year for major performances.

Film

Like all cities, Seattle has its share of shopping-center and multiplex theaters. But many of Seattle's movie theaters are a bit more distinctive than that.

Ballard: At the **Bay Theater** (2044 NW Market St.; 206-781-2229), nautical theme pervades, mahogany doors with gold-rimmed portholes mark the entrance, and glass-blown jellyfish light fixtures droop leisurely from the ceilings.

Downtown: The **Cinerama Theater** (2100 Fourth Ave. at Lenora St.; 206-441-3080), is one of Seattle's best technological efforts with fine sound. The **Market Theater** (1428 Post Alley; 206-781-9273) is in an alleyway behind Pike Place Market with a good auditorium and pleasant lobby.

University District: The most eclectic programming is at the **Grand Illusion** (1403 NE 50th St.; 206-523-3935), a very intimate little theater recently purchased by its employees. The **Seven Gables** (911 NE 50th St.; 206-781-5755) has a cozy exterior of dark, shingled sides and notorious gabled roof. Built in 1925 as an American Foreign Legion dance hall, the building was converted into a theater in 1976. The **Neptune** (1303 NE 45th St. at Brooklyn Ave.; 206-781-5755), dating from 1921, is one of Seattle's last remaining single-screen theaters. It became a Landmark Theatre in 1981 and was redecorated to live up to the Neptune name, with a concession stand created by a local boat builder, an aqua-colored rug, faux stained-glass panels, and Neptune god-heads inside the auditorium. With Dolby digital and SDDS digital, the theater offers a state-of-the-art viewing experience in a classic surrounding.

Seattle also has two IMAX theaters that show IMAX films on wraparound screens: the **Eames/IMAX Theater** (Pacific Science Center; 206-443-2001) and the Omnidome at Pier 59.

IMAX SeattleDome Film Experience
Pier 59, Waterfront Park
Waterfront
206-622-1868
www.seattleimaxdome.com
Open: 10–8:30 daily
Admission: $7 adults, $6 youth 6–12, free 5 and under
Wheelchair accessible: Yes

The IMAX movie theater located on the same dock as the Seattle Aquarium has a 180-degree viewing screen and features two shows daily, including *The Eruption of Mount St. Helens*. The St. Helens show takes viewers back to May 18, 1980, when at 8:32 am Mount St. Helens blew and 75 million tons of volcanic ash spread across the Pacific Northwest. You'll experience the eruption in dramatic close-ups and see the devastating aftermath of an explosion that unleashed the force of 27,000 atomic bombs, spewing a column of ash 16 miles into the air and heard as far as 700 miles away. It continues with dramatic views of the volcanic flows, ensuing eruptions, and intensive damage created by ash fallout and concludes with the rebirth of nature in the years following the eruption.

Music

Although the Seattle Opera and Seattle Symphony are the largest of the classical music organizations, Seattle is permeated with small groups giving concerts throughout its neighborhoods in small halls, churches, and even parks during the summer. The **Philadelphia String Quartet** (206-527-8839), Seattle Opera Association, Seattle Symphony, **Seattle Youth Symphony Orchestras** (206-362-2300; www.syso.org), **Cascade Symphony Orchestra** (425-745-5921; www.cascadesymphony.org), **Collegium Musicum** and **Contemporary Group** (206-543-1201; www.music.washington.edu/ensemble), Northwest Chamber Orchestra, **Earshot Jazz** (206-547-9787; www.earshot.org), **Seattle Classic Guitar Society** (206-365-0845; www.seattleguitar.org), and **Early Music Guild** (206-325-7066; www.earlymusicguild.org)—among others—produce regular concerts in a variety of venues. Plus there are numerous free concerts in Seattle's downtown parks and plazas nearly every lunchtime during the summer. Groups range from classical to rock and jazz.

The **Seattle Baroque Orchestra** (206-322-3119) plays at Illsley Ball Nordstrom Recital Hall at Benaroya Hall and specializes in the composers of the 17th and 18th centuries, from Monteverdi to Mozart. The **Seattle Chamber Music Society** (206-283-8710; www.scmf .org) is the largest and most active of the city's small ensemble organizations and presents soloists and groups, as well as a lecture series, throughout the summer months and during January. The **Seattle Chamber Music Festival** in July takes place at the Lakeside School near Lake Washington, where artistic director Toby Saks puts together a program utilizing 30 musicians in a gorgeous setting.

The **UW World Series** (206-543-4880; www.uwworldseries.org) at Meany Hall for the Performing Arts on the University of Washington campus is a collage of series performances that include chamber music, dance, classical piano, and world music and dance. You could easily call these series a United Nations of artistic expression, since you'll get a taste of what's going on internationally. The UW World Series has nearly 50,000 audience members each year, who watch and hear performances from diverse cultures from around the globe.

Northwest Chamber Orchestra
200 University St. (Benaroya Hall)
Downtown
206-343-0445
www.nwco.org

This 30-year-old company's concerts, a showcase for Pacific Northwest performers, are at the Recital Hall in Benaroya Hall, as well as at the Seattle Asian Art Museum in Volunteer Park. The company's repertoire is essentially the mainstay of orchestras everywhere: works by Haydn and Mozart, and an occasional thunderous Tchaikovsky. But you also get premieres of works by contemporary composers such as Alan Hovhaness. The season runs from September through May. If you want to see and hear what music sounds like in the Recital Hall, this is a low-cost (tickets are around $15) and enjoyable way of doing it.

Seattle Opera
321 Mercer St. (Marion Oliver McCaw Hall)
Seattle Center
206-389-7676
www.seattleopera.org

The Seattle Opera is one of the enduring companies in the Pacific Northwest, breaking new ground in the 1970s by staging Wagner's *Ring of the Nibelung* cycle, which gained a world-wide reputation, and it has continued to draw spectators from around the world to its summer performances of the cycle. The last cycle was performed in 2001 and the next is in 2005. In addition to the usual classics such as *Carmen, Madame Butterfly*, and *La Boheme*, the company usually stages one or two new operas a year. The company is now in McCaw Hall, whose dramatic and modern design seems more fitting for a company that has a reputation for taking chances.

Seattle Symphony
200 University St. (Benaroya Hall)
Downtown
206-215-4747
www.seattlesymphony.org

Since Gerard Schwarz's appointment in 1983, the Seattle Symphony has developed a deserved reputation for innovative and adventurous programming and recording, with the orchestra performing 46 premieres in the past 20 years. Schwarz and the 90-member orchestra have also presented often-neglected masterpieces by mid-20th-century composers, and many of these works can now be heard on remastered recordings recently issued on the Naxos label. The symphony presents nearly 220 performances annually to a combined audience of more than 325,000 people. The season is balanced among the familiar work of the classical repertoire, pops concerts, children's fare, and afternoon concerts.

Kate Mulgrew as Katherine Hepburn at the Seattle Repertory Theater Seattle Repertoire Theater Company

Theater

Theater is Seattle's most dominant live-performance discipline, with major repertory companies and smaller theater groups across the city staging works throughout the year. The theatrical options range from sweeping Shakespearean dramas to flashy contemporary Broadway to tiny experimental works seen once and forever lost to stage literature.

Capitol Hill: Theater Schmeater (206-324-5801; www.schmeater.org) stages weird and delightful comedy, including the popular live late-night stagings of episodes from *The Twilight Zone.*

Downtown: If you're a fan of Broadway shows, check the calendars at the **Paramount Theatre** (206-467-5510; www.theparamount.com) and the **5th Avenue Theatre** (206-625-1900; www.5thavenuetheater.org), both of which regularly serve as Seattle stops for touring shows.

Alas, the Seattle Fringe Theater Festival, America's oldest fringe, declared bankruptcy and closed its doors in early 2004, ending 13 years of operation. Held each September (it was moved from February so as not to compete with Vancouver's Fringe Festival held in that month), it had productions and skits that spanned a wide range of topics, with sex and violence, plays for kids, and surrealist productions that only the writer could understand. The history of Seattle theater suggests that someone will try to remount a "fringe" theater festival of some sort in the near future.

Fremont: Empty Space (206-547-7500; www.emptyspace.org) stages uncommon and provocative new works that you won't see at larger companies. It develops and premieres new scripts from regional and national playwrights, as well as taking a new look at classics.

Green Lake: Although the fringe festival has gone, there are plenty of places in which to get nonmainstream theater in Seattle. **Bathhouse Theater** (7312 W. Greenlake Dr. N.; 206-524-1300; www.seattlepublictheater.org) holds performances at the old Green Lake bathhouse, and the programs range from original musicals to updated versions of Shakespeare.

Pioneer Square: Theatre Off Jackson (206-340-1049) produces works by Asian-American writers, actors, and musicians and also stages cutting-edge, off-Broadway shows.

Seattle Center: Book-It Repertory Theatre (206-325-6500; www.book-it.org) adapts literary works for the stage and stages works by local playwrights with performances at various venues.

West Seattle: ArtsWest (206-938-0339; www.artswest.org) is a multidisciplinary company that puts on music shows, art shows, and theatrical productions, most of which have an irreverent bend.

ACT Theatre
700 Union St. (Kreielsheimer Place)
Downtown
206-292-7676
www.acttheatre.org

In operation since 1965, the ACT Theatre company was the first theater dedicated to new plays in Seattle, redesigned stagings by Arthur Miller, Tennessee Williams, and others, as well as fresh off-the-paper productions. The 15-show season runs from Septembe through May, and productions are held at ACT Theatre, which opened as Kreielsheimer Place. A $30 million makeover of the historic Eagles Auditorium, which had been left to years of neglect and abandonment, signaled the beginning of a renaissance in the Pike/Pine area of downtown Seattle in the mid-1990s.

Annex Theatre Company A
1122 E. Pike St.
Capitol Hill
206-728-0933
www.annextheatre.org

This is theater that's unpredictable from a company that prides itself on staging alternative and fringe material. Its stagings are at a variety of venues, and they include cabaret shows once a month at the Oddfellows Hall on Capitol Hill. Ever see a musical production of a Shakespearean play? Well, this is where it'll happen, as will many other nonmainstream shows.

Northwest Actors Studio
1100 E. Pike St.
Capitol Hill
206-324-6328
www.nwactorsstudio.org

Located at the corner of Pike Street and 11th Avenue, near Seattle University, the studio is both a teaching facility and a performance outlet, offering a wide scope of productions from Shakespeare to avant-garde in its 99-seat Gary A. Tucci Theatre and the 50-seat Cabaret Theatre. The studio has a history of annually producing more events than any other theater in Seattle. You'll see plays, musicals, sketch comedies, staged readings, workshops, and numerous benefits for charities. The studio also served as a host venue for the Seattle Fringe Festival.

Seattle Repertory Theatre
155 Mercer St. (Bagley Wright Theatre)
Seattle Center
206-443-2222
www.seattlerep.org

This is Seattle's top professional theater, and after attending a few performances you'll understand why. It stages the most consistently entertaining productions in the city in a season that runs from September to June, with five plays performed in the main theater and four in the more intimate Leo K. Theatre. Productions range from classics to world premieres. Its consistently high production and artistic standards won the company the 1990 Tony Award for Outstanding Regional Theatre. With an emphasis on plays of true dramatic and literary worth, the Seattle Rep also produces educational programs and new play workshops.

University of Washington School of Drama
University of Washington campus
University District
206-543-5140
http://depts.washington.edu/uwdrama

With 10 plays a year, the University of Washington drama school is one of the busiest theater ensembles in the city. On stage are a mix of undergraduate drama majors, Master of

Grover Thurston Gallery in Pioneer Square   Toshi

Fine Arts candidates training for professional careers, and doctoral students embarking on a scholarly path. The school is committed to hands-on training. The Mainstage season showcases the work of students from every program, and several smaller theaters, as well as classroom and studio spaces, also provide opportunities for students to put stagecraft theory into practice. Performances take place Wednesdays through Sundays, and tickets are a bargain at $12. Depending on the production, performances are at the Penthouse Theatre (NE 45th St. and 17th Ave. NE), the Playhouse Theatre (4045 University Way NE), or the Meany Studio Theatre (in lower Meany Hall).

Visual Art

Obviously, Seattle has an active and highly visible art scene that is supported by its population and businesses. Throughout its downtown buildings, parks, and even bus tunnels, Seattle has amassed hundreds of public artworks, from paintings and sculptures to manhole covers and sidewalk tiles. The yearly city budget for public art grew from $125,000 in 1978 to nearly $1.8 million in 2003, not counting administrative costs. And Seattleites take their art seriously. Henry Moore's cast-bronze sculpture "Vertebrae" was installed in front of the former Sea-first Bank building at 1001 Fourth Avenue in 1971, and the bank reportedly paid $165,000 for the piece. But when Seafirst unexpectedly sold the sculpture for an undisclosed price, citizens raised such a big fuss that eventually the piece was bought back for a reported $2 million. It now belongs to the Seattle Art Museum, though it still resides at its old address.

At last count, there were 151 art galleries in Seattle, without counting galleries in the suburbs. New York City, by comparison, has around 500, but New York City has a population of

8.1 million. So, in terms of population ratios, Seattle has an art gallery for every 3,728 people, whereas New York has one for about every 16,200 people. You can devote an entire vacation to walking through Seattle's art galleries. The biggest collections of galleries are located in Pioneer Square, in Ballard, and on Capitol Hill. But wander through any of the downtown streets and you'll bump into one.

The most enjoyable times for art gallery discovery are during the art walks, an activity for which Seattle has become famous. Art walks are not only for art gurus and professional artists, but for anyone who enjoys art. The **Pioneer Square art walk** (206-684-7171) is probably the most popular and the one that most visitors know about. It is held every first Thursday of each month from 6 to 8 pm Many home decor stores and coffee shops participate, making the walk feel more like an artsy shopping day. Many of the 35-plus arts venues, including galleries, museums, and sometimes restaurants, bars, and shops, time their new exhibits for unveiling on these First Thursdays, so there's always something new to see. You'll be part of a large band of schmoozers wandering from one historic brick building to the next, stopping to chat in Occidental Square's courtyard or to drop in for a drink at sidewalk pubs and cafés.

In the summer you'll likely find a live jazz trio setting the mood and sidewalk artists and street vendors trying to get your attention. Sometimes the party ambience makes it tough to really take in the art. Serious art lovers use the walk to get a feel for what's being exhibited and then come back for a more serious look. The Pioneer Square walk lasts until the galleries decide to close. It is informal, so just show up and start walking. At the same time, galleries in Pike Place Market and the Seattle Art Museum are open until 8 pm or later.

The **Ballard art walks** (206-784-9705) take place every second Saturday of each month from 6 to 9 pm, and you can take an urban hike on the **Capitol Hill art walk** (206-328-7158) on the first Saturday of every month, when more than two dozen galleries, stores, coffee shops, and museums stay open throughout the day—with some throwing receptions and performances into the night—all in the name of art. Pick up a self-guided tour map and monthly calendar at the galleries or join a tour group from May through October. Each art walk is free.

Eventually, you'll have to come to grips with glass art and Dale Chihuly, perhaps the most renowned contemporary glass artist in the world. Chihuly's work is exhibited in several places, along with that of his fellow glass artists. You'll find displays in the lobbies of the City Centre shopping mall at Fifth Avenue and Union Street in downtown Seattle, but the best place to see Chihuly's work is in Tacoma, his hometown. There, you'll find it at the downtown art museum, in the lobby of the federal courthouse at Union Station, and at the newly constructed Bridge of Glass and adjacent Museum of Glass.

RECREATION

Greater Seattle is one of the fittest cities in the country, a distinction based on the degree of outdoor activity that takes place within and outside its borders. Locals spend much less time than the national average in front of the television, and they lead the nation in participating in sailing and kayaking. This is the tip of the iceberg for activities and outdoor pursuits. Washington's large population of outdoor enthusiasts can be seen on weekends heading along the freeways and arterial roadways with their skis, mountain bikes, camping gear, golf clubs, snowboards, kayaks, fishing rods, and other outdoor recreational equipment.

Kayakers setting out from Lake Union's working waterfront   Toshi

Bicycling

King County is bike territory. Olympian Rebecca Twigg was born in the area, and the **Cascade Bicycle Club** (206-522-3222; www.cascade.org) is one of the nation's largest. Bike lanes and paths abound throughout the city and surrounding areas, and Seattleites are, frankly, proud of being bike-crazed. You'll see bicyclists wherever you drive in the city and suburbs. **King County Bicycling Guide Maps** are available free at the Road Services Division Maps and Records Center at the King Street Center Building in Pioneer Square (201 S. Jackson St.; 206-296-6548; www.metrokc.gov/kcdot/roads/planning/bicycling /bikemap.cfm). The center is open 8–4:30 Monday–Friday.

Gregg's Greenlake Cycle (7007 Woodlawn Ave. NE; 206-523-1822; www.greggscycles .com) and the **Bicycle Center** (4529 Sand Point Way NE; 206-523-8300; www.bicyclecenter seattle.com) both rent bikes by the hour, day, or week; rates range from $5–$7 per hour to $25–$30 per day. Both shops are convenient to the **Burke-Gilman and Sammamish River Trail**, a wonderful 27-mile paved pathway that is a great place for a family bike ride or for a long and vigorous ride without having to deal with traffic. The popular trail, managed by the City of Seattle, begins at Eighth Avenue NW in Ballard and follows an old railroad right-of-way along the ship canal and north along Lake Washing-ton's west shore. At Blyth Park in Bothell, the trail becomes the Sammamish River Trail and continues east another 10 miles.

Alki Beach is another good place to ride, with great views of the sound and the Olympics. You can rent a limited number of single-speed bikes at **Alki Crab & Fish Co.** (1660 Harbor Ave. SW; 206-938-0975), which charges $10 for a three-hour rental; call ahead and make a reservation. To get there you can take the water taxi from the downtown waterfront (Pier 55 at Madison St.) to West Seattle; it docks right at Alki Crab & Fish Co.

Boating

Seattle is a watersports dream: much of the city and its coastline are accessible by water-craft of all types. The opening day of boating season (first Saturday in May) is one of the biggest waterfront boating festivals of the year, held each year since 1913. Thousands of spectators line the shore of the Montlake Cut, near the University of Washington, to cele-brate Seattle's official opening of the season. The **Parade of Boats**, sponsored by the **Seattle Yacht Club** (206-325-1000; www.seattleyachtclub.com), begins with a cannon blast and the opening of the Montlake Bridge, and then hundreds of sail- and motorboats parade through, with crews in full regalia according to the parade theme. Festivities also include sailboat and crew races and a trophy ceremony.

At the **Seattle Maritime Festival** (mid-May) which celebrates Seattle's maritime heritage, the waterfront becomes a drag-strip for some 40 tugboats engaged in the ever-popular tugboat races. The Seattle International Boat Show, produced by the **Northwest Marine Traders Association** (206-634-0911; www.seattle boatshow.com), has been an annual event for more than 50 years. Sponsored by the Northwest Yacht Brokers Association, the **Lake Union Boats Afloat Show** (www.boats afloatshow.com) runs con-currently with the Seattle International Boat Show, with a complimentary shuttle between the two shows. Boats Afloat offers a look at a wide array of watercraft afloat in Lake Union, extending from the Center for Wooden Boats to the Yale Street Landing.

Canoeing

Warm summer days lure canoeists to the quiet marsh waterways around the Washington Park Arboretum. The University of Washington's **Waterfront Activities Center** (behind Husky Stadium at Montlake Boulevard and Pacific Avenue NE; 206-543-9433) rents canoes and rowboats for $6 per hour, February 1 through October 3. You can enjoy a peace-ful canoe ride on the waters of Lake Washington near the arboretum.

Kayaking

One of the most popular forms of getting on the water is kayaking. The advantage, of course, is that if you are in a kayak along any one of the many isolated inlets along Puget Sound, you're part of the environment, and sea animals often treat you as one of them. Puget Sound is home to many species of sea mammals, ranging from seals and otters to whales. In between are hundreds of small animals and birds that no one on a powerboat or from shore ever sees or hears.

Sea kayaks have a long past. Native Americans built the first about 10,000 years ago, and many traveled as far south as San Diego with animal skins stretched tightly across the light, wooden frames. The same technology is used today, though the materials have changed. Instead of animal skins, today's seagoing kayaks are made of fiberglass and plas-tics. They are extremely light, durable, and efficient.

You needn't be greatly experienced in boating or canoeing in order to kayak because kayaking is safe for anyone who can heed the safety measures. Kayaks can carry 100 or more pounds (45 kg) of goods and anywhere up to three kayakers; they can be launched or beached in a couple of inches of water. Their beauty is that they required no moorage, trailer, or fuel.

A number of sea-kayaking tour companies around Puget Sound offer inexpensive trips ranging from one day along Lake Union to wecklong adventures in the San Juan Islands for experts and novices. If you've not done this before, the **Northwest Outdoor Center** (2100 Westlake Ave. N.; 206-281-9694; www.nwoc.com) offers rentals and tours from Lake Union Dock with a popular tour circumnavigating houseboats, shipyards, and parks, with a refreshment stop. Other tours include Full Moon Paddles, Golden Gardens Sunset Tours, and Caroling by Kayak during the holiday season. Rent a kayak for an float around Lake Union or to take off-site to any of the dozens of popular kayaking locations around Puget Sound. Kayaking instruction is also available. Kayak rental is $10 per hour or $50 per day.

Sailing on Puget Sound near Seattle Toshi

If you want a break from driving between Seattle and Vancouver, the San Juan Islands, 80 miles north of Seattle, are known around the world as a kayaker's dream. The islands are home to a resident orca whale population, nesting bald eagles, sea lions, and a bounty of nature that is often viewed at close range by kayak. **San Juan Safaris** (360-378-1323, 1-800-450-6858; www.sanjuansafaris.com), operating from Friday Harbor and Roche Harbor on San Juan Island, offers guided tours led by naturalists.

Sailing

A wealth of boat charter companies offer a wide variety of sailing and small-boat cruises ranging in length from an hour to half- and full-day cruises and longer. **Emerald City Charters** (206-624-3931; www.sailingseattle.com) operates from Pier 54 on the water-front, and **Windworks Sailing Center** (206-784-9386; www.windworkssailing.com) and **Cristal Charters, LLC** (206-286-9711; www.cristalcharters.com) operate from Shilshole Bay in Ballard.

Reeling in the big one on Puget Sound Toshi

Fishing

Several charter fishing companies offer saltwater fishing on Puget Sound, and most provide tackle and equipment as well as licensed skippers or guides. Since fishing seasons and the allowable catch vary each year, check the dates with the companies. **Puget Sound Sports Fishing** (206-546-5710) operates from Edmonds, 20 miles north of Seattle, and provides tackle and experienced skippers for saltwater fishing excursions. **Puget Sound Salmon Charters** (253-565-6598; www.pugetsoundsalmoncharters.com) in Tacoma has day and evening salmon fishing trips. **Nooksack Charters** (866-360-4386) offers sport fishing, whale watching, and sightseeing in the San Juan Islands. **Possession Point Fishing Charters** (360-652-3797, 1-866-652-3797; www.possessionpointfishing.com) sails from Arlington, 50 miles north of Seattle, and has year-round saltwater fishing.

Golf

Golf in Seattle and the surrounding area is a relatively inexpensive pursuit, with many top venues playable for under $50 in the summer and most courses dropping their rates come October. The area has already attracted PGA Tour events, with the 1998 PGA Championship at Sahalee Country Club, a private course in Redmond, and the Greater Seattle Champions Classic, part of the PGA Champions Tour, being played at the Jack Nicklaus—designed Tournament Players Club at Snoqualmie Ridge, another private club, starting in 2005.

But there's more to Seattle golf than the PGA Tour and exclusive private clubs. On the Eastside, the **Golf Club at Newcastle**'s (425-793-4653; www.newcastlegolf.com) 36-hole complex is one of the finest facilities in the Pacific Northwest, offering terrific courses along with spectacular views. Designed by Bob Cupp and local golf legend Fred Couples, the two courses—Coal Creek and China Creek—have views of downtown Seattle, Lake Washington, and the Olympic Mountains. Coal Creek measures more than 7,000 yards from the tips and features some monster holes, such as the 621-yard, par-5 opener; China Creek is shorter (6,416 yards) but offers plenty of strategic options.

The city-owned municipal course at **Jackson Park** (206-363-4747; www.jacksonpark golf.com), is one of the area's best golfing bargains, at less than $30 a round. The driest public course in Seattle, it was built in 1930 and will take tee times eight days in advance. Another muni, **Jefferson Park Golf Course** (206-762-4513; www.jefferson parkgolf.com), was built in 1915 by Scotsman Thomas Bendelow, one of America's pioneer golf architects. Situated in the Beacon Hill neighborhood of Seattle, mere just minutes south of downtown, it measures more than 6,000 yards and features vistas of the city's skyline and Mount Rainier. It also includes a nine-hole executive golf course, a restaurant, and a practice range. **West** at At 6,600 yards, many consider the **Seattle Golf Club** (206-935-5187; www.westseattlegolf .com) the most challenging of the three city-owned championship courses. Home of the Seattle Amateur Championship, it boasts incredible views of Seattle and Elliott Bay.

Heading south into the suburbs, **Druids Glen Golf Club** (253-638-1200; www.druids glenglf.com) is notable for its up-close-and-personal sight of Mount Rainier as well as its water-laden test of golf over 7,146 yards of rolling fairways, massive evergreens, and numerous ponds.

Hiking

If you're a hiker, Seattle is hiking heaven. Even casual walkers can find plenty of places for walks in the city or the nearby mountains. Just be sure to pick a hike suitable to your physical capabilities and hiking experience. Within Seattle itself, several large nature parks are laced with enough trails to allow for a few good long walks. Among these are **Seward Park** (5898 Lake Washington Blvd.) southeast of downtown, and **Lincoln Park** (8011 Fauntleroy Ave. SW) south of Alki Beach in West Seattle.

The city's largest natural park and a favorite among local hikers is **Discovery Park** (3801 W. Government Way), at the western tip of the Magnolia neighborhood. This park, covering more than 500 acres, has many miles of forest paths and beaches to hike and a few meadows for lazing around in after a long walk. You'll have gorgeous views. (From downtown Seattle, follow Elliott Ave. W. north along the waterfront, then take the Magnolia Bridge west and follow Grayfield St. to Galer St. to Magnolia Blvd.)

Of course, if it's a challenge you want, plenty of mountains and passes await exploration within three hours' drive of the Seattle metro area. You can walk near glaciers, on beaches, through old-growth forests, and along ridges and on mountain peaks still sporting snow deep into August. **Alpine Lakes Wilderness** (509-852-1100; www.fs.fed.us/r6/wenatchee/cle-elum-wilderness) is the closest major hiking destination, with myriad choices for weekend wandering among the region's 700 lakes. For high-country experiences, visit **North Cascades National Park** (360-856-5700; www.nps.gov/noca/). **Mount Rainier National Park** (see chapter 2, Side Trips from Seattle) can be seen from downtown Seattle on clear days, beckoning many Seattleites to its mountainsides to climb and hike. And the **Olympic Peninsula** (see chapter 2, Side Trips from Seattle) is a microcosm of Northwest ecosystems with remote beaches, the country's oldest forests, and one of the state's most dramatic mountain ranges.

Skiing

As in Vancouver, rain in Seattle means snow in the nearby mountains. And like Vancouverites, Seattleites are avid skiers, both downhill and cross-country, and top-flight facilities are within an hour's drive of the city. Generally speaking, the ski season in the Seattle area runs from mid-November to the end of April. If you need equipment, you can usually rent it on the slopes or at **REI** (222 Yale Ave. N.; 206-223-1944).

If cross-country is your passion, you'll find it in abundance at Snoqualmie Pass, less than 50 miles east of Seattle on I-90, where the **Summit Nordic Center** (425-434-7669, 206-236-7277; www.summitatsnoqualmie.com/info/winter/nordic.asp) offers rentals, instruction, and many miles of groomed trails. Snoqualmie Pass is also the home of the major downhill facilities in the Seattle region, jointly known as **The Summit at Snoqualmie** (425-434-7669 information, 206-236-1600 snow report; www.summitatsnoqualmie.com): Alpental, Summit West, Summit Central, and Summit East ski areas together offer more than 65 ski runs, plus rentals and lessons.

Stevens Pass Ski Area (206-812-4510; www.stevenspass.com) is 78 miles northeast of Seattle, 65 miles east of Everett, on the summit of US 2. It has 10 lifts, more than 1,125 acres of skiable terrain, 37 primary runs, and an intimate base village surrounded by three day lodges. (From Seattle take I-5 north, get off at exit 194 in Everett, and follow US 2 east 65 miles).

Crystal Mountain (360-663-2265; www.skicrystal.com), located 12 miles northeast of Mount Rainier, has two high-speed detachable six-passenger lifts, two high-speed quads, two triples, three doubles, and one surface lift to serve 19,110 people an hour on the 7,100-foot (2,164 m) mountain. (From Seattle take I-5 south to WA-410 in Enumclaw—there are many ways to do this—then follow WA-410 east 33 miles (53 k) and turn left onto Crystal Mountain Blvd.)

Qwest Stadium, home of the Seattle Seahawks, is the newest addition to Pioneer Square. Toshi

Spectator Sports

Seattle is a major-league city in every sense of the word. Its professional baseball and football teams, the Mariners and the Seahawks, play in their own stadiums, which stand next to
each other near Pioneer Square, the city's old town. And the city's NBA basketball team,
the SuperSonics, play in KeyArena at the Seattle Center. Alone among Pacific Northwest
cities, Seattle has major-league teams in all three of America's primary sports. All main-
tain a national profile and can be seen regularly on a variety of sports networks throughout
the year.

Both the Mariners and the Seahawks used to play at the old King Dome, a cement-roofed
stadium that dated from the 1960s. The King Dome was torn down and replaced by Safeco
Field in 1999. Qwest Stadium, just north of Safeco Stadium and with the same skyline and
water views, hosted its first game in August 2002 and is already established as a prime venue
with state-of-the-art facilities for both football and soccer. Qwest Stadium and Safeco Field,
home of the Seahawks and Mariners, respectively, are monuments to sport itself. Both are
publicly owned and are spectacular examples of where sports stand in the world of 21st-
century Seattle. They dominate the city's sporting activities, and positioned as they are in
heart of the original Seattle, they cry out that here is a gladiator's city, one in which organized sport is a major lifestyle. Tours of their facilities are worth the time.

But Seattle has much more. KeyArena, anchored at Seattle Center, is home to the NBA
SuperSonics; the WNBA professional women's basketball team, the **Seattle Storm** (206-
281-5800; www.wnba.com/storm); and hockey's **Seattle Thunderbirds** (425-869-7825;

www.seattle-thunderbirds.com). The Thunderbirds are consistently among the best in the Western Hockey League, a development league for hockey players between the ages of 16 and 20 and the training ground for many players in the National Hockey League. The **University of Washington Huskies** (206-543-2200; http://gohuskies.collegesports.com) and a host of other spectator and participatory sports add character to one of the country's most active sporting communities. The **Seattle Sounders** (206-622-3415; www.seattle sounders.net) have been playing professional soccer in front of passionate fans since 1974, and the game is so popular that an exhibition match between the United Kingdom's legendary Celtic Football Club and Chelsea Football Club filled most of Qwest Stadium in 2004.

Qwest Stadium
800 Occidental Ave. S.
Pioneer Square
206-381-7582
www.stadium.org
Open (tours): 12:30 and 2:30 daily
Admission (tours): $7 adults, $5 children and seniors
Wheelchair accessible: Yes

The stadium is built on the spot that the old King Dome once occupied. That's somewhat appropriate, since 97 percent of the concrete from the King Dome was recycled for Qwest Stadium. The new home to the Seattle Seahawks opened in July 2002; the team had played at Husky Stadium while the construction was going on. More than 70 percent of the 72,000 seats are covered, and plans are for the stadium to have more than $1 million worth of art from local and national artists, as well as a public plaza and amphitheater to accommodate 5,000 people for public events. The open-air facility is configured in a horseshoe shape that is open at the north end, which includes an impressive tower with bleacher seating and a large, vertical scoreboard and large-format video screen. As well, you get sweeping views of Puget Sound, the Olympic Mountains, the downtown Seattle skyline, and Mount Rainier. The building surprisingly fits into the atmosphere and character of the Pioneer Square neighborhood and Safeco Field, the Seattle Mariners ballpark. At the south end, the stadium is connected to Qwest Event Center and a 2,000-car parking garage. The 90-minute tours start at the **Seahawks Pro Shop** (on Occidental Ave. S.).

Safeco Field
1250 First Ave. S.
Pioneer Square
206-346-4003
www.seattlemariners.com
Open (tours): 10:30, 12:30, and 2:30 on nongame days; 12:30 and 2:30 Tu–Sun in off-season
Admission (tours): $7 adults, $5 children and seniors
Wheelchair accessible: Yes

It wasn't easy getting the Mariners' field built. Many people in the Seattle area didn't want to spend taxpayer dollars to get separate baseball and football stadiums. But those battles have long been forgotten, and Safeco Field is now an accepted part of the landscape. The ballpark was built to resemble the great ballparks of yesteryear. It is open-air, has real grass, and features a retractable roof that covers the ballpark but does not enclose it. The roof keeps fans, 47 percent of whom come from outside the immediate Puget Sound area, protected from the wind and rain. Some 46,621 fans can enjoy a ballgame from seats that are closer to the field and offer greater sightlines compared to those of the old King Dome. A team store, picnic area, kids' play area, on-site restaurant, and baseball museum are just a few of the amenities that make the ballpark a fun experience.

Seattle Mariners
1250 First Ave. S. (Safeco Field)
Pioneer Square
206-346-4000
www.seattlemariners.com

Baseball is a longtime tradition in Seattle, going back to 1890 when the first professional team was organized. Called the Seattle Reds, the team played in the Class-C Pacific Northwest League (PNL). Two years later, the Reds won the PNL pennant when the Portland club declined to enter the playoffs because of financial problems. The Reds were renamed the Braves and in 1896 moved into their first real stadium, Athletic Park at 14th and Yesler. Baseball got a little confusing in the region between 1903 and 1919. In 1903 the Pacific Coast League (PCL) was formed and Seattle was a charter member. Thus, Seattle had two professional teams for one season, although the Braves folded one year later.

Three years later, Seattle ended its membership in the PCL and joined the Class-B Northwestern League, where it remained until 1910, when it rejoined the PCL. The team was renamed the Indians and played a 225-game schedule. In 1937 Emil Sick bought the team for $115,000 and immediately changed the name to the Rainiers, a natural move seeing as he was the owner of the Rainier Brewing Company. A year later the Rainiers moved into the newly built Sick's Stadium, which had seating capacity of 11,500. That year, local sports hero Fred Hutchinson began his rookie season and posted a 25-7 pitching record. "Hutch" would go on to a major-league pitching and managing career with the Detroit Tigers after helping lead the Rainiers to three consecutive PCL pennants.

In 1955 Hutch returned to the Rainiers as manager and led the team to another PCL crown, and the first official proposition for a domed stadium was made. For the first time, Seattle began to seriously consider becoming major league. Fans of the idea were encouraged when the Brooklyn Dodgers and the New York Giants moved to the West Coast—to Los Angeles and San Francisco, respectively. But were Seattleites willing to pay for it? Not likely. Two bond issues to support construction of the domed structure failed—in 1960 and 1964. In 1960 Sick sold the club to the Boston Red Sox and Seattle became the Red Sox AAA affiliate, staying with the organization until it was sold to the California Angels. In 1967 the population of Seattle gave permission for the raising of funds to build the domed stadium, with completion to be prior to the 1972 season. No one knew it at the time, but manager Bob Lemon would guide Seattle's baseball team to its last amateur championship in 1966.

Seattle was first awarded a baseball franchise in 1969, signaling that the city had finally become major league. But there were growing pains. The original American League team, the Seattle Pilots, lasted for only one year before folding its tent and moving to Milwaukee to become the Brewers. And that really threw a wrench into the gears of Seattle's major-league ambitions. Alas, because of the demise of the Pilots, Seattle was left with a stadium-in-waiting once the King Dome was built. Between 1972 and 1976, the city fielded a team, all right, but it was minor league, in the Class-A Northwest League. Then, on April 6, 1977,

Major League Baseball came back to Seattle for good when the new Seattle Mariners played the California Angels in the King Dome before a crowd of 57,762. The Mariners' starting pitcher that night was Diego Segui, a member of the original 1969 Pilots.

The recent crop of players has driven Seattleites on a roller coaster of highs and lows. The Mariners were a solid contender in 2001, winning 116 games for the best winning percentage in baseball (.716) that year. Alas, they couldn't translate that into a World Series appearance, losing to the New York Yankees in five games in the American League Championship series. They didn't duplicate that percentage in 2002 or 2003, winning 93 games in each season, and didn't make it to the postseason. In 2004 they were among the also-rans in their division, winning just 63 games, losing 99. But the one great high-light was the play of star right fielder Ichiro Suzuki, who made history by besting the single-season record for hits set by George Sisler in 1920, finishing with 262 while claiming the American League batting title with a .372 average.

Seattle Seahawks
800 Occidental Ave. S. (Qwest Field)
Pioneer Square
888-635-4295
www.seahawks.com

The Seahawks joined the National Football League in 1976 when the league granted an expansion team franchise to John Nordstrom, a Seattle department store owner. In the club's first season, quarterback Jim Zorn passed for more than 2,500 yards and was named the league's top offensive rookie. Jack Patera was named coach of the year in 1978 after leading the Seahawks to their first winning season. Zorn led the American Football Conference (AFC) in passing yardage that year, and wide receiver Steve Largent notched the first of his eight 1,000-yard seasons.

Former Buffalo Bills and Los Angeles Rams head coach Chuck Knox was hired in 1983 to guide the Seahawks, and that year's rookie running back Curt Warner led the AFC in rushing with the first of his four 1,000-yard seasons with the club. The Seahawks earned their first trip to the playoffs in 1983, defeating their first two opponents before losing to the Los Angeles Raiders (now the Oakland Raiders) in the AFC championship game.

Largent retired in 1989 as the most prolific wide receiver in professional football history. He became only the second receiver, after Don Hutson, to own career records in yards (13,089), receptions (819), and touchdowns (100) all at the same time. Jerry Rice, however, eclipsed them both; he now holds all three records. In recent years, the Seahawks haven't done well, posting five losing records in seven seasons from 1990 to 1996. While they returned to the playoffs in 1999, they've not yet played in the Super Bowl.

Seattle SuperSonics
351 Elliott Ave., W., Suite 500 (KeyArena)
Seattle Center
206-281-5800
www.nba.com/sonics

The Sonics came into the National Basketball Association (NBA) in the 1967–68 season but have won just one NBA championship, back in 1979. It has been slim championship pickings ever since, even though the team's season records continue to promise otherwise.

The Sonics came tantalizingly close in 1993, when the team won the second-highest number of games in its history with a record of 55–27, good for second place in the Pacific Division behind the Phoenix Suns. The playoffs were an exhilarating ride for Seattle fans as the Sonics defeated Utah, three games to two, in the first round and then prevailed in overtime of the seventh game in their conference semifinal series against Houston. The Western Conference finals pitted Seattle against the Charles Barkley–led Phoenix Suns. The series went seven games before the Suns finally vanquished the Sonics, 123–110. However, the 1990s were good to the Sonics. In 1997–98 they won the Pacific Division for the fourth time in five seasons after a 61–21 season and became only the third team ever to win 55 or more games for six consecutive seasons. The current crop of players continues to provide exciting play, but fans still hope for more.

SHOPPING

As the leading commercial center, the city offers visitors a wide range of shopping opportunities. The major stores are all centrally located, with distinctly different shopping styles. Neighborhoods offer their own style of small shops and intimate art galleries. Walk along Pine Street from Second Avenue eastward, and you'll encounter the major reasons for shopping in downtown Seattle. This section includes some stores that you might find of interest, as well as the major malls.

Centers and Malls

Seattle was one of the nation's pioneers in covered shopping malls, and many are in the outlying suburban districts, though they are really extensions of what you'll find downtown. Some of the major ones are **Alderwood Mall** (136 stores; 3000 184th St. SW, Lynnwood—north of Seattle), **Bellevue Square** (198 stores; 8 miles east of Seattle),

Nordstrom is an anchor of downtown shopping in Seattle. Toshi

Pacific Place, one of Seattle's newest indoor shopping centers, brightens up downtown. Toshi

The Commons at Federal Way (106 stores; off I-5 at 320th, Federal Way), **Northgate Shopping Center** (116 stores; NE Northgate Way at Fifth Ave. NE), **Southcenter** (127 stores; near the junction of I-5 and I-405), **University Village** (90 stores; 2673 NE University Village). University Village is a complex of small boutiques and stores including Crate and Barrel, Banana Republic, Pottery Barn, Victoria's Secret, and the Gap.

Capitol Hill: Along **Broadway** is where young Seattle goes for its upscale and avant garde clothing and fashion.

Downtown: Westlake Center (on Pine St. between Fourth and Fifth Aves.) is at the heart of Seattle's shopping district, though malls such as Pacific Place have made Westlake small by comparison. Westlake Center features a variety of upscale specialty shops; across the street is **Westlake Park,** a major gathering area for Seattle's wonderful street characters.

Nondepartment-store shopping areas include **Pacific Place** (600 Pine St.), next to Nordstrom, with six stories of upscale shopping including Cartier and Tiffany. On the top floor are several movie theaters and restaurants. Many hotels have minishops within their complexes. **Rainier Square** (on Fifth Ave. across from the 5th Avenue Theatre) has a collection of intimate boutiques. **Pioneer Square** is where you'll find small bookstores, art galleries, and specialty stores of all kinds.

Antiques

If you're looking for antiques, the **Pioneer Square Antique Mall** (602 First Ave.; 206-624-1164; www.pioneersquareantiquemall.com) has 60 dealers in the historic 6,000 sq. ft (557 sq. m) facility. It's next to Bill Speidel's Underground Tours office entrance, in Pioneer Square. Seattle may not be old enough to have the kind of centuries-old antiques found in Europe or the eastern US, but numerous shops throughout the downtown area—Queen Anne, Capitol Hill, the University District, and near Pike Place Market—have local collections.

Books

Downtown: At **Ishii's Bookstore** (212 First Ave.; 206-622-4719), David Ishii has a vast collection of books that reflect his own interests: fly fishing and baseball, including the city's largest collection of out-of-print, scarce, and used books on those subjects. Nearby is the **Elliott Bay Book Company** (101 S. Main St.; 206-624-6600, 1-800-962-5311; www.elliottbay book.com), one of the finest independent bookstores in the Northwest; downstairs is a café where you can sip coffee and read newspapers.

University Book Store (1225 Fourth Ave.; 206-545-9230), conveniently located near the Fairmont Olympic Hotel, travel, fiction, computer, business, and medical and local guidebooks as well music, posters, and University of Washington Husky gifts. Books can be shipped free in the United States. The University Book Store's main branch is in the University District, of course.

Clothing

Downtown: Banana Republic (500 Pike St.; 206-622-2333) is a young woman's dream shop, located in one of Seattle's greatest landmark restoration projects, the Coliseum Theater Building, built in 1916.

Coldwater Creek (1511 Fifth Ave.; 206-903-0830) is a Pacific Northwest clothing institution relatively new to downtown Seattle, with women's apparel from head to toe and a nice selection of petite sizes. **Mario's** (1513 Sixth Ave.; 206-223-1461) has been around for 60-plus years selling a selection of men's and women's apparel with name brands such as Armani, Calvin Klein, Hugo Boss, and Helmut Lang. **Northwest Pendleton** (1313 Fourth Ave.; 206-682-4430) is the Pacific Northwest's leading sweater store, with choices in colors, wool separates, Indian patterns, throw blankets, and all things Pendleton. **Seattle Shirt Company** (725 Pike St.; 206-623-6387) is where you'll find an impressive collection of shirt designs from formal to casual.

Department Stores

Downtown: The giant department stores, Nordstrom and the Bon Marche—Macy's, are both located within easy walking distance of the major hotels. **Nordstrom** (on Pine St. at Third Ave.), founded in Seattle, is noted for its contemporary fashions and its reputation for superb service and display technique. Its goods are high-end, with price tags to match. Its main department-store competition is the **Bon Marche** (on Pine St. at Third Ave.), now part of the Macy's empire and a well-frequented store with a full range of affordable clothing and merchandise.

International District: The **Uwajimaya** emporium (600 Sixth Ave. S.) is the largest Japanese grocery-department store on the West Coast. The centerpiece of the neighborhood, it's a tiled, Japanese-style gourmet's delight with anything Japanese you care to buy—china, fabrics, housewares, and a variety of gifts. Founded in 1928, the business moved into its large new location in 2001, but it is still owned by the original founding Moriguchi family. This is a wonderful cultural experience even if you don't buy anything. Check out the Food Court for an inexpensive international lunch.

Farmers Markets

Fremont: Every Sunday, the Fremont Market (off N. 34th; 10–4 winter, 10–5 summer) is host to more than 200 vendors from around the region who bring with them fresh flowers and produce, crafts, and world imports, rain or shine. Browse the flea market in search of the rare or funky or eat in one or the neighborhood bistros.

University District: During the summer months through October 31, the **University Farmers Market** (University Heights Community Center, 50th St. and University Way; 9–2 Sat.) is like a mini–Pike Place Market, with fresh produce from local farmers and cooking demonstrations from area chefs.

Pike Place Market
85 Pike St.
Downtown
206-682-7453
www.pikeplacemarket.org
Open: 8–5 daily
Admission: Free
Wheelchair accessible: Yes

This is one of Seattle's most cherished places, one that residents prefer never to change. Here, visitors and residents buy the freshest seafood and produce in town. It's more than just a place to buy a salmon and a head of lettuce, though; stall owners bark to passing clients and every corner has a spot occupied by street musicians, puppeteers, or mimes. You can, in fact, spend most of a day walking through the 250 permanent shops or going through the wares of more than 200 artists and artisans.

As the number of farmers decreased as the city expanded to overtake farmland, artists and artisans moved into the vacated stalls along with restaurants, antique shops, and a variety of specialty businesses and even a modern bank. Warrenlike lower levels with steps and ramps at what seem unplanned intervals invite visitors to browse the market's bowels.

Lively seafood vendors are a crowd pleaser at Pike Place Market. Toshi

Farmers in the market have to meet a strict set of rules. They must gross (or try to) at least $2,000 a year from their farm. They must grow or gather everything they sell, with the exception of a specific list of vegetables that they can buy for resale during the winter months only. They must also process all jams, vinegars, and similar products themselves, and they must produce the main ingredient in these products themselves. All farms are inspected to ensure that the farmers really grow the crops they sell.

Go early in the day on foot (parking is at a premium) and revel in the colors. The high-stall area is flanked by mountains of red tomatoes, green cucumbers, glossy purple egg-plants, and orange carrots. Silvery salmon on beds of ice, Dungeness crabs, oysters, clams, cod, bockwurst, liverwurst, cheddar cheese, mocha-java, orange pekoe, and hundreds of other foods greet your eyes and nose at every turn.

Since the market is built over the edge of a bluff, the restaurants offer a vantage point found in few places around the city. Morning coffee or lunch at any of the several restau-rants provides a view of Elliott Bay and the Olympics. Across the street from the market is the small, intimate, and elegant 65-room hotel Inn at the Market. The **Pike Place Hill-climb** takes you down several flights of stairs from the bluff on which the market is built to Piers 52 to 70 on the waterfront. Sundays are voluntary opening days for market mer-chants, and some shops do not open then. Business hours for individual merchants also vary depending on location and type of business. For instance, some high stalls and fish markets open very early in the morning, and some restaurants remain open until late at night. During the peak farm season, May through October, farmers frequently set up and are ready to sell by 8 am or earlier.

If you know what you want to buy and where to buy it, park for 60 minutes or less in the covered **market garage** (1531 Western Ave.) and your parking is free. Some merchants val-idate parking when you make purchases in their stores. Ask about parking validation stick-ers while you shop. Early shoppers who plan to spend the day at the market can currently enjoy a $7 early bird rate; just be in by 9:30 am for this special all-day rate. The garage is connected to the market's Main Arcade by an elevator and skybridge walkway.

Don't ignore the areas around the market. At first glance it might seem that they're dominated by street people, but there's more than that. Throughout the area are small shops, art galleries, and even the original **Starbucks** (1912 Pike Pl.). Be sure that you walk through **Post Alley**, a delightful narrow passageway between Pike Place and First Avenue. The lane cuts through several blocks around the market, and many small shops and restau-rants open onto it.

Gifts and Jewelry

The Sharper Image (1501 Fourth Ave.; 206-343-9125) is a toyland for adults, with gadgets and high-tech gizmos that will keep your attention for hours. **Exclusively Washington** (Pier 54, Ste. 200; 206-624-2600) has a variety of products from Washington State, in-cluding pottery, art glass, and a variety of apparel and goods such as Ivar's memorabilia and chowder.

Sporting Goods

Adidas (1501 Fifth Ave.; 206-382-4317) is located in the heart of downtown near the major department stores and specialty shops along Pike and Fifth avenues. Here you'll find com-petitive pricing for all types of Adidas sportswear and equipment that includes shoes, athletic apparel and accessories for the sporting enthusiast. **Eddie Bauer** (Pacific Place, 600 Pine St.,

2nd floor; 206-622-2766) sells a wide range of outdoor and casual apparel for active people to live, work, and play in. **NikeTown** (1500 Sixth Ave.; 206-447-6453) is the new guy in town, and though buying something here won't help you play golf like Tiger Woods, you can look just as good on the first tee. With a wide range of sports clothing and equipment, this place is dedicated to weekend athletes and the dreams they share. A block east is the major store **Recreational Equipment, Inc.** (222 Yale Ave. N.; 206-223-1944), the country's largest co-op selling outdoor equipment. REI, as it's known, is Seattle's major outdoor sports clothing and equipment store, with everything you need for muscle-powered activities.

Events

Seattle is a festival city, with every month having a major event or activity. Some are more attended than others, but together they make up part of the character that is unique to Seattle. Some, like Bumbershoot, offer hundreds of performers and draw hundreds of thousands of people. Other events, like BrasilFest, are one-day celebrations of a nation's culture in food, music, and the arts. The Seattle waterfront has ongoing festivities throughout the year. In summer, there are fireworks, eating, and boating festivals. During the winter there are Christmas and New Year's celebrations and cruises.

January
Seattle International Boat Show (Seahawk Exhibition Center; 206-634-0911; www.seattle boatshow.com); features more than a thousand boats of all kinds; mid-month

February
Northwest Flower and Garden Show (Washington State Convention and Trade Center; 1-800-229-6311; www.gardenshow.com); early February.

Seattle RV and Outdoor Recreation Show (Seahawk Exhibition Center; 206-381-8000; www.mhrvshows.com/seattle.html); early to mid-February.

Seattle Home Show (Seahawk Exhibition Center; 206-284-0960; www.seattlehomeshow .com); mid- to late February.

March
Irish Heritage Week (Seattle Center; www.irishclub.org); first and second week in March.

April
Seattle Cherry Blossom and Japanese Cultural Festival (Seattle Center; 206-993-3999); third week in April.

May
Opening Day of Boating Season (Seattle Yacht Club; 206-325-1000; www.seattleyachtclub .org); first weekend in May.

Maritime Festival (Seattle waterfront); early May.

Seattle International Children's Festival (Seattle Center; 206-684-7346; www.seattle international.org); second week in May.

Northwest Folklife Festival (Seattle Center; 206-684-7300; www.nwfolklife.org); one of the largest folk festivals in the country with arts, crafts, music, food, and performers; late May.

Pike Place Market Festival (206-587-0351); Memorial Day weekend.

Seattle International Film Festival (various locations; 206-324-9996; www.seattlefilm. com); late May through mid-June.

June
Pagdiriwang Philippine Festival (Seattle Center; 206-684-7200, www.seattlecenter.com); first week in June.

Fremont Street Fair and Solstice Parade (206-633-4409; www.fremontfair.com); mid-June.

July
Cingular Summer Nights at the Pier (Piers 62 and 63; 206-281-8111; www.summernights .org); all through July.

Washington Mutual Family Fourth at Lake Union (206-281-8111; www.onereel.org); July 4.

Fourth of Jul-ivar (Seattle waterfront; 206-587-6500; www.ivars.net); July 4.

Seafair (various locations; 206-728-0123; www.seafair.com); first week in July through first week in August.

Bite of Seattle (Seattle Center; 425-283-5050; www.biteofseattle.com); late July.

Ballard Seafood Fest (206-784-9705; www.seafoodfest.org); late July.

August
Bumbershoot (Seattle Center; 206-281-7788; www.bumbershoot.org); late August and/or Labor Day weekend.

BrasilFest (Seattle Center; 206-684-7200; www.seattlecenter.com); third Sunday in August.

TibetFest (Seattle Center; 206-684-7200; www.seattlecenter.com); August 27–28.

September
Oktoberfest (various locations in Fremont; 206-632-1500; www.fremontoktoberfest.org); mid-October.

Festa Italiana (Seattle Center; 206-282-0627; www.festaseattle.com); mid-September to first week in October.

October
Seattle Interior Show (Seahawk Exhibition Center; 206-284-0960; www.seattle-down town.com/convention-center); third week in October.

November–December

Seattle International Auto Show (Seahawk Stadium Exhibition Center; 206-542-3551; www.seattleautoshow.com); first week in November.

Christmas in Seattle Holiday Gift Show (Washington State Convention Center, www.seattle-downtown.com/convention-center); third week in November.

Bon Marche Holiday Parade and Westlake Tree Lighting (downtown; 206-467-3044); Thanksgiving.

Winterfest (Seattle Center; 206-684-7200; www.seattlecenter.com); last week in November to January 2.

Christmas Ship Festival (Argosy Cruises; 206-623-1445; www.argosycruises.com); on Elliott Bay and Seattle's lakes; December 1–23.

New Year's Eve at the Space Needle (Seattle Center; 206-443-2111; www.seattlecenter.com); December 31.

Artwork in
Tacoma's Museum
of Glass
Toshi

2

SIDE TRIPS FROM SEATTLE

Islands, Mountains, and Nearby Towns

Since Seattle is an oceanfront city, it offers unique ways of getting around. Prior to 2002, Seattle was a nonstarter for the cruise-ship industry. Virtually all of the major cruise lines traveling to Alaska left from Vancouver, British Columbia, where top-of-the-line passenger facilities have been in place for decades. From just six large-ship port calls in 1999, the Port of Seattle counted 79 in 2002, with a total passenger count of 125,000, and 94 in 2003, with 197,000 passengers. Although they are still short of Vancouver's numbers, the current figures mark a substantial increase, with Holland America, Norwegian Cruise Line, and Princess Cruises all making calls in Seattle. But the city has always been at the center for small-ship cruising; America West Steamboat Lines and Glacier Bay Cruise Lines make runs from Seattle to Alaska and the San Juan Islands. Your best bet is to book through a travel agent.

FERRIES

Washington State Ferries (from Colman Dock on the waterfront; 206-464-6400; www.wsdot.wa.gov/ferries) operates large and small vessels between Seattle and several island communities in Puget Sound, including Vashon Island, Bremerton, Bainbridge Island, and Whidbey Island. Check the schedule, because service changes constantly.

Bainbridge Island and Kitsap Peninsula

A scenic ferry ride across Puget Sound to Bainbridge Island followed by a leisurely drive through the Kitsap Peninsula leads to the naval town of Bremerton, from where you can take another ferry back to downtown Seattle. This is an easy one-day trip of about 60 miles, but you can extend your stay if you find an intriguing B-and-B for a stopover. If you don't want to hassle with ferries, you can also head south on I-5 to Tacoma, cross the Narrows Bridge, then head north on Highway 16 to Bremerton, about an hour and 15 minutes from downtown Seattle.

Bainbridge is a contradiction. Just 30 minutes by ferry from downtown Seattle, it's a combination of wildness and suburban sophistication—a semirural island haven for city professionals who want a taste of the woods in their hectic lives. Deer forage the island, eagles soar high overhead, and fresh fruit farms produce the same raspberries and black-

Bainbridge Island Ferry Toshi

berries they have for the past century. A cheap and delightfully different way of seeing Seattle's skyline is from the hourly ferry to Bainbridge Island. When you get there, you'll find a San Francisco–like area that's devoid of pavement and fumes. It's what people mean when they talk about West Coast living.

As you drive through the Kitsap Peninsula, you will find a series of attractive small communities—Poulsbo, Silverdale, and Port Orchard. Silverdale is Kitsap's commercial center, located at the northern tip of Dyes Inlet. Bangor Annex, just north of town, is a nuclear submarine base on Hood Canal. Seabeck, Holly, and Belfair line the canal, and Port Orchard is across the bay from Bremerton.

Bremerton is surrounded on three sides by water, but from there you find sweeping views of the Cascades and the Olympics. The community's one great claim to fame is that *Money Magazine* chose it America's most livable community in 1990. Since it is a major naval facility, home of the Puget Sound Naval Shipyard, there isn't much for a tourist to see except for the Naval Shipyard Museum, which has American and Japanese naval artifacts. But downtown Bremerton is being revitalized, so look for new attractions in the near future.

GETTING THERE

From Pier 52 in Seattle take a 35-minute ferry ride across to Winslow to reach tranquil Bainbridge Island. Follow the main route, WA 305, out of town and across Agate Passage to the Kitsap Peninsula and Poulsbo, from where you can take WA 3 either north to tour the northern Kitsap Peninsula (Port Gamble, Hansville, and Point No Point), returning via the Kingston ferry to Edmonds, or south to tour the southern Kitsap Peninsula via Silverdale. This leads you to back roads to Seabeck, Holly, and Belfair, where you can take WA 3 north to Bremerton and a ferry trip back to Seattle.

RESTAURANTS

At the Bainbridge pier, walk up Winslow Way to the **Streamliner Diner** for the salsa omelet.

ATTRACTIONS

Gardens and Parks

Bloedel Reserve
7571 NE Dolphin Dr.
Bainbridge Island
206-842-7631
www.bloedelreserve.com
Open: 10–4, W–Sun; reservations required
Admission: $10 adults, $8 seniors, $6 children
Wheelchair accessible: Yes

Bainbridge Island is home to the Bloedel Reserve, one of the Pacific Northwest's loveliest horticultural areas and the Bloedel family museum. It's the perfect setting for one of the Northwest's great collections of flora—150 acres of lush, tranquil gardens, woods, meadows, and ponds. Plants from all over the world make the grounds a horticulturalist's dream at any time of the year. It is also one of the best-kept secrets about the Seattle area.

You understand why reservations are required and limited the moment you drive along the entrance road on the north end of the island and you come to the wide gate that keeps the public at bay. Half of the acreage is in a constant wild state, with alders, firs, cedars, hemlocks, and native shrubs, mosses, and grasses. The untouched wilderness houses waterfowl, hawks, insects, and small animals. The rest is cultivated with formal, broad lawns and elms near the three-story, French-chateau-style house that is open as part of the tour. There's a Japanese garden, a moss garden that resembles the floor of a rain forest, a rhododendron and wildflower glen under the trees, and a fabricated pond planted with cattails and other native species to provide habitat for waterfowl.

The gardens blend one into the next, and trails lead through the woodlands. A footbridge over a ravine boardwalk takes you over otherwise untouched wetland. The land was once a Suquamish Indian summer camp, and giant trees were logged here in the 1860s. Prentice Bloedel and his wife, Virginia Merrell, bought the property in the 1930s after it had already been developed and the chateau built by its former owner, Angela Collins, the wife of Seattle's sixth mayor. Virginia Merrill Bloedel died in 1989 and is buried on the property. Bloedel once wrote, "We discovered that there is grandeur in decay; the rotten log hosting seedlings of hemlocks, cedars, huckleberries, the shape of a crumbling snag." The respect for nature that Bloedel, a forest industry millionaire, had is obvious from the time you enter the reserve. The gardens are meant for meditation, with every corner an isolated preserve. The Japanese garden, with its raked sand and stone, is a serene place where light and shadow mimic water. It was once a blue-tiled swimming pool but was later installed with geometric planes, then graded and set with basalt boulders.

Botanists and other specialists continue to shape the preserve. Future plans include a plantation of fragrant viburnums and honeysuckle near the marsh to attract butterflies— painted ladies, red admirals, tiger swallowtails, tortoiseshells, and azures—all native to Puget Sound. Tours are available with advance arrangement.

Museums
The **Marine Science Center** (18743 Front Street NE Poulsbo, WA 98370; 360-779-5549; www.poulsbomsc.org) is a major attraction in the region. In Suquamish, on the east side of the Kitsap Peninsula, the **Suquamish Museum** (15838 Sandy Hook Road, Suquamish, WA 98392; 360-598-3311; www.suquamish.nsn.us/museum) is an award-winning museum of the Suquamish and Port Madison Indian Reservation. Chief Sealth's grave overlooks Puget Sound in a small cemetery on the Port Madison Indian Reservation. Painted canoes high above the headstone mark his resting place.

Tours and Sightseeing
The **Bainbridge Island Vineyards and Winery** (206-842-9463; www.bainbridge vineyards.com) on Bainbridge Island is a small, family-run vineyard and winery just a 35-minute ferry trip across Puget Sound. Take a self-guided tour through the vineyard Monday through Sunday 12 pm to 5 pm, or let a professional guide you on Sundays at 2 pm The wine tasting is complimentary with a wine purchase or $2 without purchase.

On the very northern tip of the Kitsap Peninsula, at the mouth of Hood Canal, you'll find the **Point No Point Lighthouse** (360-337-5350; www.kitsapgov.com/parks), where you can take daily tours. It's on the Hansville Road off WA 104 between the Hood Canal Bridge and the Kingston ferry dock to Edmonds.

RECREATION
Fishing
At the mouth of Hood Canal on the northernmost tip of the Kitsap Peninsula is the town of **Hansville,** the acknowledged best place on Puget Sound to catch salmon.

Golf
There is a cluster of excellent golf courses on the Kitsap Peninsula. Several wonderful options include some of the newer layouts, such as **Gold Mountain Golf Complex** (360-415-5432; www.goldmt.com), **McCormick Woods Golf Course** (1-800-323-0130; www.mccormickwoodsgolf.com), and **Trophy Lake Golf and Casting Club** (360-874-8337; www.trophylakegolf.com).

SHOPPING
The **Kitsap Mall** in Silverdale has some 200 shops, including the major department stores.

EVENTS

Silverdale's **Whaling Days,** held in late July, is the town's biggest event, with boat races and a general carnival atmosphere. **Chief Seattle Days,** an annual weekend affair held in August at the downtown Suquamish waterfront park, has traditional Native American dancing, story telling, and a salmon bake.

Tacoma

When Capt. George Vancouver and his entourage accidentally stumbled onto Puget Sound in 1792, Peter Puget was ordered by Vancouver to sail past Point Defiance and the Narrows. In 1833 members of the Hudson's Bay Company built Fort Nisqually at Point Defiance; today, the fort has been rebuilt to its original specs. Another sea captain, Charles Wilkes, surveyed the sound in 1841 and gave his starting point the name it still bears, Commencement Bay.

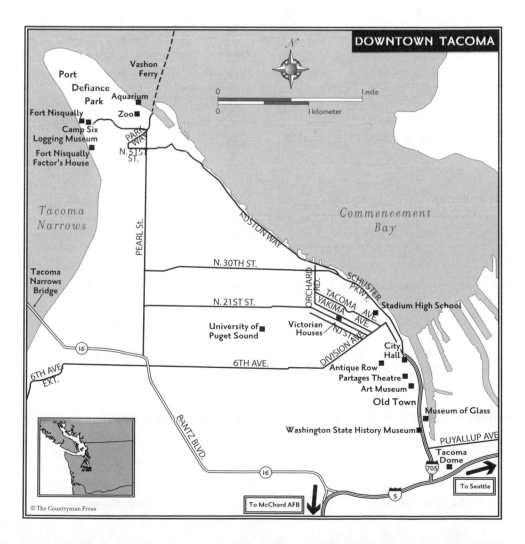

The first settlers were lured to Commencement Bay in the 1850s and 1860s by the vast lumber potential. Among them was Nicholas De Lin, a Swedish immigrant and entrepreneur who built a water-driven mill and eventually opened a brewery, barrel factory, and salmon-packing plant. Originally the settlement was called Commencement City because of its location—sided by Commencement Bay and the Narrows and backed by Mount Rainier. In 1855 city fathers gave the town the title City of Destiny in the hope it would boost its growth. Alas, the future was not as bright as civic leaders had hoped. The town was renamed Tacoma in 1869. The name comes from the Native American word *tahoma*, which means "mother of waters" (their name for Mount Rainier).

Tacoma was a small village until 1873, when the Northern Pacific Railroad chose it as its western terminus, and from that time onward, the city has competed with Seattle for dominance on Puget Sound. For the next decade, Tacoma's population erupted, increasing from 1,000 to 36,000 as the railroad brought industrial development (its population is now 194,000). The president of the railroad, Charles Wright, was a free spender, donating money for parks and schools.

Tacoma's stability was seriously shaken in the depression of 1893, and its commercial universe folded quickly. Another rail company, the Great Northern Railroad, chose Seattle as its western terminus that same year. Although Tacoma rallied with the Klondike gold rush, its growth slowed down considerably by the turn of the 20th century, and in the 1920s, the Northern Pacific moved its western headquarters to Seattle.

Tacoma has always had an intense rivalry with its larger neighbor to the north. Throughout its history, Tacoma never quite lived up to its billing as the City of Destiny, and it has had to endure jokes about its industrial character, unfavorable lifestyle comparisons, and the acrid odor coming from the Simpson Tacoma Pulp Mill, which manufactures cardboard and other paper products. Nevertheless, those days of bad jokes and second-class citizenship have fairly well passed. Seattle's southern neighbor now has its own share of attractive sites, fine restaurants, cultural activities, sports teams, and enshrined historical regions. Tacoma has undergone a cultural revitalization over the past decade, and the city once known for its neutrality to the arts is now, in fact, a home to them. It makes a worthy destination for a day's visit from Seattle.

GETTING THERE

Tacoma is an hour's drive south of Seattle via I-5. Exit at I-705 to reach downtown Tacoma; exit at WA 16 West to reach Point Defiance, then exit WA 16 at Pearl Street. You can also reach Point Defiance from downtown by following Stadium Way and either Schuster Parkway or Ruston Way north.

RESTAURANTS

Restaurants are plentiful in Tacoma, and you'll find virtually any cuisine. For steaks, **El Gaucho Tacoma** (2119 Pacific Ave.; 253-272-1510) is a local favorite owned by the same El Gaucho chain that's in Seattle. The **Harmon Pub and Brewery** (1938 Pacific Ave.; 253-383-2739) near Union Station offers tasty pub fare. And for seafood, **Johnny's Dock** (1900 East D St.; 253-627-3186) on the waterfront commands some of the city's best views.

ATTRACTIONS

Tacoma has preserved its past while embarking on a cultural renaissance. From the book-stores and small boutiques in the Old Town district to a waterfront avant-garde public arts project to city-subsidized artists' housing in the historic warehouse district and a glass museum that has hands-on glass-blowing furnaces, the arts and history are now fashion-able here. The **University of Puget Sound** (1500 North Warner, 800-396-7191; 253-879-3211, www.ups.edu) in the north end and **Pacific Lutheran University** (12180 Park Street S., 253-531-6900, www.plu.edu/external) in the south each provide a variety of cultural programs and art events open to the public.

Gardens and Parks

Tacoma's waterfront attracts locals and visitors alike to its many restaurants, trails, piers, and parks. **Ruston Way waterfront** (along the south shore of Commencement Bay) allows beautiful walks along the wide expanse of the bay, framed by steep-cliffed islands, the Olympic and Cascade ranges, and Mount Rainier. A promenade for pedestrians and bicy-clists stretches the length of the 2-mile (3.2 km) waterfront.

The city's most famous landmark is 700-acre **Point Defiance Park** (5400 N. Pearl St.; 253-591-5337), which encompasses Fort Nisqually Historic Site at the northern tip of the city. The original structure was on the Nisqually Delta but was relocated to Point Defiance in 1935 as part of a Works Progress Administration project during the Great Depression. There are 10 buildings, including the Factor's House (1854) and the Granary (1850), the only surviving original example in Washington State of the French-Canadian post-and-sill construction used in the Hudson's Bay Company's forts of the period. A museum features exhibits on the role of the fort in Puget Sound history. Within the park is also the **Point Defiance Zoo and Aquarium** (253-591-5337; www.pdza.org), which covers 29 acres and has 792 animals representing 98 different species. It is open 9–4 September–May and 9–6 May 30–Labor Day. Admission is $8.75 adults, $8 seniors, $7 youth ages 4–13, and free to tots 3 and under. It is wheelchair accessible and has wheel-chairs available for rent.

Historic Buildings and Sites

In downtown Tacoma, the **Old City Hall Historic District** (Pacific Ave. to Tacoma Ave., Ninth St. to 13th St.) reflects the activity that flourished in the railroad town at the turn of the 20th century. The **Old City Hall** (625 Commerce St.), built in 1893 in a style described by its builders as "Italian Renaissance," now houses offices. The nearby **Northern Pacific Headquarters Building** (S. Seventh and Pacific) is a handsome Italianate structure built in 1888. The **Elks Temple** (565 Broadway), constructed in 1916, is in the Beaux Arts– style, and the 1889-built **Bostwick Hotel** (S. Ninth St. at Broadway and St. Helens) is a classic example of a triangular Victoria "flatiron." The **old train depot** (1717 Pacific Ave.), located in the warehouse district on Pacific Avenue, is an heirloom from the golden age of rail-roading and one of Tacoma's most cherished sites, now housing a federal courthouse.

Students still use **Stadium High School** (6229 S. Tyler St.), a turreted, chateaulike structure. Designed as a luxury hotel in 1891 for the Northern Pacific Railroad, it was con-verted to a high school after a fire left only the outer shell.

At Pantages Center, the restored 1,100-seat **Pantages Theater** (901 Broadway), origi-nally designed in 1918 by B. Marcus Priteca, is the focal point of downtown cultural life,

The Bostwick Hotel, built in 1889, is a triangular Victorian "flatiron"-style building.
Courtesy of Tacoma Regional Convention & Visitor Bureau

holding stage, music, and dance performances. The building is an example of early 20th-century Greco-Roman music-hall architecture, similar to old Orpheum theaters across the continent, with classical figures, ornate columns, and arches. Now the home of the Tacoma Symphony, it was a stop on the vaudeville tours. W. C. Fields, Mae West, Will Rogers, Charlie Chaplin, Bob Hope, and Houdini all appeared here.

The **Tacoma Narrows Bridge**, connecting Tacoma to the Kitsap Peninsula via WA 16, is the fifth-largest suspension bridge in the world. The original, dubbed "Gallopin' Gertie" because of its undulating motion in windy weather, collapsed in a windstorm within four months of its completion in 1940. The current structure spans 5,979 feet (1,822 m) and was completed in 1950. It doesn't sway.

Victorian Houses

If cities are defined by their architecture, then Tacoma is decidedly eclectic—historically speaking—with a good supply of intriguing old houses. Tacoma was a small mill town that was changed into a sophisticated city over a very few years by Eastern capitalists involved in the railroad, the shipping industry, mining, timber, and land. Their tastes varied greatly, and many of the owners demanded designs that set them apart.

Several factors contributed to the eclectic architectural styles of the mid-1800s to 1900. The post–Civil War era evolved from the traditional Greek Revival to Victorian picturesque. And the opening of the Orient brought influences from new sources and provided a wider range of inspiration. So Tacoma's burghers produced houses that included fish-scale shingles, bay windows with curved glass, pillars, pilasters, terra-cotta tiles, stained-glass and leaded-glass windows, cupolas, wrought-iron fences, gothic arches, dormers, gables, and quoins. The glitzy styling included brackets, pendants, dentils, corbels, tall chimneys, projected porches, cornices, and pediments until nothing more could possibly be added. This wealth of detail was seen in the most modest of cottages as well as in pretentious mansions, and all are examples of what Tacoma once was.

Many of these elegant homes are still standing. The stately homes and cobblestone streets in the north end of Tacoma are often used as sets for Hollywood films. Most of the homes have been restored by private owners and are currently being lived in, so they cannot be visited except by driving past them. But there are some unique architectural examples worth a visit even if it is at arm's length. They can be found in the area west of Stadium High School, near Tacoma Avenue from North First Street to Orchard Street.

The **William Laird McCormich House** (509 N. Tacoma Ave.) is a stone example of Italian Renaissance. The post-Victorian mansion that once belonged to **Henry Rhodes** (701 North J St.), Tacoma's most famous mercantilist, still stands. The post-Victorian **H. F. Alexander House** (502 N. Yakima) has a series of Ionic columns and ornate corbel trim that recall an opulent past. The colonial mansion that once belonged to **William R. Rust** (1001 North I St.) is known as "Tacoma's Greatest Town House" because the interior of the majestic sandstone structure has been divided into apartments.

Museums

If you had to rename Tacoma today, it would likely be the City of Glass, since everywhere you go you'll find glass sculpture. Even the **Federal Courthouse** (1717 Pacific Ave.) is now a tribute to glass art, with glass sculptures by Dale Chihuly dominating the high-ceilinged atrium entranceway of the former train depot. You can walk along the top of the atrium and closely examine the works.

Among the museums in town are several that fit the "unusual" category, including the **Children's Museum of Tacoma** (936 Broadway), the **Shanaman Sports Museum** (in the Tacoma Dome, 2727 E. D St.; 253-272-8543), **Karpeles Manuscript Library Museum** (407 S. G Street; 253-383-2575), the **Fort Lewis Military Museum** (Bldg. 4320, Fort Lewis; 253-967-7206), and the **Maritime Center** (705 Dock St.; 253-272-2750).

The **Camp Six Museum** (in Point Defiance Park, 5400 N. Pearl St.) is a 20-acre open-air museum featuring restored bunkhouses, hand tools, and historical logging equipment. It features a Dolbeer donkey steam engine, a restored water wagon, and a ride on an original, 90-ton Shat steam locomotive.

Glass art by Dale Chihuly hangs in the foyer of Tacoma's federal courthouse. Ioshi

The Asia Pacific Cultural Center

1123 Pacific Ave.
Downtown
253-383-3900
www.apccusa.org
Open: 9–5 M–F
Admission: Depends on exhibit; call
in advance
Wheelchair accessible: Yes

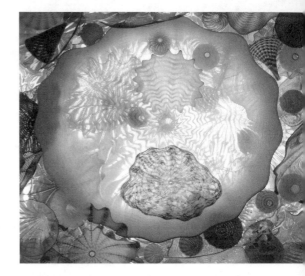

Glass art in the overhead Seaform Pavilion, part of the Chihuly Bridge of Glass that connects the Museum of Glass to downtown Tacoma. Toshi

The Asia Pacific Cultural Center opened in December 2004 in the former home of the Tacoma Art Museum; it promotes the cultures of 47 Asian and Pacific groups ranging from Japan, China, and Korea to Indonesia, Polynesia, and New Zealand. There are rotating art exhibits, an upscale Asian restaurant on the ground floor, a 250-seat performance/meeting space, and classrooms on the second floor where, among other things, classes in ikebana (flower arranging), Asian languages, and tea ceremonies are taught.

Museum of Glass: International Center for Contemporary Art

1801 E. Dock St.
Downtown
253-284-4750
www.museumofglass.org
Open: 10–5 T–Sa, noon–5 Su
Admission: $10 adults, $8 seniors, $4 children 6–12, free under 6
Wheelchair accessible: Yes

The Museum of Glass is, as its name suggests, totally devoted to the medium of glass. Opened in July 2002, the $58 million museum features state-of-the-art facilities, including the Hot Shop Amphitheater, housed in a 90-foot-tall, angled cone, 100 feet in diameter at the base, where visitors can watch glass artists at work. Outdoor plazas on the roof feature large works of glass art, reflecting pools, and seating areas for relaxing and enjoying views of the city skyline and waterfront. The roof of the museum connects with the Chihuly Bridge of Glass, a 500-foot-long pedestrian bridge that spans I-705 to connect the Thea Foss Waterway and the Museum of Glass to the Washington State History Museum and downtown Tacoma. The glass art itself, created by Dale Chihuly, is valued at some $12 million, and you can stroll across it, pausing to admire the 1,500 pieces in the overhead Seaform Pavilion, the 109 jewel-toned glass creations in the 80-foot-long Venetian Wall, and the 30-foot-high, glacial blue twin Crystal Towers.

Tacoma Art Museum
1701 Pacific Ave.
Downtown
253-272-4258
www.tacomaartmuseum.org
Open: 10–5 Tu–W and F–Sa, 10–8 Th, noon–5 Sun
Admission: $6.50 adults, $5.50 seniors and students, free under 6
Wheelchair accessible: Yes

After years in a too-small former bank building, the Tacoma Art Museum opened in its own new place in 2003. The galleries feature a permanent collection of Northwest artists and 19th- and 20th-century American, European, and Asian art, including Chinese jades, imperial robes, and works by Renoir, Degas, and Pissarro. The museum has a permanent children's gallery and a glass art collection that includes the world's largest collection of early Chihuly glass. A museum store, a café, art-preservation areas, collections storage, and a 125-space parking garage are also on-site.

Washington State History Museum
1911 Pacific Ave.
Downtown
253-272-9747
www.wshs.org
Open: 10–5 M–W and F–Sa, noon–5 Su, 10–8 Th
Admission: $7; free 5–8 Th
Wheelchair accessible: Yes

This 106,000-square-foot space features interactive, multimedia, and storytelling exhibits on Washington State, its people, and its places. You can experience life in a Salish plank house, eavesdrop on Lewis and Clark, discover the realities of life on the frontier and during the Depression, enter the complex world of Washington's early labor movements, and learn about major industries that shaped the state. The museum contains the largest collection of pioneer, Native American, and Alaskan artifacts on the Pacific Coast, including canoes, baskets, and masks from British Columbia and Puget Sound. It also has the state's largest permanent model railroad exhibit.

Tours and Sightseeing
Across the Tacoma Narrows Bridge via WA 16 is **Gig Harbor**, a delightful harbor town with old-style shops and plenty of restaurants, plus bed-and-breakfast inns.

Across Dalco Passage from Point Defiance Park is **Vashon Island**, a 15-minute ferry trip from the Point Defiance dock. Its most enduring charm is its rural character, with plenty of cows and quiet roads perfect for bicycle touring.

For an even slower pace, **Anderson Island** might be for you. It's west of Tacoma near Steilacoom. The last ferry leaving the island is at 6:30 pm, and if you miss it, you'll have to sleep under someone's porch because there are no motels on the island.

Gig Harbor is a quaint saltwater town across the Narrows from Tacoma.
Courtesy of Tacoma Regional Convention & Visitor Bureau

RECREATION

Spectator Sports

The **Tacoma Dome** (2727 East D St.; 253-272-3663) is the largest domed-wood structure in the world, measuring 530 feet in diameter and 150 feet in height—equal to a 15-story building—and covering 6.1 acres. Its 288 triangular wooden sections support the urethane-composition roof, and each section weighs 5,000 pounds.

The Tacoma Dome has seating configurations that include 16,000 movable sideline and end-zone seats, which readily convert the facility from large-scale stadium events such as soccer to arena events including concerts and ice shows, and it can pack in 25,000 enthusiastic concertgoers. If it has one disadvantage, it's the fact that it is somewhat removed from downtown. Located just off I-5 to the southeast of the downtown core, however, it is near Freighthouse Square and its Public Market and within several blocks of the Visitors Center. The location does allow for easy entrance into and exit from the 2,900-capacity parking lot. So, unlike the case in Seattle, major events don't tie up traffic for blocks around downtown.

Shopping

Antiquing is a favorite pastime of locals, with **Antique Row** (Broadway between Seventh and Ninth Aves.; 253-272-0334—Antique Row Association) located in the heart of Tacoma's historic district. There's a unique blend of specialty shops with more than a dozen antique stores. The district boasts one of the largest concentrations of antiques and collectibles in the Northwest, with more than 80,000 square feet of midcentury antiques, local galleries, funky collectibles, vintage automobiles, jewelry, and furniture. Thursdays June– September, the district hosts Tacoma's **Farmers Market** (on Broadway between 9th and 11th Streets; 253-272-7077; www.tacomafarmersmarket.com).

Mount Rainier

On a clear day, if you look southeast from the Seattle waterfront, you'll see Mount Rainier looming in the distance, its snowy bulk dominating the southeastern skyline. No one in the area calls it Mount Rainier. It is simply "the Mountain." Located 74 miles (119 km) south-east of Tacoma, the 14,410-foot (4,392 m) mountain is the fifth highest in the Lower 48; it is so big that it creates its own weather system.

Local Native Americans called the mountain Tahoma, and considered the mountain a god. And indeed, there are moments when anyone living within the influence of its potential anger sometimes thinks the Native Americans just might have been right.While the native peoples called the mountain Tahoma, it got its current name when Capt. George Vancouver named it after his friend, Admiral Peter Rainier, although the admiral had never seen it.

Mount Rainier is the tallest of the Cascade volcanoes, and though it's quiet now—not dead, but sleeping—it wasn't always so. It's estimated that it was 16,000 feet (4,877 m) tall about 75,000 years ago but that glaciers later stripped about 2,000 feet (650 m) off its top. Today, encased in 26 glaciers comprising 35 square miles of snow and ice, the mountain is host to the single largest glacier system in the continental United States. On clear days, Mount Rainier can seem a cuddly, coned giant, but its gentleness is deceiving, and every now and then you can see the hidden power deep in its bowels. Steam hisses from fumaroles high on the glacier-clad cone, where stranded climbers have survived by gathering around the steam vents for warmth. Even the first white climbers to make it to the top, in 1870, gathered around a vent.

Geologist claim that Rainier will again erupt, but they claim that day will not be soon. The bigger worry is mud slides, which can happen if the steam vents melt the snow surrounding the cone. There is ample evidence that this has happened before, at the 1947 Kautz Creek mudflow. Geologists also claim that about 5,800 years ago such a mud slide buried the site of present-day Enumclaw 70 feet (21 m) deep and almost reached the present-day suburbs of Tacoma.

Because Rainier towers over the other mountains in the Cascades—with other peaks guarding its flanks—it helps force the incoming ocean air to drop moisture on its west face. Thus, the influence of Rainier, along with the rest of the Cascades, on Washington's climate is that the western part of the state is wet and the east, in the rain shadow of the Cascades, dry. The mountain's height also catches high winds, which account for its lenticular clouds, the upside-down saucer-shaped clouds that hover just above the summit on clear days. The largest amount of snowfall ever recorded anywhere was on Rainier, in 1972, when the Paradise Ranger Station snowpack reached 93.5 feet (28.5 m).

Mount Rainier National Park (Tahoma Woods, Star Rte., Ashford; 360-569-2211; www.nps.gov/mora) was established in 1899 with 235,625 acres (97 percent is designated

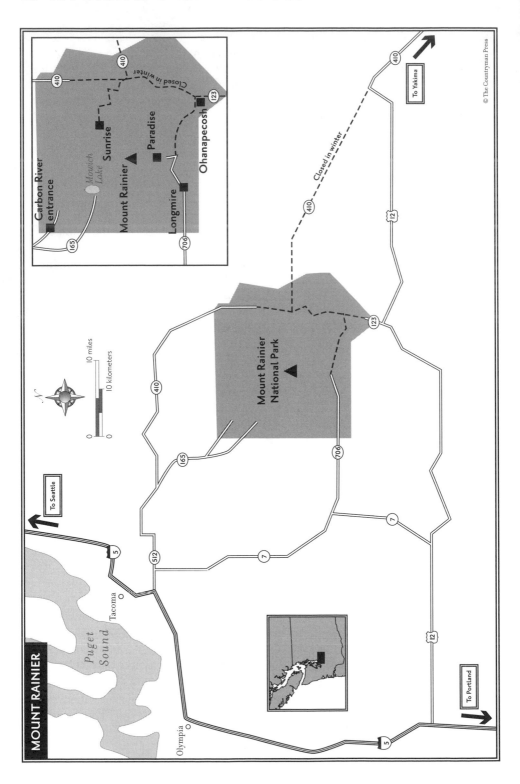

MOUNT RAINIER

Puget Sound

Tacoma

Olympia

To Seattle

To Yakima

To Portland

Mount Rainier National Park

Carbon River entrance

Mowich Lake

Sunrise

Mount Rainier

Paradise

Ohanapecosh

Longmire

Closed in winter

Closed in winter

10 miles

10 kilometers

© The Countryman Press

Mount Rainier Tacoma Regional Convention

wilderness). The park contains outstanding examples of old-growth forests and subalpine meadows surrounding the imposing peak. You won't be alone up there. Nearly two million people come to enjoy the grandeur and beauty of Mount Rainier each year.

Most people, of course, drive to Mount Rainier rather than climb it. There are 147 miles of roads and 240 miles of maintained trails in the park and five areas that serve as bases for exploration: Longmire (southwest corner), Paradise (south side), Ohanapecosh (southeast corner), Sunrise/White River (northeast side), and Carbon River/Mowich Lake (northwest corner).

GETTING THERE

Year-round access to Mount Rainier National Park from Seattle and Tacoma is via WA 7 and WA 706 to the Nisqually entrance in the southwest corner of the park, which leads to Longmire and Paradise. Summer access is available via WA 410 on the north and east sides of the park, which leads to Sunrise and also provides summer access to WA 123 in the southeast corner of the park (at Ohanapecosh). The Carbon River/Mowich Lake area (in the park's northwest corner) is accessed via WA 410 and WA 165 through Wilkeson.

Admission to Mount Rainier National Park is $10 per motor vehicle or $5 per person for pedestrians, motorcyclists, and bicyclists. Park roads are winding and road shoulders are narrow. The maximum speed limit is 35 miles per hour (56 kph) in most areas, so allow plenty of travel time during your visit. Parking can be difficult or impossible to find on sunny summer weekends at Paradise, Sunrise, Grove of the Patriarchs near Ohanapecosh, and trailheads between Longmire and Paradise. Try to visit these areas on weekdays, arrive early in the day, and carpool to the park. Parking is not permitted along road edges.

ACCOMMODATIONS

Accommodations in the park range from camping to staying at lodges. Two of the park's campgrounds—**Cougar Rock** and **Ohanapecosh Campgrounds**—take reservations (National Park Reservation Service; 800-365-2267; http://reservations.nps.gov), which should be made several months in advance for summer weekends.

The **National Park Inn** (360-569-2275 for reservations), located in Longmire in the southwest corner of the park, is a rustic lodge built in 1917 and opened in 1920. The guest lodge features 117 guest rooms, the Glacier Lounge, and a gift shop offering Native American crafts. In 1919 Hans Fraehnke, a German carpenter, designed and built much of the decorative woodwork that exists today, including a rustic piano and a 14-foot grandfather clock.

Paradise Inn (360-569-2275 for reservations) is high on the south flanks of Mount Rainier in an area aptly known as Paradise. The lodge should be booked early because it is popular. Cedar-shake siding, huge exposed beams, cathedral ceilings, and a gigantic stone fireplace make this the quintessential mountain retreat. It offers breathtaking views of the mountain. Paradise is also the starting point for miles of trails.

The nearby town of **Ashford** (www.gonorthwest.com/washington/cascades/ashford/ashford.htm) also offers a range of accommodations including B&Bs, lodges, and motels.

RESTAURANTS

In the park, the **National Park Inn's dining room** at Longmire provides a wide selection of meals and is fully accessible to those using wheelchairs. The **Paradise Inn dining room** (summer only) is also accessible to wheelchairs by a walkway leading from the lobby. The **Jackson Grill** in the Jackson Visitor Center at Paradise is accessible to wheelchair users with help via steep paved ramps. The **Sunrise Lodge** snack bar is accessible by ramp.

The Henry M. Jackson Memorial Visitor Center at Paradise in Mount Rainier National Park
Courtesy of Tacoma Regional Convention & Visitor Bureau

ATTRACTIONS

Just inside the Nisqually entrance is Longmire, where you'll find the National Park Inn; the **Longmire Museum,** which has exhibits on the park's natural and human history; a hiker information center that issues backcountry permits; and in winter a ski-touring center where you can rent cross-country skis and snowshoes. From Longmire, take the road up to **Paradise viewpoint** at an elevation of 5,400-feet (1,646 m), and you'll have a view of the mountain itself, weather permitting. It's a popular place, so expect crowds. In July and August, the meadows are ablaze with wildflowers. The circular **Henry M. Jackson Memorial Visitor Center** provides 360-degree panoramic views, and nearby is a spot from which you can see the Nisqually Glacier. The visitor center has a variety of exhibits, including 3-D maps, educational discussions with Park Service personnel, and a food concession.

Tours and Sightseeing

If you don't want to make the drive yourself, **Gray Line Tours** (206-626-5208, 1-800-426-7532) offers daily trips from Seattle to Paradise from May 1 to September 30. The **Rainier Shuttle** (360-569-2331) offers daily shuttle service from Sea-Tac Airport to Ashford on WA 706 just outside the park or to Paradise from May 3 to October 10. The **Ashford Mountain Center** (360-569-2604) offers shuttle services from June through September from Sea-Tac Airport to destinations within the park. Most visitors are satisfied with the trip to Paradise, where they can find the Paradise Inn, the Jackson Memorial Visitor Center, and nearby wildflower walks in summer.

RECREATION

Climbing to the top of Mount Rainier can be extremely dangerous. Over the years, many knowledgeable climbers have lost their lives doing so. Depending on your route, it takes two to three days for most parties to reach the top. Guided groups start at Paradise Ranger Station for Camp Muir at 10,000 feet (3,048 m) the first day and then head to the top the next day. There are two ways to make the climb: on your own or with a guide service such as **Rainier Mountaineering** (360-569-2982). Unless you're an experienced climber with a long list of credits, you are required to climb with a guide service. If you plan to climb with your own party, you have to register at one of the ranger stations in Mount Rainier National Park. Rangers will make sure you have adequate experience and the proper equipment, collect the climbing fee, and tell you about routes, avalanche conditions, and the weather forecast. You must also check in with them when you come down.

Hiking

At 6,400 feet, **Sunrise** (northeast side) is the highest spot in the park accessible by car, and an old lodge serves as the visitor center. From here, you can see not only Mount Rainier but also Mounts Baker and Adams. Some of the park's most scenic trails begin at Sunrise, which is usually less crowded than **Paradise** (south side). At both places, you choose from a good variety of hikes ranging from short, flat nature walks to long, steep, out-and-back hikes—or the around-the-mountain Wonderland Trail.

At the southeastern corner of the park is the **Ohanapecosh** region, where a short hike takes you to Silver Falls. The trail starts at the Ohanapecosh Campground and heads north through the Ohanapecosh Hot Springs, then follows the Old Boundary Trail out to the falls. Here the Ohanapecosh River falls almost 80 feet, producing a silver mist. You can take the bridge at the base of the falls to make the hike a 3-mile loop or simply return as you came. At Stevens Canyon just north of Ohanapecosh, be sure to stop and hike the

Grove of the Patriarchs Trail. This 1.2-mile self-guided interpretive trail passes through ancient stands of 1,000-year-old western red cedar and Douglas fir, which rise above you and block out the sun.

Olympic Peninsula

On the northwestern coast of Washington State is the Olympic Peninsula, which on a map looks like a giant thumb sticking out of Puget Sound. With mountains and seashores that are often shrouded in fog or rain-laden clouds, this vast area embraces some 5,000 square miles, about the size of the island of Kauai in the Hawaiian Islands. Like Kauai, it could easily eat up a week's vacation time. Dominated by Olympic National Park, it is sparsely inhabited along a narrow sliver of land that rims its borders. The park is a primeval place where glaciers drop off sheer cliff faces into the temperate rain forest (one of only three in the entire world) below, and where America's largest herd of Roosevelt elk roam mostly unseen. The coastlines are just about the only part of the peninsula anyone sees, because its core is wild and roadless, accessible only to hikers.

Near Cape Alava on the Olympic Peninsula are the remains of Ozette, an ancient Makah hunting and fishing village that was buried in a mud slide 500 years ago. It had been occupied for at least 2,000 years, and archaeologists working at the site have found more than

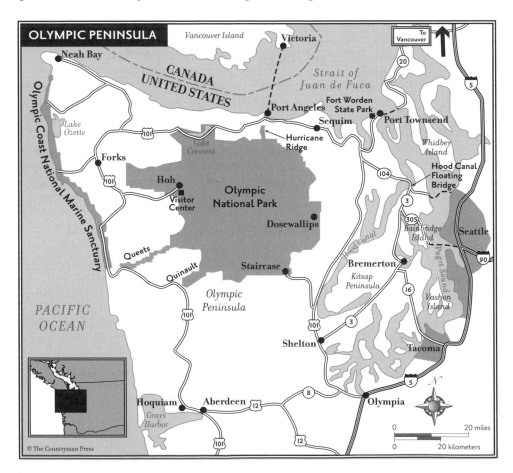

50,000 artifacts, including a remarkable effigy of an orca whale. At a fishing station near the mouth of the Hoko River, at the north end of the Olympic Peninsula, artifacts date back 3,000 years.

On the west side of the Olympic Peninsula, the Hoh, Queets, and Quinault river valleys make up most of the Olympic rain forest. Only about 150 inches (381 cm) of rain falls here yearly, as compared to more than 400 inches (1,016 cm) on the island of Kauai in the Hawaiian chain. But it does the job. Some of the largest trees in the world are found here, including the world's largest western hemlock (in the Quinault river valley), the largest Douglas fir (in the Queets), and the largest red alder (in the Hoh river valley). The four major species that grow in the rain forest—Sitka spruce, western red cedar, Douglas fir, and western hemlock—average 200 feet (61 m), with the tallest being in excess of 300 feet (91 m).

Although the largest mountains on the peninsula are not particularly high, with the tallest, Mount Olympus, being 8,000 feet (2,438 m), they do capture the moisture-laden clouds that sweep off the coast at the end of a 2,000-mile (3,218 km) ocean voyage. The area creates its own ambience, a pillow of quiet in which the smells and silence are almost smothering. The areas protected by the park have never been logged, so life here has been uninterrupted since prehistoric days, with nature growing upon itself generation after generation. Enormous trees grow out of long-decayed "nurse logs" that serve as a breeding ground for new life; club moss drapes eerily over branches and hangs down like uncut hair; ferns and mosses, skunk cabbage, lichens, bunchberry, and vanilla leaf cover nearly every inch of the forest floor so that you won't hear your own footsteps as you pass through. In summer, the sunshine, delightful as it might be, seems out of place.

Port Townsend, named in 1792 by Capt. George Vancouver, is a picture-perfect town situated on the northwestern corner of the Olympic Peninsula, where the Strait of Juan de Fuca meets Puget Sound in full view of the Olympic Mountains. Founded in 1851, a few months before Seattle, the town was soon crawling with sawmills and gold seekers. Anticipating a linkup with the transcontinental railroad—after building its own rail line—the community was soon the home of elegant Victorian mansions and a collection of commercial buildings. Today it's a working artists' colony, restored by writers, artists, and preservation-minded citizens into one of the most livable communities in the state. And, yes, it can be a tourist trap if you let it, but there's more than enough real character to the place.

GETTING THERE

US 101 circles the Olympic Peninsula, with main entrances to Olympic National Park at Lake Crescent south of Port Angeles and at the Hoh River south of Forks. There are several ways to access the entire peninsula from Seattle. One way is via I-5 south through Tacoma and Olympia, and then US 101 north along Hood Canal and the east side of Olympic National Park, past Staircase and Dosewallips at the foot of the Olympic mountain range. At Discovery Bay, WA 20 detours into the charming town of Port Townsend, a place you definitely should not miss; US 101 continues on to the towns of Gardiner, Sequim, and Port Angeles on the peninsula's north side. Port Angeles is the northern entry into Olympic National Park (and from there you can catch a ferry across the Strait of Juan de Fuca to Victoria; see below).

You can also travel around the west coast of the peninsula from Olympia by taking US 101 north and then US 12 west to Aberdeen and Hoquiam, where you link up with US 101 north again. The drive along the west coast of the peninsula takes you through the town of Forks and the park's temperate rain forest along the shores of Lake Crescent on the peninsula's north side, eventually reaching Port Angeles.

Combining these two routes circumnavigates the entire peninsula. But if you want to skip the long drive up the peninsula's west coast, you can take the ferry from downtown Seattle to Bainbridge Island (described earlier in this chapter), from where you can take WA 305 to WA 3 at Fort Madison and then cross the Hood Canal Bridge via WA 104 to US 101. The 6,471-foot (1,972 m) Hood Canal floating bridge connects the Kitsap Peninsula to the Olympic Peninsula. Hood Canal is not really a canal but a tidal inlet. This route cuts hours off the drive to Port Townsend, Port Angeles, and the national park's northern entrance or to the east side of the park along Hood Canal. The downside is that you miss some spectacular scenery.

Horizon Air (1-800-547-9308; www.horizonair.com) flies between Sea-Tac Airport and Port Angeles. Rental cars are available in Port Angeles from **Budget Rent-A-Car** (www.budget.com).

Two ferries, one for foot passengers only and the other for vehicles and foot passengers, connect Port Angeles and Victoria, British Columbia. The ferry terminal for both is at the corner of Laurel Street and Railroad Avenue in Port Angeles. **Victoria Express** (360-452-8088, 1-800-633-1589; www.victoriaexpress.com) is the faster of the two and carries foot passengers only. This ferry runs only between Memorial Day weekend and the end of September. The **Black Ball Transport** (360-457-4491, 250-386-2202 in Victoria; www .cohoferry.com) ferry operates year-round except for two weeks in late January or early February and carries vehicles as well as walk-on passengers. The crossing takes slightly more than one and a half hours.

You can also reach the peninsula via the year-round **Keystone ferry** (www.wsdot.wa .gov/ferries), a 30-minute run between Port Townsend and Whidbey Island, which is connected to the mainland north of Seattle by the Mukilteo ferry.

INFORMATION

For more information on Port Angeles and the rest of the northern Olympic Peninsula, contact the **North Olympic Peninsula Visitor and Convention Bureau** (338 W. First St., Ste. 104, P.O. Box 670, Port Angeles, WA 98362; 360-452-8552, 1-800-942-4042; www .northwestsecretplaces.com) or the **Port Angeles Chamber of Commerce Visitors Center** (121 E. Railroad Ave., Port Angeles, WA 98362; 360-452-2363, 1-877-456-8372; www.port angeles.org). For information about the national park, contact **Olympic National Park** (600 E. Park Ave., Port Angeles, WA 98362-6798; 360-565-3131, 360-565-3130; www.nps .gov/olym). Park admission is $10 per vehicle and $5 per pedestrian or cyclist.

ACCOMMODATIONS

There's lots of lodging in the region, ranging from motels in Aberdeen/Hoquiam, Forks, and Port Angeles to elegant living in Port Townsend. The **Bishop Victorian Hotel** (714 Washington St., Port Townsend; 360-385-6122; www.bishopvictorian.com) is a Victorian-built brick building a block off Water Street and has suites with kitchenettes and a lovely garden. The **Tides Inn** (1807 Water St., Port Townsend; 360-385-0595; www.tides-inn .com) is another Port Townsend set; it was used in filming *An Officer and a Gentleman* and has a good view of the town. The **Ann Starrett Mansion** (744 Clay St., Port Townsend; 360-385-3205; www .starrettmansion.com) is an elegant B&B and the most ornate in Port Townsend. Today, the perfectly restored rose and teal mansion has a three-story turret that towers over the front door, and in every room are period antiques. Several of the former officers' houses at **Fort Worden State Park** (200 Battery Way, Port Townsend; 360-344-4434; www.parks.wa.gov/vacationhouses/ftworden.asp) are available for rental, and with up to six bedrooms each, this is a bargain for large families or a small group. The **Palace Hotel** (1004 Water St., Port Townsend; 360-385-0773, 1-800-962-0741; www.palacehotelpt. com) is a restored Victorian hotel that was built in 1889 and was used as a hotel and brothel. Today, only the hotel is still active!

RESTAURANTS

In all the towns you encounter on the Olympic Peninsula, you'll find places to fill up when you're hungry. For a memorable meal, Port Townsend locals eat at the **Landfall Restaurant** (412 Water St.; 360-385-5814), but for a unique dining experience try the **Manresa Castle** (Seventh and Sheridan, Port Townsend; 360-385-5750), located in an 1897 hilltop inn that overlooks the town.

The view of Mount Olympus from Hurricane Ridge is spectacular. Valerie Henschel

Port Townsend Historic District and its waterfront as seen from Port Townsend Bay

ATTRACTIONS

Gardens and Parks

Fort Worden State Park (360-344-4400), once a military installation that guarded the mouth of Puget Sound, is north of the Port Townsend Historic District. Built at the turn of the 20th century, it is now a 360-acre state park. Many of the fort's old wooden buildings have been restored and put to new uses. The Fort Worden Commanding Officer's House has been fully restored and is filled with period antiques.

Olympic National Park encompasses three distinctly different ecosystems: rugged, glacier-capped mountains; more than 60 miles of wild Pacific coast accessed via Lake Ozette; and magnificent stands of old-growth temperate rain forest. It's a wilderness park, with most of its interior accessible only by hiking trails. In the park are eight wildflower species found nowhere else, the continent's largest elk population, and world-record-size trees. There are no poisonous reptiles or insects, and the only problem plants are stinging nettle and devil's club.

The park's wilderness information center is located near Port Angeles, with access to Hurricane Ridge, one of the most popular destinations in the park. This northern part of Olympic National Park is the most accessible, and it's where you'll find the most tourists. If you take the Heart of the Hills/Hurricane Ridge Road from Port Angeles into Olympic National Park, you'll climb 5,200 feet (1,585 m) in just 17 miles (27 km). From Hurricane Ridge you have a breathtaking view of Mount Olympus, the highest in the Olympics range at 7,965 feet (2,428 m). Visitors to Hurricane Ridge can eat in the day lodge and walk through meadows atop the mountain while deer, for which the ridge is famous, wander nearby. In winter, the lodge serves as a ski lodge for downhill and cross-county skiers.

The annual snowfall of 400 feet (122 m) is how the area's 50 glaciers stay icy during the summer. Down below, the Bogachiel, Hoh, Queets, and Quinault river valleys are the park's rain collectors, with between 150 and 200 inches (381–508 cm) falling annually.

If you take winding US 101 west from Port Angeles through the mountains you'll reach another of the park's accessible sites, Lake Crescent, with a handsome lodge, lake access, and short paths to waterfalls and pools. US 101 continues around the peninsula's west side, where, about halfway along the coast at Forks, you can drive about 19 miles east into the park to the Hoh Rain Forest Visitor Center. Here, vast amounts of information is available about the wildlife, botany, and history of the region, and short trails wander through the immense, mossy forest.

Historic Buildings and Sites

Strolling through the **Port Townsend Historic District,** you have the impression that time has stood still. Many of the restored old homes have become bed-and-breakfast inns, antiques shops line the streets, and grand old mansions are open for viewing. It was in 1961, just prior to the opening of the Seattle World's Fair, that residents decided to do something about the decaying town and set about restoring its old buildings. By 1976 they had achieved enough to be granted status as a National Historic District. Water Street is the main thoroughfare in the historic district, where you'll find art galleries, craft shops, and antique stores as well as an unending series of small delis and restaurants. Because much of the town was erected at about the same time as Seattle's Pioneer Square, there's a similarity in architectural styles. Most notable are the Daniel Hogan House, the Bartlett House, and the Ann Starett Mansion (see Accommodations). The Starrett Mansion was built in 1889 for $6,000 as a wedding present for Ann Starrett from her husband, George. He was the city's leading contractor and once boasted that he had built up to 350 houses. Even if you're staying elsewhere, you can take a tour of the house for $2.

There are a number of wonderful Victorian house restorations in the uptown district atop the hill. The Rothschild House (Franklin and Taylor Streets) has original furniture and is regularly open to the public. Built in 1868, it's a good example of the Greek Revival houses that were prefabricated in New England and transported to Pacific coast settlements.

Museums

The **Jefferson County Historical Museum** (end of Water St., Port Townsend) is worth a stop. At Fort Worden State Park, you can learn about life below the waters of Puget Sound at the **Port Townsend Marine Science Center** (532 Battery Way, Port Townsend; 360-385-5582; www.ptmsc.org). Tide-pool touch tanks are alive with crabs, starfish, anemones, and other marine life, and an exhibit on the area's natural history has fossils from around the peninsula.

Nightlife and Other Pleasures

If old things aren't what you have in mind, Port Townsend has the **Upstage** (923 Washington St.; 360-385-2216), formerly the Back Alley Tavern, for food mixed with live music, theater, and a lot of local color. The historic **Maxwell's Pub** (636 Waterfront Pl.—at the corner of Quincy St. and Water St.; 360-379-6438) has an assortment of pool tables, a huge bar, and fine music; you may recognize it from *An Officer and a Gentleman,* which was filmed here, when it was called the Town Tavern.

Tours and Sightseeing

Port Townsend's biannual house tours in May and September bring visitors to the multi-colored Victorian homes. Stop off at the **Port Townsend Chamber of Commerce** visitor information center (2437 E. Sims Way; 360-385-7869; www.ptchamber.org/tourism.html) for historic site maps. The Jefferson County Historical Museum at the end of Water Street is open for tours, as are the City Hall, Customs House, Jefferson County Courthouse, and Bell Tower.

The only way to see the town at its best is to walk it. Guided one-hour walking tours of the Port Townsend Historic District are at 2 pm every Saturday, beginning at the Jefferson County Historical Museum in **Old City Hall** (540 Water St.; 360-385-1003).

Entertainment and the Arts

In Port Townsend, the **Key City Playhouse** (419 Washington St.; 360-385-7396) provides live theater throughout the year.

RECREATION

Hiking

Because so much of the Olympic Peninsula is accessible only on foot, bring along your hiking boots to get a good feel for the place. There's no end to where you can hike. **Olympic National Park** is a logical venue, with 600 miles of designated trails and 955 designated campsites. But you don't have to go inside the park itself to satisfy your hiking cravings; many trails and back roads lace the entire region. There are beaches to comb, rain forests to explore, and a lot of mountain and high-country trails.

On the northwest side of Sequim, on the north shore of the Olympic Peninsula, are Dungeness Spit and the **Dungeness National Wildlife Refuge** (360-457-8451), a remarkable stretch of sand 7 miles long. Open daily from sunrise to sunset, this narrow strip of sand and gravel is the longest natural sand spit in the United States, jutting into Dungeness Bay and providing a haven for hundreds of species of birds. If you're up for the 14-mile round-trip hike, you'll find a lonely lighthouse at the end of the spit, but check tide tables to make sure that you don't get stuck out there. Note that pets are not allowed on the spit.

North of the Kalaloch information station on US 101, on the Pacific shore, six different beaches can be reached by short paths from the road. The wave action can be spectacular, especially during the storm season, November to March. Besides the many camping areas here, **Kalaloch Lodge** (157151 US 101; 866-525-2562) has cozy oceanfront cabins, log cabins with Franklin fireplaces, and a variety of guest rooms that suit any vacationer's lifestyle.

SHOPPING

On Water Street in Port Townsend, you'll find a wild collection of stores for virtually every interest. And the **Port Townsend Antique Mall** (802 Washington St.) has some 40 shops under one roof, certainly enough to create cobwebs in anyone's mind.

Events

Port Townsend's **Rhododendron Festival** (in May) is colorful. The **Centrum Summer Arts Festival** (July/August) is one of the most successful cultural programs in the state, is held at Fort Worden State Park in Port Townsend. The **Wooden Boat Festival** (in September) is a combination of sailboats and eclectic design in Port Townsend.

VANCOUVER

Gastown's steam clock in Vancouver's birthplace
Toshi

3

VANCOUVER

Saltwater Sophisticate

Vancouver is a physical city. That fact dictates virtually everything that is done within and outside the city limits. Stand at any point in the city, look around, and it becomes obvious why Vancouver is an outdoor enthusiast's dream. Worldwide, only Rio de Janeiro and Hong Kong can compete with Vancouver's spectacular setting which integrates mountains, city, and ocean.

Five minutes from downtown, to the north, are the Coast Mountains, where you can ski in the winter and hike the many trails that lace the North Shore in the summer. The well-sheltered harbor opens up into the Strait of Georgia and Howe Sound to the west, beckoning visitors to explore the beauty of the region. The mountainous forests across Burrard Inlet dominate the North Shore communities of West Vancouver and North Vancouver, whose residents regularly encounter black bears, deer, and the occasional mountain lion. Waterways including the Fraser River still carry migrating salmon to their spawning areas upstream. Now and then an orca whale takes a wrong turn at the entrance to English Bay and swims into the harbor. Coyotes are seen throughout Vancouver's city parks, and amused golfers often wait until the wily critters have crossed fairways. And bald eagles are so common a daily sight that when they hover overhead, they're usually ignored.

Vancouver has a casual play ethic, and residents and visitors alike enjoy the city to the hilt. Surprising to many visitors, Vancouver is literally surrounded by sand, beginning at Stanley Park (Third Beach, Second Beach, English Bay Beach, and Sunset Beach) and winding along both sides of Point Grey (Kitsilano Beach, Jericho Beach, Locarno Beach, and Spanish Banks Beach). Each beach has a distinct character with different activities. For a real adventure, walk over to Wreck Beach, on the southern shore of Point Grey just below the University of British Columbia's sand bluffs. This is Vancouver's unofficial nude beach, where suntanning is, well, complete and those wearing clothes are viewed as suspicious characters.

When you walk around Vancouver, look at the faces. It's like being in the lobby of the United Nations. The city is arguably the most international city on the continent, exceeded only by New York in its ethnic diversity. Whole sections of the city and suburbs have become ethnic centers, with large populations of East Asian, Chinese, Japanese, Italian, Greek, and other cultural origins giving the city its unique international flavor. A large part of the city's character is borrowed from and exhibits the myths of the aboriginal peoples who inhabited the region thousands of years ago as well as today.

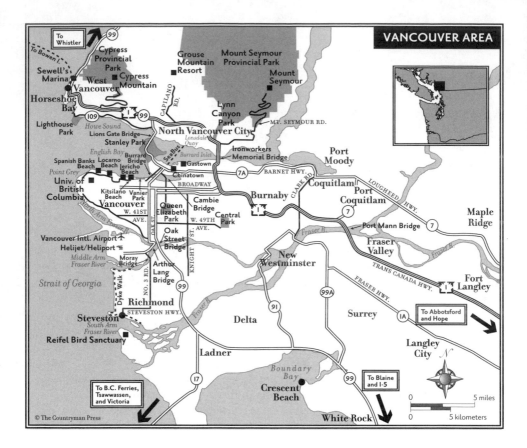

The old Vancouver of 25 years ago, with its prim and proper, staid British traditions, where a stiff upper lip was a sign of position, no longer exists. Because Vancouver is Canada's major entry point from the Far East, expect a United Nations of languages, colors, costumes, and foods. It's because of this rich cultural mix that Vancouverites tend to be more tolerant of lifestyles and customs than are other cities. It's why the city, with just a little discourse, willingly accepted shopping centers that had only Chinese writing on all of their signs.

After English and Chinese, the most common languages spoken in Vancouver are Punjabi, German, French, Italian, Tagalog (Filipino), and Spanish. But languages aren't necessarily an accurate indicator of the diverse population, much of which is composed of third- and fourth-generation Vancouverites who have been integrated into the mainstream of Vancouver society and whose mother tongue is now English.

In the late 1960s and early 1970s, a movement tried to create a series of expressways leading out of the city, just as in Seattle and other North American cities. It would have cut through portions of Chinatown's residential district. That was the first big battle between city planners/developers and those who refused to bow to progress. The city has been fighting that kind of progress ever since.

Vancouver is, after all, the birthplace of Greenpeace, the international ecological organization that had its origins in a Vancouver basement in 1969 after the United States detonated a nuclear weapon in the Aleutians. Since then, the organization has been active worldwide, with branches in 30 countries and a total membership of more than five million. Oddly, in Vancouver the organization receives no more or less support than anywhere else in the world, because Greenpeace is often at odds with the local forestry industry and politics.

Life in Vancouver is a sensual collection of lifestyles, with more restaurants for the city's population than anywhere else in Canada and the most varied cuisines imaginable. According to national statistics, Vancouver dwellers read more, shop more, eat out more, drink more wine, spend more on sporting equipment, smoke less, and take longer coffee breaks than those who live in the more wintery climates in the rest of Canada.

HISTORY

Unlike most of Canada's major cities, Vancouver has had a somewhat bland history, with no experiences of war, rebellion, or foreign occupation, although hostilities once almost broke out between Canada and the United States over a pig that was shot on a nearby island (see History in chapter 1). The first permanent residents were the Coast Salish native peoples, split into a group of tribes that included the Musqueam, who lived by the mouth of the Fraser River and along the shores of Burrard Inlet and English Bay. Between the Musqueam, the Kwantlen, and the Squamish tribes who lived north and east of present-day Vancouver, thousands of seasonal and permanent residents lived in the Vancouver region long before the first Europeans arrived.

When Spanish explorer Jose Maria Narvaez sailed into what is now English Bay in 1791, he was greeted and shown the area by the local native settlement. A year later, in 1792, Capt. George Vancouver explored the area and named Point Grey, Burrard's Inlet, and Robert's Bank for his fellow explorers. Burrard Inlet, as it's known today, is now Vancouver's busy harbor.

Haida totem pole at the Museum of Anthropology on the University of British Columbia campus Toshi

Vancouver's namesake himself was of Dutch descent. He joined the British Navy at the age of 13 and eventually served with Captain Cook on his second and third voyages around the world. In 1791 Captain Vancouver was on his own, in charge of the HMS *Discovery* on a voyage around the Cape of Good Hope on commission from the British government to survey the northern Pacific coast of North America.

Vancouver was also told by the British Admiralty to negotiate a land settlement with Spanish Capt. Bodega y Quadra at Nootka Sound, on what is now known as Vancouver Island. But the Spaniard had already charted the entire region well in advance of Vancouver's arrival and so claimed all of the land he saw for King George III. Pleased with himself, he returned to England in 1797, where he died three years later at age 40. The Spanish, in what became a major bad decision, were involved with the Mexican revolution and simply walked away from their claims to the Pacific Northwest. Spain became an ally of Britain during the French Revolution, but by 1795 it's influence in the region had diminished and it abandoned the West Coast.

Capt. Vancouver nonetheless relied on Spanish charts and never changed the area's Spanish names. So the original names, such as those of the Strait of Juan de Fuca and Quadra Island, still reflect Spain's former glories. In 1808 British explorer Simon Fraser, looking for fur-trading routes, arrived at the mouth of what's now known as the Fraser River and found himself face to face with the resident native peoples, who proceeded to chase him away. But Fraser's explorations opened the door for other European expeditions, mostly British, and in 1824 a Hudson's Bay Company expedition arrived, building a trading post three years later at Fort Langley, about 12 miles (20 km) up the Fraser River from what is now Vancouver.

The first significant immigration of white settlement came in the mid-1860s, attracted by the trees and their lumber potential. In 1862 Sewell Prescott Moody, originally from Maine, established the area's first sawmill at the eastern end of Burrard Inlet in what's known today as Port Moody. The city really took off with the linking of British Columbia to the rest of Canada through the Canadian Pacific Railway (CPR) in 1886, the same year in which Vancouver was incorporated. Many of the 10,000 Chinese who had been brought to Canada specifically to build the transcontinental railway for the CPR settled in Vancouver when the project was finished, establishing what is the present Chinatown just south of Gastown. They were forced into their own community because of racist housing policies at the time.

Since then, not only has Vancouver been a gateway into Asia, but it also serves as an entryway into America. Consequently, business interests on both sides of the Pacific became familiar with the city. Thus, investing in the city after the Second World War seemed a natural extension of Asia's many business interests. The result has been almost continuous growth since the 1960s. Viewed as neutral territory between Asia and the United States, the city is one of North America's busiest ports.

Vancouver's historical financial roots have always been based on the forestry industry. Though forestry employs the most people overall throughout British Columbia even today, the past couple of decades have seen the city make a conscious effort to diversify its economy. There is a vibrant high-tech industry, an international banking community, and a burgeoning film industry. In some ways Vancouver is a branch-plant city, with many of the city's businesses having their corporate head offices in Toronto or Montreal. That's not surprising, considering that the economic center of the nation resides east of Manitoba. Nonetheless, Greater Vancouver is headquarters for some 160 major corporations, accounting for $60 billion a year in total worldwide revenue.

Thanks to the fact that Burrard Inlet, Vancouver's major harbor, is one of the world's largest natural harbors, deep and ice free all year, Vancouver is a major North American port. Along with the nearby coal superport of Roberts Bank in Delta, south of Vancouver, the area handles more tonnage than any city on the West Coast and is among the top five ports in the Western Hemisphere. Freighters anchored in English Bay awaiting their cargoes of grain, sulfur, coal, potash, iron ore, forest products, and copper are as much of the Vancouver landscape as the mountains and city skyline.

Downtown Vancouver's green spaces and high-rises Toshi

The average cost of doing things in the city doesn't seem different from that of other major cities in North America. But the difference in the Canadian dollar in relationship to other currencies makes Vancouver considerably cheaper than Chicago, New York, San Francisco, Tokyo, and London.

WEATHER

It rains a lot here. But the annual rainfall of 57 inches (144 cm) translates to good skiing weather on the local mountains in winter and to green shrubs in spring and summer. Between July and October, the weather is sunny and mild. On average, Vancouver gets 45 days of fog, 168 days of rain, and 80 days without measurable sunshine, usually between the end of October and April. Monthly hours of sunshine average 305 in July and 44 in December. Spring comes early, and winter never stays long. Moderated by the Pacific Ocean currents, Vancouver's weather is the mildest in Canada, with daytime temperatures averaging 70 degrees F (20 degrees C) in summer and 35 degrees F (2.4 degrees C) at the coldest periods during the winter.

Once a decade, there's a snowstorm that lasts two or three days. Residents generally just wait for the rain to melt it. But there can also be 45 or even 60 straight days of sunshine in the summer, and the falls are gorgeous, with a combination of fresh, fog-shrouded mornings, sunny afternoons, and often clear, crisp evenings.

The diversity of terrain results in huge variations in average hours of sunshine, rainfall, snow, and average temperatures, sometimes over short distances. For example, the average yearly precipitation in White Rock, a small community just south of Vancouver, is 43 inches (109.2 cm). Less than 30 miles (50 km) away in North Vancouver, the North Shore mountains force clouds to rise and release their moisture, producing yearly rainfall averaging 73 inches (185.9 cm). Vancouver Airport, located south of the city in Richmond, records about 39 inches (100 cm) of rain each year.

Summertime is reliably sunny and warm (not hot), and with a frequent ocean breeze. June is a wet month. July, August, September, and October are the driest months. Summer average highs are 70–80 degrees F (mid-20s C), but evenings can be cool, so a sweater, even in July, is not out of place, though you may not need it. Just bring along a light jacket in the summer, rain gear year-round, and light winter wear for December through March.

If it's blossoms you want, visit in March and April, when a succession of ornamental cherry and plum trees bloom. From May onward, it's simply glorious when the rhododendrons and azaleas are in full bloom. Remember, however, that while June may be wonderful in many parts of the world, it's not so in Vancouver, where it can be cool and wet.

GETTING THERE

By Car

If you're arriving by car from the south, you'll likely travel via I-5 through the border crossing at Blaine, Washington. It becomes BC 99 on the Canadian side and takes you into Vancouver via the Oak Street Bridge. Watch the signs at the bridge for directions. The most direct route into downtown is via Granville Street; though Oak Street is a six-lane thorough-fare, it ends at False Creek, short of the downtown core. But you won't get lost following Oak Street. A sign directs you to turn west at 19th Avenue, which links up to Hemlock Street, where you turn right, go down the hill across Broadway, and across the Granville Street Bridge into downtown. The view driving across the Granville Street Bridge is spectacular, so pay attention to the road. No one drives the 30-miles-per-hour (50 kmph) speed limit. A U.S. driver's license is good in Canada.

If you're arriving from Victoria via **BC Ferries** (250-386-3431 (US and outside British Columbia); 1-888-223-3779 (in BC); www.bcferries.bc.ca), exit the ferry and drive straight along BC 17 until you reach the freeway, BC 99. Cross the Oak Street Bridge and drive along Oak as described above.

By Air

If you arrive by air, you'll most likely arrive at Vancouver International Airport (YVR), located in the suburb of Richmond, about 10 miles (16 km) from downtown Vancouver. Virtually every major North American and international airline serves the city, including American, United, Air Canada, Lufthansa, Continental, Singapore, Northwest, Alaska, Horizon, Delta, Qantas, Air New Zealand, Japan Airlines, and KLM.

But there are other air gateways into and out of Vancouver. The seaplane terminal, near the Westin Bayshore Hotel, services a variety of coastal communities. There's also helicopter service between downtown Vancouver and Victoria, with a heliport next to the Convention Centre downtown. The old terminal at Vancouver International Airport services both land and seaplane service into British Columbia communities, lodges, and resorts.

Vancouver International Airport

When you land at **Vancouver International Airport** (www.yvr.ca) and walk through the terminal, take a look around you. The 46 large skylights, generous open spaces, and nearly 300,000 square feet (27,000 sq. m) of glass walls offer dramatic views of the surrounding mountains and water. Pillars of local stone and hardwood floors soften the public places; carpet patterns mimic log booms in the nearby Fraser River. Steel columns resemble trees gracefully supporting the roof while branchlike column-struts reduce roof-beam spans, giving the 1.25-million-square-foot (116,000 sq. m) interior an expansive quality.

The two international and domestic terminals are laid out in a crescent shape, with the international wing at the eastern end and the domestic wing in the west, bordering a wide access ramp with ample drop-off zones.

The short-term parking garage is just paces from the arrivals and departures levels. It's an easy, unimpeded walk between wings, with a children's play area between them. Connecting passengers from the United States (E Wing) can quickly walk to the overseas departure gates (D Wing) and a variety of shopping possibilities. Canada flight connections are on the second floor after you exit Customs. Some 175 volunteers in green blazers roam seven days a week, 7 am– 9 pm, awaiting questions.

Vancouver International Airport has a concourse connected directly to the Fairmont Vancouver Airport Hotel. Courtesy of Fairmont Hotels

The terminal is a dramatic combination of technology and tradition, reflecting both contemporary Vancouver and the culture and lifestyle of the Musqueam, the aboriginal peoples who have lived at the mouth of the Fraser River near where the airport is located, for more than 8,000 years. All YVR telephones are data compatible and the Business Center, just behind baggage storage in the International Arrivals area, meets the needs of anyone with a laptop. Copying machines, faxing facilities, Federal Express pickup, and cell phone and pager rentals are available.

Airline lounges, behind security, have better facilities than the Business Center. Air Canada honors United Airlines's Red Carpet Lounge members and Premier Executives cardholders at its Maple Leaf Lounges in the international, transborder, and domestic wings. You also gain entry with a same-day international or transborder first- or business-class boarding pass from any of the Star Alliance partners. The lounges have the latest copying equipment, fax machines, laser printers, and scanners. All facilities are free except for long-distance calls and faxes. The individual workstations have telephones, dataports, and stand-alone computers with Internet access. If privacy is essential, the lounges have workstations in an enclosed area with air conditioning and lighting controls.

If you have a long wait before your flight, look around. Time goes quickly on the main concourse as you walk the length of the international and domestic wings, looking in stores and admiring the art. Native art is everywhere. A dramatic cedar spindle whorl in front of the cascading waterwall confronts you at the customs and immigrations area; traditional hand-created weavings hang from the ceilings everywhere; 20-foot-tall (6 m) red-cedar welcome figures greet you at three arrivals areas; and the massive, $1.3 million "Spirit of Haida Gwaii," a jade green patina bronze casting by the late Native American artist Bill Reid, is the centerpiece of the new international terminal. "Spirit of the Haida Gwaii" is the focal point of the international terminal, spanning 20 feet by 10 feet (6 m by 3 m) and backdropped by a 131-foot by 32-foot (40 m by 10 m) floor-to-ceiling glass structure by artist Lutz Haufschild called "The Great Wave Wall."

Entertaining your children is easy, with the play area between the international and domestic terminals in constant use. The domestic wing has a new shopping concourse, restaurants, art displays, and services including a barber shop. Retail "streets" are located on the departure levels of both the domestic and international wings and behind the international security gates. Storefronts and passageways reflect British Columbian themes, and the airport's fair pricing policy means that there's no difference between airport and downtown prices. Any retail outlet charging more than the cost of similar items or services in downtown Vancouver can be fined Can$1,500.

Taxis, limos, public bus transportation, courtesy hotel shuttles, and long-term parking transport are accessed immediately outside the international and domestic arrivals areas. Six large baggage carousels—four of which are the world's largest—deliver your bags while separate conveyors sort baggage transfers for international and cruise-ship passengers. Baggage carts are plentiful and free.

Taxis to downtown (30 minutes) are between Can$25 and $30. The Airporter bus leaves every 30 minutes with rates at $12 one-way and $18 round-trip, with discounts for seniors (65 and older), children (5–12 years), and families. There's also scheduled service from the airport to communities in the Central Fraser Valley and to Whistler Village, the heart of the internationally known ski center ranked North America's number-one ski resort by *Mountain Sports and Living Magazine* (formerly *Snow Country*) for seven consecutive years and by *Skiing Magazine* for the second time in the past three years.

A connecting concourse leads to the **Fairmont Vancouver Airport Hotel** (www.fairmont.com/vancouverairport), a 14-story, $65 million facility managed by Fairmont Hotels and Resorts, a luxury hotel management company jointly owned by Fairmont Hotels and Canadian Pacific Hotels. The hotel, which opened October 7, 1999, is the first hotel in the world to offer guests a seamless connection from hotel room to airline seat. It is one of the world's most technologically advanced hotels and the first in the world to allow airline check-in from your hotel room. (The Fairmont and other nearby hotels in Richmond are described under Accommodations.)

The cruise-ship information counter is directly outside the customs hall, with nearby banking services, currency exchange, and American Express automatic teller machines (ATMs). Be sure to pick up your goods and services tax (GST; 7 percent on all sales items) rebate form at any YVR customer service counter.

By Train

Vancouver is served by **Amtrak** (1-800-872-7245; www.amtrak.com) from Los Angeles, Portland, and Seattle on the Coast Starlight and by **Via Rail Canada** (1-800-561-8630; www.viarail.ca) from eastern Canada. The terminus for both is the old Canadian National Railway station, now called the Pacific Central Station, on Main Street on the southern edge of Chinatown. You can reach the heart of downtown in just a few minutes by cab for about $10 or take the Sky Train from the Main Street station two blocks away. Pacific Central Station is also where you leave and return from Alberta via the superluxurious **Rocky Mountaineer** (1-800-665-7245; www.rockymountaineer.com).

By Bus

The **Airporter** (604-946-8866; www.yvrairporter.com) takes you to and from Vancouver Airport. **Quick Shuttle** (1-800-665-2122; www.quickcoach.com) provides service to Sea-Tac and Bellingham Airports in the United States.

Greyhound Canada (604-482-8747; www.greyhound.ca/en), **Maverick Coach Lines** (604-940-2332; www.maverickcoachlines.bc.ca), and **Pacific Coach Lines** (604-662-8074; www.pacificcoach.com) all provide intercity service throughout British Columbia and beyond, and all leave from Pacific Central Station.

CUSTOMS AND IMMIGRATION

Entering Canada and going through Canada Customs and Immigration is relatively speedy, and there are few entry restrictions. One significant restriction is that Canada considers all drunk-driving convictions as felonies and doesn't permit felons to enter the country. However, visitors from the United States are seldom asked whether they have a criminal record, though that would likely show up if passports are scanned. Much is up to the discretion of the border guard, as it is in crossing the U.S. border. Since 9/11, security has been beefed up at all entry points, so make certain that you have proof of citizenship such as a birth certificate at the minimum. Passports are best. No guns are allowed into Canada except under hunting guidelines, and handguns will be confiscated at the border. Liquor and cigarettes are limited to one liter and 200, respectively, but customs officials are lenient if you're slightly above the limits. Be prepared for long lines, some as long as an hour or more, at the border crossing at Blaine, Washington, on weekends and holidays.

CURRENCY AND LOCAL TAXES

Canadians use the decimal system and the dollar, but the Canadian dollar is worth less than the U.S. dollar. Always try to make your money exchanges at a bank, where you'll get the best exchange rate. ATMs are everywhere—banks, many grocery stores, and even hotels. VISA, Mastercard, and other bank cards will work in them. Canadian bills, like most European currencies, are colored according to their value. The $5 bill is blue; $10 is purple; $20 is green; $50 is red; and $100 is beige. There are $1 coins (nicknamed "loonies") and $2 coins (nicknamed "two-nies").

Taxes include the federal goods and services tax (GST) at 7 percent. Visitors can get it back if they buy more than $100 worth of goods by filling out a rebate form. The British Columbia provincial sales tax is 7 percent, hotel tax is 10 percent, and there's a 10 percent sales tax added to the cost of liquor consumed in bars and restaurants.

INFORMATION

Tourist information is available at Vancouver International Airport just outside the International Arrivals area. In downtown Vancouver, **Tourism Vancouver** (Plaza Level, 200 Burrard St.; 604-683-2000; www.tourismvancouver.com) is located near the cruise ship terminal. If you want business information, contact Vancouver's **Board of Trade** (604-641-1260; www.boardoftrade.com). Remember that in Vancouver you have to dial the 604 prefix even when making a local call.

Vancouver is awash with newspapers. Both dailies—the *Vancouver Sun* and the *Province*—are morning publications. There are also two national newspapers: the *Globe and Mail* and the *National Post*. Entertainment news can be found in both dailies, but Vancouverites go to the *Georgia Straight*, a free publication similar in character to the *Seattle Weekly*. In addition, numerous neighborhood weeklies can be found throughout the city.

Because of the surrounding mountains, Vancouver is almost 100 percent cable saturated, with access to hundreds of Canadian, U.S., and international channels from a variety of cities and countries. Depending on where you're staying in the Lower Mainland, television channel settings can vary. Weekly listings can be found in the Friday editions of the *Vancouver Sun* and *Province*, in *TV Guide*, and in the locally published *TV Week*.

If you're from the United States, you'll notice that Canadians spell things differently, for instance, metre, labour, and centre. Americans pay bills with checks and Canadians do it with cheques. In reality, most Vancouverites and Canadians have adopted a mix of American and British spellings in daily use. Newspapers, for example, use mostly American spelling, even in the use of names. This book uses American spellings except for proper nouns such as the Ministry of Labour or the Pacific Centre Mall.

Metric System

American visitors immediately notice that once they cross the border, weights and measures are in the metric system. Canada uses the metric system, the standard of weights and measurements used in most parts of the world. Instead of miles per hour, speed signs in Canada are in kilometers per hour. If you've traveled to Europe, South America, or Asia, you're likely familiar with this system. If not, most cars have speedometers that provide both kilometers per hour and miles per hour. One meter is 39.4 inches, very close to the 36 inches in a yard. One kilometer is a little more than a half mile. One kilogram is 2.2 pounds.

One liter is a quart plus a quarter cup. Water freezes at 0 degrees Celsius and at 32 degrees Fahrenheit; it boils at 100 degrees C compared to 212 degrees F. You'll soon get the hang of it. Even if you ask for something in pounds or ounces, you'll get what you want.

Holidays

New Year's Day (January 1)
Good Friday (late March or early April)
Victoria Day (May 24 or the preceding Monday)—often close to the U.S. Memorial
    Day holiday
Canada Day (July 1)—close to the United States' July Fourth/Independence Day
British Columbia Day (August 1)
Labor Day (first Monday in September)
Thanksgiving Day (second Monday in October)
Remembrance Day (November 11)—same as Veterans Day in the United States
Christmas Day (December 25)
Boxing Day (December 26)

Telephone Area Codes

In the Vancouver regional district, the area code is 604, which you must dial before dialing the rest of the local number. The rest of the province of British Columbia has the area code 250.

GETTING AROUND

The Greater Vancouver area consists of the city itself plus the suburbs of North Vancouver and West Vancouver on the North Shore; Burnaby, New Westminster, Richmond, Delta, and White Rock to the south; and East Vancouver, Port Moody, Coquitlam, Surrey, and Langley to the east. But don't look for signposts. It's often difficult to recognize where one city ends and the next begins. Because these communities have grown together, moving from one to another often goes unnoticed. Although the region's combined population adds up to about two million, Vancouver proper is only about 521,000.

Collectively, the communities in the Greater Vancouver area are called the Lower Mainland. You'll hear the term *Lower Mainland* mentioned quite often, especially in weather reports. It includes Vancouver and the suburbs, and the region extends, roughly, to the Port Mann Bridge that crosses the Fraser River just beyond New Westminster. The Lower Mainland spreads out between the Fraser River to the south and Burrard Inlet to the north. Beyond its borders are the southern bedroom communities of Richmond (the location of Vancouver International Airport), Delta, Ladner, Surrey, Crescent Beach, and White Rock. Eastward are Burnaby, New Westminster, Port Moody, Coquitlam, Port Coquitlam, Langley, Fort Langley, and Maple Ridge. North of downtown, along the sides of the mountains, are North Vancouver and West Vancouver. Beyond the Lower Mainland are the Lower Fraser Valley and the Upper Fraser Valley, farmland that extends eastward about 93 miles (150 km) to the community of Hope.

The city's outward growth is limited by mountains to the north, the ocean in the west, the U.S. border to the south, and land preserved for agriculture to the east. So the city grows upward, where clouds pose no barrier whatsoever. That's why the downtown core

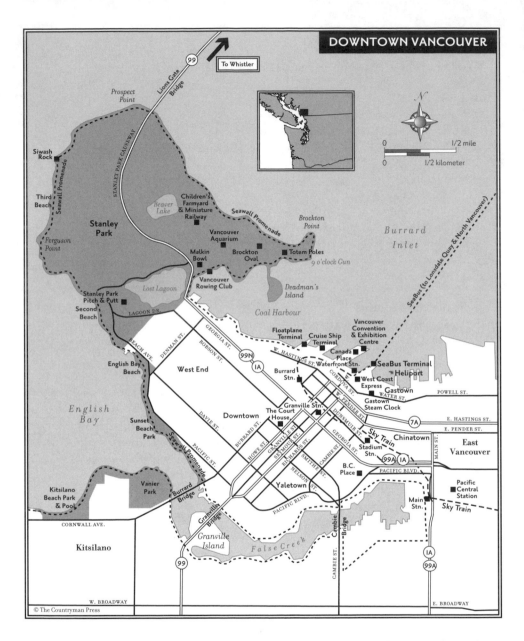

consists of both office towers and high-rise condominiums. The result is a city that isn't deserted after working hours.

Vancouver is downtown oriented, with the major hotels, nightclubs, restaurants, and theaters mainly located within the downtown core, making getting around easy. Vancouver is also one of the most wheelchair-friendly cities in North America, with sidewalks, public transportation, theaters, attractions, most restaurants, museums, and galleries having wheelchair accessibility.

The streets of downtown Vancouver are logical and gridlike, so it's difficult to lose yourself. Find a mountain: that's north. Once you know that, the rest falls into place. Grouse

Mountain in North Vancouver looks down on the Vancouver skyline, and its ski-run lights act as a beacon both in winter and in summer. Beneath it lie the communities of North Vancouver and West Vancouver, spread out along the mountain terrain.

You learn quickly that Vancouver is a walker's city—safe, colorful, vibrant—and that it's a city of neighborhoods. The downtown area, for example, is split into several distinct zones, as important in their character differences as those in San Francisco. There's Chinatown, the third largest in North America behind the ones in San Francisco and New York. Chinatown is such a distinct area that it stands alone, a little nation within the city. There's also Gastown (the historical area), Yaletown, and the West End, all of which are in the downtown area.

The area between Chinatown and the West End is where you'll find the major theaters, the public library, and sports facilities. The West End is downtown's primary residential area, and Yaletown, adjacent to the old Expo '86 grounds, is the city's latest rehabilitation project, where old warehouses are being converted into high-end condos, restaurants, and small shops. The south end of Yaletown and the downtown area, on the south side of Pacific Boulevard, is where you'll find blocks of new high-rise condos, restaurants, and small shops along False Creek. It's a shiny collection of the very new where penthouse condo apartments cost $2 million and upward.

There are also 21 other "local areas" defined within the city limits. You likely won't be able to experience them all, but you can make an entire visit of the city's most colorful, historical, and lively areas.

Driving in the City

Because Vancouver is bounded on three sides by water, you'll eventually have to come to grips with the bridges that connect parts of the city and the suburbs. Be sure you cross them before or after the morning rush hour (7:30–9) and before or after the evening rush hour (3:30–6), or you could be in bridge gridlock. Burrard Inlet, which separates downtown from the North Shore, is spanned by the Lion's Gate Bridge at the north end of Stanley Park and by the Second Narrows Bridge (also called the Ironworkers Memorial Bridge) from the east end of Vancouver. False Creek juts into the heart of the city and is crossed by three bridges: the Cambie Street Bridge (by the BC Place Stadium), the Granville Street Bridge, and the Burrard Street Bridge. The Fraser River is spanned by the Oak Street Bridge (connecting Vancouver to Richmond, the U.S. border, and the ferries to Victoria), the Knight Street Bridge (to eastern Richmond), the Arthur Laing Bridge (to Vancouver International Airport), the Alex Fraser Bridge (from New Westminster and Richmond to Surrey and Delta), the Port Mann Bridge (to the interior of British Columbia), and the Pattulo Bridge (from New Westminster to Surrey).

Several routes in Vancouver are named Marine Drive. Fortunately, they have directional prefixes to designate which one they are. In Vancouver, NW Marine Drive and SW Marine Drive navigate around the Point Grey peninsula, offering magnificent views of the Vancouver skyline, the North Shore, and Howe Sound. On a clear day you can see almost to Whistler. From downtown, go over the Burrard Street Bridge and follow Cornwall Street through Kitsilano. You'll eventually merge into Dunbar; four blocks later, turn right and travel along Fourth Avenue, which merges into NW Marine. It takes you along the waterfront and past beaches where you can stop for photos or to walk in the sand. The road goes around the perimeter of the University of British Columbia and the University Endowment Lands and then becomes SW Marine Drive on the south

Lion's Gate Bridge from Stanley Park leads to Vancouver's North Shore. Toshi

side of the peninsula, taking you along the Fraser River and past several golf courses, public and private.

On the North Shore, Marine Drive takes you along English Bay and Howe Sound, through West Vancouver to Horseshoe Bay. It's a spectacular drive in which you can see downtown Vancouver and the entire length of Point Grey, and it takes you past Lighthouse Park, several small coves and islands, and magnificent homes that edge the waterfront. It eventually links up with BC 99 to Whistler and to the ferry system that takes you to mid–Vancouver Island at Nanaimo and to nearby Bowen Island, a residential community that has a quaint dockside village.

Downtown has a series of one-way streets to ease the flow of traffic. The result is an on-road civility that's a cross between British tradition and contemporary necessity. When three lanes of traffic merge into two, cars alternate in a smooth transition like a line of dancers all knowing their place. There's no cramming into a vacant spot and no horn blowing (it's illegal in Vancouver except in emergencies), and obscene gestures are as rare in the city as snow in winter. You're expected to give a friendly wave back to the driver who let you get in line. Many neighborhoods, such as the West End, have blocked some streets to control traffic and have also placed roundabouts at strategic spots.

The Vancouver area has a large number of car break-ins—in fact, the city leads the country in this dubious statistic. Make sure your car is secure. If you have a lock on your trunk release switch, use it.

If you're just visiting the cruise-ship terminal, try to avoid parking there because it's the most expensive place to park in town. The rule of thumb is that the closer to the waterfront you park, the more you'll pay per hour. Try the Hudson's Bay Company Store (known as "The Bay;" see "Shopping") parking lot on Seymour Street between Georgia Street and

Dunsmuir. It's secure and relatively inexpensive. The cheapest downtown parking is beneath the main library on Hamilton between Robeson and W. Georgia streets, but it is often full. If you park in a no-parking area, your car could be impounded. Downtown has tough on-street parking regulations, with prime shopping and business streets always full. Expect to pay between $1.50 and $3 an hour for parking garages and $1 for 30 minutes on the street.

In Vancouver, pedestrians have the right of way. When someone steps off the curb at a cross street, you're required by law to stop and let that person cross.

Public Transportation

The Greater Vancouver Regional District maintains an integrated system of buses, rapid-transit computerized trains called Sky Train, and a ferry service called the Seabus, which crosses Burrard Inlet. Fares are the same for all systems. Serving about 695 square miles (1,800 sq. km), the entire system is wheelchair accessible. About 50 percent of all Vancouver buses have wheelchair ramps for easy access. Look for the wheelchair symbol on the front of the bus. And, depending on the route, some buses have bicycle holders. For help in planning your transit tours, call **TransLink** (604-953-3333; www.translink.bc.ca). Ticket vending machines at Sky Train and Seabus stations accept payment from Canadian $5, $10, and $20 bills and coins.

Sky Train is an elevated system connecting downtown Vancouver with Burnaby, New Westminster, and Surrey, stopping at 20 stations along the way. It's a safe and cheap way ($2–$4, depending on how many zones you cross) to see the general layout of the city. But don't look for a conductor; the entire system is computerized. The Lower Mainland is split into three zones. With cross-zone travel, there's an increase in prices. One zone is $2, two zones is $3, and three zones is $4. There are deep discounts for seniors over age 65, students 14–19 years old who attend school in Vancouver, and children ages 5–13. Children under age 5 travel free if accompanied by an adult.

The Aquabus ferry crosses False Creek. Toshi

Seabus is a passenger-only ferry service that connects downtown Vancouver with North Vancouver via a 12-minute ride. Terminals are located in Vancouver at the foot of Granville and Seymour streets in the old Canadian Pacific Railroad terminal and in North Vancouver at the Lonsdale Quay, where you can shop at the farmers market or enjoy the view from a waterfront café. You can transfer to a Seabus at both ends.

And don't forget the water taxis—the Aquabus—that traverse a series of routes between the West End, Granville Island, and False Creek. It's a neat, relaxed way of traveling the False Creek waterfront for a $2 fare.

Taxis are best found at a hotel, but they can be flagged down.

NEIGHBORHOODS

Vancouver's neighborhoods are separated by water and bridges, and they are recognizable by distinct character and ethnic makeup—Italian (along Commercial Drive), Greek (on West Broadway), and Indo-Pakistani (near Main and 49th). From the downtown core, to the north is the waterfront and, across Burrard Inlet, the North Shore. To the northwest of downtown is the West End, adjacent to Stanley Park; due west are Kitsilano and Point Grey. To the east of downtown are Gastown, Chinatown, and East Vancouver. South of downtown are Yaletown, Granville Island and the False Creek area, Kerrisdale and Southlands, and Richmond and Steveston.

A Chinatown grocery store Toshi

Chinatown

Vancouver is home to Canada's largest Chinese community, which dates from the late 1800s. In this six-block region, two blocks southeast of Gastown, narrow sidewalks are vibrant with humanity, elbow to elbow in a crowded swirl of chatter and haggling, day or night. East Pender Street, in the heart of the district, transports you thousands of miles within the space of a few blocks. It is lined with Mandarin, Cantonese, and Szechwuan restaurants and shops selling wickerwork, bamboo bird cages, and jade jewelry. Smells of outdoor vegetable stalls, meat shops with their hanging ducks, restaurants, and pastry shops float in the air. Walk into any of the crowded specialty shops and you'll find everything from mysterious Oriental herbal remedies to finely lacquered pots, jade, carved wood, and embroidered dresses. The **Sam Kee Building** (Carrall and Pender Sts.) is the narrowest in the world at 5.9 feet by 98.3 feet (1.8 m by 30 m); the **Chinese Cultural Centre** (50 E. Pender St.; 604-658-8850) is marked by an enormous red gateway.

Downtown

This is where people gather at all hours every day. It is where you'll find the city's major performance centers, the art gallery, the crafts museum, and major hotels. Georgia Street, which runs east and west, is the main artery through downtown. A block south is Robson

Street, which runs parallel to Georgia, with a myriad of restaurants, boutiques, and shops. Granville Street, which runs perpendicular to Georgia, is one of the city's major shopping areas and the longtime entryway into other sections of the downtown core. The Orpheum, home to the Vancouver Symphony, is located a half block south of Granville and Robson Streets. In Pacific Centre, accessed through any of the stores on the corner of Georgia and Granville, are some 200 stores and services on three floors beneath three city blocks.

Robson Street is what Vancouverites have always considered the best strolling street in the city. It's said that if you wait at the corner of Robson and Thurlow, eventually every person you know in the city will saunter by. And some days and nights, especially on weekends, it seems true. In the late 1960s, the street was called Robsonstrasse for its many German restaurants. Now the street is dominated by chic boutiques and upscale restaurants of all flavors, and the German restaurants have long disappeared. Though it extends from BC Place Stadium, the most popular sections of Robson Street begin where the street separates the Vancouver Art Gallery from the contemporary Court House complex.

On the northeast corner of Georgia and Granville streets stands the Hudson Bay Company (the Bay), part of the old fur-trading company that had its beginnings in the 1600s. Across the street is the Sears downtown shopping center. Three blocks west along Georgia Street is the $100 million Vancouver Public Library at Library Square. In addition to more than one million books and a collection of electronic databases, the building is home to 15,000 square feet (1,394 sq. m) of retail space and 15 stores. With the library as its core, the area is the heart of Vancouver's theater district, with the Queen Elizabeth Theatre complex, the 1,824-seat Centre for Performing Arts, the Canadian Broadcasting Corporation (CBC) building, and BC Place and the nearby General Motors Place, home of the British Columbia Lions football team and the Vancouver Canucks hockey team, respectively. The Grizzlies, the former NBA franchise, used to be housed in GM Place, but they moved to Memphis in 2001.

Commercial Drive in East Vancouver is home to Italian markets. Toshi

East Vancouver

The East Vancouver area roughly rests to the east of Main Street and includes some of the most colorful areas of the city. Because land and housing values are considerable in this area, you'll find a young population and diverse ethnic neighborhoods. Just a decade ago, this was an area dominated by Italians. If you wanted to experience it to its fullest, you were advised to know some Italian phrases that would gain you access to special dishes at restaurants and the most chic of clothing. Now Commercial Drive, the cultural center of East Van, as locals call it, is a mix of other ethnic minorities, giving it an international flavor. There's still enough Italian

character for the region to retain its original name of Little Italy, and it still has a certain Italian ambience. Along its vibrant sidewalks are inexpensive grocery stores, cafés, coffee-houses, and funky shops.

Commercial Drive is the heart of commerce and community in the area officially known as Grandview/Woodland. As Vancouver's first suburb, it has seen many changes over the years and is an area rich in history and cultural diversity. The area's first house was built in 1891, and the first businesses were established along Commercial Drive soon after. As early as 1907, residents organized to have Park Drive improved so children would not have to walk along rail lines to school.

The face of the community changed after the First World War when Italian, Chinese, and Eastern European immigrants arrived in the area. After World War II, a second wave of Italian immigrants made the area home. They renovated old houses and noticeably changed the look of Commercial Drive with new shops and restaurants. Grandview's Chinese residents increased in number in the 1950s and 1960s as some of the earlier Italian and Eastern European residents moved on to other neighborhoods. In the late 1960s, Grandview's first East Indian residents also made the community their home.

Although thousands of Indo-Canadians live throughout the city, the cultural focal point is on Main Street between 49th and 51st, where you'll find the many jewelry stores and fabric shops that make up the Punjabi market. Also here are a variety of food stores as well as a gorgeous Sikh temple designed by architect Arthur Erickson.

False Creek and Granville Island

Many an early sailor came into this inlet only to find a dead end, thus the name False Creek. Today the eastern end of the creek is marked by the Science Centre, while North False Creek embraces Yaletown and to the south are Granville Island and condos and town-houses that march up the hill above Second Avenue. A walkway rings the two shorelines of False Creek, with restaurants and shopping areas set among the anchored sailboats and condos. At Stamps Landing, at the shore's south edge of a condo complex, are restaurants and pubs.

The evolution of Granville Island has been one of North America's great urban renewal projects. In the 1960s it was a cesspool of industrial pollution that infected the entire downtown core. In 1972 the Canadian federal government, which owned the island and leased it out to a variety of heavy industries, created the Granville Island Trust and leased the land to a variety of city-backed activities with an emphasis on art and artisans. The idea behind the revitalization was to convert run-down waterfront industrial property to public markets and avant-garde retail space.

But no one could have envisioned what the island would become. Stylish restaurants, art galleries, artists' studios, crafts shops, and live theaters have produced a formula that has proven so potent that it is being mimicked in other cities. Buskers add a carnival atmosphere, and dockside restaurants offer sweeping views of downtown, the mountains, countless sailboats, and the tiny Aquabus ferries that run to and from Granville Island seven days a week year-round.

The former industrial site, under the south end of Granville Street Bridge, is now 37 acres (15 hectares) of parks, walkways, renovated warehouses, and a successful combina-tion of 200 commercial, cultural, and boating enterprises, including theater companies, countless artists' galleries, and the Sea Village Dockside, a residential complex that floats on barges in front of a colorful collection of rural mailboxes near the Granville Island

Condominiums line the walkway along False Creek. Toshi

Hotel. All across the island, former empty sheds have been reawakened as studios, stages, sets, and scenery for art exhibits, theatrical plays, street performers, and music shows. There's also the Granville Island Brewery, with its assortment of beers that you can buy on the spot or in restaurants.

Because it's in the middle of the city, Granville Island is easy to get to by car, by bus, by bicycle, or on foot. A word of caution: On weekends traffic is horrendous. Take the ferry or a cab to the island. Across from the Public Market is the Granville Island Information Centre. Stop there for brochures, information, and a touch of history before venturing farther onto the island. There's a detailed map of the area, a money exchange, and an ATM, as well as a couple of desk people to answer questions.

The heart of the island is the Granville Island Public Market and its waterfront plaza. Much like Pike Place Market in Seattle, the Public Market is an irresistible emporium of greengrocers, butchers, bakers, fishmongers, importers, ethnic food sellers, craft vendors, sweets stands, florists, and casual eateries. It also features a wine shop and a microroaster of organic coffee. Everything in the Public Market is on display, from bakery backrooms to a mini fudge-making factory. Fifty permanent vendors and a constantly changing array of farmers, artisans, and cottage-industry food producers are open 9 am to 6 pm seven days a week.

The Sea Village Dockside on the north side of the Emily Carr College of Art and Design, tied up to the dock away from the mainstream bustle of the island, is an intricate community of houseboats, many luxurious though small, in a series of interlocked floating docks. This is West Coast living at its most picturesque. The houseboats are a rainbow of colors against the comparative whiteness of the high-rises across False Creek. Residents are the only ones who live on Granville Island, and they do it in style, often lounging on tiny balconies. This is a terrific photo opportunity of what must be the most unique West Coast lifestyle.

Sea Village, a picturesque houseboat community on Granville Island   Toshi

Gastown

Gastown is where the city began, as the site of Stamps sawmill, in the vicinity of Water, Carrall, Cordova, and Powell Streets. In 1867 "Gassy Jack Deighton," a compulsive Yorkshire talker, came to town and gave what was then officially known as Hastings the nickname Gastown. It was renamed Granville in 1870 and 16 years later incorporated as the City of Vancouver. The Canadian Pacific Railway terminal (around the corner from the Convention Centre/Pan Pacific), where the first CPR train steamed in 1887, is now restored and is the main terminal for the Seabus that goes to the North Shore and for the Sky Train system. About 300 yards (100 m) around the corner lies Gastown, where renovated turn-of-the-20th-century brick buildings, mews, courtyards, and passages host shops filled with the good, the bad, and the tacky.

Gastown was leveled by fire in 1886 but rose again as a commercial area. Now the warehouses and shops have been converted to boutiques and restaurants, and the turn-of-the-20th-century atmosphere attracts thousands of visitors by day and cabaret patrons by night. A focal point of Gastown is an old steam clock at the corner of Cambie and Water Streets.

Maple Leaf Square, at the intersection of Water and Carrall Streets at Gastown's east end, is the transition area between Chinatown to the south and the Gastown business core; it's where you'll find a mix of local yuppies, tourists, and Vancouver's less affluent downtown eastside residents mixing daily. It's a mini–melting pot of economic and social zones. Storefronts attract your attention more than the occasional panhandler. At Maple Leaf Square is the bronze statue of Gassy Jack Deighton standing on a whiskey barrel; he built a saloon on the site in 1867 and now faces the pie-shaped Hotel Europe, converted in recent decades to an office building. The statue guards the entranceway into the busiest part of Gastown to the west. Read the plaque on the wall of Miriam's Ice Cream Parlor behind the statue for a history of the corner and of Jack's second saloon. Behind the statue is Gaolers Mews, a labyrinth of alleyway shops in the area of what was Vancouver's first gaol (jail). Here you'll find some of the city's most unusual shops, including several specialty stores such as Cigar Connoisseurs, where a wide selection of Cuban cigars is available.

Kerrisdale and Southlands

Kerrisdale and Southlands are where the city's Establishment lives. This is one of the best shopping neighborhoods, in terms of variety and quality of selection, in town. Also known as Kerrisdale Village, the area has an Olde English character, with specialty shops offering everything from rich chocolates to flavorful cheeses. There are shops for the fashion-conscious as well as for the do-it-yourselfers and home decorators. The surroundings of Kerrisdale are well maintained, courtesy of the residential community's strong support for the area's businesses. Kerrisdale Village extends east–west along West 41st Avenue from Larch to Maple Streets and north–south along East and West Boulevards from West 37th to West 49th.

The area had its beginnings in 1867, the year Canada became a nation, when Samuel and Fitzgerald McCleery decided to farm the area now occupied by the Marine Drive Golf Club. The first interurban train forged through Kerrisdale on July 4, 1905, traveling along West Boulevard en route to the Steveston canneries. Those tracks still remain, and they may be destined to become part of the city's Sky Train system.

In Southlands, south of fashionable SW Marine Drive, you'll find a neighborhood unlike any other North American urban center. Imagine living on a horse ranch within the city boundaries, just 25 minutes from downtown. What you'll find here is a fascinating mix of multimillion-dollar mansions complete with stables and corrals. The mini-ranches are bounded by SW Marine Drive to the north and the Fraser River to the south. The area is laced with horses and walkers on bridle paths, blackberry bushes, and river-front walks. What little traffic there is moves at a snail's pace. Just beware the country-style fertilizer that spots the streets.

Kitsilano

What was once a gathering place for the long-haired set of the 1960s is, like its former residents, now more mature. Yet it remains one of Vancouver's liveliest neighborhoods. It was Vancouver's answer to San Francisco's Haight-Ashbury counterculture of the 1960s, but it wasn't long after the hippies got jobs that its market potential caught up with the area. Bounded by Fourth Avenue to the south and the waterfront to the north, Kits (no one calls it Kitsilano) is where you go for a view of the city overlooking Stanley Park, the North Shore mountains, and the skyline. It's an easy drive over the Burrard Street Bridge to a spectacular route along Cornwall Avenue.

Baby boomers now make up about 60 percent of the area's population, so you'll find plenty of shopping, restaurants, and even a lingering thread of those hippie roots as boomers and their well-heeled offspring park their 4x4s to walk along Fourth Avenue and sip lattes at Starbucks or Capers. And nothing is more picturesque than walking along Kits Beach at sunset, watching a big ball of fire settling behind Bowen Island, lighting up the midsummer sky in bright red and glowing orange.

At Vanier Park in Kitsilano, on the waterfront, you'll find the *St. Roch*, the old Royal Canadian Mounted Police ship that was the first vessel to navigate the Arctic Ocean west to east, in the 1940s. Also in Vanier Park are the Planetarium and the Centennial Museum complex. From Vanier you can walk along the seawall clear to Granville Island.

The Seabus crosses Burrard Inlet to Lonsgate Quay on the North Shore. Toshi

North Shore

If you stand anywhere in the downtown area and look across Burrard Inlet to the mountains, you'll be looking at the North Shore, extending 17 miles (28 km) from Horseshoe Bay in the east to Lion's Bay on Howe Sound, where you can catch the ferry to mid–Vancouver Island at Nanaimo. There's little that's flat on the North Shore. Pressed up along the North Shore mountains, the communities of North Vancouver and West Vancouver are studies in contrast. The Lion's Gate Bridge offers access to both communities, as does the Second Narrows Bridge, also called the Ironworkers Memorial Bridge.

North Vancouver, which stretches from the Second Narrows Bridge to the Lion's Gate Bridge, is easily accessed by the Seabus from the old Canadian Pacific Railway terminal near Gastown to the foot of Lonsdale Road in North Vancouver. The hub of North Van is along Lower Lonsdale, where numerous small shops and restaurants are found. The Seabus lets you off at the Lonsdale Quay and its many cafés, hotel, and specialty shops. North Van is a combination of middle-class homes and high adventure. At the base of Lonsdale Road is the Lonsdale Quay Market; higher up the mountains are Lynn Canyon Park, the Capilano Suspension Bridge, and the tram to the top of Grouse Mountain.

West Vancouver is a city of spacious homes, one of Canada's most exclusive communities, with a higher per-capita income than anywhere else in British Columbia. West Van's Ambleside Drive is an exclusive shopping district that passes through the heart of the community. If you take the street westward, you'll pass some of the loveliest waterfront terrain in the city, with spectacular views of English Bay, Vancouver Island, and the city of Vancouver. For a taste of high-end living, cruise along Marine Drive, stopping at Lighthouse Park, and you'll eventually end up at Horseshoe Bay, where the BC Ferry terminal is located in a charming, seaside village.

Point Grey

From Stanley Park looking south across the water, the strip of land stretching out into the Strait of Georgia is Point Grey. It sprawls westward from Burrard on the east and includes Pacific Spirit Park and the University of British Columbia (UBC). It encompasses some of Vancouver's most livable areas, including Kitsilano, Southlands, the beaches along English Bay, and the University Endowment Lands. This is an area of big homes and lots of trees. Rule of thumb: The farther west toward UBC, the costlier the housing.

Point Grey was named for Capt. George Grey, a friend of—you guessed it—Capt. Vancouver. In the early 1790s, the British, along with Spanish navigators whose presence is remembered in the name Spanish Banks, visited this forested peninsula that for centuries had been home to native peoples. At what's now Jericho Beach, a native village stood at the edge of a meadow of mossy grass, hemmed in by enormous Douglas firs and hemlocks that were later logged. The colonial government of the time recognized the area's strategic importance by establishing government reserves at the point and along Jericho, which eventually became UBC and Jericho Park, the School for the Deaf and Blind, and the Jericho army base.

Richmond and Steveston

Across the Oak Street Bridge, south of Vancouver and on Lulu Island, lies Richmond, sitting much like the forgotten sister of a beautiful film star. Her virtues are too often overlooked, her physical assets are skipped over, and while her charm is acknowledged, it is seldom scrutinized. If the airport—which sits on Richmond property—had been called the Richmond International Airport instead of Vancouver International, who knows what might have happened in terms of development?

In Richmond, signs are bilingual in English and Chinese. Toshi

Richmond has character, a rich history, a wide variety of activities, a performing arts theater, shopping centers, and quaint out-of-the-way places. It's where you can find good hotels (which are usually much less expensive than those of the same standard in Vancouver), plenty of historical sites, sport fishing, a host of charming boutiques and restaurants, scenic splendor, and great tourist attractions such as the Richmond Nature Park and the Buddhist Temple on Steveston Highway. You'll definitely need a car; unlike Vancouver, Richmond is a community that isn't always easy to navigate. It is former farmland that over the years has been developed in a haphazard way, with street patterns that match the development.

Although Richmond has many parks, recreational facilities, and attractions, its most fascinating area is Steveston, located 20 miles south of downtown Vancouver. The crown jewel of the area is the fishing village of Steveston, at the southwest corner of Lulu Island, where Richmond is located, with its historical buildings, small stores and restaurants, and working fishing docks where you can buy freshly caught salmon at dockside off the boats. Steveston is home to the largest fleet of commercial fishing vessels on Canada's west coast. Moncton Street, the main artery through Steveston, has several seafood restaurants, marine supply shops, and antique shops. Art lovers like the Canoe Pass Gallery, which sells traditional coastal Native American art. The Steveston Museum, the only site remaining of the original 350 Northern Banks that operated across western Canada in the 19th century, has a fascinating collection of photos as well as farming, fishing, and blacksmithing tools used by early Japanese settlers.

Waterfront

The waterfront along Vancouver's northern downtown extends west from the Second Narrows Bridge through Gastown, the West End, and Stanley Park. The area between Gastown and Stanley Park is the most interesting and offers the most activities. The newest section is west of the Convention Centre, where condominiums, restaurants, and waterfront activities add to Vancouver's casual lifestyle.

West End and Stanley Park

The West End is a massive area, extending from Burrard Street westward to Stanley Park and from Georgia Street south to the waters of English Bay. This is the most densely populated Vancouver neighborhood, with a population of about 43,000. It's a vital, young community that is filled with action day and night. The West End is home to Vancouver's gay community and the site of the annual Gay Pride Parade held on the Sunday of every BC Day weekend (a provincial holiday on the first weekend in August).

Robson Street is the city's most vibrant shopping district, with name-brand stores, boutiques, and plenty of high-end shopping. Cutting through the West End from west to east, Robson leads back to downtown's Hudson's Bay Company, the Vancouver Art Gallery, the courthouse complex with its skating rink and restaurants, and the underground shopping beneath Granville Street.

North–south Denman Street, on the other hand, is laid back, offering inexpensive shopping and dining. Denman is a mass of character and characters, of small shops, tree-lined streets where you'll find B&Bs in restored Victorian houses, restaurants, and people crushed together on sunny days when high-rises empty. Denman Street is the closest Vancouver has to a European ambience. The vast majority of residents live in modest

The Stanley Park seawall has great views of downtown Vancouver. Toshi

low- and high-rise apartments and condos. Along English Bay is one of the city's beaches where every clear evening hundreds go to watch the sunset and walk, cycle, or roller skate the seawall, a 6-mile (9 km) route around the periphery of Stanley Park.

Yaletown

If you want to see the way urban change takes place before your eyes within days, then spend time in Yaletown, leave, and come back in a week. You'll likely find new shops being opened, more condos, and yet another warehouse conversion getting underway. In its 19th- and early 20th-century heyday, Yaletown boasted more saloons per acre than anywhere else in the world. Now this heritage area along Pacific Avenue is home to art galleries, furniture and fashion boutiques, and restaurants.

Yaletown was a run-down warehouse district of Vancouver, but the elevated loading docks with their cantilevered canopies now house sidewalk tables, providing shelter for patrons of the many dining and drinking establishments. Today's Yaletown covers a much wider area than before its rebirth; it's now considered to be the area bounded on the north by Georgia Street, on the west by Richards Street, on the south by False Creek, and on the east by Cambie Street.

Originally Vancouver's garment district, Yaletown still retains links to its past through its fashionable boutiques and local designers. The seawall along False Creek hosts a mix of walkers, joggers, cyclists, and roller skaters. The walk has extensive landscaping, lighting, artifacts, and green spaces. At the foot of Davie Street, newly developed marina berths house everything from modest sailboats to floating palaces. The Aquabus boats leave here on a frequent schedule for destinations such as Granville Island, Stamps Landing, and Science World.

Located in the heart of Yaletown is probably Vancouver's most trendy food store, Urban Fare. This not only is an up-market food store, but it also houses a restaurant and a coffee bar in its open layout. Across the street from Urban Fare is the neighborhood community center, transformed from a locomotive roundhouse originally built by Canadian Pacific Railway as the turning point for trains. Today the roundhouse not only serves as the community center but also houses steam locomotive no. 374, which first entered Vancouver in 1887 and is on exhibit to the public year-round.

Accommodations

Vancouver offers a wide array of hotels in the downtown core and throughout the rest of the city and suburbs, fitting all budgets and tastes. Some properties, such as the Hotel Vancouver, are not just superb places to stay but also have enormous historical significance to Vancouver and Canada. Many B&B establishments are in heritage buildings, but most are located in homes throughout the area. On the North Shore, for example, there are few hotels but many B&Bs. Waterfront hotels, downtown hotels, bed-and-breakfasts, motels, short-term apartment rentals, and suburban hotels can be booked through **Tourism Vancouver** (Plaza Level, 200 Burrard St., Vancouver, BC, Canada V6C 3L6; 604-683-2000; www. tourismvancouver.com), which acts as a clearinghouse for all Vancouver accommodations.

Hotels and Motels

As in most other cities, hotel prices depend on the day of the week, time of year, and space available. The most expensive time is, of course, during the summer, when tourists compete with the robust cruise-ship industry for available rooms. It is impossible to list all of the hotels in the Greater Vancouver area, so check with Tourism Vancouver if what you want isn't listed here. This book lists virtually every hotel and motel in the downtown area, but there are more outside the downtown area. All Vancouver hotels must provide handicap access, but some of the heritage buildings are exempt, though many are trying to accommodate handicapped guests. Always check before committing to a property. The following listings are arranged alphabetically by neighborhood.

Airport Area

Hotels near Vancouver's airport are different from those near Seattle's airport because Richmond, where the airport is located, is a destination in itself. On the south side of the Fraser River, which separates Vancouver from Richmond, there are hotels within five minutes of the airport and in the city of Richmond itself, just a few minutes farther from the airport's closest properties. Since the hotels in Richmond are only 20 minutes or so from downtown Vancouver, travelers often stay there because of the quality of lodging for the money. Hotels in Richmond are considerably less expensive than those in downtown Vancouver, and each offers free airport shuttle service. Some offer free parking while you're traveling. The City of Richmond, within whose boundaries you'll be staying, boasts unique shopping at its Asian malls and ample cuisine from different countries. There's also a wide range of cultural activities to enjoy, such as the nearby quaint fishing village of Steveston and its Cannery Museum.

Accent Inn

10551 St. Edwards Dr.
Richmond, BC V6X 3L8
604-273-3311, 1-800-663-0298
www.accentinns.com
Price: Inexpensive
Credit cards: AE, DC, MC, V
Special features: Excellent value
Pets: Yes

The Accent Inn is located just minutes from the main airport terminal, where a free shuttle bus will pick you up and drop you off. And downtown Vancouver is just minutes away. Rooms are spotless and comfortable at this family-owned and family-operated inn that's good for short or longer stays.

Best Western Abercorn Inn

9260 Bridgeport Rd.
Richmond, BC V6X 1S1
604-270-7576
www.abercorn-inn.com
Price: Incxpensive to moderate
Credit cards: AE, DC, MC, V
Special features: Close to casino
Pets: Small OK

This country-style white stucco and brown-beamed hotel/motel has become a Lower Mainland landmark. It's a British-style inn with character. With a series of high-rise hotels sprouting up around it, the Abercorn sits like a friendly old house just waiting to greet guests. Sitting next to the Oak Street Bridge, it provides easy access into the heart of downtown. And like most of the near-airport hotels, it has complimentary shuttle service to the airport and complimentary breakfast.

Best Western Vancouver Airport

7551 Westminster Hwy.
Richmond, BC V6X 1A3
604-273-7878, 1-800-663-0299
www.richmond-hotel.ca
Price: Inexpensive to moderate
Credit cards: AE, DC, MC, V
Special features: Convenient location
Pets: Small OK on approval

Situated in the heart of Richmond, it is within walking distance of malls, movie theaters, sports facilities, parks, and restaurants. Within a short driving distance are golf courses, ocean beaches, and interesting historical sites. This hotel is located within a 10-minute drive of Vancouver International Airport, with 24-hour complimentary airport shuttle, and is only a short trip from Vancouver's downtown core.

Coast Vancouver Airport Hotel

1041 SW Marine Dr.
Vancouver, BC V6P 6L6
604-263-1555
www.coasthotels.com
Price: Inexpensive to expensive
Credit cards: AE, DC, MC, V
Special features: Near the airport
Pets: Small OK at $20 a night

This 134-room property is only five minutes away from the airport, but on the Vancouver side of the Fraser River at the foot of the bridge leading to the airport. It's in the South Vancouver area, well located if you're looking to explore the western Point Grey region. There's free shuttle service to and from the airport.

Comfort Inn Vancouver Airport Hotel

3031 No. 3 Rd.
Richmond, BC V6X 2B6
604-278-5161, 1-800-663-0974
www.comfortinnvancouver.com
Price: Moderate
Credit cards: AE, DC, MC, V
Special features: Rated AAA three-diamond
Pets: OK at $10 each

The Comfort Inn Vancouver Airport Hotel is 10 minutes away from the Vancouver International Airport. It's a AAA three-diamond hotel with a wide collection of amenities such as voice mail, data-port telephones, high-speed Internet access on request, free local calls, no long-distance access fees, and a coffeemaker.

Delta Vancouver Airport Hotel

3500 Cessna Dr.
Richmond, BC V7B 1C7
604-278-1241, 1-800-268-1133
www.deltavancouverairport.com
Price: Moderate to expensive
Credit cards: AE, DC, MC, V
Special features: Five minutes from airport
Pets: OK

Just 2 kilometers from Vancouver International Airport, it's on the middle arm of the Fraser River, so if you want to be close to the airport, you can still get a taste of what it's like to have a waterfront environment, with the marina right on the doorstep. It's a good place for a layover, because you can ride a bike or walk along the top of the dike that keeps the Fraser River from drowning Richmond. It is near a casino and shopping, and kids under six eat free in the hotel's dining rooms.

Executive Airport Plaza Hotel
7311 Westminster Hwy.
Richmond, BC V6X 1A3
604-278-5555, 1-888-388-3932
www.executivehotels.net
Price: Inexpensive to expensive
Credit cards: AE, DC, MC, V
Special features: Business focused
Pets: No

Geared for the traveling businessperson, the complex includes a hotel tower and state-of-the-art convention center and is five minutes from Vancouver International Airport and 20 minutes from downtown Vancouver. It has 350 luxury apartments, deluxe suites, and corporate club rooms and 16 meeting rooms, the largest of which seats 675. Apartments are designed for relaxing, dining, and entertaining in one-, two-, and three-bedroom and penthouse units featuring full kitchens with a dishwasher, oven, microwave, fridge, and in-room laundry. Deluxe suites offer a separate sitting area, Jacuzzi bathtubs, and kitchenettes. Corporate club rooms offer office amenities.

Fairmont Vancouver Airport Hotel
Vancouver International Airport
Richmond, BC V7B 1X9
604-207-5200, 1-800-441-1414
www.fairmont.com
Price: Expensive to very expensive

Credit cards: AE, DC, MC, V
Special features: In the airport
Pets: No

The Fairmont Vancouver Airport Hotel, a 14-story, $65 million facility, is the first hotel in the world to offer guests a seamless connection from hotel room to airline seat and is just an elevator ride up from the international departures terminal. Incoming passengers can check in at counters situated adjacent to the luggage carousels in the domestic and international arrivals halls while awaiting delivery of luggage. After guests get their key cards and identify their baggage, hotel bellhops bring the luggage directly to their rooms. The hotel is also one of the most technologically sophisticated in North America. Touch-screen and push-button consoles give guests fingertip control over everything: lighting, temperature, television, electronic "do not disturb" indicators, and even the drapes.

Four Points by Sheraton Vancouver Airport
8368 Alexandra Rd.
Richmond, BC V6X 4A6
604-214-0888, 1-888-281-8888
www.fourpoints.com
Price: Moderate to expensive
Credit cards: AE, DC, MC, V
Special features: Business oriented
Pets: No

Situated in the heart of Richmond, the Four Points by Sheraton Vancouver Airport is convenient to the suburb's shopping, dining, entertainment, and business district. Hotel services combine the needs of business and leisure travelers, and include an indoor pool, Jacuzzi, restaurant and lounge, fully equipped fitness center, free 24-hour airport transportation, 24-hour business center, high-speed Internet access in the business center, and complimentary high-speed wireless Internet access in all common areas.

Hampton Inn Vancouver Airport Hotel

8811 Bridgeport Rd.
Richmond, BC V6X 1R9
604-232-5505, 1-888-488-0101
www.hamptoninn-vancouver.com
Price: Moderate
Credit cards: AE, DC, MC, V
Special features: downtown Richmond
Pets: No

This Richmond hotel offers 111 guest rooms equipped to make you feel comfortable and right at home. Hotel amenities include complimentary shuttle service to the airport and shopping centers, in-house fitness facilities, and a business and conference center.

Hilton Vancouver Airport

5911 Minuro Blvd.
Richmond, BC V6X 4C7
604-273-6336
www.vancouverairport.hilton.com
Price: Moderate
Credit cards: AE, DC, MC, V
Special features: Great views
Pets: No

The hotel's suites and junior suites feature views of the Coast Mountains and the Fraser River. Most suites have balconies plus separate living and bedroom areas. Many suites feature high-speed Internet access and large work desks with ergonomic chairs. Carmichael's, the hotel's dining room, offers premium steak and a West Coast fusion-inspired menu. The Sax on Minoru lounge has casual fare with a martini menu and a touch of jazz.

Holiday Inn Express Vancouver Airport

9351 Bridgeport Rd.
Richmond, BC V6X 1S3
604-273-8080, 1-877-273-8080
www.hiexpress.com
Price: Moderate
Credit cards: AE, DC, MC, V
Special features: Near casino
Pets: No

Located near the Oak Street Bridge, the hotel is five minutes away from the airport. It has basically the same amenities as the Holiday Inn Vancouver Airport hotel but is not as centrally located to the Richmond core activity. It is near the casino and local shopping areas.

Holiday Inn International Vancouver Airport

10720 Cambie Rd.
Richmond, BC V6X 1K8
604-821-1818, 1-888-831-3388
www.hi-airport.bc.ca
Price: Moderate
Credit cards: AE, DC, MC, V
Special features: Kids eat free with parent
Pets: No

This Holiday Inn (not to be confused with the Holiday Inn Express Vancouver Airport) has 163 guest rooms designed for corporate, leisure, group, and family travelers. Business floors feature high-speed Internet access, ergonomic chairs, house robes, and a work desk. Kids' rooms feature bunk beds in addition to a separate queen-size bed, plus two TVs, a VCR, a video game system, a fridge, and a microwave. Breakfast, lunch, and dinner are served in the lively Fogg 'n' Suds restaurant and lounge, which features 100 beers from around the world. Children 12 and under eat free in the restaurant when accompanied by a dining parent. The hotel offers free gated underground parking.

Marriott Vancouver Airport Hotel

7571 Westminster Hwy.
Richmond, BC V6X 1A3
604-276-2112, 1-877-323-8888
www.marriott.com/yvrsa
Price: Moderate
Credit cards: AE, DC, MC, V
Special features: Business oriented
Pets: Small OK

This high-rise hotel is conveniently located in the heart of Richmond, directly across from the Richmond Centre Shopping Mall and five minutes from the airport. It is within walking distance of restaurants, shopping, cinemas, and outdoor recreation. Its 18 floors, 65 rooms, and 172 suites are all specifically designed for the business traveler. On-site parking is available for $8 a day.

Park Plaza Vancouver Airport

10251 St. Edwards Dr.
Richmond, BC V6X 2M9
604-278-9611, 1-866-482-8444
www.vacr.bc.ca
Price: Inexpensive to expensive
Credit cards: AE, DC, MC, V
Special features: Many family activities
Pets: OK at $25 a stay

This high-rise is just south of the Oak Street Bridge and just off the east side of BC 99. It has indoor and outdoor swimming pools, a health club, squash courts, tennis courts, a 225-foot waterslide, a children's center program, restaurants, lounges, and Nintendo in the rooms. Among the 227 units are a generous number of nonsmoking rooms. There's a wide selection of room combinations to suit large families as well as a free airport shuttle.

Quality Hotel Vancouver Airport

7228 Westminster Hwy.
Richmond, BC V6X 1A1
604-244-3051, 1-877-244-3051
www.qualityairport.ca
Price: Moderate
Credit cards: AE, DC, MC, V
Special features: Convenient location
Pets: No

Ten minutes away from the airport, this hotel is surrounded by a variety of restaurants and nightspots and is within walking distance of Richmond Centre Mall, movie theaters, and a fitness center. The hotel is next to Minoru Park and is convenient to many unique historical sites, as well as superb cultural, entertainment, and recreation facilities.

Radisson President Hotel and Suites

8181 Cambie Rd.
Richmond, BC V6X 3X9
604-276-8181, 1-800-333-3333
www.radisson.com/vancouver.ca
Price: Moderate to expensive
Credit cards: AE, DC, MC, V
Special features: On-site Buddhist temple
Pets: No

The luxurious ambience of this 184-room hotel is just one aspect that makes it so exceptional. Its real charm is in its location: the heart of the new Richmond Chinatown. And next to it is one of the most fabulous Chinese grocery stores you'll see this side of Shanghai, as well as a Buddhist temple. It's also just five minutes from the airport and only 25 minutes from downtown Vancouver. But this location offers its own fascination. Around the corner is a Japanese food center and nearby is an Asian mall. Rooms are discerning rather than opulent but very comfortable.

Sandman Hotel Vancouver Airport

3233 St. Edwards Dr.
Richmond, BC V6X 3K4
604-303-8888
www.sandmanhotels.com
Price: Moderate to expensive
Credit cards: AE, DC, MC, V
Special features: One block from GM Place, Queen Elizabeth Theatre, and BC Place Stadium
Pets: Small OK

Five minutes from the airport, the Sandman is next to the Travelodge and across the highway from the Holiday Inn Express. Complete with Internet access, the 172 rooms have coffeemakers, hair dryers, and in-room movies. Available suites include executive, kitchen, loft, and Jacuzzi. There's an indoor pool, a whirlpool, and fitness facilities. Moxie's Classic Grill is a restaurant and a sports lounge. Parking is free if you're leaving town and returning within 10 days.

Steveston Hotel

12111 Third Ave.
Richmond, BC V7E 3K1
604-277-9511
www.stevestonhotel.com
Price: Inexpensive to moderate
Credit cards: AE, DC, MC, V
Special features: In historic Steveston
Pets: No

This is a hotel with character in the heart of historic Steveston, about 15 minutes from the airport. Since it's the only hotel in this part of Richmond, the hotel pub is a local hangout. It's a clean but basic property in the middle of the Lower Main-land's most unusual area. Steveston is to Vancouver what Sausalito is to San Fran-cisco. The hotel has a beer and wine store, a pub, and a restaurant. Rooms have both shared and private baths. The 25 units have cable TV. They are not wheelchair accessible.

Travelodge Hotel Vancouver Airport

3071 St. Edwards Dr.
Richmond, BC V6X 3K4
604-278-5155, 1-800-578-7878
www.travelodge.com
Price: Inexpensive to moderate
Credit cards: AE, DC, MC, V
Special features: Mostly nonsmoking
Pets: No

This unpretentious property is within five minutes of Vancouver International Airport and is near some of Richmond's major stores. Smokers might have trouble getting accommodation since of the 159 rooms, 90 per cent are non-smoking. But for basic, clean and efficient lodging, it's good value. There are restaurants within easy walking distance although the hotel does have one plus a lounge. If you're a business person needing work room, ask for the Executive Floor where you'll find mini-suite that includes an ottoman and easy chair.

The Fairmont Hotel Vancouver is a downtown landmark. Courtesy of Fairmont Hotels

DOWNTOWN

Because the downtown area is also where you'll find high-rise apartments, the area is active well into the night with people walking the streets, especially in the West End. So walking at night is safe and relatively secure. The downtown core is safe, but you'll find young panhandlers in parts of the area, such as around S. Granville Street.

Barclay Hotel

1348 Robson St.
Vancouver, BC V6E 1C5
604-688-8850, 1-800-359-4827
Price: Moderate
Credit cards: AE, MC, V
Special features: At the quieter end of one of the busiest streets in Vancouver
Pets: No

Located on one of the city's hottest streets, the Barclay places you in the action without actionlike rates. This European-style hotel is a cordial family place with a casual restaurant and lounge near Stanley Park.

A heritage hotel nestled in the heart of downtown Vancouver, it is surrounded by charming boutiques, shops, bistros, restaurants, and art galleries. Within walking distance are Vancouver's attractions: Stanley Park, English Bay, the Vancouver Aquarium, the financial district, and major shopping malls. It's especially good for anyone expecting to spend more than a couple of days.

Blue Horizon

1225 Robson St.
Vancouver, BC V6E 1C3
604-688-1411, 1-800-663-1333
www.bluehorizonhotel.com
Price: Moderate to expensive
Credit cards: AE, DC, MC, V
Special features: Every room has a view
Pets: No

It's a pleasant place to be, in the heart of Robson Street, especially since you're right in the middle of the action. You're just minutes away from Stanley Park, English Bay, the Vancouver Aquarium, GM Place, BC Place, the Queen Elizabeth Theatre, Theatre Row, Chinatown, Gastown, the Canada Place Convention and Cruise Center, the Vancouver Planetarium, and the Granville Island Market. A family plan and spacious units make this long-established hotel a good choice.

Century Plaza Hotel

1015 Burrard St.
Vancouver, BC V6Z 1S5Y
604-687-0575, 1-800-683-1818
www.century-plaza.com
Price: Moderate to expensive
Credit cards: AE, DC, MC, V
Special features: Nonsmoking floors
Pets: No

Completely renovated in 2001, the hotel is right across the street from the luxurious Wall Centre Hotel and next to St. Paul's Hospital, so you might hear the occasional

siren during the night. Originally built as an apartment building, it has 235 suites, a restaurant, a lounge, a nightclub, a cappuccino bar, and an indoor pool and spa, plus nonsmoking floors. A lot of tour groups stay here.

Comfort Inn Downtown Vancouver

654 Nelson St.
Vancouver, BC V6B 6K4
604-605-4333, 1-888-605-5333
www.comfortinndowntown.com
Price: Inexpensive to expensive
Credit cards: AE, DC, MC, V
Special features: Free continental breakfast in Doolin's Irish Pub
Pets: OK at $25 per stay

This heritage building, located in the heart of downtown, is one of the city's finest boutique hotels, thoroughly modernized to include all of the technical wizardry that businesspeople look for, and in a fresh setting. High-speed Internet access, voice mail, in-room pay movies, and air conditioning subtly blend into the inviting colors. The building used to be the Hotel Dakota before it changed hands. Upscale rooms have high ceilings with crown moldings, luxurious duvet covers, and ceiling canopies.

Crowne Plaza Hotel Georgia

801 W. Georgia St.
Vancouver, BC V6C 1P7
604-682-5566, 1-800-663-1111
www.hotelgeorgia.bc.ca
Price: Expensive to very expensive
Credit cards: AE, DC, MC, V
Special features: European elegance
Pets: OK

This hotel combines old-fashioned charm with up-to-date innovations and is located in the heart of the city across from the Vancouver Art Gallery. Built in 1927, the 12-story stone hotel, with 313 guest rooms, had a complete face-lift in late 1998 and now combines the look and feel of a first-class business hotel with the elegance of European style. All guest rooms have custom-designed furniture, fabrics, and artwork that reflect the hotel's original era. The meeting place has been brought back to its original grandeur, and meeting rooms now include refurbished woodwork, moldings, and ornate chandeliers. Walk into the lobby and you're met with modern furnishings on original tile floors, fancy woodwork, marble accents, and a fireplace.

Delta Vancouver Suite Hotel

550 W. Hastings St.
Vancouver, BC V6B 1L6
604-689-8188, 1-877-814-7706
www.deltahotels.com
Price: Expensive to very expensive
Credit cards: AE, DC, MC, V
Special features: Fine restaurant
Pets: Only small OK

Across the street from the Simon Fraser University downtown campus, this new property is one block from the old Canadian Pacific Railroad terminal and on the edge of everything. All 226 full-service suites offer a separate bedroom and parlor area. The Manhattan Restaurant is one of Vancouver's favorite dining spots, with cuisine that's a meld of Asian and West Coast. The hotel does have a strange check-in area: Although you can drive up to the front for check-in, the main drop-off area is behind the hotel.

Empire Landmark Hotel

1400 Robson St.
Vancouver, BC V6G 1B9
604-687-0511, 1-800-830-6144
www.asiastandard.com
Price: Inexpensive to expensive
Credit cards: AE, DC, MC, V
Special features: Revolving restaurant
Pets: No

This property has been a Vancouver institution for several decades and has never lost either its character or its importance as a major West End property. Its caters to many meetings and conventions with remarkably intimate public rooms. The revolving restaurant atop the hotel on the 42nd floor, Cloud 9, is one of Vancouver's great viewing spots and has a menu featuring Continental and West Coast cuisine. As is the case in most revolving eateries, you're getting views rather than haute cuisine, but it's a wonderful way to see the city. Nonsmoking floors, a fitness center, a family plan, and off-season rates are available for the hotel's 357 units.

Fairmont Hotel Vancouver

900 W. Georgia St.
Vancouver, BC V6C 2W6
604-684-3131, 1-800-441-1414
www.fairmont.com/hotelvancouver
Price: Expensive to very expensive
Credit cards: AE, DC, MC, V
Special features: A grand historic hotel
Pets: OK at $25 a stay

This is more than just a hotel. At one time, the hotel's roofline was the town's symbol, but now it's dwarfed by surrounding buildings. Nonetheless, it's at the heart of the

The grand lobby of the historic Fairmont Hotel Vancouver Courtesy of Fairmont Hotels

downtown core. The Hotel Van (no one calls it the Hotel Vancouver) is to Vancouver what the Waldorf Astoria is to New York and the Mark Hopkins is to San Francisco: a major part of the city's hotel history. The imposing château-style hotels that dot the Canadian landscape between Halifax and Victoria are as Canadian as baseball is American, and this is one of those great historic hotels. Built by Canadian–Pacific Railway as it moved from east to west, the stylish hotels were inspired by the picturesque châteaus of Scotland and France, with steepled roofs and gargoyles.

Vancouver's version, the Hotel Vancouver, is at the heart of downtown, right across the street from the Vancouver Art Gallery and one block from where Canadian Pacific Railway built the original Hotel Vancouver in 1887, which is now the site of a shopping complex. After the original burned down, the hotel was rebuilt with renaissance details in 1939, a deadline imposed because of the impending visit of King George VI and Queen Elizabeth. Although it was rival Canadian National that built the hotel, Canadian Pacific agreed to joint management of the hotel in exchange for use of the hotel's name. Now owned by Fairmont Hotels, the hotel is in terrific shape and has recently had a complete multimillion-dollar makeover. The renovations have exposed the wonderful stone arches and other designs that had been covered up by previous renovations. Be sure to stop at the Canadian Pacific store in the shopping arcade on the lobby floor even if you're not a guest. There you'll find memorabilia of all kinds dating from when the railway first came to the city. The executive floor, Entre Gold, has premium rooms with a private concierge desk. The lounge on the first floor is where downtown businesspeople gather after hours.

Four Seasons Hotel
791 W. Georgia St.
Vancouver, BC V6C 2T4
604-689-9333, 1-800-268-6282 in Canada, 1-800-819-5053 in the U.S.
www.fourseasons.com/vancouver
Price: Very expensive
Credit cards: AE, DC, MC, V
Special features: Above Pacific Centre Mall
Pets: OK

This is one of the finest hotels on the West Coast. Although it may seem hard to determine where the shopping center ends and the hotel begins, you'll have no trouble adapting once you get into the place. This hotel has been rated five stars from the day it was built some 25 years ago, and it has since undergone several updates. Everything is impeccable. Amenities include complimentary shoe shines, hair dryers, 24-hour valet service, and bath robes. Kids are welcomed with complimentary milk and cookies. Voice mail is in English, French, or Japanese. Some of the city's best shopping is right beneath your room. The Four Seasons is adjacent to the Hotel Georgia, and across the street from the Vancouver Art Gallery. Chartwell, the main dining room, has a European and West Coast menu.

Georgian Court Hotel
773 Beatty St.
Vancouver, BC V6B 2M4
604-682-5555, 1-800-663-1155
www.georgiancourt.com
Price: Expensive to very expensive
Credit cards: AE, DC, MC, V
Special features: Across from BC Place Stadium
Pets: Small OK

While listed as an expensive to very expensive property, the Georgian Court Hotel offers intimate and luxurious rooms at less cost than you'll find at hotels of similar stature. During the off-season, November to March, the same room categories dip into the moderate to expensive range, providing some of the best hotel value in the city. The 180-room European-style building is located directly across the street from BC Place Stadium and near the Queen Elizabeth Theatre, the Centre for the Performing Arts, and GM Place. It's also the location of one of the city's finest restaurants, the William Tell. What you save on the hotel bills, be sure to spend in the restaurant. The strong point of this brick-faced hotel is that you get luxury for value. All of the rooms have terrific reading lamps, turn-down service on request, desks, three telephones, and the sense that you're being pampered.

Greenbrier Hotel

1393 Robson St.
Vancouver, BC V6E 1C6
604-683-4558, 1-888-355-5888
www.greenbrierhotel.com
Price: Inexpensive to expensive
Credit cards: AE, DC, MC, V
Special features: Long-term stays
Pets: No

In an area of expensive and luxurious hotels, the Greenbrier is a throwback to what Robson Street once was: down-home. The hotel has newly renovated and spacious one-bedroom suites, with large living rooms, complete kitchens, and full bathrooms. Extra touches include complimentary coffee served in your suite each morning. Ample parking is available. The hotel is particularly well suited for long-term stays.

Hampton Inn and Suites Vancouver

111 Robson St.
Vancouver, BC V6B 2A8
604-602-1008, 1-877-602-1008
www.hamptoninnvancouver.com
Price: Expensive to very expensive
Credit cards: AE, DC, MC, V
Special features: Suites
Pets: No

When you walk into this relatively new hotel, located on Robson Street in the heart of Vancouver's theater district, you're impressed by a marble lobby decorated with a fireplace and comfortable seating. On the cozy second-floor mezzanine, you receive a free daily continental breakfast and newspapers. The glassed-in rooftop Jacuzzi offers spectacular views, as does the fitness and entertainment facility. Each of the rooms has been decorated in West Coast pastels and includes a microwave oven, minifridge, and coffeemaker.

Holiday Inn Hotel and Suites Vancouver

1110 Howe St.
Vancouver, BC V6Z 1R2
604-684-2151, 1-800-663-9151
www.hivancouverdowntown.com
Price: Moderate to expensive
Credit cards: AE, DC, MC, V
Special features: Convenient location
Pets: Only small OK

A standard Holiday Inn, with some rooms having kitchens, it's located just minutes from most major Vancouver tourist attractions. There's underground parking, a bistro, a sports bar, and a kids' activity center, and it's located right near Theater Row.

Hotel Le Soleil

567 Hornby St.
Vancouver, BC V6C 2E8
604-632-3000, 1-877-632-3030
www.lesoleilhotel.com
Price: Very expensive
Credit cards: AE, DC, MC, V
Special features: Opulent quality
Pets: OK at special rates

This is not your usual upscale, downtown hotel, and that becomes clear the second you walk into the regally appointed lobby. Every piece of art, furniture, and fabric was handpicked from the best local and European designers. And that attention to detail and quality is evident throughout the hotel, from satin sofas to floor-to-ceiling marble bathrooms. In addition to top-of-the-line amenities in its 122 rooms, this luxury boutique hotel also offers a selection of natural aromatic oils for aromatherapy. Four rooms have been designated as Elle suites. Besides the pantyhose and fruit juices in the minibar, they're stocked with lifestyle magazines such as *Martha Stewart Living*, discount vouchers for clothing stores and beauty salons, admittance to the YWCA facilities next door, and information about special events around town that are of interest to women. The hotel's restaurant, Oritalia's, features Japanese, Chinese, and Southeast Asian ingredients prepared with a distinctive Mediterranean flair.

Hyatt Regency Vancouver

655 Burrard St.
Vancouver, BC V6C 2R7
604-683-1234, 1-800-233-1234
www.vancouver.hyatt.com
Price: Expensive to very expensive
Credit cards: AE, DC, MC, V
Special features: Above a shopping center
Pets: No

After an $18 million renovation, the Hyatt Regency Vancouver reopened in March 2002 with a new design that gives the hotel a West Coast look. The restaurant and bar were completely redone, and a new bistro was added in the lobby. Guest rooms were upgraded in 1999. Former U.S. president Bill Clinton stayed here during his 1996 summit meeting with former Russian president Boris Yeltsin. The hotel is built directly above and next to the Royal Shopping Centre complex, so guests have easy access to a major shopping complex—not that they need it, since the hotel is just two blocks north of Robson Street in the heart of the city's action. With 644 rooms, it's the city's largest hotel, so you can expect a lot of activity in the massive lobby. The Gallery Bar is one of the city's great after-work meeting places, and the quieter Peacock Lounge offers respite from the bustle; both are just off the lobby.

Kingston Hotel

757 Richards St.
Vancouver, BC V6B 3A6
604-684-9024, 1-888-713-3304
www.kingstonhotelvancouver.com
Price: Inexpensive to moderate
Credit cards: AE, MC, V
Special features: Good value
Pets: No

Looking for a clean, no-frills hotel in the middle of the action? This backpacker's special is European, complete with continental breakfast. It won't break your bank account because a lot of the usual hotel amenities such as TVs have been eliminated in the 60 rooms. And not all of the rooms have private baths. Four stories high, the hotel has no elevator, but it is close to the theater, GM Place, and BC Place. There are senior discounts and off-season rates. A neighborhood pub, the Rose and Thorn, is on the main floor. The facade includes cut granite and heavy wood along with Tudor-style windows.

Landis Hotel and Suites

1200 Hornby St.
Vancouver, BC V6Z 1W2
604-681-3555, 1-877-291-6111
www.landissuitesvancouver.com
Price: Expensive to very expensive
Credit cards: AE, DC, MC, V
Special features: Long-term stays
Pets: No

Located on the corner of Davie and Hornby Streets, this all-suites hotel is one of the more elegant long-stay establishments in the downtown core. It has fully equipped kitchens and all the comforts of home, including up-to-date technology for computer systems. It is within easy walking distance of the downtown sights and near False Creek.

Listel Vancouver

1300 Robson St.
Vancouver, BC V6E 1C5
604-684-8461, 1-800-663-5491
www.listel-vancouver.com
Price: Expensive to very expensive
Credit cards: AE, DC, MC, V
Special features: Nonsmoking throughout; live jazz in the bar
Pets: No

Located midway along Robson Street, this is a decidedly upscale property with 130 rooms, a restaurant, and a lounge, and it's within walking distance of both Stanley Park and the main shopping area of Robson. That said, the real story is in the 52 gallery rooms, where pieces of art line the walls of the hallway and the rooms. The hotel's partnership with the University of British Columbia's Museum of Anthropology and private galleries has enabled the hotel to present a tribute to all things British Columbian. Rooms on the Museum Floor feature distinctive furniture made of hemlock and cedar set against walls reflecting the soft, muted colors of Pacific Northwest forests while showcasing contemporary Northwest Coast art. With a sidewalk view, O'Doul's restaurant is a great place along Robson Street to people watch.

Metropolitan Hotel Vancouver

645 Howe St.
Vancouver, BC V6C 2Y9
604-687-1122, 1-800-667-2300
www.metropolitan.com
Price: Expensive to very expensive
Credit cards: AE, DC, MC, V
Special features: Top of the line
Pets: Small OK

This high-end boutique hotel has a pedigree of excellence. It began as the

The Pacific Palisades Hotel's lobby is contemporary chic. Courtesy of Pacific Palisades

Mandarin Hotel built for Expo '86, was sold to Delta Hotels, and is now owned by the Metropolitan chain. During all of these transitions, it has never lost its edge as a top-of-the-line facility. All of the 197 rooms have down quilts and four-piece marble bathrooms, and the lighting dimmer switches are next to the beds. There's still a touch of the Mandarin influence, with Chinese art tastefully placed throughout the lobby and in the rooms. Across from the Pacific Centre Mall, this hotel has first-class concierge service, a full-scale business center, limo service, and one of the best health clubs in town. There's a wonderfully understated and quiet elegance to this place, even though the generous use of marble would suggest otherwise. Its restaurant, Diva at the Met, is a culinary delight that delivers contemporary, international fare as well as regional specialties.

Pacific Palisades Hotel

1277 Robson St.
Vancouver, BC V6E 1C4
604-688-0461, 1-800-663-1815
www.pacificpalisadeshotel.com
Price: Expensive to very expensive
Credit cards: AE, DC, MC, V

Special features: Complimentary evening wine reception
Pets: Small OK

This was always one of Vancouver's finest hotels, but it became an even classier establishment when it was bought by the Shangri-La chain back in 1991, and it is now part of the California-based Kimpton chain. This is another movie-industry favorite because of its spacious rooms and minikitchen facilities that include a microwave and fridge. It is composed of two towers with an open palazzo and garden area between. The hotel exemplifies chic style, from the intimate lobby with its Murano glass chandelier and handmade glass-mosaic registration desk to the custom-designed furnishings. The feeling you get walking into the lobby is that it is contemporary and cool. Along with the light palette, there's a watery theme with elements such as frosted glass, backlit and supported by brushed-steel beams behind the registration desk. The main hotel's Monterey Grill is one of Robson Street's best eateries, and the location is right in the heart of the Robson Street action.

Ramada Inn and Suites Downtown
1221 Granville St.
Vancouver, BC V6Z 1M6
604-685-1111, 1-888-835-0078
www.ramadavancouver.com
Price: Moderate to expensive
Credit cards: AE, DC, MC, V
Special features: Good value
Pets: OK at $20 a day

Basic, clean, and functional, all guest rooms come with in-room coffee and tea, an iron and ironing board, a 27-inch color TV with cable (CNN and MSNBC) and pay-per-view movies, a data-port telephone with voice mail, and a hair dryer. The rooms are individually temperature controlled. A complimentary national newspaper is delivered to your door daily. You also have complimentary full access to Fitness World, located just a two-minute walk out the front door. In the middle of everything, it's good value for the money.

Residence Inn by Marriott Hotel
1234 Hornby St.
Vancouver, BC V6Z 1W2
604-688-1234, 1-800-663-1234
www.marriottresidenceinnvan.com
Price: Expensive to very expensive
Credit cards: AE, DC, MC, V
Special features: Longer stays
Pets: OK at $25 per stay plus $5 per day cleaning fee

The longer you stay at this place, the less your daily rate. It's a six-year recipient of the CAA/AAA three-diamond award. With 201 studio suites offering luxury and comfort, the hotel is ideal for business or leisure travelers\. Each suite includes a fully equipped kitchen and living room area featuring a work desk with high-speed Internet connection. Complimentary hors d'oeuvres are served in the evening. Vancouver's major attractions, such as GM Place, Stanley Park, the Centre for Perform-ing Arts, entertainment, shopping, and business districts, are just blocks away. There is 3,000 square feet of meeting space for groups from 10 to 200. Most conference spaces offer full windows and access to a private balcony.

Riviera Hotel
1431 Robson St.
Vancouver, BC V6G 1C1
604-685-1301, 1-888-699-5222
www.rivieraonrobson.com
Price: Inexpensive to expensive
Credit cards: AE, DC, MC, V
Special features: Weekly rates
Pets: No

From the balconies, there are views of the mountains, the harbor, and the city, and the hotel is a short walk from Stanley Park. The only problem is that often rooms are not available in this popular, 41-suite property. It has free parking for all guests—that in itself is worth staying here, since parking anywhere in downtown is expensive. Little wonder that word got around quickly about this place; it's perfectly located near Stanley Park and Robson's shopping area, every room has a view, and it has fully equipped kitchenettes. The one-bedroom suites and the large family suites are brightly decorated and have ample room. It has the look and feel of an apartment block, and the staff maintains a "glad you're here" atmosphere.

Robsonstrasse Hotel

1394 Robson St.
Vancouver, BC V6E 1C5
604-687 1674, 1-888-667-8877
www.robsonstrassehotel.com
Price: Moderate to expensive
Credit cards: AE, DC, MC, V
Special features: Family friendly
Pets: No

If you're traveling with a large family, this may be the best bargain in the downtown core because you can have a suite for up to eight persons. Executive guest rooms, deluxe studios, and spacious suites all offer kitchenettes and large living areas. Being in the middle of the Robson Street action, the hotel gets its name from when the street was the favorite hangout for those eating at the many German restaurants that once lined the street. It has security-monitored underground parking, and rooms have one queen-size bed, two double beds, or two double beds and one queen, plus a pull-out sofa bed, voice mail, a high-speed modem connection, a TV with remote and cable, and a kitchenette.

Rosedale on Robson Suite Hotel

838 Hamilton St.
Vancouver, BC V6B 6A2
604-689-8033, 1-800-661-8870
www.rosedaleonrobson.com
Price: Moderate to very expensive
Credit cards: AE, DC, MC, V
Special features: Business oriented
Pets: OK at $10 a day

Rosie's is the name of the New York–style restaurant that's attached to the hotel, but it's also what Vancouverites call the property itself. It's one of those places where you feel comfortable the second you walk in. It's next to the public library, two blocks from the theater district, next to Yaletown, and a short 20-minute walk from Chinatown. The all-suites rooms are bright and functional and offer everything a long-stay client might need, including business facilities and a good fitness room, pool, and sauna. Although the rooms are somewhat small, the bay windows and the light furnishings make them seem larger. The corner suites have more room.

Sandman Hotel Downtown Vancouver

180 W. Georgia St.
Vancouver, BC V6B 4P4
604-681-2211, 1-800-726-3626
www.sandmanhotels.com
Price: Inexpensive to expensive
Credit cards: AE, DC, MC, V
Special features: Good value
Pets: Small OK

The Sandman chain is British Columbian to the core. Originally a company serving the province's smaller communities, it has since spread into virtually every city. Its raison d'être is to offer functional and clean downtown facilities at affordable prices. And that's what you'll get here. There's nothing pretentious, just value for the money—and the potential for a lot of fun. The Shark Club and Grill, located on the ground floor, is a popular nightspot well known for its sports bar, pool tables, and large-screen TVs. Moxie's Classic Grill offers a wide choice of basic cuisine. The hotel is across the street from the Queen Elizabeth Theatre and the CBC Building and one block from BC Place

Stadium and GM Place. If you're here for 12 days, you get the 13th night free.

Sheraton Vancouver Wall Centre Hotel
1088 Burrard St.
Vancouver, BC V6Z 2R9
604-331-1000, 1-800-663-9255
www.sheratonvancouver.com
Price: Expensive to very expensive
Credit cards: AE, DC, MC, V
Special features: High-tech with style
Pets: Small OK

Imagine waking up one morning and saying, "I'm going to build the city's best hotel," and then doing it. That's exactly what Peter Wall, one of the city's most prominent financiers and arts patrons, did about 10 years ago. The result is an exceptional property that has quickly vaulted to near the top of the list of Vancouver's quality hotels. Upon arrival to the grand courtyard, it is apparent that you've entered a special place, with its spectacular gardens, cascading water, and Roman-style hand-laid paving stones providing a dramatic counterpoint to the hotel's innovative glass design. Two towers contain a total of 733 units in this Sheraton-managed facility located on downtown Vancouver's highest point (114 feet above sea level), and a full one acre is devoted to a garden. The hotel has a relatively small lobby that has bright furnishings set within a marble decor. Guest rooms, with floor-to-ceiling windows and stunning panoramic vistas, have duvets and personal-care items, including an iron and ironing board, a hair dryer, a make-up mirror, luxury bath amenities, lush bathrobes, and a guest "build your own" refreshment center. These set the tone along with numerous high-tech items including an in-room safe, high-speed Ethernet (10 Mbps), in-room Internet access via wireless keyboard, and a TV monitor for e-mail and Internet connec-

tions, fax/data ports, in-room movies, personal voice mail, and multiline telephones. Executive club level residents share exclusive access to the private club boardroom and the sophisticated club lounge. Try to get a one-bedroom corner suite, where the windows offer views of Grouse Mountain.

Sutton Place Hotel
845 Burrard St.
Vancouver, BC V6Z 2K6
604-682-5511, 1-800-961-7555
www.vancouver.suttonplace.com
Price: Very expensive
Credit cards: AE, DC, MC, V
Special features: Extended stays
Pets: Small dogs and cats OK

Originally a Le Meridien property, it still has a decidedly French style that's reflected in its decor and manner. Located one block south of Robson and one block from the key shopping areas, the hotel is elegant and warm, with rooms that are small but richly appointed in warm colors with wood furniture. Suites are marked by French doors separating the bedroom from the sitting area. Amenities include thick terry bathrobes, in-room movies, business traveler facilities, and twice-daily maid service. The nearby towers contain suites for long-term guests. Created for discerning guests seeking accommodation for extended stays, each of the 164 terraced residences of the 18-story apartment complex is fully furnished, complete with kitchen facilities. Valet parking, concierge service, a business center, and maid, laundry, and room service are also available for tower guests.

Terminal City Club Tower Hotel
837 W. Hastings St.
Vancouver, BC V6C 1B6
604-681-4121, 1-888-253-8777
www.tctowerhotel.com
Price: Expensive to very expensive

Credit cards: AE, DC, MC, V
Special features: Business oriented
Pets: No

Some private club. Founded in 1892, the Terminal City Club has sat near Vancouver's waterfront as a beacon to draw the city's old-boy's network. The club's new tower has five floors devoted to hotel rooms. The Terminal City Club lobby exudes comfort and prestige. Overhead, an arched golden ceiling reflects the light of a brilliant chandelier over the elaborate cherry-wood desk. Beyond the main lobby, the foyer becomes the introduction to all the club's facilities. When you stay in one of the 60 studio or one-bedroom apartments, you receive all of the club's amenities and privileges. This is the perfect location for any businessperson spending a few days in the city. Take a look at the club's billiards room; some of the tables date back to the turn of the 20th century.

Tropicana Suites Hotel
1361 Robson St.
Vancouver, BC V6E 1C6
604-687-6631
www.tropicanasuites.com
Price: Moderate
Credit cards: AE, DC, MC, V
Special features: Good value
Pets: No

Another of the comfortable, clean, and affordable Robson Street suites hotels, the Tropicana offers one-bedroom units with either a double bed or twin beds, plus a living room with a sofa bed, easily accommodating up to four adults. Well located on Robson Street in the downtown core, the hotel is within walking distance of restaurants, shopping, the business district, theaters, and Stanley Park.

Victorian Hotel
514 Homer St.
Vancouver, BC V6B 2V6
604-681-6369, 1-877-681-6369

www.victorianhotel.ca
Price: Inexpensive to moderate
Credit cards: AE, DC, MC, V
Special features: Historic building
Pets: No

When you walk up the entranceway into the Victorian, you'll understand immediately why this is one of the most popular hotels in Vancouver. The building was constructed in 1898 as one of the first guesthouses in Vancouver and has been meticulously restored with high ceilings, hardwood floors, and gorgeous period pieces. Now newly renovated in the style of the Victorian era, the Victorian Hotel is comfortable and homey.

Wedgewood Hotel
845 Hornby St.
Vancouver, BC V6Z 1V1
604-689-7777, 1-800-663-0666
www.wedgewoodhotel.com
Price: Expensive to very expensive
Credit cards: AE, DC, MC, V
Special features: Across from Courthouse Square
Pets: No

This Continental-style hotel is directly across the street from the British Columbia Supreme Court buildings, and it's a favorite for those in the legal profession. Half a block from the Vancouver Art Gallery, the 83-room property has large, finely appointed rooms, and the attention to detail is meticulous throughout. The hotel is one of Vancouver's leading intimate boutique establishments, with flowers, fine antique pieces, and original works of art throughout the rooms, suites, and public areas. A fine dining room specializes in Continental cuisine, and the Bacchus Lounge—the most cordial in the city—completes the package. You can indulge yourself in the spa with a massage, body treatment, or facial.

Westin Grand Vancouver
433 Robson St.
Vancouver, BC V6B 6L9
604-602-1999, 1-888-680-9393
www.westingrandvancouver.com
Price: Expensive to very expensive
Credit cards: AE, DC, MC, V
Special features: Business oriented
Pets: Two to a suite OK at $50 per stay

Directly across the street from the Vancouver Public Library and next door to the Centre for the Performing Arts, the Westin is within walking distance of Yaletown, Gastown, the Vancouver Art Gallery, the Queen Elizabeth Theatre/ Playhouse complex, and all downtown shopping areas. The 206-room, all-suites hotel features in-house minikitchens in all of its suites. The 46 office suites all have an ergonomically designed desk chair, laser printer, fax, copy machine, and speaker-phone with data port. The suites are light colored, and modern furnishings give a cheery atmosphere. As a Westin, with all of the attention to fine detail the chain brings to its properties, this hotel offers the finest service at all levels, as you would expect. Its restaurant, Aria, emphasizes local and West Coast cuisine.

EAST VANCOUVER
Holiday Inn Express Atrium Inn
2889 E. Hastings St.
Vancouver, BC V5K 2A1
604-254-1000, 1-888-428-7486
www.hievancouver.com
Price: Moderate to expensive
Credit cards: AE, DC, MC, V
Special features: Close to Pacific National Exhibition grounds
Pet: One maximum

A few blocks from Exhibition Park, this newly opened Holiday Inn Express hotel offers a variety of rooms in a wide range of price ranges. Although its drawback is that it's on one of Vancouver's main thor-oughfares, it's also a delightfully airy and bright property. The three-storied, 101-room glass-domed atrium is the setting for regular concerts and often for weddings. There's a shuttle to downtown, which is about 20 minutes away, and rooms have business peripherals and cable TV, including a movie channel. There's an airport shuttle pickup, a restaurant, and a pub. The hotel is situated next door to the Hastings Park Racecourse and 10 minutes from the Gastown Historic Area, and a complimentary shuttle is provided for trips within a three-mile radius of the hotel.

FALSE CREEK AND GRANVILLE ISLAND
Best Western Chateau Granville
1100 Granville St.
Vancouver, BC V6Z 2B6
604-669-7070, 1-800-663-0575
www.bestwestern.com
Price: Inexpensive to expensive
Credit cards: AE, DC, MC, V
Special features: All suites
Pets: OK on approval

Right on Granville Street in the heart of Vancouver's theater district, the hotel is conveniently located within easy walking distance of Yaletown and most of the downtown museums and attractions. It is located at the corner of busy Helmcken and Granville streets, and its chief advantage is the fact that its suites are relatively inexpensive. It has gated parking and a surprisingly quiet courtyard.

Executive Hotel Downtown Vancouver
1379 Howe St.
Vancouver, BC V6Z 2R5
604-688-7678, 1-800-570-3932
www.executivehotels.net
Price: Expensive to very expensive
Credit cards: AE, DC, MC, V
Special features: Great views
Pets: No

Looking more like an apartment block than a hotel, the property is just one block away from False Creek and the tiny Aquabus ferries that transport you back and forth to Granville Island. And it's located next to Yaletown. There are 130 luxury apartments and deluxe rooms with spectacular panoramic views of waterscapes, city skylines, and mountains. The hotel has everything that you'd expect from a long-term businessperson's facility, including same-day turnaround on laundry. The in-house business and information center has a complete selection of faxes and e-mail data ports. Views of Vancouver's South Slope and out to Point Grey are terrific. It is in a somewhat awkward location, but there is complimentary shuttle service within the downtown core on request.

Granville Island Hotel and Marina

1253 Johnson St.
Vancouver, BC V6H 3R9
604-683-7373, 1-800-663-1840
www.granvilleislandhotel.com
Price: Expensive to very expensive
Credit cards: AE, DC, MC, V
Special features: Spectacular setting among boats
Pets: No

Tired of sailing around the world? Tie your yacht up here. On the eastern tip of Granville Island, this unusual hotel is a combination of sailing motif and big-city meeting place. It's on a spectacular waterfront setting that provides views of False Creek, the North Shore mountains, and the old Expo '86 grounds that are now a series of high-rise condos. Take a walk down to the Granville Island Market in the morning, pick up your bread and cheese, and head out for a day of exploring. The 54 units feature marble floors, oversize bathtubs, and balconies in some rooms. The dockside lounge is one of Vancouver's hot singles gathering spots.

Holiday Inn Vancouver-Centre

711 W. Broadway
Vancouver, BC V5Z 3Y2
604-879-0511, 1-888-211-9874
www.hivancouver.com
Price: Moderate to expensive
Credit cards: AE, DC, MC, V
Special features: On the south side of False Creek
Pets: Small OK

The hotel is located in the middle of the Broadway shopping district and close to False Creek. It's an easy drive or walk from the hotel to Granville Island and the south side of the False Creek area, where you have wonderful views of the new city skyline. Try to get a room facing the North Shore mountains and downtown Vancouver. The views from the upper rooms are fabulous. The rooms are fairly standard Holiday Inn, clean and bright with cable/satellite TV, a free morning newspaper delivered to the room, high-speed Internet access, in-room pay-per-view movies, and windows that actually open. Included in the hotel complex is a casino.

Howard Johnson Hotel Downtown

1176 Granville St.
Vancouver, BC V6Z 1L8
604-688-8701, 1-888-654-6336
www.hojovancouver.com
Price: Inexpensive to expensive
Credit cards: AE, DC, MC, V
Special features: Family friendly
Pets: No

In line with the Howard Johnson style, this recently renovated hotel is great for families and is within walking distance of the False Creek area of the city. It has 110 rooms, five stories, and two elevators, and all rooms have cable TV and an "in house" movie channel. Coffeemakers and hair dryers are in every room. All rooms are air-conditioned and have electronic locks.

Travelodge Vancouver Centre
1304 Howe St.
Vancouver, BC V6Z 1R6
604-682-2767, 1-800-578-7878
www.travelodge.com
Price: Moderate to expensive
Credit cards: AE, DC, MC, V
Special features: Close to False Creek
Pets: No

It's located in what at first sight seems an unusual place for a motel: at the north end of the Granville Street Bridge next to the on-ramp. Stay in the right-hand lane of Howe Street as you approach the bridge, or you'll find yourself on the other side of False Creek. Nonetheless, you're close to everything here and the traffic noise is surprisingly low since the hotel is on the down slope of Howe Street, below the bridge. There's cable TV, a restaurant, a lounge, and an elevator, and it's just a couple of blocks from the False Creek waterfront and the small water taxis that sail to the island.

NORTH SHORE

Lonsdale Quay Hotel
123 Carrie Cates Crt.
North Vancouver, BC V7M 3K7
604-986-6111, 1-800-836-6111
www.lonsdalequayhotel.com
Price: Moderate to very expensive
Credit cards: AE, DC, MC, V
Special features: Part of Lonsdale Quay Market complex
Pets: No

This is one of Vancouver's most unusually placed hotels. On the North Shore, directly opposite downtown Vancouver and across Burrard Inlet, the hotel lies at the end of the Seabus line, so it's an easy "sea voyage" from the hotel to downtown Vancouver and back again. When the hotel opened for Expo '86 it was an instant hit because of its waterfront location, and it has been popular ever since. The hotel is located within a multifunctional complex that also houses a series of boutiques and the Lonsdale Quay Market; its main lobby is on the third floor of the market, and its facilities spread out over three floors. Moreover, the rooms are so discreet that there is little awareness of being in a hotel. Many of the rooms have cross-water views of the Vancouver skyline, and the multilevel complex is home for more than 90 shops and services.

WATERFRONT

Days Inn Vancouver Downtown
921 W. Pender St.
Vancouver, BC V6C 1M2
604-681-4335, 1-877-681-4335
www.daysinnvancouver.com
Price: Moderate to expensive
Credit cards: AE, DC, MC, V
Special features: Good value
Pets: No

This is arguably one of the best values in the downtown area. One block from the waterfront, it's located in the middle of everything—shopping, restaurants, museums, Gastown, and theaters. It's a recently refurbished European-style hotel with 85 guest rooms with business-friendly facilities such as voice mail and data ports. Rooms also include a closet safe, voicemail message service, and in-room coffeemaker. The executive suites have harbor views. The Chelsea Restaurant serves three meals daily; the Bull and Bear is a warm, English-style lounge that's popular with downtown businesspeople.

Fairmont Waterfront
900 Canada Place Way
Vancouver, BC V6C 3L5
604-691-1991, 1-800-441-1414
www.fairmont.com/waterfront
Price: Very expensive
Credit cards: AE, DC, MC, V
Special features: Business oriented
Pets: Only small OK

Third-floor terraces at the Fairmont Waterfront have stunning North Shore views.
Courtesy of Fairmont Hotels

Right across the street from the Pan Pacific, here you'll find a collection of amenities not usually found in a city hotel. The third-floor rooms, for example, have small terraces. And there's a club floor, called Entre Gold, that has a concierge, continental breakfast, nightly hors d'oeuvres, and a private conference room. Like the Pan Pacific, the Fairmont is on the edge of Gastown and is one block from the downtown core. As you'd expect from a five-star hotel, it has everything a business traveler needs, including communications and computer technology in its rooms. The ground-floor Herons Restaurant is one of the city's finest. The art collection—made up of works from Canadian artists—is seen throughout the lobby areas and in all rooms.

Pan Pacific Hotel
300-999 Canada Pl.
Vancouver, BC V6C 3B5
604-662-8111, 1-800-663-1515 in Canada,
1-800-937-1515 in the U.S.
www.panpacific.com
Price: Very expensive
Credit cards: AE, DC, MC, V
Special features: Part of Canada Place Convention Centre
Pets: Only small OK

More than a hotel, this is part of a complex that is the city's symbol, every bit as noticed by visitors as is the Space Needle in Seattle. Even if you don't stay here, a walk through the Pan Pacific Hotel's lobby is a tourist "must" on its own. Be sure to watch your step at the top of the two flights of escalators that seem to rise straight into a magnificent cavern of glass, because the tendency is to look upward in awe. In a city of exceptional hotels, the 350-room Pan stands out as an opulent dwelling of thick carpets, marbled commons, waterfalls, and floor-to-ceiling windows. Princess Diana and Prince Charles stayed here during Expo '86. It's an integrated part of the Canada Place complex: a convention center, cruise-ship terminal, hotel, and home of the Board of Trade. The complex, shaped like a ship and recognized by its five towering white sails, has become the city's symbol. In the early evening, sit in the glass-fronted Cascade's Lounge in the late twilight, facing the harbor and the craggy North Shore mountains. Rooms and suites are exquisite, with tasteful art and furniture in leathers and textured fabrics. It's easy to work here, as all rooms have halogen lighting with burnished bronze bedside and desk lamps sitting on amply sized desks with close-by data ports. There's a superb fitness center with a running track, massage facilities, and four restaurants.

Renaissance Vancouver Hotel Harbourside
1133 W. Hastings St.
Vancouver, BC V6E 3T3
604-689-9211, 1-800-468-3571
www.renaissancevancouver.com
Price: Expensive to very expensive
Credit cards: AE, DC, MC, V
Special features: Asian influence
Pets: OK at $30 per stay

This is probably Vancouver's most Asian downtown hotel, with Chinese art motifs throughout the lobby area. It has some of the finest harbor views of any of the water-front hotels. Atop the hotel is a revolving restaurant that makes one complete cycle an hour. It's a great way to see the city from all perspectives without getting tired. The hotel's 432 units are close to everything and just three blocks from the Convention Centre. But it's just far enough from the sometimes frantic cruise-ship facilities to almost qualify as an off-the-beaten-path location.

Vancouver Marriott Pinnacle Hotel
1128 W. Hastings St.
Vancouver, BC V6E 4R5
604-684-1128, 1-800-207-4150
www.vancouvermarriottpinnacle.com
Price: Expensive to very expensive
Credit cards: AE, DC, MC, V
Special features: One block from waterfront
Pets: No

The Marriott is a short block from the city's waterfront and only two blocks from the Vancouver Conference and Exhibition Centre. It's an easy walk to Stanley Park along the seawall, and you're just four blocks north of Robson Street. With 434 rooms, some with fabulous views of the inner harbor and the North Shore mountains, the hotel has three floors of exclusive concierge-level accommodations and a separate concierge lounge on the 25th floor, with a clear view of the mountains and Coal Harbor. In the Show Case Restaurant and Bar, the menu offers Pacific Northwest cuisine and the best from British Columbia wineries. The hotel has a 24-hour pool and health club, and you can enjoy a jog in Stanley Park.

Westin Bayshore Resort and Marina
1601 Bayshore Drive
Vancouver, BC V6G 2V4
604-682-3377, 1-888-625-5144
www.westinbayshore.com
Price: Very expensive
Special features: Good location
Pets: OK

The Westin Bayshore on the Vancouver waterfront Toshi

If you haven't time to go to an island resort while you're in the Vancouver area, this is the next best thing to island living. The hotel is located next to Stanley Park and on the waterfront facing the Royal Vancouver Yacht Club docks. There is easy access to the Coal Harbor marina and to the downtown seaplane airport, and it's connected to the Stanley Park seawall for those wanting a 6-mile workout in the mornings. The hotel tower—which once served as Howard Hughes's headquarters for more than a month in the 1980s—has been totally renovated, and each room has a balcony. There's a Kids Club Program, and the 510 rooms are served by a superb health club. Walk along the newly developed Coal Harbor waterfront for an easy 15-minute walk to downtown shopping.

WEST END

Aston Rosellen Suites at Stanley Park

2030 Barclay St.
Vancouver, BC V6G 1L5
604-689-4807, 1-888-317-6648
www.rosellensuites.com
Price: Moderate to very expensive
Credit cards: AE, DC, MC, V
Special features: Two-bedroom penthouse Katherine Hepburn suite
Pets: OK with $75 cleaning fee

It may look plain, but this West End suite hotel is one of the city's best-kept secrets, just a couple hundred yards from Stanley Park and two blocks from the action. Katherine Hepburn, who was a frequent visitor to Vancouver, called this her favorite hotel. The Rosellen caters to the film industry, families, and executive travelers with a minimum stay of three nights. The beige and peach designer furniture gives you an upbeat feel even when it's raining. Suites have a fully equipped kitchen, one or two bedrooms, separate living and dining areas, a stereo, and cable TV. Some suites have a cozy fireplace, and all have voice mail. The building was converted from an apartment block to a suite hotel in the 1960s but has undergone extensive renovations since then. There's no lobby, just a manager's office.

Buchan Hotel

1906 Haro St.
Vancouver, BC V6G 1H7
604-685-5354, 1-800-668-6654
www.buchanhotel.com
Price: Inexpensive to moderate
Credit cards: AE, DC, MC, V
Special features: Homey atmosphere; nonsmoking only
Pets: No

Built in 1926, the Buchan Hotel is ideally located on a tree-lined cul-de-sac in the heart of residential West End in downtown Vancouver, next to Stanley Park. You'll have to park on the street—and parking spots are rare in this high-rise part of town—or pay for parking in lots nearby. The great location and character of the place are offset by the lack of individual telephones in the 90 rooms. But kids under 12 stay free, there's cable TV and in-house bicycle and ski storage, and you're only one block from restaurants and shopping. The rooms on the east side are brighter and overlook a minipark. The largest are the four front-corner executive suites.

Coast Plaza Hotel and Suites

1763 Comox St.
Vancouver, BC V6G 1P6
604-688-7711, 1-800-663-1144
www.coasthotels.com
Price: Expensive to very expensive
Credit cards: AE, DC, MC, V
Special features: Extended stay
Pets: OK at $20 a day

You want to be close to Hollywood? Well, you can rub elbows with a lot of industry people who stay at this place when they're in town for a month working on flicks. The stars, of course, stay elsewhere. But this is a great location for anyone staying a week or so. Among the 269 rooms of this former apartment building are 170 suites. And of those, 12 have two bedrooms. A block away from the main West End streets, the hotel is next to Stanley Park and a short walking distance from tennis courts. All rooms have balconies; some have a great view of the park. And many of the rooms have kitchen facilities to augment 24-hour room service.

Lord Stanley Suites on the Park
1889 Alberni St.
Vancouver, BC V6G 3G7
604-688-9299, 1-888-767-7829
www.lordstanley.com
Price: Expensive to very expensive
Credit cards: AE, DC, MC, V
Special features: On the edge of Stanley Park
Pets: No

You can't ask for a more at-home quality or greater location. Open since July 1, 1998, the building offers fully furnished one- and two-bedroom deluxe suites with panoramic harbor, park, and mountain views—ideal for daily, weekly, and extended stays. The one-bedroom suites, approximately 500 square feet in size, have a separate bedroom with an open living, dining, and kitchen area. Each of these suites features a fully equipped kitchen with state-of-the-art appliances, cable TV and a VCR, in-suite washer and dryer, and office; each has either an enclosed solarium or an open balcony. Smoking and nonsmoking rooms are available. The two-bedroom suites are about 1,000 square feet in size and have two balconies each, are on the top floor, and have great views of downtown Vancouver, Stanley Park, Coal Harbor, and the North Shore mountains. Each of these suites has a master bedroom with queen bed, TV, en suite bathroom, and balcony. The second bedroom has two twin beds. Two-bedroom suites also have a full kitchen, a washer/

dryer, a second full bathroom, a living area with pullout sofa bed, a TV and a VCR, a gas fireplace, a dining area, and a den and/or enclosed balcony. All of the two-bedroom suites are designated nonsmoking and have a minimum stay requirement.

Oceanside Hotel
1847 Pendrell St.
Vancouver, BC V6G 1T3
604-682-5641, 1-877-506-2326
www.oceanside-hotel.com
Price: Moderate
Credit cards: AE, DC, MC, V
Special features: In residential area
Pets: OK

For a taste of West End residential living, you can't get more at home than this. The hotel is located in the English Bay area of downtown Vancouver, half a block from the beach and just two blocks from Stanley Park. It is a block away from Davie Street, one of the West End's major restaurant and small-shop areas. This is an all-suites hotel, each having a separate bedroom, a living room with a sofa bed, and a full kitchen. The suites are comfortable though not luxurious; some have twin beds and others have a queen-size one. The recently renovated kitchens have a clean, fresh look. However, there's no air conditioning and you might get a bit of street noise. There's free parking beneath the building, a plus in an area where parking is difficult to find.

Sunset Inn Travel Apartments
1111 Burnaby St.
Vancouver, BC V6E 1P4
604-688-2474, 1-800-786-1997
www.sunsetinn.com
Price: Moderate
Credit cards: AE, DC, MC, V
Special features: Good value
Pets: No

Don't mind the occasional high C. This tall, gray concrete structure is the choice for many opera singers and actors in town for extended stays. Located in the heart of the West End residential area, two blocks off one of the West End's major streets and close to the beaches and Stanley Park, it's an exceptional bargain with free hotel parking. In fact, it is a home away from home, with fully equipped kitchen facilities and private balconies. The room decor can best be described as 21st-century miscellaneous, but the rooms are spacious and have large closets.

Sylvia Hotel

1154 Gilford St.
Vancouver, BC V6G 2P6
604-681-9321
www.sylviahotel.com
Price: Inexpensive to moderate
Credit cards: AE, DC, MC, V
Special features: Heritage site
Pets: OK

This is the old salt of Vancouver, the place that locals recommend to their out-of-town friends. It's an official Vancouver heritage site, and the ivy-covered building overlooks English Bay. On the south side of the West End, it's a favorite for anyone looking for the best combination of price and setting. Two blocks from Stanley Park and Denman Street (the West End's main thoroughfare), the hotel was originally built as an apartment complex in 1912. The 119 rooms are comfortable, though some are quite small, and many have housekeeping facilities. Across the street are the English Bay beaches. Families should ask for the one-bedroom suites that sleep four and have a living room and kitchen. There's a restaurant and a lounge that looks out to the beaches.

Bed & Breakfasts

Many of the B&Bs have their own associations, including the **Vancouver Bed and Breakfast Network** (www.vancouver bb.com), the **Association of B&B**

Accommodations (www.bbvancouverbc .com), and the **Downtown Vancouver Bed and Breakfast Group** (www.downtown accommodations.com).

English Bay Inn

1968 Comox St.
Vancouver, BC V6G 1R4
West End
604-683-8002, 1-866-683-8002
www.englishbayinn.com
Price: Expensive to very expensive
Credit cards: AE, DC, MC, V
Special features: Hideaway location
Pets: No

This is more than just a place to sleep. It's an experience curling up in your Louis Phillippe sleigh bed under a down comforter in this romantic, five-room establishment. The best of the lot is the top-story, two-level suite, which has a fireplace in the bedroom. All rooms have private baths, and two back rooms open up onto a garden. Among the extras are terrycloth robes, evening port or sherry, and phones in each room. The formal dining room, where you'll have breakfast, is complete with a gas fireplace that crackles and a wonderful old ticking grandfather clock. To the south of the Tudor-style inn is English Bay, with four beaches within easy walking distance. To the north is Burrard Inlet, and one block to the west is Stanley Park. The house is tucked away from the street with high-rise apartments on both sides and a small landscaped garden in the backyard.

Heritage Harbour B&B

1838 Ogden Ave.
Vancouver, BC V6J 1A1
Kitsilano
604-736-0809
www.vancouver-bc.com/heritageharbour
Price: Moderate to expensive
Credit cards: None

Special features: Great view; no children; nonsmoking
Pets: No

This quiet waterfront home is directly across from English Bay and near the Kitsilano beaches across from the Maritime Museum. You simply won't find a more stunning view anywhere in the city: You face the entrance to False Creek and the West End skyline with the mountains as a backdrop. In the mornings there's a sweetness in the air that you'll never match anywhere else in the city. In the summer it can get a bit busy since you're in the heart of Vanier Park, with the museums and beach activities outside the door. But there's a sense of life and joy that's infectious. There are just two units, but the place has all of the amenities you find in your own home: private baths, a balcony, full gourmet breakfast, and a guest lounge with a fireplace, TV, VCR, and fridge.

Johnson House

2278 W. 34th Ave.
Vancouver, BC V6M 1G6
Point Grey
604-266-4175
www.johnsons-inn-vancouver.com
Price: Inexpensive to moderate
Credit cards: None
Special features: Antiques galore
Pets: No

This immaculately restored 1920s craftsman style home is in the middle of Kerrisdale, on a quiet street in the city's very well-heeled Point Grey district. You like antiques? Go no farther. Staying in this delightful home is like being in a richly decorated antiques store. It is furnished with antique Canadian heritage furniture, Persian rugs, and collectibles such as hand-carved wooden carousel horses, gramophones, collector clocks, and ancient stone statues. In fact, the porch light is an old Vancouver street lamp. The three guest rooms have fir floors, Oriental carpets, cathedral ceilings with ceiling fans, TVs, high-speed cable Internet lines, guest extension-phones, clock radios, robes, irons and ironing boards, and desks. The private, themed bathrooms all have showers or shower/tub combinations, tiled floors, and antique wood-framed mirrors. The best of the three units is the Carousel suite, with a mermaid-theme bathroom en suite. Each room has a large Vancouver map and guidebook. Breakfast is in the airy cottage-style room on the first floor.

West End Guest House

1362 Haro St.
Vancouver, BC V6E 1G2
West End
604-681-2889, 1-888-546-3327
www.westendguesthouse.com
Price: Moderate to expensive
Credit cards: AE, DC, MC, V
Special features: Heritage building
Pets: No

One block from Robson Street, this early 1900s Victorian-style home is a longstanding Vancouver landmark, and its service is just as legendary. Its pink exterior makes it stand out from the surrounding homes and gives a hint of the warmth you'll find inside. Each of the eight rooms is furnished with antiques and has a private bath. Beds have feather and lambskin comforters, robes and telephones are in every room, and breakfast is a feast served family style or delivered to your room. The original builders and occupants of the circa 1906 house also owned Edwards Brothers Photo Supplies, so the early years of the West Coast are chronicled in the photographs throughout the rooms. The setting is completed with accents of old-world comforts such as overstuffed parlor furniture and a Belgian-made mahogany dining suite circa 1920.

Budget Options

C&N Backpackers Hostel
927 Main St.
Vancouver, BC V6A 2V8
Downtown
604-682-2441, 1-888-434-6060
www.cnnbackpackers.com
Price: Inexpensive
Credit cards: AE, DC, MC, V
Special features: Convenient location
Pets: No

This clean and renovated hostel is in the heart of downtown, one block from the Main Street Sky Train station and Science World and next door to the Via Rail station. There's a kitchen, Internet access, bike rentals, an elevator, free parking, and non-smoking rooms.

Hosteling International Downtown
1114 Burnaby St.
Vancouver, BC V6E 1P1
West End
604-684-4565, 1-888-203-4302
www.hihostels.ca/hostels/vancouver
downtown
Price: Inexpensive
Credit cards: MC, V
Special features: Fabulous location; wheelchair accessible
Pets: No

Few would ever expect a hostel to look like this. This centrally located property is bright and basic but an incredible value. In the West End residential neighborhood, close to colorful Davie Street with its many shops, restaurants, and cafés, the hostel is a two-minute walk from English Bay Beach, the Aquatic Centre, and False Creek ferries to Granville Island. There are seven double rooms, which is unusual for a hostel since they usually have just dormitory sleeping areas. The facility can handle about 240 people and has a fully equipped kitchen and a large dining area. If you're interested in going to the beach, there's

free shuttle service between the downtown and the Jericho Beach hostels. Every guest is provided a key card, and there's a full travel-service information and guest-activity desk in the lobby. And, unlike the Jericho Beach property, this one is wheelchair accessible.

Hostelling International—Jericho Beach
1515 Discovery St.
Vancouver, BC V6R 4K5
Point Grey
604-224-3208, 1-888-203-4303
www.hihostels.ca/vancouverjerichobeach
Price: Inexpensive
Credit cards: MC, V
Special features: Fabulous location; no children under 5
Pets: No

Few hostels in North America are as well located as this. In the middle of Jericho Park just off the Point Grey strip of beaches, it's only 20 minutes from downtown by car (35 minutes by bus) and right next to Jericho Beach. The view of downtown Vancouver is spectacular. The facility is open to individuals or families, but it's off-limits to children under five and pets. Bring your own sleeping bag or rent linens on the spot. Private rooms are available. If you're planning to be here between June and September, you'll have to leave a one-night advance deposit via credit card or cash. The hostel is closed October 1 to April 30. It is not wheelchair accessible.

Simon Fraser University Residences
Room 212, McTaggart-Cowan Hall
Simon Fraser University
Burnaby, BC V5A 1S6
East Vancouver
604-291-4503
www.sfu.ca/conference-accommodation
Price: Inexpensive to moderate
Credit cards: AE, V
Special features: Magnificent architecture
Pets: No

Simon Fraser University opens its residences to the public from May to August, when classes aren't in session. Located atop Burnaby Mountain, the university itself was hailed as an architectural marvel when it was constructed in the 1960s. There are kitchen facilities, laundry rooms, a TV lounge, and plenty of parking. The one disadvantage is that it's 12 miles (16 k) east of downtown. The big advantages are that it's cool in summer and it has spectacular mountain views during the day.

University of British Columbia Resident Housing

Conferences and Accommodation
Reservations Office
5961 Student Union Blvd.
Vancouver, BC V6T 2C9
Point Grey
604-822-1000
www.conferences.ubc.ca
Price: Inexpensive to moderate
Credit cards: AE, DC, MC, V
Special features: Suites and apartments
Pets: No

You may be surprised by the range of guests staying at these budget accommodations; they include businesspeople trying to keep the budget in line while attending conferences. Nearby are the UBC Museum of Anthropology, the UBC Botanical Gardens, and Wreck Beach, the unofficially sanctioned nude beach at the western tip of Point Grey. There's a wide array of seasonal accommodations, from 47 fully equipped suites year-round to 3,000 rooms May to August, including single or shared apartments and dormitory and hostel-style rooms. Parking is free during the summer, and the primary residence building, the Walter Gage, is easily accessible from downtown by bus.

YWCA Hotel

733 Beatty St.
Vancouver, BC V6B 2M4
Downtown
604-895-5830, 1-800-663-1424
www.ywcahotel.com
Price: Inexpensive to moderate
Credit cards: AE, DC, MC, V
Special features: Great value and location
Pets: No

This is a Y that's impressive for its care of its residents. The hotel/residence with 155 rooms on 12 floors was built with security in mind, so you'll have keys for parking, the front door, your room, and hall bathrooms. The rooms are immaculate and functional, and there's air conditioning, minifridges, TVs, meeting rooms, a nearby YWCA fitness center, a coffee shop, and Internet terminals. There's also a communal kitchen, laundry, and lounges. You won't find accommodations this clean and secure as cheaply anywhere downtown, and it's within a couple blocks of theaters and sports venues.

RV Parks

RV parks are located throughout the Lower Mainland. For a list contact **Tourism British Columbia** (604-435-5622 or 1-800-435-5622 in North America, 250-387-1642 for international callers; www .hellobc.com) and ask for the listings and the accommodations guide. You can also search at www.welcometobc.ca /vancamping. Here's a sampling.

Capilano RV Park

295 Tomahawk Ave.
North Vancouver, BC V7P 1C5
North Shore
604-987-4722
www.capilanorvpark.com
Price: Inexpensive
Credit cards: MC, V
Special features: Waterfront location in town
Pets: OK at $2 per day

This private ground offers some of the best views on the Lower Mainland, catering to a lot of young families with a pool, a playground, and a Jacuzzi. In most cities, you can expect any RV park to be well outside the city limits, out in the boonies. That's why this one is so special: not only is it within 10 minutes by car from downtown Vancouver, but you also have a great location on the Capilano River across the water from Stanley Park. It's surprisingly quiet for a campground that is virtually under the Lion's Gate Bridge. Reservations in summer are a must. It's open year-round.

Hazelmere RV Park and Campground
18843 Eighth Ave.
South Surrey, BC V3S 9R9
East of Vancouver
604-538-1167
www.hazelmere.ca
Price: Inexpensive
Credit cards: MC, V
Special features: Riverfront location, tranquil setting
Pets: OK

This is a golfer's location, virtually next door to two of the area's finest courses—Hazelmere and Peace Portal—and you'll find campers with golf clubs nearby; it's also near beaches and shopping. The Campbell River runs through the tranquil, parklike property. The campground has laundry, showers, cable TV, a store, a recreation room, a covered picnic area, and cabins. (From BC 99, the first exit north of the Canadian–U.S. border, drive east on Eighth Avenue.)

RESTAURANTS

There are literally hundreds of eateries in Vancouver and its suburbs, restaurants that reflect the region's cultural diversity. For example, in what is described as the most Asian city in North America, you'll find some 65 Japanese restaurants and that doesn't count those in nearby suburbs. Vancouver is a city where restaurants aren't just a place to eat—they're cultural experiences. Whatever you want, you'll find in profusion, whether it's sushi, won tons, Italian sausage, grilled salmon or venison, or a plate of fern leaf.

Vancouver has seen vast increases in Asian immigration and the area's markets and restaurants now offer a plethora of food varieties, with European culinary traditions integrated into the newer cuisine, creating something unique. There is now a West Coast cuisine, one with the sophistication of the French, combining with indigenous Pacific Northwest foodstuffs and Asian invention.

Chinatown is obviously the place to go for Chinese food. The restaurants there range from interchangeable to exquisite. Walk through Chinatown and you'll be in restaurant heaven, with eating options every few feet. Along West Broadway, past Granville Street and on the way to the University of British Columbia, are numerous Greek restaurants; Robson Street has contemporary Northwest cuisine on every block; and on Commercial Street you'll find Italian. Once you get into Richmond, there's a dazzling array of Asian restaurants in every shopping center and on virtually every block.

Most people have had experiences with Chinese restaurants. Not so familiar, perhaps, are Japanese eateries, and since Vancouver is the Japanese restaurant capital of North America, you might want to know something about eating Japanese. No, you don't always have to remove your shoes; not all the food swims or is eaten raw, nor do you have to like seaweed, eel, or sea urchin. You can, if you want, walk away stuffed from barbecued meats, noodles, and cooked salmon and vegetables. You won't have any problem in finding just the right Japanese restaurant for your palate.

What you get in a good Japanese restaurant is 900 years of art, history, and culture. The cuisine is part food and part presentation, and its preparation and presentation involve good taste, some mystique, a lot of graciousness, and immaculate cleanliness; every customer is treated as though a guest in the owner's home. Just as proper form is everything in Japanese society, appearance in a Japanese restaurant is everything, and the way food looks is as important as its taste. Presenting raw fish (sashimi) in colorful surroundings and carefully placing it on the tray as one would design a bouquet of flowers for a table is an art form.

Frankly, it's rare to find a substandard restaurant in Vancouver, as in San Francisco and Seattle. You have unlimited choices in variety and price, and every neighborhood gives you plenty of options. Even in Stanley Park you'll find two fine restaurants. In Richmond, you'll see Chinese and Japanese restaurants no matter where you are. And in Steveston's dock area, many small restaurants serve seafood and snacks. It's restaurants include the Steveston Seafood House for gourmet dining, Dave's Fish and Chips, the Steveston Cannery Cafe, the Dockside Cafe, the Charthouse Restaurant, and O'Hares Pub and Bistro, to name just a few.

If it's just a burger you want, try Earl's, a local chain with outlets throughout the city and suburbs. And you won't run short of McDonald's, Wendy's, or any other international chain. The White Spot, at some 30-and-growing locations in the Lower Mainland, is a homegrown franchise with a broad menu, but for a taste of what made the chain successful, try the legendary Triple O Burger with its special (undisclosed formula) sauce.

With the vast numbers of choices in the Greater Vancouver area, it's impossible to list here every eatery in town. And every guide offers its own views of which places you should experience. This one is no different, except that what follows is a sampling that reflects the city's unique international and West Coast culinary experiences—those that offer a difference without missing what's essential.

By law, all Vancouver restaurants are non-smoking. Pubs allow it if the smoking areas are isolated and ventilated. And as for dressing up, in Vancouver (as in Seattle), you can wear anything, casual to tux, and no one will care.

Seafood

Like Seattle, Vancouver is a seafood town, and you'll have seafood choices in virtually every restaurant and eatery throughout the city. Frankly, however, Vancouverites are not as passionate about seafood as are Seattleites. Nevertheless, most restaurants feature salmon in all varieties, and each species has it own taste and firmness (see "Seafood" in chapter 1). In recent years, farmed salmon has appeared on restaurant menus. But many restaurants, bowing to local tastes, serve only wild varieties.

Wine

Like Washington State, British Columbia has a thriving wine industry. And if you like wines from Washington State or Oregon, chances are you'll love British Columbia's varietals. British Columbia wines, available throughout the province from vineyards south of the Okanagan to Vancouver Island, are produced in a wide variety of reds, whites, and blushes.

As in California's Napa Valley, France's Bordeaux, and Italy's Chianti region in Tuscany, in the Okanagan Valley grape growing and wine production compose a vigorous wine industry. Between the town of Osoyoos in the south and Vernon in the north is a 125-mile-long (200 km) string of some 60 wineries, one vineyard after another beckoning locals and visitors alike to sample the region's seductive products. About a five-hour, 185-mile (300 km) drive east of Vancouver, the Canadian Okanagan is also a prime tourist destination, a popular place to rest awhile in one of the cozy restaurants or resorts that overlook Lake Okanagan. The Okanagan valley is especially popular in late September and early October during the wine festivals. (Take Trans-Canada Highway 1 east to the town of Hope and then Hwy. 3 east.)

CHINATOWN

Floata Seafood Restaurant
400–180 Keefer St.
604-602-0368
Cuisine: Chinese, Asian
Meals served: L, D
Open: Daily
Price: Moderate
Credit cards: AE, DC, MC, V
Reservations: Not necessary
Wheelchair accessible: No

It's as much a cultural experience as a culinary one to eat in this vast restaurant, Canada's largest, that seats more than 1,000 people. Oddly, it's a surprisingly intimate place, as floor-to-ceiling partitions turn the space into a series of smaller rooms. The menu has more than just the usual Chinese fare, with options for Cambodian and Vietnamese dishes. The choices include Peking duck that is barbecued on premises and lobster and crab in a ginger and garlic sauce. The restaurant has a sister operation in Richmond at the Parker Place (4380 No. 3 Rd., Richmond, 604-270-8889). Be sure to try the lobster in cream sauce or the braised mushrooms with mustard greens.

Sun Sui Wah Seafood Restaurant
3888 Main St.
604-872-8822
Cuisine: Chinese
Meals served: L, D
Open: Daily
Price: Moderate

Credit cards: AE, DC, MC, V
Reservations: Recommended
Wheelchair accessible: Yes

This has been named the best Cantonese restaurant in the Lower Mainland by a Chinese-language radio poll as well as by major North American magazines and newspapers. It's the place for dim sum in an area where dim sum is a specialty of almost every restaurant. A signature dish is the roasted squab marinated with a blend of seasonings and spices and then roasted until crispy and tender. Squab is a delicacy more familiar to Asian cultures; according to Chinese tradition, it has healing properties to aid in liver and kidney functions and contains antitoxins for cleansing the internal organs. Regardless, it tastes great. Alternatives are the king crab steamed with minced garlic, steamed scallops on silky bean curd, and Alaskan king crab dressed in wine and garlic. There's also lobster hot pot with egg noodles and lightly sautéed geoduck paired with coconut milk in a fluffy crust. Chinese weddings, many of which are huge, compete for place settings, especially on weekends.

DOWNTOWN

Bacchus Ristorante
845 Hornby St. (Wedgewood Hotel)
604-689-7777
Cuisine: Italian, Northwest
Meals served: B, L, D
Open: Daily
Price: Moderate to expensive
Credit cards: AE, DC, MC, V
Reservations: Recommended
Wheelchair accessible: Yes

This is the power-lunch place for lawyers, judges, and others in the legal profession, because the restaurant is across the street from the courthouse complex and it's a favorite for the local barristers. The flavor of the place is luxurious, and the cuisine is northern Italian with an emphasis on the use of British Columbian products such as salmon. The restaurant is a combination lounge/café and high-style dining room. You must try afternoon tea in front of the fireplace (2–4 pm), especially on a rainy winter's day. The evening menu changes often, but the pan-seared wild British Columbia salmon with olive oil–forked fingerling potatoes, shaved fennel, and cilantro salad is a constant. And behind a set of elegant doors is a cigar room stocked with fine Cuban cigars.

Bishop's

2183 W. Fourth Ave.
604-738-2025
Cuisine: Pacific Northwest
Meals served: D
Open: Daily
Price: Expensive
Credit cards: AE, DC, MC, V
Reservations: A must
Wheelchair accessible: Main level only

When you walk into this two-level restaurant, it's almost like being in someone's dining room. It's an intimate space where owner John Bishop makes himself an important element in the dining experience. Consistently on everyone's "Best" list, Bishop's has maintained its position as one of Vancouver's finest restaurants because of its simplicity in presentation. Bishop has cooked not only for Bill Clinton and Boris Yeltsin, but also for a long list of Hollywood's who's who, such as Glenn Close, Robin Williams, and Robert DeNiro. Although the menu changes often, rack of venison is a house specialty, as is the pan-seared scallops scented with lemongrass. The restaurant, like the food, is subtly presented, with gentle tones creating an at-home atmosphere. It is located along Fourth Avenue's bustling area of boutiques and small shops.

Chiyoda

200-1050 Alberni St.
604-688-5050
Cuisine: Japanese
Meals served: L, D
Open: Daily
Price: Inexpensive to moderate
Credit cards: AE, MC, V
Reservations: Not necessary
Wheelchair accessible: Yes

If you like the experience of seeing what you eat cooked in front of you, you'll love this place. Everything here, down to the beer glasses, was designed in Japan. For those who want something other than sushi, the emphasis here is on grilled food (robata) and it draws in Japanese visitors at lunch and locals in the evenings for moderately priced dinners.

Diva at the Met

645 Howe St. (Metropolitan Hotel)
604-602-7788
Cuisine: Continental, Pacific Northwest
Meals served: B, L, D
Open: Daily
Price: Expensive
Credit cards: AE, DC, MC, V
Reservations: Recommended
Wheelchair accessible: Yes

Diva is an airy space, with a decidedly business atmosphere for lunch. And you'll be surprised to see that the menu has none of the pretensions you might automatically associate with a restaurant of this caliber. Yet chef Scott Baechler has consistently produced an innovative and award-winning menu. Try the Queen Charlotte scallops, the wild sockeye salmon, or the Pacific halibut. The chilled tomato martini is a great starter; finish with the Stilton cheesecake. The meticulous service melds with an elegant yet casual West Coast ambience. The layout has tiered seating, a semi-open kitchen, spot lighting, and an airy, naturally lit bar and lounge.

Ichibankan

770 Thurlow St.
604-682-3894
Cuisine: Japanese
Meals served: L, D
Open: Daily
Price: Inexpensive to moderate
Credit cards: AE, DC, MC, V
Reservations: Not necessary
Wheelchair accessible: No

Like your food served on a conveyor belt? Sit around the long sushi bar and watch as the chefs work in the middle, placing a variety of sushi items on color-coded dishes that are then put on a moving conveyor belt. When something you like passes by, reach over and grab it. A waitress collects your dishes before they get too high and marks off on your tab what you've had. Be careful about the dish colors. You might be surprised when you get the bill and realize you should have had the green instead of the black.

Imperial Chinese Seafood Restaurant

355 Burrard St.
604-688-8191
Cuisine: Chinese
Meals served: D
Open: Daily
Price: Inexpensive to moderate
Credit cards: AE, DC, MC, V
Reservations: Not necessary
Wheelchair accessible: Yes

Located in the historic Marine Building, a restored heritage site at the north end of Burrard in the middle of hotel row, the Imperial Chinese Seafood Restaurant is in keeping with a stately and opulent restaurant in Hong Kong. In what just might be the grandest dining room in town, you walk up a sweeping staircase that looks as though it came out of a 19th-century-period movie. The chandeliered dining room, a fusion of traditional Chinese furnishings and smart modern decor, offers panoramic views from two-story windows of Burrard Inlet and the North Shore mountains. This is a decidedly upscale Chinese restaurant, with classical music and Dom Perignon accenting the menu of lobster, pan-fried scallops, and pan-smoked black cod.

Joe Fortes

777 Thurlow St.
604-669-1940
Cuisine: Seafood, West Coast
Meals served: L, D
Open: Daily
Price: Moderate
Credit cards: AE, DC, MC, V
Reservations: Recommended
Wheelchair accessible: Yes

Located adjacent to the busiest part of Robson Street, Joe's is one of downtown Vancouver's most popular eateries. The place is named after Vancouver's most famous lifeguard, whose real name was Seraphim Fortes. He was a seaman who arrived in 1885, took up residence on English Bay in a squatter's shack, and took pride in scaring hoodlums who harassed local picnickers. The restaurant is a high-energy place in a multilevel, brick interior that has a large U-shaped bar. The menu is varied, with seafood and a wide selection of meats with Creole accents.

William Tell

765 Beatty St. (Georgian Court Hotel)
604-688-3504
Cuisine: Swiss, Continental
Meals served: D
Open: Tu–Sun (Sunday Swiss farmer's buffet only)
Price: Expensive
Credit cards: AE, DC, MC, V
Reservations: Recommended
Wheelchair accessible: Yes

Across from the BC Place Stadium, "the Tell" is a longtime Vancouver institution that has never lost its edge and remains an award-winning fine dining restaurant even after

40 years. One of the reasons for its long-lasting success is a menu that moves with the times and is served with a passion for detail. Specialties include potato-crusted wild salmon fillet with sautéed spinach and lemon cream sauce; smoked poached Alaskan cod with whisky velouté and parsley potatoes; and *Zürcher Geschnetzeltes*—sliced veal and mushrooms sautéed in a white wine sauce. The Sunday Swiss farmer's buffet is a combination of hot and cold appetizers and entrees that include Swiss-style soup, leg of lamb, prime rib, bratwurst and Schüblig sausages on sauerkraut, braised red cabbage, and *Berner rosti* (Swiss potatoes with onions). Close to the theater area, the restaurant is convenient for dinner prior to a concert or for a dessert afterward. And if you were born before 1943, you'll get 20 percent off the bill.

Yaletown Brewing
1111 Mainland St.
604-681-2739
Cuisine: Pizza, pub fare
Meals served: L, D
Open: Daily
Price: Inexpensive
Credit cards: AE, DC, MC, V
Reservations: Recommended
Wheelchair accessible: Yes

Like that of virtually every restaurant in the area, Yaletown Brewing's space is carved from a warehouse, and the pub/restaurant makes use of the original character. Home-brews accent the pub-fare menu. It's always crowded late in the afternoon and evening, so the best bet for uncrowded moments is weekend lunchtimes around opening time. It isn't a traditional pizza place, not with grilled crusted salmon with stone ground mustard on the dinner menu, so purists may find it just too yuppie for their tastes. But the real story is the homebrew the restaurant serves. You'll likely want a pint of Frank's Nut Brown Ale or Red Brick Bitter to wash down the pizza.

FALSE CREEK AND GRANVILLE ISLAND
Bridges
1696 Duranleau St.
604-687-4400
Cuisine: West Coast
Meals served: L, D
Open: Daily
Price: Inexpensive to moderate
Credit cards: AE, DC, MC, V
Reservations: Not necessary
Wheelchair accessible: Yes

Bridges has four dining possibilities, ranging from exquisite to bar room, all with water, mountain, and city views. Go here on a sunny day and you'll never want to leave the casual wharfside patio next to the Granville Island yachts. Across the dock from the Granville Island Market, it's the quintessential West Coast eatery. The enclosed restaurant on the second floor is the fine dining area, featuring seafood, lamb, and beef. In the summer, you can dine al fresco on the second-floor terrace. Downstairs, in winter, the Bistro offers everything from grilled salmon to pizza, steamed mussels to steak, plus the warmth of a fireplace. But in summer, the Dock restaurant is where you want to be: 300 chairs on the waterfront attract visitors and residents of the nearby condos.

C
2-1600 Howe St.
604-681-1164
Cuisine: Pacific Northwest
Meals served: L, D
Credit cards: AE, DC, MC, V
Open: Daily (dinner), M–F (lunch)
Price: Expensive
Reservations: Recommended
Wheelchair accessible: Yes

The restaurant with a single letter for a name is one of Vancouver's newer, located on the shores of False Creek directly across from Granville Island. The menu is seafood and the environment is decidedly 1980s with a

Bridges, a quintessential West Coast restaurant with great water views Toshi

semi-industrial character. Expect bread baskets to be made from sheets of industrial-grade rubber and the washrooms to be lined with false vinyl siding. The dining area is open and airy, with minimalist decor and dramatic touches. Floor-to-ceiling windows extend two stories for a view of joggers, cyclists, sea kayakers, and ferries. An outdoor patio is open in summer. The menu has a cosmopolitan character and features local, seasonal seafood in dishes such as albacore tuna sashimi, spot prawn and oyster cocktail, pan-roasted wild salmon, and baked halibut. Specialties include a roasted pork shoulder and gold potato terrine for those who want a nonseafood meal. For a seafood experience, ask for the chef's collection, an innovative assortment of what the seas have to offer.

Il Giardino Di Umberto
1382 Hornby St.
604-669-2422
Cuisine: Italian, Northwest
Meals served: L, D

Open: M–Sat
Price: Moderate to expensive
Credit cards: AE, DC, MC, V
Reservations: Recommended
Wheelchair accessible: Yes

Umberto Menghi is an institution in the city, having no less than three popular restaurants in town and two in Whistler. This is his corporate flagship. Located near False Creek, the restaurant has an ambience that is perfect for talking or just sitting back and looking around. The decor is Tuscan villa, not surprising since Menghi has a popular cooking school in Tuscany. There's a garden patio for sunny days and warm evenings. Ask for the wonderful table set above the small, intimate dining area just to the right of the entrance. High above the floor, it's in a small alcove that can't be equaled anywhere in the city for its romantic intimacy. While the menu is heavily weighted to Tuscan fare, it offers a good variety of flavors. Try the salmon carpaccio medio-rente or a thick chop of grilled veal in a rosemary-accented wine jus. Farm-raised pheasant is a specialty, as is the veal with a mélange of lightly grilled wild mushrooms.

Monk McQueen's

602 Stamp's Landing
604-877-1351
Cuisine: Seafood
Meals served: L, D
Open: Daily
Price: Moderate
Credit cards: AE, DC MC, V
Reservations: Not necessary
Wheelchair accessible: Yes

Not technically on Granville Island, Monk's is directly east of it along the seawall that connects the island to the False Creek Marina. On the water near the east end of False Creek's south side, it is in the heart of both the residential and the sailboating community. There's a terrific view of the Vancouver skyline, and brilliant sunsets accent a menu that provides something for both casual and formal diners. The restaurant it has a light, spacious ambience, with an upstairs room for more formal dining and the casual downstairs oyster bar. Anyone who wears a tie is looked upon as weird. Prices are budget-focused downstairs, but the upstairs salmon braised in a prawn sauce is worth the extra cost.

GASTOWN

Borge Antico

321 Water St.
604-683-8376
Cuisine: Italian
Meals served: L, D
Open: M–Sat
Price: Moderate to expensive
Credit cards: AE, DC, MC, V
Reservations: Recommended
Wheelchair accessible: Yes

Former visitors might remember this third of Umberto Menghi's Vancouver restaurants as Al Porto. Although the name has changed and some structural changes were made in this red-brick converted warehouse in the heart of Gastown, it has remained one of the most authentic Italian menus in the city. The downstairs area seats 150, plus there's a terrace and an upstairs dining room, each of which seats 40 to 50. The atmosphere is created with wood and artwork, and the place overlooks the railway tracks along Coal Harbor next to the Convention Centre. You won't go wrong if you start with grilled calamari salad and a roulade of smoked salmon before moving on. The Beef Fiorentina or rib pork roast serves two. Other main dishes include smoked sea bass and roasted chicken.

The Cannery

2205 Commissioner St.
604-254-9606
Cuisine: Seafood
Meals served: D
Open: Daily
Price: Moderate to expensive
Credit cards: AE, DC, MC, V
Reservations: Recommended
Wheelchair accessible: No

To begin with, it's really midway between Gastown and the Second Narrows Bridge in East Vancouver, but you can easily get there by driving through Gastown along Hastings Street. The Cannery is on the industrial waterfront, across from countless railway tracks, near warehouses, and isolated from the city. But it has been a Vancouver seafood institution for going on 25 years, because all it does is produce satisfied customers. The rugged cedar restaurant looks out toward North Vancouver and to the downtown area with views of fishing boats and freighters. A new dock now accommodates boats, yachts, and charter boats for those who want to arrive differently. The menu features most anything that swims or lives in the ocean, and the staff will even pack a picnic basket for you. (Access is via either the Commissioner St. overpass, located just off McGill St., or the Clark Drive overpass at Hastings St.)

Steamworks Brewery
375 Water St.
604-689-2739
Cuisine: Burgers, Italian, Pacific Northwest, Continental
Meals served: L, D
Open: Daily
Price: Inexpensive to moderate
Credit cards: AE, MC, V
Reservations: Not necessary
Wheelchair accessible: Yes

This place has the best selection of beers in town, in a location adjacent to the old Canadian Pacific terminal on the edge of Gastown. It's a two-story restaurant that serves great burgers and everything-on-it pizzas as well as Continental and Pacific Northwest items that would not be out of place in trendy restaurants. Upstairs is a pub/lounge that has become an unofficial downtown, boy-meets-girl-on-their-respective-lunch-hours place—or after work when it's time to unwind. Downstairs are three more sedate, separate dining rooms. Because the restaurant is next to and below the Landing minimall, it attracts a lot of youngish, upscale shoppers.

NORTH SHORE
Beach House Restaurant at Dundarave Pier
150 25th St. (West Vancouver)
604-922-1414
Cuisine: West Coast
Meals served: L, D
Open: Daily
Price: Moderate
Credit cards: AE, DC, MC, V
Reservations: Recommended
Wheelchair accessible: Yes

This waterfront restaurant is located at the foot of Dundarave Pier, where even locals

shoot a lot of film of its dramatic views across English Bay. In recent years, the restaurant was restored to its original 1912 character, with wooden floors, creamy walls, and a glass-walled front that allows everyone to look out. Although the menu leans toward seafood, you'll also find many traditional Italian favorites and West Coast cuisine. Try the vanilla- and saffron-marinated Atlantic scallops, fanned on baby spinach with blood-orange yogurt. There's also one of the best selections of British Columbia estate wines anywhere in the city, with 450 selections, many of them international medal winners.

The Salmon House on the Hill
2229 Folkestone Way (West Vancouver)
604-926-3212
Cuisine: West Coast
Meals served: L, D
Open: Daily
Price: Moderate to expensive
Credit cards: AE, DC, MC, V
Reservations: Recommended
Wheelchair accessible: Yes

If you want a view of the city, this is as close to an eagle's-eye view as you're likely to get, especially if you have a window table in this restaurant perched on a high bluff overlooking the city and ocean. The window-wrapped dining room offers an unparalleled view of Vancouver and Burrard Inlet. The decor is West Coast Native American culture, and you'll notice the distinct odor of the burning green alder that's used in cooking the seafood. The salmon choices are terrific, but for something different try the alder-grilled cajun shark dusted with pistachio prawn butter and basmati rice. The restaurant is only a 15-minute drive from downtown Vancouver. (From downtown, cross Lion's Gate Bridge and take the West Vancouver exit to Taylor Way; turn right. Head north under the freeway and turn left onto H westbound; take exit

10/21st St. and Folkestone Way to the stop sign and continue west. Take the first right at Folkestone Way to the restaurant entrance and parking.)

The Tomahawk
1550 Philip Ave. (North Vancouver)
604-988-2612
Cuisine: American, burgers
Meals served: B, L, D
Open: Daily
Price: Inexpensive
Credit cards: AE, DC, MC, V
Reservations: No
Wheelchair accessible: Yes

It's not often you find a consensus among food and travel writers in recommending a burger joint, but this is an exceptional place. Located on the Burrard Band Native reserve just east of the Lion's Gate Bridge, it is part restaurant, part art gallery. Beginning more than 80 years ago, the original owner, Chick Chamberlain, started accepting carvings and other art objects from Burrard Band members in lieu of payment for food. Included in the collection are handmade pots, drums, cooking utensils, large and small totem poles, masks, and other carved objects. They've since gained great historical value. The Chamberlain family still owns the place, and North Shore and West Coast Native American artifacts grace the restaurant. You'll need a jaw hinge like a python's to get around the burgers. The sweet smell of bacon permeates the place. The burgers are named after First Nations chiefs. Be sure to have the fried egg on your burger for a real man's tummy filler.

POINT GREY
Lumiere
2551 W. Broadway
604-739-8185
Cuisine: French, Continental
Meals served: D

Open: Tu–Sun
Price: Expensive to very expensive
Credit cards: AE, DC, MC, V
Reservations: Required
Wheelchair accessible: Yes

The first thing you notice here is the minimal decor. In fact, it's downright sparse. It's a quiet place with a menu that offers sophisticated French cuisine created by chef/owner Rob Feenie. Think of French cuisine gone 21st century and you'll begin to appreciate what's in store for you. The appetizers are especially superb, giving customers a severe case of overchoice. The seafood menu includes the signature dish, sable fish marinated in sake and maple syrup and served with potatoes and leeks, shimiji mushrooms, and a soy and hijiki broth. The lamb has shreds of preserved lemon and finely chopped Niçoise olives added just at the last second so the flavors complement rather than clash.

Ouzeri
3189 W. Broadway
604-739-9378
Cuisine: Greek
Meals served: L (summer only), D
Open: Daily
Price: Moderate
Credit cards: AE, DC, MC, V
Reservations: Not necessary
Wheelchair accessible: Yes

An *ouzeri* in Greece is a place where you have a drink and snacks before you go off to dinner. And this is exactly what this place is—a local restaurant where you're treated just as well for eating a light snack before dinner as for ordering a full meal. The restaurant is located in the middle of Vancouver's Greek district along West Broadway. Envision a trendy Greek restaurant and you have the flavor of this place. The interior is bright and modern Mediterranean. Framed photographs and prints are on the walls, and small tables and chairs are placed back to back on tiled floors. The moussaka, Kitsilano style, is vegetarian, and the prawns dressed with ouzo and mushrooms are yummers. It's a terrific place to spend 30 minutes or three hours.

Quattro on Fourth

2611 Fourth Ave.
604-734-4444
Cuisine: Italian
Meals served: D
Open: Daily
Price: Moderate
Credit cards: AE, DC, MC, V
Reservations: Recommended
Wheelchair accessible: Yes

There are three Quattro restaurants: this one, another on the North Shore at the foot of Lonsdale Avenue near the ferry terminal, and one at Whistler Resort. Each has the same basic menu, with the spaghetti "piga" advertised as being "for Italians only." But don't worry about your ethnic origins when ordering it; it's a crowd-pleaser guaranteed to warm and fill you. The list of antipastos is extensive, and each is worthy of a full meal in itself. On the main menu, L'Abbuffata (Roman feast) is the chef's creation designed for four people.

WATERFRONT

Bravo Bistro

100-550 Denman St.
604-688-3714
Cuisine: West Coast, Moroccan
Meals served: L, D
Open: Daily
Price: Moderate to expensive
Credit cards: AE, DC, MC, V
Reservations: Recommended
Wheelchair accessible: Yes

There's a definite Moroccan influence in this relatively new restaurant on the edge of Coal Harbour, almost directly across from Cardero's. Chef/owner Abdel Elatouabi has created a cheerful, intimate, modern room with harbor views and a menu blending French and West Coast cuisine. Try the escolar marinated in Moroccan chermoula, seared and served with couscous, or the potato-wrapped halibut with corn salsa and beurre blanc.

Cardero's

1583 Coal Harbour Quay
604-669-7666
Cuisine: Seafood, West Coast
Meals served: L, D
Open: Daily
Price: Inexpensive to moderate
Credit cards: AE, MC, V
Reservations: Not necessary
Wheelchair accessible: Yes

The interior is designed with a nautical motif. Named after Joseph Cardero, the marine surveyor who sailed these waters with Capt. Vancouver, the restaurant is nestled amid the boats, seaplanes, and yachts of Coal Harbour Quay near the Westin Bayshore Inn. The menu of this casual, waterfront bar and dining room could fit easily into several different categories—seafood, steaks and meat, or even pub fare. The spectacular views of the Coal Harbour marina and North Shore mountains will knock back your eyeballs. If the patio is open, it's one of the city's prime porches for eating, drinking, and viewing. The menu is essentially seafood, with meat entrées prepared with invention. If all you want is a salmon burger, you can get that as well. The value-oriented wine list is well chosen.

The Five Sails

999 Canada Pl. (Pan Pacific Hotel)
604-662-8111
Cuisine: Seafood, Pacific Northwest
Meals served: D
Open: Daily
Price: Very expensive

Credit cards: AE, DC, MC, V
Reservations: Recommended
Wheelchair accessible: Yes

The Five Sails offers the perfect fusion of the elegance of Europe and the robust flavors of Asia. In addition, you'll get a sweeping view of Canada Place, the Lion's Gate Bridge, and the lights of the North Shore. The seasonally changing menu's primary focus is seafood. If you want a taste of everything, order the Voyage of Discovery, a seafood platter that features tuna-crab roll, freshly shucked oysters, smoked wild sockeye salmon, and several other ocean delicacies. There's also a wide selection of duck, beef, and lamb dishes. The service is impeccable, and the clientele is mostly well-heeled businesspeople. That doesn't prevent locals from eating here for a special occasion, especially since it has the best dining view in town.

WEST END AND STANLEY PARK
The Fish House at Stanley Park
2099 Beach Ave.
604-681-7275
Cuisine: Seafood
Meals served: L, D
Open: Daily

Cardero's casual dining room on the waterfront
Toshi

Price: Moderate
Credit cards: AE, DC, MC, V
Reservations: Recommended
Wheelchair accessible: Yes

This is a combination of Olde England, Pacific Northwest, and uniquely Vancouver. When you enter Stanley Park from Beach Avenue, the large house on the left is the Fish House. Tucked in behind the Stanley Park tennis courts and next to a croquet lawn and the nearby pitch-and-putt golf course, it's an ideal location. The earth-toned interior immediately relaxes you. The menu is mainly seafood, featuring such unusual items as grilled wild salmon wrapped in cornhusk, with buttermilk mashed potatoes on the side. A wide range of white wines will make you want to linger.

Liliget Feast House
1724 Davie St.
604-681-7044
Cuisine: Native seafood
Meals served: D
Open: Daily
Price: Inexpensive to moderate
Credit cards: AE, DC, MC, V
Reservations: Recommended
Wheelchair accessible: Yes

No restaurant in either Seattle or Vancouver is like this one. This West End eatery near Stanley Park is a West Coast First Nations restaurant. But this is more than just a restaurant. Designed by architect Arthur Erickson in the early 1970s, it had a series of owners until Liliget owner Dolly Watts, a Native caterer, bought it. Down the stairs, you enter into a world you'll find nowhere else. You eat in a simulated longhouse of poles and beams, graveled walkways, and sunken tables. Subdued lighting illuminates cedar tables and benches, creating an atmosphere reminiscent of a Northwest Coast longhouse. Haida folk songs accompany oolichan, bannock bread, caribou, salmon cheeks,

The Five Sails, a Vancouver waterfront landmark. Toshi

and whipped soapberries. Authentic regional dishes cooked over the green-alderwood grill include the Feast Platter, with alder-grilled wild salmon, Pacific oysters, mussels, venison strips, smoked buffalo, duck breast, sweet potatoes with hazelnuts, wild rice medley, steamed vegetables, and wild blueberry and juniper berry sauces. The Bounty of the Sea platter has wild salmon, halibut, mussels, clams, scallops, and prawns in a roasted-garlic, tomato, and basil base. There's also a vegetarian menu.

Sequoia Grill
Stanley Park Dr. (in Stanley Park)
604-669-3281
Cuisine: West Coast
Meals served: L, D
Open: Daily
Price: Moderate to expensive

Credit cards: AE, DC, MC, V
Reservations: Recommended
Wheelchair accessible: Yes

This used to be the Ferguson Point Teahouse, but it has undergone a change in owners and name. It is now owned by the same people who own and operate Cardero's near the Bayshore Inn. But even with some renovation to the interior of the restaurant itself, the menu has stayed essentially the same. Yes, it's a magnet for tourists, with a view of Point Grey and English Bay that is unequaled in the city. But it's a fine dining experience as well, especially in the evening. Salmon here is always a good bet, but try the lamb in a fresh herb crust, a meal that locals have favored for years. (The restaurant is located on the southwest side of the park; drive around the perimeter.)

ATTRACTIONS

Seeing the attractions that make Vancouver unique is relatively simple because walking is both a pastime and a way of life here. It's a walker's city. Stroll a few blocks in any direction and you'll find something worth experiencing—a building, a view, a garden. If you have to drive, the distances are not lengthy. Vancouverites like to brag that within sight of downtown you can ski in the morning, play tennis or golf in the afternoon, and sail in the evening. Those who have the physical endurance of a moose actually do it just to say they have.

There are some things that every visitor to Vancouver must see and do. The gondola ride to the top of Grouse Mountain (see Tours and Sightseeing) offers the greatest view this side of the moon, with the city, the Strait of Georgia, and Vancouver Island laid out before you. Not going there is like visiting Seattle without going to the top of the Space Needle. The Museum of Anthropology (see Museums), located on the University of British Columbia campus, has one of the world's great collections of indigenous art. And you must visit Steveston (see Historic Buildings and Sites), the fishing village that's part of Richmond. There you can browse unique shops and eat at the many seafood restaurants that dot the wharves.

Not all attractions have an admission fee. For example, the five giant sails atop the downtown cruise-ship terminal/convention center have become the city's symbol, drawing visitors to its unique design. A visit to the center during the cruise season—May through October—will give you a free, up-close view of the huge ships that cruise to Alaska.

Gardens and Parks

Vancouver likes to think of itself as a city that's really a series of forests separated by areas of pavement. Although the crown jewel is 1,000-acre (405-hectare) Stanley Park at the tip of the West End, there are some 175 public gardens and parks in Vancouver proper and hundreds more in the surrounding neighborhoods and region. In addition, the Greater Vancouver Regional District has 17 regional parks. When you add the thousands of home gardens that abound, this city is a floral masterpiece, a combination of British traditions and wilderness realities. The cultivated parks do have severe competition from the natural surroundings of the city.

With the temperate coastal climate, Vancouver and its suburbs are a kaleidoscope of colors year-round—pinks and whites in the spring, green in the winter, bright oranges and yellows in the fall, and every color in the rainbow during the summer. Still, though locals take great pride in the cultivation of their parks and gardens, the fact is that they live on the edge of a wilderness, one that makes human efforts at floral and faunal organization impressive but often insignificant by comparison.

Central Park
Kingsway and Imperial St.
Burnaby
604-294-7450
Open: Daily
Admission: Free
Wheelchair accessible: Yes

One of the oldest parks in the city, this park is to Burnaby what Stanley Park is to Vancouver, with a variety of activities including a pitch-and-putt golf course, horseshoe pitches, tennis courts, a swimming pool, and lawn-bowling greens. Trails ring and cut through the 222-acre (90-hectare) park that was once a naval reserve and a source of ship masts for the Royal Navy. It was called Central Park after New York's famous landmark, as a tribute to the wife of Vancouver's second mayor, who was born in New York City. Vancouver's professional soccer team, the Whitecaps, plays its games at Swangard Stadium at the entrance to the park. There are wheelchair-accessible washroom facilities and paths. (Follow either Kingsway or Trans-Canada Hwy. to Boundary Rd. Or from the south, take 49th St. south. Central Park is also easily accessible by Sky Train at Patterson Stn.)

Dr. Sun Yat-Sen Classical Chinese Garden
578 Carroll St.
Chinatown
604-662-3207
www.vancouverchinesegarden.com
Open: 10–5 daily with seasonal variations
Admission: $8.25 adults, $6.75 seniors, $5.75 students, free children under 5, $18 families (children under 18)
Wheelchair accessible: Yes

This was the first authentic classical Chinese garden to be built outside of China. Constructed during Expo '86, this Ming Dynasty–style garden was created with the help of 52 artisans from Suzhou, China's foremost garden city. It's not just a place to witness pretty flowers. Sit and watch, think Asian, and try to explore what's in your heart. The Taoist balance between yin and yang—light and shadow, smooth and rough, large and small—creates perfect harmony in pebbled patios, moon gates, lattice windows, see-through shrubbery, placid jade pools, and craggy gray limestone. Rocks, wood, plants, and water are used with remarkable, deceptive simplicity. Eventually the differences reveal themselves—hard and soft, straight and winding, artificial and natural. Everything is in perfect symmetry. After the dazzle of Chinatown, the gardens are passive, with a collection of soft colors, greens and stony grays with milky jade water ponds. White lilies line walkways leading from pavilion to pavilion among the gnarled trees and natural rock sculptures. A guided tour is included in the admission cost.

Garry Point Park
12015 Seventh Ave.
Richmond
604-276-4000
Admission: Free
Wheelchair accessible: Yes

Once the permanent fishing camp of the Musqeaum Indians, Garry Point Park is the entrance to a well-defined path to the Richmond dike, which has magnificent views along it's top. Because the community is below sea level, it is surrounded by a dike that holds back the water, and along its top you'll walk past open marshes, the Quilchena Golf and Country Club, and the old Steves Farm (at one time the only construction in the area and for which the community of Steveston is named). You'll have unrestricted views to Vancouver Island and the North Shore mountains. Eventually, you'll find yourself opposite the Vancouver International Airport.

Dr. Sun Yat-Sen Garden, the first classical Chinese garden outside of China Toshi

George C. Reifel Migratory Bird Sanctuary
Robertson Rd.
Ladner
604-946-6980
www.reifelbirdsanctuary.com
Open: 9–4 daily
Admission: $7 (includes parking)
Wheelchair accessible: Yes

If you like to watch what birds do in the privacy of their nests or resting places, you'll find a lot to occupy your entire day here. Located in the Delta area, just south of Vancouver along BC 99 to the U.S.–Canadian border, these 650 acres (260 hectares) of marsh and waterfront are devoted entirely to birds, some 250 species of which use the area. The peak viewing time is between October and April; in November the sanctuary is devoted to the Snow Geese Festival, when hundred of the giant birds stop off here on their way south. Call ahead because the parking lot has limitations. (Take BC 99 to the Ladner exit, then take River Rd. to Westham Island.)

Lighthouse Park
Point Atkinson
North Shore
604-925-7200
www.westvancouver.net

Open: Daily
Admission: Free
Wheelchair accessible: Limited accessibility

Lighthouse Park features an old-growth rain forest of Douglas fir, western hemlock, and western red cedar trees, the largest uncut, coastal-elevation trees in the Lower Mainland. Because logging in this area was stopped and the region set aside as a reserve in 1881, the Douglas firs are enormous, some 200 feet (61 m) tall and 6.5 feet (2 m) in diameter. The park is also home to Point Atkinson, one of Canada's first manned light stations. Built in 1912, the lighthouse is a landmark that can be seen from several viewpoints. If you're here in the moody winter months, you'll likely feel like a stranded traveler. It's an ideal place to walk and picnic and to get some of the finest photos of the surrounding ocean, islands, and English Bay. (Drive west along Marine Dr. from Lion's Gate Bridge to West Vancouver.)

Mount Seymour Provincial Park and Lynn Canyon
Mount Seymour Pkwy.
North Shore
604-987-1273
www.britishcolumbia.com/parksandtrails
Open: 8–10 daily
Admission: Free
Wheelchair accessible: Limited accessibility

Here you'll find yourself in the middle of a multiple-sport mountain. A few hundred yards up the mountain is the entrance to the difficult Northlands Golf Club. In winter, the top of Mount Seymour is one of three major ski hills just minutes from downtown Vancouver. And in summer, it's a prime location for hiking. Within the park is the Seymour demonstration forest, where you can be guided through the different species of trees that make up the vegetation. The Suspension Bridge and Ecology Centre make an ideal starting point for a hike, with guided walks available. But be careful. Every year there are deaths on this mountain when people wander off well-marked trails. Get caught here at night and you could walk off into one of several deep canyons that mark the region. (In North Vancouver, turn left off Mt. Seymour Rd. at the well-marked entrance.)

Nitobe Memorial Garden
Across from UBC Botanical Gardens
6804 SW Marine Drive, Point Grey
604-822-3928
www.nitobe.org
Open: 10 a.m.–dusk daily in summer; 10–2:30 M–F in winter
Admission: $4 adults, $3 seniors, children under six free; double-entry ticket to Nitobe Memorial Garden and UBC Botanical Gardens $8.
Wheelchair accessible: Yes

This is considered the best traditional, authentic Japanese tea and stroll garden in North America and among the top five Japanese gardens outside Japan. The Nitobe Garden includes a rare authentic tea garden with a ceremonial tea house. Walkways meander past pruned cherry, maple, and pine trees. This is a must-see when the cherry trees bloom in

April or May and the irises bloom in late June. The admission charge allows entry to both Nitobe Gardens (a couple hundred feet south of the Museum of Anthropology) and the UBC Botanical Gardens (see below).

Pacific Spirit Regional Park
Between NW Marine Dr. and SW Marine Dr. (on the UBC campus)
Point Grey
604-224-5739
www.gvrd.bc.ca/parks
Open: 24 hours, 7 days a week
Admission: Free
Wheelchair accessible: Limited

This regional park is both a research area for the University of British Columbia's forestry students and a recreational area for walkers, cyclists, and horseback riders. Its intertwined 34 miles (55 km) of horse and walking paths wind throughout the 2,000 acres (800 hectares) of this forest on the university at the end of Point Grey. Known as the Endowment Lands, bestowed to the university by the provincial government in 1911; it was officially created in 1989. You can enter the forest at several points, including from the north above Lucarno Beach, where you'll find wildflowers and ravines, and from the south just up from the Fraser River, where the tallest trees and small wildlife, including raccoons and coyotes, can be seen.

Park and Tilford Gardens
333 Brooksbank Ave.
North Shore
604-984-8200
www.parkandtilford.ca
Open: 10–5 daily
Admission: Free
Wheelchair accessible: Yes

In this garden created in 1968 by a privately owned distillery, 3 acres (1.2 hectares) offer eight separate gardens, including the Rose Garden, with nearly 300 plants in 24 varieties. The Oriental Garden showcases traditional bonsai trees with a tranquil pond. If you have the urge to see a wedding, you'll likely see a happy couple strolling these gardens. The former distillery buildings are now a shopping center and a film studio. (Take Second Narrows Bridge into North Vancouver, get off at exit 23A, and follow Main Rd. to Brooksbank and Main.)

Queen Elizabeth Park and Bloedel Floral Conservatory
Cambie St. at 33rd Ave.
East Vancouver
604-257-8570
www.city.vancouver.bc.ca/parks
Open: Daily (park); 9:30–5 daily; (conservatory) 10–5
Admission: Free (park); $4.10 adults, $2.90 seniors, discounts for families, students, children (conservatory)
Wheelchair accessible: Yes

Located on the city's highest point, this is a photographer's delight. Not only does it offer dramatic vistas of the North Shore mountains and the city skyline, but it's a destination in itself, with flowers, manicured bushes, and tranquil ponds filled with ducks and other wild birds. When shrubs bloom in the spring, the place is alive with colors from rhododendrons, azaleas, and other local varieties. The park, at the top of 500-foot (150-m) Little Mountain—its original name but really just a large hill—was created from two quarries. There's a fine restaurant, **Seasons in the Park** (604-669-7666), as well as tennis courts, pitch-and-putt golf, disc golf, and sculptures such as Henry Moore's bronze sculpture "Knife Edge," atop the water reservoir on the plaza. Inside the large silver dome atop the hill is the Bloedel Floral Conservatory, which contains a moist rain forest plus a dry desert environment. The tropical plants inside are from Mexico, South America, and Africa. Beware of the many species of birds flying around overhead.

Robson Square
Robson, Howe, Hornby, and Smithe Sts.
Downtown
Wheelchair accessible: Yes

Robson Square is a public open space designed by architect Arthur Erickson that is the absolute heart of downtown. The square begins with the massive slopes of glass covering the Law Courts Building that's opposite the Wedgewood Hotel. The courthouse opens up into a public space with a waterfall, trees, and many stairs and a ramp. It's the gathering point of young people in the summer. The lower level has restaurants, conference rooms, and a skating rink. Erickson provided a functional structure that is also a testament to the idea that high-rises are not the only choice for inner cities. After the courthouse was constructed, the classical-styled former courthouse on Georgia Street at the north end of the site was adapted to become the home of the Vancouver Art Gallery.

Stanley Park
Georgia St./Beach Ave.
West End
604-257-8400
www.city.vancouver.bc.ca/parks
Open: Daily 24 hours
Admission: Free
Wheelchair accessible: Yes

Visiting Vancouver without ever seeing and walking through Stanley Park is like going to New York and missing Central Park. This 1,000-acre (400 hectare) park opened in September 1888 and has been Vancouver's prime walking and doing place ever since. It is a mix of wilderness, sophisticated restaurants, and recreational facilities and also has an aquarium and an outdoor theater. The park used to be a military reserve, but local residents convinced the federal government to give the city the land, and it was immediately turned into a park, with Lord Stanley's name attached to it. Stanley, the same fellow whose name adorns the Stanley Cup, the National Hockey League trophy, was Governor General of Canada from 1888 to 1893, the time during which Vancouver was given the land.

   The best way to see the city and the park is to take the 6.5-mile (10.5 km) **seawall** (split down the middle for walkers and cyclists) or to drive the road that circles the entire park.

It offers a magnificent view of downtown and, as you progress, across Burrard Inlet to the North Shore, English Bay, and Point Grey. From the seawall you can branch out to take through the park numerous hiking, cycling, and horse trails (and roads) that will almost make you think you're in virgin wilderness as the city sounds disappear. Lily-covered **Beaver Lake** is a perfect place for contemplation. Bike rentals—and maps—are available at the park's entrance on Georgia and Denman Streets. The Lion's Gate Bridge heads across Burrard Inlet from Prospect Point at the tip of Stanley Park.

Walking or jogging the seawall is a daily routine for many residents in the West End. The route around the 6.5-mile (10.5 km) seawall is not just for exercise but a local rite to meet and watch Vancouverites up close—sand-castle builders, windsurfers, mature ladies dressed in pink sweat suits walking their apartment-size dogs, joggers, walkers, cyclists, roller skaters, the weird and the wonderful. Along the east end of the walkway you'll pass the Tudor-style **Vancouver Rowing Club**, the **Nine O'Clock Gun, Brockton Point**, and **Lumberman's Arch**; on the north end is **Prospect Point**; on the west are **Siwash Rock** and **Second Beach**. Citizens gather at many points on their determined walks around the park in all kinds of weather. It's also the best place in the city for a dramatic close-up photo of the Vancouver skyline. The nine o'clock gun is an old English sea canon that for about 100 years has been a part of Vancouver's tradition. Every evening at 9 pm, seven days a week, it is automatically shot to signal the hour. It was originally used to signal the end to fishing hours in English Bay and Vancouver harbor and used to shoot blank shells. Now, the sound is electronically produced and the cannon has no particular significance—except as a part of Vancouver's history.

There's also plenty of "civilization" in the park to keep you occupied. The **Vancouver Aquarium** (see Kids' Favorites) is home to more than 8,000 animals from around the world—from the Amazon to the Arctic—including sea lions, octopuses, and beluga whales.

Brockton Point in Stanley Park Toshi

Nearby **Lost Lagoon** is a haven for many varieties of birds and marine life. A **miniature train and petting zoo** keep the kids happy (see Kids' Favorites); tennis courts and a pitch-and-putt golf layout entertain, too.

Not far from Stanley Park's former Teahouse Restaurant, now called the Sequoia Grill (see Restaurants), near the hollow tree at **Third Beach** on the west side, is a monument to Pauline Johnson, the Ontario-born daughter of a Mohawk chief and an Englishwoman. Her real name was Tekahionwake, and at the age of 31, in 1892, she dressed as an Indian princess and began publicly reciting her poetry. It was the start of an 18-year career touring North America. By the time she eventually settled in Vancouver, she was well known and she learned local legends that she eventually turned into poems. She retold the stories she learned from Chief Capilano in a collection called *Legends of Vancouver.* She could often be seen canoeing in Lost Lagoon, the small body of water in Stanley Park that she named. She said it was there that she found tranquility. She died in 1913, and her ashes were buried near Ferguson Point, the site of the current restaurant. A memorial to her was erected in 1922 even though she had expressly wished that no monument would ever be erected.

Deadman's Island, southwest of Brockton Point directly across from downtown Vancouver and now a naval training station, is where the Coast Salish native peoples once buried their dead. It's a small island connected to Stanley Park by a causeway, and during the smallpox epidemic of 1888, it was used to quarantine the ill, most of whom were prostitutes and Chinese. It's said that on misty nights the occasional ghost walks across the causeway.

Nearby to the west is **Malkin Bowl,** an outdoor theater where, during the summer, you can see popular Broadway shows enacted by a local semiprofessional theater group. It's also where local artists display their work for sale in an informal, gorgeously set manner. And at **Brockton Oval** due north of Deadman's Island, you can sit on the grass and watch (or simply be confused by) a cricket match. The **Nature Centre** is near the entrance to the park, and it's where you can learn about the park's complex ecological system, flora, and wildlife (raccoons, squirrels, beavers, coyotes, owls, and other animals).

Opposite Deadman's Island, between it and Brockton Point, stands a series of **totem poles** carved by the Kwakiutl and Haida peoples. It's a natural draw for photos, especially for newlyweds attracted to the one with the woman with outstretched arms. They obviously have not been told that the woman represents the mythical crazed bear-woman who comes out of the mountains to steal children. The poles are near the **Nine O'Clock Gun,** which was used to call fishermen home at night and which residents still use to check their watches and clocks. Keep walking on the seawall and you'll eventually come to Prospect Point, which overlooks the Lion's Gate Bridge and the North Shore, then a series of beaches and eventually **Ferguson Point,** where you can have a meal and look out toward the mountains and harbor.

(University of British Columbia) Botanical Gardens

6804 SW Marine Dr.
Point Grey
604-822-9666
www.ubcbotanicalgarden.org
Open: 10 a.m.–dusk daily in summer; 10–2:30 M–F in winter
Admission: $6 adults, $4 seniors, $3 non-UBC students; double entry to Nitobe Gardens $8
Wheelchair accessible: Yes

Virtually across the street from the UBC football stadium is the oldest and arguably the finest botanical garden in the country, spread over 70 acres (28 hectares). It is really five gardens in one: the Asian Garden, the British Columbia Native Garden, the Alpine Garden, the Physick Garden, and the Food Garden, each with an amazing collection of the best plants of its kind. Home farmers, for example, will love the Food Garden, which must be the best-organized garden on the planet. In just ¾ acre (.30 hectare), a dozen raised beds and some 180 fruit trees give bloom to a succession of crops—all of which are donated to the Salvation Army.

VanDusen Botanical Garden

5251 Oak St.
West Side/Shaughnessy
604-878-9274
www.vandusengarden.org
Open: 10 a.m.–dusk daily
Admission: $7.50 adults Apr–Sep 30, $5.20 rest of year; discounts for seniors, youth, students
Wheelchair accessible: Yes

Have an old golf course you want redesigned? Go no farther than this place for ideas. Named after W. J. Van Dusen, former president of the Vancouver Foundation, British Columbia's largest philanthropic organization, this once-prestigious golf course of 55 acres (23 hectares) was transformed into a series of small gardens in the 1970s. Criss-crossing paths wander through 40 theme gardens, skirting lakes and ponds and passing bamboos and redwoods. Sprinklers restaurant (604-261-0011) on the grounds offers a West Coast menu among the plants and shrubs.

Vanier Park

1100 Chestnut St.
Kitsilano
604-257-8400
Open: 7 days, 24 hours
Admission: Free
Wheelchair accessible: Yes

Vanier Park is within easy walking or cab distance of downtown, on the south shore of False Creek just west of Granville Island, on the eastern edge of Kitsilano. The park offers a wide range of activities and places to explore, including the Vancouver Space Museum and H. R. MacMillan Planetarium, the Vancouver Museum, the Gordon Southam Observatory, the Vancouver Maritime Museum and the *St. Roch*, and the Vancouver Academy of Music. In addition, it's the site of two major annual events: the Bard on the Beach Shakespeare festival in summer and the International Children's Festival in early May.

Historic Buildings and Sites

Blood Alley Square

Lane between Abbott and Carrall Sts.
Chinatown

Between 1860 and 1900, this area was where smugglers hung out, where opium (it was legal then) was sold, and where you could usually expect to find a dead person in the mornings. It's more civilized and gentle these days, with the alleyway leading into a variety of stores and restaurants. But, unfortunately, the drug identity has remained, and the area is one of downtown Vancouver's drug sites. Police keep it well patrolled, and chances are you'll never see anything you might not want to.

Burnaby Village Museum
6501 Deer Lake Ave.
Burnaby
604-293-6500
Open: 11–4:30 daily
Admission: Free
Wheelchair accessible: Yes

An entire turn-of-the-20th-century village was constructed from scratch on what was once an Indian encampment to celebrate British Columbia's centenary in 1958. The open-air museum depicts a typical tram-stop community, complete with costumed schoolmarm, town printer, blacksmith, and Chinese herbalist, who all double as interpreters. There are 30 buildings depicting life between 1890 and 1925. Take a look at the 1890s dentists office and your jaw will tighten; see what a printer used back then and you'll appreciate the Internet. Try being a kid again riding the colorful 1912 carousel.

Canadian Pacific Railroad (CPR) Roundhouse
181 Roundhouse Mews (Davie St. and Pacific Blvd.)
Downtown
604-713-1800
www.roundhouse.ca
Open: 9 am–10 pm M–F, 9–5 Sa–Su
Admission: Free
Wheelchair accessible: Yes

This is all that remains of the once massive CPR marshalling yard, where passenger trains were serviced. It is now a combination of performance spaces: theater, restaurant, community center, and museum. Built in 1888, it was where the large locomotives were driven in on a single track, turned around on a giant pivoting wheel, and sent off on one of several service tracks. Engine no. 394, the steam locomotive that brought the first passenger train into Vancouver, is now located here.

Capilano Suspension Bridge
3735 Capilano Rd.
North Shore
604-985-7474
www.capbridge.com
Open: 8 a.m.–dusk daily in summer; 9–5 daily except Christmas Day in winter
Admission: $21.95 adults; discounts for seniors, students, children
Wheelchair accessible: No

If you don't like heights or swaying footbridges, this isn't for you. But this is one of Vancouver's oldest and most popular attractions. The swinging metal footbridge, only 5 feet wide (1.5 m) and suspended 230 feet (70 m) above the 450-foot-wide (137 m) Capilano Canyon, was originally built by George Grant Mackay and two local Native Americans in 1889 to join the sides of his recently purchased North Vancouver property. Yearly, about 500,000 tourists walk across the secure bridge for a safe thrill and to explore the canyon along well-marked paths on the west side. From May to September, there are anthropology and forestry tours, and a native carver works on-site all year long.

Chinatown Historic Site
Bounded by Hastings, Keefer, Gore, and Taylor Streets
Chinatown
www.vancouverchinatown.ca

Vancouver is home to Canada's largest Chinese community, which dates from the late 1800s when Chinese immigrants were brought to Canada to work as laborers in the building of the Canadian Pacific Railway. Between 1890 and 1920, early Chinese immigrants settled in what was known as Shanghai and Canton Alleys near what is now Pender and Carrall Streets, about when the City of Vancouver was incorporated in 1886. The alleys were the convergence of vibrant nightlife, opera music, shopping, and political and cultural activities. The typical Chinatown building was a two-story wooden structure with a storefront on the ground floor and a residence and meeting rooms tucked in on the second floor. The neighborhood has been declared a historic site, assuring that its character will be preserved and enhanced.

Just steps west of Shanghai Alley is the Millennium Gate on Pender at Taylor Street. It opened in July 2002 to inaugurate the new millennium, and it represents both the past and the future. It incorporates both Eastern and Western symbols, with traditional and modern Chinese themes in its construction and appearance.

Chinatown's Millennium Gate at Shanghai Alley Toshi

Go south a few steps from the Millennium Gate and you will find a replica of a West Han Dynasty bell unearthed in Guangzhou, China, in 1983, a gift from the City of Guangzhou to the City of Vancouver in honor of the 15th anniversary of the twinning of the two cities. The bell hangs from two crossbeams supported by four columns. Three bronze bands on the tip of the bell bear the names of the early settlers and sponsors of this project.

Christ Church Cathedral
690 Burrard St.
Downtown
604-682-3848
www.cathedral.vancouver.bc.ca
Wheelchair accessible: Yes

Located across from the Fairmont Hotel Vancouver, this sandstone Gothic Revival church, with its gabled roof, buttresses, and stained-glass windows, sticks out like a lush olive tree against the sterile high-rise skyline. You must go in to see the rich, multicolored windows. The oldest surviving church in Vancouver, it was completed in 1895 and is at the heart of the Cathedral Place complex, a city block that houses several important buildings, including Cathedral Place Tower and a lovely plaza that separates the buildings from one another.

Fort Langley National Historic Park
23433 Mavis Ave.
Fort Langley
604-513-4777
www.pc.gc.ca
Open: 10–5 daily Mar 1–Oct 31; 10–4:30 M–F excluding holidays in winter
Admission: $5.75 adults, $5 seniors, $3 youth
Wheelchair accessible: Yes

About an hour's drive east of Vancouver, Fort Langley is a Hudson's Bay Company trading post that has been lovingly preserved and restored. The fort was founded in 1827 by Chief Trader McMillan and named after Thomas Langley, a director of the Hudson's Bay Company. In 1839 the original fort was abandoned and replaced with a new one. By 1896 the Hudson's Bay Company had closed its store, leaving the fort to deteriorate, until its restoration was completed in 1957. It was here that British Columbia was declared a British Crown Colony in 1858. There's now only one original building, the storehouse. But everything else has been built to original 1850s specs. Period-costumed entertainers/guides re-create the crafts of the original pioneers. (Take Trans-Canada Hwy. 1 east and follow signs from the Fort Langley turnoff.)

Gastown Historic Area
Richards, Cordova, and Columbia Sts.
Gastown
604-683-5650
www.gastown.org

There's a statue of "Gassy" Jack Deighton on the plaza at the corner of Water and Carrall Streets. In a real sense it's a tribute to heavy drinking and tall tales, because "Gassy" was famous for his storytelling and for his ability to drink anyone under than table. Deighton was born in Hull, England in 1830, and became a sailor at the age of 14. On one of his voyages, he landed on the west coast and decided to stay. Odd jobs gave him enough money to buy a tiny pub in New Westminster, an enterprise in which he managed to go bankrupt. Meanwhile, Deighton married a native woman who suggested there were better pickings further along the Fraser River. So, Deighton and his wife canoed around Point Grey to Burrard Inlet in 1887 and set up another grog shop in what is now the Gastown area. He knew that a new bunch of sawmill workers in the area would keep the place hopping and, this time with a built-in clientele, he made a lot of money. Before long the area began to be built up with stores and houses, the first growth spurt for what would become Vancouver. Deighton died from unknown causes just eight years after opening his saloon. After his death, the city grew outward and soon the Gastown area was eclipsed by other parts of town that had become more eco-

Gassy Jack Deighton, founder of Gastown Toshi

nomically important. In the 1960s, Gastown was slated to be demolished for redevelopment, but a groundswell of indignant architects and city activists put that idea to rest. In 1971, the provincial government declared Gastown an historic area and the region slowly came back to life as shops and restaurants began to open. Today, it's a major tourist draw with shops selling everything from tacky souvenirs to upscale clothing and native art. Restaurants of all kinds are sprinkled throughout the 11- or 12-block area that stretches between Burrard Inlet to the north, Columbia Street to the east, Hastings Street to the south, and Richards Street to the west. It's a part of town that's busy from about 10 a.m. to early the next morning. In summer, it's crowded with cruise-ship passengers who embark and disembark for Alaskan cruises at the nearby cruise ship terminal at Canada Place, and with locals who just like the area.

Gulf of Georgia Cannery National Historic Site

12138 Fourth Ave.
Steveston
604-664-9009
www.gulfofgeorgiacannery.com
Open: Apr–Oct; prebooked tours Mar–Nov
Admission: $6.50 adults, $5 seniors, $3.25 youth, $16.25 families
Wheelchair accessible: Yes

Built in 1894 in historic Steveston, this was once the biggest cannery on the West Coast. And it still retains many of the smells and harsh working character of those days. At one time, the 10,000-member workforce consisted mostly of Japanese immigrants, attracted to the area by what seemed then an unending supply of salmon. The Cannery Store and Canning Line exhibit takes you through the process of salmon canning on a 1930s production line with accompanying noise and clatter. As you'll quickly discover, there's more to salmon fishing than pulling in a net.

Hotel Europa
43 Powell St.
Gastown

If Gastown has a building that symbolizes its finest moments, Hotel Europa is it. Originally built in 1892, it's no longer a hotel, so forget about staying overnight. Now restored, although not to its original grandeur (the grand lobby was gutted to expand the beer hall before the 1960s movement to save Gastown from the wrecking ball), this was Vancouver's first steel and concrete structure, modeled after Manhattan's Flatiron Building. It was once the grandest hotel in Vancouver, with a lobby famous for its brass and marble detailing. Today you'll find the bottom level devoted to small stores selling antiques.

Gastown's Hotel Europa is a Victorian flatiron building. Toshi

Sam Kee Building
8 W. Pender (at Carrall St.)
Chinatown
www.tourismvancouver.com

This building looks as though it has been on a diet for a long time. The narrowest building in the world, built in 1913 and only 6 feet (1.8 m) wide, 100 feet (30 m) long, and two stories tall, it looks bigger than it really is because of the bay windows on the upper floor. There's a basement under the sidewalk with a glass-paneled roof. Sam Kee (whose real name was Cheng Toy) was a poor immigrant who became a successful import merchant. He constructed his building after the street was widened, leaving him with just a narrow space. The building was originally a store that sold gorgeous silks; it's now an insurance office, and though you can go inside, you'll find yourself in a working office.

Steam Clock
At the corner of Water and Cambie Sts.
Gastown

The Gastown steam clock has been a regular stop for every visiting tourist since 1977, when clockmaker Ray Saunders decided that the underground steam pipes that heated local buildings was a great source of power. Standing at 16.4 feet (5 m), the clock has a four-sided glass face with a 44-pound (20 kg) gold-plated pendulum and a Gothic roof. It is powered by the same steam system that passes underground to heat nearby buildings. The clock erupts in a cloud of steam and sound every 15 minutes. Vancouver has some of the weirdest "clocks" in North America. There's the Nine O'Clock gun at Stanley Park that blasts a *boom* across Burrard Inlet every evening; Canada Place announces noon every day with a blast of the first four notes of "O Canada"—and then there's Gastown's steam clock.

Steveston Heritage Site
SW corner of town
Richmond
604-271-8280 (Tourism Richmond)
www.steveston.bc.ca

Steveston was once its own community at the southwesternmost point of what's now Richmond, primarily along the waterfront at the foot of Moncton Street, where Third Avenue intersects it. To reach it from downtown Vancouver, cross the Oak Street Bridge and follow Hwy 99 South until you reach the Steveston Hwy Exit. Travel west on Steveston Hwy. until you reach No. 1 Road, and follow it south to the end. Built in 1894, the Gulf of Georgia Cannery (see above) in Stevestonwas part of the industry that once dominated Richmond. This complex turned out canned food, fish oil, and fish meal until 1979. In 1897 there were 14 canneries stretching along the Steveston channel, and by 1901 there were 49. Steveston was also home to Vancouver's Japanese, who settled here in the late 1800s and early 1900s, until they were evacuated during the Second World War in the 1940s. Much of that Japanese culture still lives. Today the richness of both heritages is in abundance. The area, now a heritage site, and the original buildings still stand, an integral part of the Steveston waterfront.

Farther down Moncton Street, past No. 1 Road, there's a turnoff to the old **Britannia Heritage Shipyard** (open May–September, Wed–Sat 10am–4pm, Sun noon–4pm; free;

Steveston's historic wharf Toshi

604-718-8050)—8 acres (3.2 hectares) of boardwalk and buildings. You'll find traditional Japanese dwellings, a Native American dwelling, two former boat works, and a cannery house. While walking on a self-guided tour, you'll find carvers and woodworkers restoring old boats. At the Murakami Visitor Centre, you'll get a taste of what life was like for a Japanese fisherman's family in the early part of the 20th century.

Waterfront Station (Canadian Pacific Building)
601 W. Cordova St.
Downtown
604-683-3266 (Tourism Richmond)
Open: 5 am–1 am daily
Wheelchair accessible: Yes

The old Canadian Pacific Railway station, meticulously restored to its original 1914 beaux-arts style, is now a terminal for the Seabus and Sky Train system. It lies next to Gastown and is adjacent to the Convention Centre and the Pan Pacific/Canadian Pacific Waterfront Hotel properties. The interior of the building is one of the city's most impressive, with a series of paintings by the wife of a former CPR executive decorating the walls. It's also a gathering place for young people, where they can get coffee and a muffin at Café Zoom or at the Starbucks franchise outlet.

Kids' Favorites
Capilano Salmon Hatchery
4500 Capilano Park Rd. (in Capilano River Regional Park)
North Shore
604-666-1790
www-heb.pac.dfo-mpo.gc.ca/facilities/capilano/capilano_e.htm
Open: Daily; seasonal hours
Admission: Free
Wheelchair accessible: Yes

Science World on False Creek is a Vancouver landmark. Toshi

The fish and salmon hatchery is designed to restore the dwindling stocks of coho salmon and steelhead trout. Each year, the Capilano Salmon Hatchery produces more than 1 million coho, up to 2.5 million chinook, and 10,000 to 20,000 steelhead fry. During the fall, returning salmon make their way up the fish ladders to spawn. This federal government display takes you through the entire process, and you can watch the wild salmon leaping up the ladders to the container tanks. It's a spectacular event and also very sad. By the time the fish reach the holding tanks, they're ready to lay their eggs or fertilize them and then die. Some are already beginning to change shape and color as they reach the end of their cycle. But the story of life and death is handled very well in the nearby supporting information. (After you pass the Capilano Suspension Bridge entrance, take the first left and follow the road to the end.)

Children's Farmyard and Miniature Railway
In Stanley Park (Georgia St./Beach Ave.)
West End
604-257-8530
www.city.vancouver.bc.ca/parks
Open: 11–4 Sa–Su Oct–Easter; 11–4 daily Easter–Sep
Admission: $2.50 adults, $1.25 seniors, $1.75 youth 12–17, $1.25 children 2–11, free under 2
Wheelchair accessible: Yes

The old, traditional zoo closed some time ago, and in its place is a wonderland of peacocks, rabbits, donkeys, goats, llamas, cows, and other barnyard animals. The miniature railway is nearby. The farmyard is well-marked with explanations of animals and what to do at every exhibit. It's a user-friendly place where you'll find local children in school groups and with their parents melding into the wildlife of the area. Later, take a ride on the small steam engine that pulls a series of open cars through the woods, where you'll also see animals. The combination is one of Vancouver's most popular children's attractions, especially in the summer, so it could get crowded. To reach it follow Georgia Street west until you reach the Stanley Park turnoff and then just follow directions. Look for a directional sign immediately on your left as you enter the Stanley Park from downtown. It will lead you up Pipeline Road to a parking lot adjacent to the farmyard. If you miss that turnoff, don't worry. The one-way road along the seawall will lead you to the Aquarium, about a half mile (.8 km) from the Stanley Park turnoff. From the Aquarium parking lot it's a short walk to the farmyard.

Gordon MacMillan Southam Observatory
1100 Chestnut St. (Vanier Park)
Kitsilano
604-738-7827, ext. 228
www.hrmacmillanspacecentre.com
Open: 1 p.m.–3 p.m. M–F, sunset–midnight F–Sa
Admission: By donation
Wheelchair accessible: Yes

A small-domed building right next to the H. R. MacMillan Space Centre, the observatory is equipped with a 0.5-m Cassegrain telescope to explore the day and night skies around Vancouver. Telescope observing sessions are held daily, organized by staff and volunteers who will tell you how it works and let you look through it to see stars and galaxies, and you can also listen to National Aerospace and Space Administration broadcasts. You're even allowed to take your own photos of the moon on a clear night.

Science World

1455 Quebec St.
Downtown
604-443-7443
www.scienceworld.bc.ca
Open: 10–5 M–F, 10–6 Sa–Su and holidays
Admission: $12.75 adults, $17.75 including Omnimax Theatre ($11.25 for just the theater); discounts for children, families, groups
Wheelchair accessible: Yes

When it's lit up at night, the silver geodesic dome of Science World looks like a giant dimpled golf ball. Inside are some of the most wonderful hands-on exhibits that have ever turned an adult into a child. You can play the piano with your toes, create a cyclone, or take a picture of your shadow. Located at the east end of False Creek, the center houses five permanent galleries and a feature exhibition gallery that has regular changes in content. Yet another legacy of Expo '86, the center begins on street level with a Gravitram for experimenting with potential energy and the force of gravity; the IBM Info Windows, which introduce the world of computers; and the puzzling optical effects of the Visual Illusions exhibit.

The second level encompasses a world of physics where you can actually touch a tornado, lose your shadow, or stretch an echo. In the Search Gallery, which focuses on British Columbia's natural history, you find tree roots hanging from the ceiling, a crawl-through beaver lodge, and a see-through beehive. The Music Machines Gallery allows you to step on sound and compose music on a giant walk-on synthesizer that can be programmed by the user for 120 sound selections. And you can play in booths filled with keyboards, drum pads, and an assortment of electronics.

The centerpiece, and biggest draw, of course, is the 400-seat Omnimax Theatre, where the audience is surrounded by huge images on the five-story, domed screen (one of the world's largest) and engulfed in wrap-around sound. The larger-than-life shows cover a wide variety of subjects, such as the vast icy world of Antarctica, the explosive ring of Pacific Rim volcanoes, and the history of transportation.

Storyeum

142 Water St.
Gastown
604-687-8142, 1-800-687-8142
www.storyeum.com
Open: 10–5 W–F, 11–5 Sa–Su and holidays
Admission: $22 adults 19–64 (in summer), $20 (in winter); discounts for seniors and youth
Wheelchair accessible: Yes

Storyeum is like a combination of Disneyland and the History Channel. It's a unique 70-minute tour through time, set in a multimedia underground performance theater the size of six hockey rinks located in the heart of Gastown. Two passenger lifts that take you to and from the underground theater are part of the show. Here you can get an entertaining and exciting summary of the city, the province of British Columbia, and also what else to see and do in the city and elsewhere. Storyeum opened in July 2004 and immediately became a "must see" experience. You're surrounded by extravagant movie sets with passionate performances by actors and state-of-the-art effects and lighting techniques, as well as a full original score. Witness the geological events that shaped the Northwest coast, and then travel inside a rushing salmon stream. Experience the oral histories of the First Nations and the arrival of European explorers; go on a trip to Barkerville, a once-thriving gold-rush town in central British Columbia; and watch the first steam train arriving at the docks in Gastown in the mid-1800s.

Vancouver Aquarium
845 Avison Way (in Stanley Park)
West End
604-659-3474
www.vanaqua.org
Open: 10–5:30 daily
Admission: $16.50 adults; $12.50 seniors, youths 13–18 and students; $9.50 children 4–12; free 3 and under
Wheelchair accessible: Yes

Canada's largest aquarium is marked by Haida artist Bill Reid's massive 18-foot (5.5 m) bronze statue of a killer whale in its own reflecting pool. Inside are more than 8,000 species of aquatic life, including beluga and killer whale exhibits. The facility is essentially designed for research and education, but it's also a highly entertaining and sometimes hands-on place where children and adults alike enjoy themselves. What can give greater pleasure to a child than to see beluga whales, seals, and other sea mammals up close? It's magical and it's easy to do because the beluga and harbor seal pools were designed to be seen from both outside and inside the facility. Beyond the show-biz aspect of the aquarium is the fact that it's also Canada's largest marine mammal rescue and rehabilitation center, and the rescue techniques are explained at the several exhibits. At the outdoor Max Bell Marine Mammal center, you meet a variety of recuperating animals—otter, seals, beluga whales. The facility has several ongoing exhibits from the tropics, northern climates, and North America featuring tropical fish, octopuses, and reptiles.

Museums
Vancouver is a community that places great importance on social movements and the city's cultural past, so you'll come across museums devoted to the social, economic, and scientific past and present. Throughout the city and suburbs, Native Americans, Asians, and Europeans are all represented in a variety of specialty and general museums and science centers. Where does science begin and art end? Or vice versa? After your tour of the city's museums and galleries, you may no longer have the answer.

BC Golf Museum
2545 Blanca St.
Point Grey

604-222-4653
www.bcgolfmuseum.org
Open: 12–4 Tu–Su
Admission: Free
Wheelchair accessible: Yes

Canada's only golf museum is between the 16th green and the 17th tee-box at the University Golf Club on the eastern edge of the University of British Columbia. The club's original 1931 clubhouse now houses six galleries depicting the evolution of the game and an extensive golf library of more than 1,200 volumes and 100 videos covering instruction, history (including Ben Hogan playing in the 1967 Masters), biography, fiction, architecture, and current environmental concerns. Two halls display exhibitions of special interest, featuring golf from all over the Pacific Northwest. The museum gift shop has calendars, plus Pringle sweaters and prints. There's a small putting and chipping green outside the door for practice.

BC Sports Hall of Fame and Museum
777 Pacific Blvd. S., Gate A (BC Place Stadium)
Downtown
604-687-5520
www.bcsportshalloffame.com
Open: 10–5 daily
Admission: $8 adults; $6 seniors, students, and youth
Wheelchair accessible: Yes

This place highlights British Columbia's greatest athletes—including the efforts of disabled athletes such as Terry Fox and Rick Hanson. It also offers a hands-on experience in which you can test your skills at climbing, throwing, or racing. The exhibitions in 18 rooms cover 150 years of sports history. You can also take a tour of the stadium itself.

Chinese Cultural Centre Museum and Archives
555 Columbia St.
Chinatown
604-658-8880
www.cccvan.com
Open: 11–5 Tu–Su
Admission: $5
Wheelchair accessible: Yes

On Pender Street, just a few steps east of Columbia, is a big red arch that frames the entrance into the Chinese Cultural Centre Museum and Archives. Inside the museum you'll find a variety of cultural exhibits and classes for tai chi and other Chinese arts. Attached to the building is the Dr. Sun Yat Sen Classical Chinese Garden (see Gardens and Parks). The museum also houses the Chinese Canadian Military Museum on the second floor. Its purpose is to educate the public about the Chinese Canadian soldiers who fought for Canada in the First and Second World Wars. The center also does research on the history of the Chinese people in Canada, as well as collecting and preserving historic artifacts, memorabilia, and photographs.

Geology Museum

6339 Stores Rd. (Geological Science Centre, UBC campus)
Point Grey
604-822-2229
www.geology.ubc.ca
Open: 10–5 M–F
Admission: Free
Wheelchair accessible: Yes

The Geology Department of the University of British Columbia maintains significant collections of rocks, minerals, and fossils displayed to the public throughout most of the first floor of the building. Virtually unknown to tourists, this is a gem in every sense of the word. Not only will you find displays of every stone and rock found in Canada that glows and sparkles, but there's even a collection of 80-million-year-old lambeosaurus dinosaur bones. Want to know what's happened in the past four billion years or so? This is the place to find out.

Granville Island Sports Fishing, Model Trains, and Model Ships Museums

1502 Duranleau St.
Granville Island
604-683-1939
www.sportfishingmuseum.ca, www.modeltrainsmuseum.ca, www.modelshipsmuseum.ca
Open (all three): 10–5:30 Tu–Su
Admission (to each): $7.50 adults, $6.00 students and seniors
Wheelchair accessible: Yes

Here are three museums in one. The Granville Island Sports Fishing Museum is home to an extensive collection including hardy reels, rare art, fly plates, salmon fishing history, and interactive technology. At the Model Trains Museum, you'll find the world's largest collection of toy trains, plus exhibits and memorabilia from train enthusiasts all over North America and Europe. And the Model Ships Museum has an international collection of submarines, warships, sailing ships, working vessels, and remote-control racers, with the showpiece of the museum being a 13-foot-long cast replica of HMS *Hood*.

Hasting Mills Store Museum

1575 Alma
Point Grey
604-734-1212
Open: 11–4 daily Jun–Sep; 1–4 Sa–Su after Sep
Admission: By donation
Wheelchair accessible: Yes

This was Vancouver's first building; built in 1865, it was the city's first general store, its first meeting place, its post office, a church, and, as the headquarters of the British Columbia and Vancouver Island Spar, Lumber and Sawmill Co., the city's first employer. It was also one of the very few buildings that survived the great fire of 1886. In 1930 it was moved from Gastown to its current location. Once inside the store, you're met with notions, furniture, hardware, toiletries, and dry goods dating from Queen Victoria's time.

Totem poles, some dating to the 1800s, at the University of British Columbia's Museum of Anthropology Toshi

Museum of Anthropology

6393 NW Marine Dr. (UBC campus)
Point Grey
604-822-5087
www.moa.ubc.ca
Open: Variable; call ahead
Admission: $8 adults, $7 seniors 65-plus, $6 students, free under 6
Wheelchair accessible: Yes

This is a world-class facility devoted to mankind's journey through time. The large, magnificent cement and glass structure was built in 1976 on a bluff overlooking Howe Sound. Located on the University of British Columbia campus, this is a hands-on way to explore native cultures of the Pacific Northwest. Though the building complex is relatively new, the university's anthropology program and collection is recognized as a world-class; the museum goes hand in hand with the university anthropology degree courses.

This is a magical place whether you're an adult or a child. When you walk in, you're faced with monumental totem poles that stare down at you. The poles have been collected from Native American communities in the interior of the province and from along the coast; some date to the 1800s. Outside, in back of the museum, are other poles and an authentic Haida longhouse.

A dozen galleries reflect complex indigenous cultures from around the world. In the Great Hall, light streams in from 46-foot-high (14 m) windows that highlight weathered cedar totem poles. In the Masterpiece Gallery, you'll find intricately carved small pieces of argillite, ivory, gold, silver, bone, and wood, most of which date from the 18th century. The old merges with the new in artist Bill Reid's massive sculpture, "The Raven and the First Men," which depicts how Raven fooled the First People into emerging from their clamshell. It's the most spectacular of what amounts to the best collection of Northwest Native American art anywhere in the world. And like the best of indigenous art, it's impossible to tell where art begins and culture ends.

Other exhibit halls have work from European, South Pacific, and Vancouver artists. Outside, you can explore a sculpture garden and two facade-carved Haida houses, plus totem poles and a magnificent view of the Strait of Georgia.

Vancouver Art Gallery

750 Hornby St.
Downtown
604-662-4700
www.vanartgallery.bc.ca
Open: 10–5:30 M–W and F–Su; 10–9 Th; closed Monday's in winter, Christmas Day, New Year's Day
Admission: $15 adults; discounts for students, seniors, children
Wheelchair accessible: Yes

The art gallery is located in the heart of the downtown core in the old Vancouver Provincial Courthouse, designed by Francis Rattenbury, the same architect who designed Victoria's Legislative Buildings, and was renovated by Arthur Erickson in 1983. It now houses historical and contemporary exhibitions of paintings, sculpture, graphic arts, photography, and video by distinguished regional, national, and international artists. A portion of the permanent collection, which covers four centuries of Canadian art as well as Dutch paintings from the 17th and 18th centuries and modern British paintings and sculpture from 1933 to 1955, is always on view. So too are the paintings and drawings by Emily Carr from the largest permanent collection of her work in Canada. Tours, lectures, and family workshops are regularly scheduled. The gallery also contains a 25,000-volume noncirculating reference library, a restaurant, and a gift and bookshop.

You'll hear the name Emily Carr mentioned often when you're in Vancouver.

The Vancouver Art Gallery is located in the old Vancouver Provincial Courthouse, designed by Francis Rattenbury, who also designed Victoria's Legislative Buildings. Toshi

There's an art school on Granville Island named after her, and the Vancouver Art Gallery has devoted an entire wing to her work. She was and still is British Columbia's artistic heart. Born in 1871, she painted and drew the natural and native environments in British Columbia long before it was easy to travel. Always dressed in a shapeless coat and high laced shoes and with her hair held in place by a dark hairnet, she spent a lifetime having her "modern" art lambasted by the artistic establishment. Chronically poor, she painted on paper using house paint or oils thinned by gasoline. When not painting, she bred sheep dogs and made pottery. By the 1930s her work was finally recognized internationally, but it didn't contribute to her finances. While recovering from the first of four heart attacks, she began writing about her experiences, and at the age of 70, her first book about travels with the Native Americans of the Pacific Northwest (*Klee Wyck*, 1941) was published and earned her a Governor General's Award, Canada's equal to the Pulitzer. She died in 1945. Her birthplace in Victoria, at 207 Government Street, has been restored for public viewing. Her works are on permanent display both in Vancouver and in Victoria.

Also in the gallery are works by the Group of Seven: In 1920 J. E. H. MacDonald, Lawren Harris, A. Y. Jackson, Arthur Lismer, Franklin Carmichael, F. H. Varley, and Frank Johnston officially formed this group of painters bitten by the Canadian north who, for the first time, took on the task of painting the great power, scenery, and spirit of the land. All—except Harris who was independently wealthy—made their living as commercial artists, and several of them even worked together in the same shop.

The Vancouver Maritime Museum houses a National Historic Site, The St. Roch. Toshi

Vancouver Maritime Museum
1905 Ogden Ave.
Kitsilano
604-257-8300
www.vancouvermaritimemuseum.com
Open: 10–5 M–Sa, noon–5 Su
Admission: $8 adults, $5.50 seniors and students
Wheelchair accessible: Yes

In front of this building is a Kwakiutl totem pole towering 100 feet (30.5 m) into the sky. Inside is the wooden 1928 sailing ketch the *St. Roch* in its own permanent building, a glass encasement that surrounds the now National Historic Site. The former Royal Canadian Mounted Police craft was the first sailing vessel to circumnavigate the Northwest Passage through the Arctic from west to east. The ship was brought on shore and the building was built around it. Check out the permanent collection in the museum for the hands-on interactive area where kids can maneuver an underwater robot.

Vancouver Museum
1100 Chestnut St.
Downtown
604-736-4431
www.vanmuseum.bc.ca
Open: 10–5 Tu, W, F–Su; 10–9 Thu
Admission: $10 adults, $8 seniors, discounts for youth
Wheelchair accessible: Yes

The roof atop this place, which also houses the Space Museum, is shaped in the form of a traditional Coast Salish cone hat, giving you an indication of what awaits you inside. Here's where you go to see how the city grew from a wilderness on the edge of the ocean to a major North American city in 100 years. There's a replica of a sawmill, elaborate dresses and clothing, and thousands of individual items ranging from Native American carvings to railway passenger cars.

Vancouver Police Centennial Museum
240 E. Cordova St.
East Vancouver
604-665-3346
www.city.vancouver.bc.ca/police/museum
Open: 9–3 M–F
Admission: $6 adults, $4 seniors and students
Wheelchair accessible: Yes

Housed in the old Coroner's Court Building near the main police station, this museum has on display wanted posters, a preserved larynx fractured by a fatal karate chop, plus the old morgue and autopsy room where actor Errol Flynn ended up in 1959 after dying at a local hotel. There's also a crime scene re-creation of "Babes in the Woods," a 1953 murder that's still unsolved. On January 14, 1953, the skeletal remains of two children were found in the bushes of Stanley Park. They were covered by a woman's fur coat and leaves that had fallen from the trees over the years. It was estimated that the bodies, of two boys, seven to 10 years old, had been there since the fall of 1947. Though police suspected who they were and who killed them, the case is still unsolved.

Vancouver Space Museum/H. R. MacMillan Planetarium Star Theatre
1100 Chestnut St.
Kitsilano
604-738-7827
www.hrmacmillanspacecentre.com
Open: 10–5 daily May–Sep; 10–5 Tu–Su rest of year
Admission: $13.50 adults 19–64, $10.50 seniors 65 and over; discounts for children, families, groups
Wheelchair accessible: Yes

This is the place for *Star Trek* wannabes to play in space and use space gadgets. The space museum is a recent natural outgrowth of the H. R. MacMillan Planetarium that occupies the top floor and has one of the finest star-gazing programs in North America. It's not quite the *Enterprise*'s holo-deck, but the Space Museum's Cosmic Courtyard will give you a good idea of what it might be like.

Nightlife and Other Pleasures

Drinking establishments in Vancouver are a bit different from those in Seattle, though the differences are rapidly disappearing, as British Columbia recently changed its drinking laws to reflect the realities of the 21st century. Pubs and bars in downtown Vancouver are open until 3 am, and the legal drinking age is 18. In Vancouver's nightclubs, you'll find a variety of musical forms, ranging from ear-blasting rock to folk and jazz and everything in between. Many nightclubs offer dancing to rock, fusion, or 1940s music. Always call before you go to find out about cover charges, show prices (if any), and—the business being what it is—whether the establishment is still open.

A great source for news about live entertainment is the *Georgia Straight*, a weekly tabloid with the best listings in the city. The Thursday edition of the *Vancouver Sun* newspaper has a weekly entertainment section. The **Vancouver Cultural Alliance Arts Hot Line** (100-938 Howe Street; 604-684-2787; www.allianceforarts.com) is a great source for all entertainment events. Tickets can be ordered through Tickets Tonight (www.ticketstonight.ca), a joint venture between the Alliance for the Arts and Culture and Tourism Vancouver.

This is the city that gave the world rock singer Bryan Adams, so expect there to be a legacy of pop culture in this town, where music of all kinds permeates the city's consciousness. You name it, Vancouver has it in spades—blues, jazz, rock, country and western. The **International Jazz Festival** (604-872-5200; www.jazzvancouver.com) is located around the city at various venues every June and includes a number of free concerts. The **Coastal Jazz and Blues Society** (604-872-5200), organizer of the jazz festival, has the latest news about local performances. The **Vancouver Folk Festival** (604-602-9798; www.thefestival.bc.ca) in July attracts the biggest names in the discipline.

Because Vancouver has the largest gay and lesbian population west of Toronto, there are several gay clubs downtown. They're located primarily in the West End area. And in Vancouver, one of the most tolerant of North American cities, they have become almost mainstream, with straights and gays often attending the same clubs to see the same performers. If you want to know the current hot spots, contact the **Gay Lesbian Transgendered Bisexual Community Centre** (2-1170 Bute St.; 604-684-5307) or pick up a copy of *Xtra West*, a tabloid that's available at most newsstands. Among the popular clubs is **Heritage House Hotel** (455 Abbott; 604-685-7777) on the edge of Chinatown, which has three gay bars, each with a different character, and is one of the trendiest places in town; on Saturday, it's women only at the **Milk Lounge** on the main floor. The **Odyssey** (1251 Howe St.; 604-689-5256) is one of the hottest hip bars in town for both gays and straights. The dance floor, with mirrors overhead, is usually packed, especially on weekends. A DJ spins CDs nightly, and there's a variety of live entertainment during the week, including male go-go dancers and live drag.

Visitors are always surprised that there's a lot of gambling activity throughout the Lower Mainland. The gambling may not match up to the great casinos of Vegas or Atlantic City, but there is now enough around town to keep your interest. At the **Gateway Casino** (611 Main St., third fl.; 604-688-9412), you'll find gambling with a difference. Along with the usual blackjack, poker, and other table games, this Chinatown casino caters to the cultural realities of the neighborhood with games such as Pai Gow Poker and Sic Bo. It's about as close as you'll get to Macao, where Chinese from Hong Kong jet-boat for gambling. Here, at times you may think you need a Mandarin or Cantonese phrase book, but simply get absorbed by the atmosphere. There are no slots. The **Great Canadian Casino** (1133 W. Hastings; 604-682-8415) is located in the Renaissance Hotel downtown, and the games reflect both the traditional Western style and the hotel's Asian clientele. And at the **Royal Diamond Casino** (750 Pacific Blvd.; 604-685-2340), located at the Plaza of Nations— across from BC Place Stadium— you'll find a comfortable atmosphere with a $500 limit on card games. And you can play Pai Gow Poker.

The live theaters are open year-round, though some of the arts organizations take the summers off. From mid-September to early June, however, the live theater and music scene is in full bloom. Local humor can be found at **Vancouver Theatresports League** (604-687-1644) at the Arts Club Revue Stage on Granville Island. The material is sometimes raunchy, definitely insulting, and always innovative; ignoring the politically correct about anything—politics, religion, race, family—is the standard that this longtime comedy institution has always held dear. So don't go if you're particularly sensitive about these topics. The comics work as teams, taking themes shouted to them by the audience and then competing against one another, with a referee determining the winner. Shows are Wednesday through Saturday. Check for specific start times since they differ from day to day.

Purple Onion Jazz Cabaret
15 Water St.
Gastown
604-602-9442

You'll be glad you took the hike to this Gastown institution. It features a variety of music forms, though live jazz is its mainstay. This is a Vancouver hot spot, so expect to wait in line an hour or so on Friday. There is a dress code (no shorts, jeans, or T-shirts). During the jazz festival, this place really moves.

Richard's on Richards
1036 Richards St.
Downtown
604-687-6794

This has been a mainstay of the nightclub scene for several generations, and it continues to move with the times. What was once Vancouver's primary club for the hormone-overloaded youth of the city has become one of the trendier, more established music places downtown. The interior is high-tech and tasty and there's valet parking, plus two floors, four bars, laser lighting, and live and taped top-40 hits. Live acts have included James Brown and 2Live Crew.

The Stone Temple
1082 Granville St.
Downtown
604-488-1333

Here's one of the primary hangouts for the very young, a cruiser bar with a huge dance floor and a DJ spinning music that spans virtually every musical form—except Mozart.

The Yale Hotel
1300 Granville St.
Downtown
604-681-9253

This home for R&B, located at the north end of the Granville Street Bridge, has been around for more than 100 years, and some of the players seem like they may have been there at the original opening. The musicians are old pros, and they're good, really good. Ignore the sense of seediness that permeates the place. This section of Granville isn't the nicest, but the musical rewards make coming here worthwhile.

Quieter Pursuits
Pubs, quiet bars, and cozy places permeate the downtown area as stand-alones or in hotels. You'll get a more discreet atmosphere and clientele; many are refuges from the hectic life outside the walls and windows.

Downtown: At the **Bacchus Lounge** in the Wedgewood Hotel (845 Hornby St.; 604-689-9321), there's soft jazz for the genteel crowd. A pianist plays during the cocktail hour, and then a gentle duo or trio takes over the evening. The **Barclay Lounge** (1348 Robson St.; 604-688-8850) is a cabaret-style bar with singers whose repertoire is broad—from the songs of Judy Holiday to weepies from the past three decades. Attached to O'Doul's restaurant, and decorated in pastels with paintings on the walls, the lounge is a high-end way to spend an evening. Just down the street, at **Joe Fortes** (777 Thurlow St.; 604-669-1277; see Restaurants), a pianist plays nightly for the suited set that drops in after work and on Saturday night.

At the **Gallery** in the Hyatt Regency (655 Burrard St.; 604-683-1234), you get soft music, comfy chairs around the bar, warm reds and browns, and TVs with no sound. Sit for a few minutes and you're convinced you're in a private club—and you're treated as such by an attentive staff. The **Garden Terrace** at the Four Seasons Hotel (791 W. Georgia St.; 604-689-9333) is located in a high atrium next to the hotel's lobby area, with a large number of potted plants carefully placed around the 120 seats. The floor plan provides a high degree of privacy, with luxuriously soft chairs and a piano player who caresses the keyboard. Elegance permeates the place.

Granville Island: The **Backstage Lounge** at the Arts Club (1585 Johnson St., Granville Island; 604-687-1354) is one of Vancouver's little secrets. Most visitors to the island don't realize that here is one of the comfiest pubs in the city—and it's on the waterfront. Originally designed as an intermission place where theater patrons could relax between curtains, it has become busy on weekends, when the live entertainment is usually a blues band.

Waterfront: Cascade's Lounge in the Pan Pacific Hotel (300-999 Canada Pl.; 604-682-5511) is one of the most tranquil places in the city. Get there in the late twilight and look out over the water to the dark-edged mountains outlined in the orange sky. Try hard enough and you might find a bald eagle heading toward Squamish. Located along a glass-walled side of the Pan Pacific's lobby area, this spot overlooks the cruise ships, out toward Stanley Park and downtown's waterfront area.

Tours and Sightseeing

Although much of Vancouver is best seen on your own, there may be times when you want to let someone else do the driving. Taking a tour when you get into town gives you a good overall impression of the city and what you'd like to explore in greater detail.

Chinatown: One of the best ways to experience and get to know Chinatown is by taking **A Wok around Chinatown** (604-736-9508; www.awokaround.com), a guided culinary and cultural walking tour.

The cruise-ship terminal on Vancouver's waterfront Toshi

Gastown: Each summer from June 15 to August 30, Gastown merchants offer **free historic walking tours of Gastown** (604-683-5650), usually leaving from the steam clock on the corner of Water and Cambie Streets. These 90-minute tours run daily at 2 p.m. and provide information about the architecture and history of Vancouver's birthplace.

Canada Place
Foot of Burrard St.
Waterfront
604-641-1987
www.canadaplace.ca
Wheelchair accessible: Yes

The iconic Canada Place complex, which includes the city's main convention center, a cruise-ship terminal, the Pan Pacific Hotel, the Vancouver Board of Trade, restaurants, and shopping, is recognizable by its five towering white sails. It's the departure point for cruise ships sailing to Alaska between May and October. To the east helicopter passenger service flies between Vancouver's harbor and Victoria's. To the west is the seaplane launching pad. Built for Expo '86, the convention complex faces the craggy North Shore mountains.

Granville Island Brewery
1441 Cartwright St.
Granville Island
604-687-2739
www.gib.ca
Open: Variable; call ahead
Admission: $6 adults, $5 seniors and students
Wheelchair accessible: Yes

This microbrewery is one of the island's most popular stops, if for no reason other than you can have a sampling of the product in a 30-minute tour. Granville Island Lager is one of the city's most popular local brews, found in every pub in town. It's a preservative-free Bavarian-style Pilsner. If you've never been in a brewery and have always wondered how the golden stuff is made, you can't find a more user-friendly way.

Gray Line Vancouver Tours
900 Georgia St. (Fairmont Hotel Vancouver)
Downtown
604-879-3363, 1-800-667-0882
www.grayline.ca

Although the main pickup stop is the Fairmont Hotel Vancouver, the Gray Line buses will pick you up at your hotel. A variety of trips are available, including city tours, a cruise to Victoria or Whistler, and much more.

Grouse Mountain
6400 Nancy Greene Way
North Shore
604-984-0661

www.grousemountain.com
Open: 9 a.m.–10 p.m. daily
Admission (Skyride): $26.95 adults 19 years and over; discounts for seniors, students, children, families
Wheelchair accessible: Limited

This is both a tourist destination and one of Vancouver's favorite ski hills, and you get there in a gondola that takes you straight up the mountain. The Skyride takes you to the 3,600-foot (1,100 m) mountaintop winter or summer, offering spectacular views of the city, English Bay, Mount Baker in Washington's Cascades, and the Strait of Georgia. In summer, walking paths and nature trails provide some of the most spectacular hiking on the West Coast, all of it just a few minutes from downtown Vancouver. Check the mountain map at the Skyride. During the summer there are 15-mile (25 km) mountain-bike tours of the nearby trails. Helicopter tours as well as tandem paragliding are also available. During winter there is skiing day and night. The Peak chair, which in winter takes skiers to the very top, stays open in summer; the chair ride up the Peak is included in the Skyride fee. Round out the day with a visit to the multimedia Theater in the Sky presentation. Also within the building at the top are restaurants, a pub, and gift shops.

Harbour Air
Coal Harbour
Waterfront
604-274-1277
www.harbour-air.com

Departing from Coal Harbour, near the Bayshore Inn Hotel, seaplanes offer a complete aerial tour of the city and surrounding mountains. The seaplane airline operates daily year-round with 30-minute or 20-minute flights. It also has packages for golf on Vancouver Island, fishing, and other activities.

Harbour Centre Tower
555 W. Hastings St.
Downtown
604-689-0421
www.vancouverlookout.com
Open: 8:30 a.m.–10:30 p.m. daily
Admission: $10 adults; discounts for students, seniors
Wheelchair accessible: Yes

This former department store is one of the city's most energetic places, where shoppers, students, and tourists mix on an ongoing basis. Not only is it the downtown campus of Simon Fraser University, it has an observation tower that lets you see the entire waterfront area. The observation deck was opened on August 13, 1977, by the first man on the moon, Neil Armstrong. Look for his footprint in concrete on the lookout level. A glass-encased Skylift takes you up 553 feet (168.5 m) to the roof for the view. The Harbor Mall beneath the building has more than 50 shops, and the Top of Vancouver revolving restaurant is a great way to take a turn around the city.

TRIUMPF
4004 Wesbrook Mall (UBC campus)
Point Grey
604-222-1047
www.triumf.ca
Open (tours): 1 p.m. W and F Sep 1–May 31; 11 a.m. and 2 p.m. M–F Jun 1–Aug 31
Admission: Free
Wheelchair accessible: Yes

There aren't many places where you can tour an atomic research center that specializes in the uses of subatomic particles. And don't worry about anything blowing up. It's as safe as a walk in the nearby park. The free 90-minute tour lets you watch the world's largest cyclotron in action. For the curious, it's a circular particle accelerator in which charged subatomic particles are accelerated spirally outward by an alternating electric field; it's capable of generating millions of volts. Tours begin with a general description of the history and operation of the facility. Afterward the guide will walk you through part of the experimental building. You will see several experimental areas, the central control room, and more. (The center is located south of 16th Ave.)

University of British Columbia Campus
West end of NW Marine Dr.
Point Grey
604-822-2211
www.ubc.ca
Open (tours): 10 a.m. and 1 p.m. M–F (excluding holidays) in summer
Wheelchair accessible: Yes

Students must have a focus of steel to be able to study and yet ignore the spectacular views toward Vancouver Island on a campus that overlooks Howe Sound and the Gulf Islands. The views, especially driving to the university along the NW Marine Drive water-front, are stunning, with mountains offering a backdrop to the city and the ocean. The university is home to about 40,000 students, but it's much more than just a place of study. It combines academics with forests, beachfront, gardens, theaters, and remarkable architecture.

ENTERTAINMENT AND THE ARTS

More than a century ago, Vancouver had an opera house that attracted the luminaries of the time—Sarah Bernhardt, Mark Twain, Henry Irving. That tradition has lasted, both indoors and out. In live theater, for example, there are some 30 professional theatrical groups, two major theater festivals, and more than 21 venues, balancing mainstream and experimental programming. In music and dance, the list of professional and amateur organizations has exploded during the past 15 years to the point where you can find a wide range of classical, jazz, and world music. Performers from Asia and Europe sometimes perform at sold-out concerts at the city's largest venues without so much as a classified ad in the newspapers.

In film, it's no surprise that the city, now the third-largest movie-making center in North America, behind Hollywood and New York, has a major film festival. Yet no single art form so clearly defines the city's cultural explosion as its staggering number of choirs—there are some 140 in Greater Vancouver. These range from the large 150-member Vancouver Bach Choir to the small, 12-member Musica Intima, and they consist of church, male, female, ethnic, and general performance choirs. Although the Vancouver Symphony and Vancouver Opera—as in most major cities—remain the biggest and most moneyed of Vancouver's arts scene, Vancouver is blessed by literally hundreds of small spin-off ensembles.

For a daily listing of what's going on in Vancouver's arts scene, read the *Georgia Straight* newspaper, which has the city's most complete listings.

Main Venues

Most of Vancouver's prime concerts sites are located downtown. There are several major live-theater complexes in Vancouver. The Orpheum (see below) hosts the Vancouver Symphony and a variety of other major concerts. The **Queen Elizabeth Theatre** complex (600 Hamilton St.; 604-665-3050) is home of the Vancouver Opera and major dance and theater companies. The **Centre in Vancouver for the Performing Arts** (777 Homer St.; 604-280-3311) was originally built as the Ford Centre and is the home to large touring theater companies. The **Vancouver East Cultural Centre** (1895 Venables; 604-251-1363) stages contemporary theater, small music ensembles, and children's programming. And the recently opened **Scotiabank Dance Centre** (677 Davie St.; 604-606-6400) offers performance and rehearsal space for 30 dance companies.

Outside of downtown, the **Chan Centre for the Performing Arts** (6265 Crescent Rd., UBC campus, Point Grey; 604-822-2697) is the home of the Vancouver Recital Society and campus music and acting programs. The **Gateway Theater** (6500 Gilbert Rd., Richmond; 604-270-1812), in the heart of Minoru Park, is home to professional live theater and music.

The Orpheum Theatre
801 Granville St.
Downtown
604-665-3050

When the Orpheum opened in 1927 as one in a chain of the Orpheum theaters across North America, the hall's interior was in a conservative Spanish Renaissance style with a basic color scheme of antique ivory and gold and ornamental colonnades and gold leaf contrasted with black and gold arabesques. Glittering chandeliers lit the hall. Below the stage was an electrically operated elevator that lifted three huge Wurlitzer organs, one of which is still played here once a year. When the Famous Players movie theater chain announced in the early 1970s that the Orpheum would be transformed into a series of small movie theaters, City Hall was besieged by a letter-writing campaign to save the hall for use as a concert hall. Consequently, the city bought the theater for about $4 million and spent an equal amount bringing it up to standard for its 1977 opening. It is now the city's premier hall, the home of the Vancouver Symphony, and a declared National Historic Site. When you're in the 2,900-seat hall, be sure to look up at the mural on the massive dome. The original artist and decorator, Tony Heinsbergen, supervised the interior decorations. See if you can spot the left-handed cellist.

Tickets

Most music, theater, and performance companies sell tickets directly. Others work through a variety of brokers and ticket services. And for sporting events, there are always scalpers outside the stadiums waiting for someone willing to pay a premium. Sometimes, when an event is not sold out, scalpers are willing to sell at a loss just to rid themselves of the ducats. It's illegal only if they try to sell on the venue property. **One Stop Ticket Shop** (604-689-5500) promises to get you the best prices for the city's sporting events, concerts, and theater productions. **Pacific Northwest Ticket Service** (604-683-3515) not only has local events on its schedule but can also get tickets for the Super Bowl, Indy, Seattle sporting events, the Kentucky Derby, and the World Series. **Showtime Tickets & Tours** (604-688-5000) is a broker that'll find you the ticket you need; buys, sells, trades, and consigns. **Ticketmaster** (604-280-4444) is the biggie in town, offering tickets to virtually everything. **Tickets Tonight** (604-684-2787) is fashioned after similar outlets in New York and London, whereby half-price tickets are available on the day of the performance.

Dance

Ballet British Columbia (604-732-5003; www.balletbc.com) is a leading company in the Pacific Northwest. It's both an umbrella organization that brings in such renowned companies as the National Ballet of Canada and a performance organization that mounts exciting and courageous performances. Classical and contemporary dance is presented between September and June as part of its Dance Alive series at the Queen Elizabeth Theatre.

    Dancing on the Edge Festival (604-689-0926; www.dancingontheedge.org), held each July for two weeks, is North America's largest festival of independent choreographers, with some 70 performances conceived by choreographers from around the world. This dance orgy is held at numerous venues ranging from the **Firehall Arts Center** (280 E. Cordova St.) to beaches and even street corners. **Kokoro Dance** (604-662-7441; www.kokoro.ca) is a Japanese modern dance company that fuses a form called butoh with Western dance techniques. The results are stagings that incorporate live music, strong visuals, and physically demanding dance. Performances are at the Firehall Theatre (see above) and sometimes at the Vancouver East Cultural Centre.

Film

The **Vancouver International Film Festival** (604 685 0260; www.viff.org) is the biggest film event in the city, with 400 or so screenings of about 300 films from 50 countries at seven theaters over 17 days in September and October. It's the third-largest film festival in North America, with everything from avant-garde to mainstream to experimental drama and documentaries. Many of the films refuse categorization, breaking normal boundaries.

    Downtown, along Granville Street between West Georgia and Smithe Streets, has several major movie houses, as do major shopping centers around the city. As in most cities, the trend is to multiple screens, so expect downtown theaters to have five, six, or more films from which to choose. The downtown theaters include **Capitol 6** (820 Granville St.; 604-669-6000), **Granville 7 Cineplex** (855 Granville St.; 604-684-4000), **Royal Centre** (1055 W. Georgia St.; 604-669-9791), and **Vancouver Centre** (650 W. Georgia St.; 604-669-4442). The **Pacific Cinematheque** (1131 Howe St.; 604-688-3456; www.cinematheque.bc.ca) features films from around the world.

The entrance to Dr. Sun Yat-Sen Classical Chinese Garden, site of Chinese opera and traditional music Toshi

Music

Most Vancouver choirs perform in a variety of locations. **Musica Intima** (604-839-6612; www.musicaintima.com), the newest Vancouver choir, has won awards for its 12-member ensemble. The **Phoenix Chamber Choir** (604-437-9200; www.phoenixchamber choir.bc .ca), formed in 1983, has won international competitions, including the Canadian Broad-casting Corporation (CBC) Choral competitions. The **Vancouver Bach Choir** (604-921-8012; www.vancouverbachchoir .com), the largest (with 130 members) and oldest (formed in 1930) of the Vancouver area choirs, has a grand repertoire, often performing major works by Beethoven, Britten, and Mahler with the Vancouver Symphony. The **Vancouver Cantata Singers** (604-921-8588; www.cantata.org) is an international-award-winning, 40-member ensemble led by conductor and artistic director Eric Hannan. The **Vancouver Chamber Choir** (604-738-6822; www.vancouverchamberchoir.com), led by its founder/conductor/music director Jon Washburn, was formed in 1971 as one of Canada's two professional choirs. Its Vancouver season emphasizes short and Canadian works, but it is also a major interna-tional force, touring the world independently and for Canada's External Affairs ministry.

Chinese Opera

578 Carroll St. (Dr. Sun Yat Sen Classical Chinese Garden)
Chinatown
604-662-3207
www.vancouverchinesegarden.com

The gardens are the unique site of two quite different series of Asian arts: Chinese opera and traditional music and dance. Chinese opera is a formalized, colorful art form that's presented by local Chinese organizations using both local and international companies during the win-ter. In July and August, try to catch Enchanted Evenings, in which the gardens are bathed in soft light from traditional lanterns and musicians and dancers perform and tell stories.

Early Music Vancouver
Various venues
604-732-1610
www.earlymusic.bc.ca

Besides having 10 main concert series during the season, this society also has a joint sum-mer program with the University of British Columbia offering a series of workshops and concerts. Its collection of 20 accurate replicas of old instruments—built by Vancouverite craftsmen—is among the finest in the country.

Friends of Chamber Music
600 Hamilton St. (Queen Elizabeth Theatre)
Downtown
604-437-5747
www.friendsofchambermusic.ca

This organization stages only the very best in international small ensembles. Between October and April, the Beaux Arts Trio, Emerson Quartet, Tokyo String Quartet, and other international standard ensembles are regular visitors here.

Uzume Taiko
Various venues
604-683-8240
www.uzume.com

North America's first professional taiko drumming ensemble, formed in 1988, performs tra-ditional Japanese drumming that will get your blood flowing! Fusing three drummers, a flautist, a cellist, and African and Latin percussionists, Uzume blends old and new styles of drumming, bringing a vibrant, contemporary sensibility to an ancient art.

Vancouver Opera
600 Hamilton St. (Queen Elizabeth Theatre)
Downtown
604-682-2871
www.vanopera.bc.ca

The Vancouver Opera has grown from one opera a season when it was founded in 1960 to five. The company also stages a recital series in conjunction with other music organizations such as the Vancouver Recital Society, bringing in such international operatic stars as Jessye Norman, Kathleen Battle, Dmitri Hvorostovsky, Ben Heppner, and Samuel Ramey.

Vancouver Recital Society
6265 Crescent Rd. (Chan Centre for the Performing Arts, UBC campus)
Point Grey
604-602-0363
www.vanrecital.com

Founder and music director Leila Getz travels the world to find the best of international talents before they become unaffordable. In addition, one or two special concerts during the year feature big-name performers. In recent seasons, the organization has gone into joint sponsorships of major concerts with the Vancouver Opera and other organizations. Getz is also in charge of the International Chamber Music Festival.

Vancouver Symphony Orchestra
801 Granville St. (Orpheum Theatre)
Downtown
604-876-3434
www.vancouversymphony.ca

Remember that haunting theme from Oliver Stone's war film *Platoon*? Well, the music that drove the film's pathos and drama was American composer Samuel Barber's "Adagio for Strings," and the film score was played by the Vancouver Symphony Orchestra (VSO). It's not the first time the VSO has played for major films. It also played the sound track for *The Changeling* and for the TV film *Baby M*, among others. *Platoon* won an Oscar for best sound track and *The Changeling* for best sound. The orchestra has 11 different concert series through a regular season of about 40 weeks, playing music ranging from traditional concert fare to contemporary and children's concerts. In addition to its Orpheum Theatre concerts, the VSO plays in unlikely venues such as at the top of Whistler Mountain and Grouse Mountain and on Granville Island during the summer.

Theater
The **Arts Club** (604-687-1644; www.artsclub.com) owns and operates two theaters and a performance lounge on Granville Island plus the renovated **Stanley Theatre** (2750 Granville Street) less than a mile further south. The company holds its major productions at both the Stanley Theatre and at the **Main Stage Theatre** on Granville Island. In the same building as the Granville Island Main Stage Theatre is the intimate **Backstage Lounge** where musical groups and singers strut their talents. Directly across the mall from the Granville Island Main Stage is the **Revue Theatre** where **Vancouver Theatresports League** (see Nightlife) stages its action.

Bard on the Beach Shakespeare Festival
1100 Chestnut St. (Vanier Park)
Kitsilano
604-739-0559
www.bardonthebeach.org

Performances are in a large performance tent in Vanier Park on the south side of the entrance to False Creek, opposite the West End, where you just cannot ignore the sunsets, the mountains, and the high-rises. Spread a blanket on the grass and have a picnic before the often exciting Shakespearean plays performed every summer. Bring a cushion for the hard benches inside the tent.

Fringe Festival
Various venues
East Vancouver
604-257-0350
www.vancouverfringe.com

Vancouver's Fringe Festival is alive and well, with 92 shows spread over 11 days in early September. Some 100 companies are accepted on a first-come, first-served basis. Held in indoor theaters and outdoor stages around the Commercial Drive area, some really bad theater performances are mixed in with innovation and the never-tried-before.

Theatre Under the Stars
Malkin Bowl (Stanley Park)
West End
604-687-0174
www.tuts.bc.ca

This is a Vancouver institution. Casts are enthusiastic, and the under-the-stars atmosphere in Stanley Park makes this an enchanting evening of theater unlike anything else you'll see in town. Bring a sweater or light jacket for the mid-July to mid-August season.

Vancouver Playhouse Theatre Company
600 Hamilton St. (Vancouver Playhouse at the Queen Elizabeth Theatre)
Downtown
604-873-3311
www.vancouverplayhouse.com

This company's repertoire blends the classical with the contemporary, using many of the country's best actors and directors. It's the most established of the city's major companies and is the resident company of the Vancouver Playhouse. Here's where you'll likely find works by Shakespeare, Tennessee Williams, and Tom Stoppard.

Visual Art

Art in Vancouver is a reflection of what the city is: young, vibrant, fresh, multicultural, and West Coast. Mix that in with an abundance of Native American art, showings by local and national art legends, and outdoor and indoor public art, and you have an idea of what Vancouver's art gallery and museum scene is all about. With more than 100 private galleries, Vancouver's art scene is rich with enthusiasm, with many of its artists gaining laudable reputations in the international community. Among the city's artists who have reached major status now and in the past are Jack Shadbolt, Emily Carr, Gordon Smith, Lawren Harris, Bill Reid, Toni Onley, and Fred Varley.

The private galleries, which specialize in a wide range of art forms, are located primarily in Gastown, on or near Granville Island, and along Granville Street just south of the Granville Street Bridge. All of Vancouver's public galleries are wheelchair accessible unless otherwise stated. Art dealers are found throughout the downtown area and feature a wide variety of work. Although Vancouver does not have nearly as many as Seattle does, its galleries offer unique collections.

Art Beatus
108-808 Nelson St.
Downtown
604-688-2633
www.artbeatus.com

This gallery is devoted to Chinese artists from Canada and around the world. It's a great change from when much of Vancouver's art scene was a throwback to when the city was very British and European focused. This gallery reflects what the city has become in recent years: the most Asian of North American cities. You'll find a wide range of form and substance—traditional to contemporary—including painting, small sculptures, and silk print.

Bau-Xi Gallery

3045 Granville St.
False Creek
604-733-7011
www.bau-xi.com

The Bau-Xi Gallery is the oldest contemporary gallery in Vancouver, established in April 1965. The gallery was opened by Bau-Xi Huang (pronounced "boe she," meaning "great gift") to create a showcase for the many emerging and established Canadian artists in need of a gallery on the West Coast. The philosophy of the place is to focus on the art, not the surroundings, so the paintings, prints, and watercolors are presented on plain walls. Ask to see the gallery's storage area, where visitors can explore more than just what's displayed in the main gallery.

Crafthouse Shop

1386 Cartwright St.
Granville Island
604-687-7270
www.cabc.net/mem_sect/Chshop.html

This popular craft shop, located in the Loft across the street from the Granville Island Market, has just about everything and anything made from glass, clay, cloth, wood, paper, or delicate wiring. There's a wide variety of work, from small brooches to napkins to major art pieces. Artists are British Columbian from throughout the province, and the work is exquisite.

Emily Carr Institute of Art and Design

1399 Johnston St.
Granville Island
604-844-3811 (Charles Scott Gallery 604-844-3800)
www.eciad.ca

Visitors are welcomed with enthusiasm to view works of art in the Charles Scott Gallery, located in the college's lobby area. Situated between the Granville Island Hotel and the Granville Island Market. Huge picture windows frame budding artists as they do their work. The college is one of the few Canadian art institutions that offer a bachelor's degree, and it all began as a federal project to utilize three abandoned metal-fronted industrial buildings. If you're really keen and you'll be in town awhile, you can sign up for visitors' art courses.

Inuit Gallery

206 Cambie St.
Gastown
604-688-7323
www.inuit.com

In the heart of Gastown, this place is one of North America's leading Inuit art gallery and is staffed by knowledgeable salespersons. One of the hottest items in the gallery is its show catalog, itself a collector's item because of its fine reproductions. You'll find plenty of soapstone carvings; the Inuit use soapstone because it's a soft stone and it doesn't chip, making it a good medium for carving. You'll also find a wide range of masks, jewelry, and wood carvings.

Khot-La-Cha Coast Salish Handicrafts

270 Whonoak St. (Capilano Indian Reserve)
North Shore
604-987-3339
www.khot-la-cha.com

Located off the northern end of the Lion's Gate Bridge, this is the source for wood carvings and jewelry by local and Vancouver Island Native American artists and craftspeople. The items include hand-carved yellow and red cedar totem poles and plaques and ceremonial masks. As well, you'll find hand-knit Indian sweaters, moccasins, and silver and gold carved jewelry. Artists are from the Queen Charlotte, Haida, Tlingit, and Tahitan tribes.

Leona Lattimer Gallery

1517 W. Sixth Ave.
Granville Island
604-742-2330

On the southern edge of Granville Island, ensconced in what looks like a longhouse, this collection contains a wide range of art pieces, including immaculate carved wood boxes, silver and gold jewelry, argillite carvings, and button blankets. The masks are particularly fascinating, as they represent animals (Raven, Bear, and others) important to First Nations culture.

A carver working on a totem on the Univeristy of British Columbia campus Toshi

Marion Scott Gallery

481 Howe St.
Downtown
604-685-1934
www.marionscottgallery.com

Dating from 1975, this is one of the oldest galleries in Vancouver, housed in a spacious and airy gallery. It used to be an all-encompassing gallery that sold virtually all Pacific Northwest

Native American art. But in recent years it has refocused to specialize in only Inuit pieces, making this one of the city's most complete collections of stunning eastern Canadian Inuit prints, stone carvings, and jewelry. The collection frequently includes works by recognized master artists such as Karoo Ashevak, Jessie Oonark, Osuitok Ipeelee, and Lucy Tasseor.

Morris and Helen Belkin Art Gallery
1825 Main Hall (UBC campus)
Point Grey
604-822-2759
www.belkin-gallery.ubc.ca

This gallery also houses the university's 2,000-piece permanent art collection. The collection, established primarily through donations, emphasizes contemporary Canadian art and is also the home of various archives, including the Morris/Trasov Archives of the Seventies and the Peter Day Collection of Concrete Poetry. The gallery is not wheelchair accessible.

Richmond Art Gallery
180-7700 Minoru Gate
Richmond
604-231-6440

Located in the Richmond Library/Cultural Centre, this gallery has 5,000 square feet of exhibition space for contemporary art by local and international artists. The gallery is quite involved in community art, so you'll likely see programs for children and adults alike, including artist-run workshops. And each year a show is mounted especially for children. There's about 20 exhibits a year as well as 20 at the outreach gallery located at the Gateway Theatre. Exhibitions reflect a wide variety of media and styles, so you can expect anything. Programs and tours provide the public with opportunities to meet artists as well as to create their own art. The gallery is not wheelchair accessible.

Robert Held Art Glass
2130 Pine St.
Granville Island
604-737-0020
www.robertheld.com

Being here is much like watching construction of an office building from a viewing area. Held is a glass blower, and in this large, cavernous studio workshop, you can watch how he and his staff do it. The red-hot furnaces are used to form glass designs by a number of artists who use the facility, so in the studio you'll find delicate vases, glasses, and a variety of decorative pieces. The work is exquisite, and the colorations found within the glass emphasize the delicate nature of the items. The shop is located west of the Granville Street Bridge.

Three Vets
2200 Yukon St.
East Vancouver
604-872-5475
www.3vets.com

This clothing and outdoor equipment store hides one of the city's best-kept art secrets: At the back of the store, behind all the hiking and camping gear, is a small storage room/ gallery filled with Northwest Native American art, paintings, prints, bowls, jewelry, rattles, and plaques from about 300 different artists, many of whom you won't find elsewhere. Why rent another gallery elsewhere in town, after all, when you have a ready-made store with a little extra room?

RECREATION

Vancouver is a hockey town, unlike Seattle with its major-league baseball, football, and basketball teams. It is also an outdoor city. On a clear winter's evening, if you look toward the North Shore mountains, you'll see three well-lit mountaintops. As you're facing the mountains, to the right is the Mount Seymour ski area, in the middle is Grouse Mountain, and to the left is Cypress Bowl—all calling out to local residents to come and do some downhill skiing. The city has remarkably easy access to its ski areas, which are just minutes from the downtown core.

But if skiing and snowshoeing don't get your attention, the countless sailboats in English Bay, as well as hikers and walkers throughout the city, kite fliers, cyclists, and equestrians certainly will. Vancouver is one of the most golf-friendly cities in Canada, with courses in the middle of nearby neighborhoods. Tennis is also big, with 180 free public tennis courts as well six semiprivate clubs that offer indoor and outdoor pay-for-play facilities. Vancouver's Stanley Park tennis tournament, held every July–August, is the country's largest.

Jericho Beach's view of Vancouver's skyline Toshi

The Steveston dike is a great place for bicycling or walking. Toshi

Beaches

Vancouver is a city virtually surrounded by beaches, and they're a focal point for recreation and relaxation at all times of the year. Since the Vancouver area has fairly active movements of tides during the year, its beaches can sometimes stretch out from the high-tide shoreline for some distance. Every now and then, a sailboat makes a miscalculation and is stranded on the sand until the next high tide.

Kitsilano: Kitsilano Beach (along Cornwall Ave. between Arbutus and Trafalgar Sts.) fronts the most spectacular views in the city, and it's also one of the cultural centers of the city, with Vanier Park (see Gardens and Parks) attached to the east end of the beach. Take your camera, because when you look west, the entire vastness of English Bay opens up to Vancouver Island. Kids love the **Kitsilano Pool**, (604-257-8400 at Vancouver Parks Board; www.city.vancouver.bc.ca/ parks/rec/ pools/) a heated saltwater pool that fronts the **Kitsilano Showboat**, (604-734-7332) a local institution that has provided free seaside entertainment since 1935. Local amateur groups sing and act three days a week, weather permitting, during the summer months.

    Locarno and **Jericho Beaches** (along NW Marine Dr. between Trimble and Blanca Sts.) are really one continuous beach. Stand on the beach and you see the entire North Shore mountains, Howe Sound and its islands, Stanley Park, the city skyline, cruise ships, and glorious sunsets. At low tide it seems as though you can walk miles right across the bay, and it's a great place to explore for shells and to play in the tidal pools. A dirt path runs along its length, and there are grassy picnic areas between the road and the sand.

West End: English Bay Beach (along Pacific St. between Denman and Burrard Sts.) is a strutting area as well as a cooling-off place during the summer where young things male

Scullers at practice on False Creek Toshi

and female display their assets. During August, the spectacular Symphony of Fire (see Events), an international fireworks show, takes place over four days. And this is the site, every New Year's Day, of the annual Polar Bear Swim (see Events). A wonderful ginger-bread bandstand is still used for summer concerts.

Biking

Vancouver is a cycling mecca, and the best way to investigate a neighborhood is often by bike. Wide thoroughfares and cycling lanes make biking safe and enjoyable. Headgear is mandatory; it's a $25 ticket if you're caught without a helmet.

Kitsilano and Point Grey: A great cycling area is around western Point Grey, along the shoreline of Kitsilano past Vanier Park and Kitsilano Beach. If you're in great shape, bicycle Point Grey Road through Jericho Park and past the beaches along SW Maine Drive. You'll have great views of the mountains and English Bay, with places to stop and take photos and eat. Refreshment stands beachside are open during the summer.

Richmond: You can bicycle along the Steveston dike. And you can walk or bike around Richmond's Gulf of Georgia and Fraser River dikes, which take you virtually around the entirety of Lulu Island—with minor detours. If you start at the Moray Channel Bridge, you can bike the length of the Vancouver International Airport along the Middle Arm of the Fraser River, then along Sturgeon Bank with its lush wildfowl, and then along the Steveston waterfront past London Farm, the public fishing pier, Finn Slough, and Horseshoe Slough. Along the way you'll have the finest view of Vancouver Island, the gulf, and the North Shore mountains you can find in the Lower Mainland.

West End: The Stanley Park seawall is a great cycling path, shared with walkers. The path around the seawall is marked for both walkers and cyclists. The route around the seawall is 6.5 miles (10.5 km).

Bicycle Rentals

Near the entrance to Stanley Park, where Robson and Denman Streets meet, are several bike-rental shops. These include **Alley Cat Rentals** (1779 Robson St.; 604-684-5117), **Bayshore Bicycles** (745 Denman St.; 604-688-2453), **Spokes Bicycle Rental** (1798 W. Georgia St.; 604-688-5141), and **Stanley Park Rentals** (1741 Robson St.; 604-608-1908).

Under sail in English Bay Toshi

Competition for prices is fierce. For cycling western Point Grey and the University of British Columbia area, there's **West Point Cycles** (3771 W. 10th St.; 604-224-3536).

Boating

Blue Pacific Yacht Charters

1519 Foreshore Walk
Granville Island
604-682-2161

If you charter a Blue Pacific yacht, you can take the boat anywhere in the "inside" waters of British Columbia and the state of Washington, including all of Puget Sound, the Strait of Juan de Fuca as far west as Cape Flattery, and the waters inside Vancouver Island as far north as Port Hardy. The sailing fleet includes a variety of sizes, from a Catalina 27 to a Sparkman/Stephens 55.

Sunsail

450 Denman St. (Bayshore West Marina)
Waterfront
604-320-7245

Sunsail is the largest yacht charter company in the world, with 1,200 yachts operating from 39 bases in 23 countries, including a base in the heart of Vancouver's downtown waterfront. You can opt for a holiday in which you're the skipper, or the charter can include the services of a private skipper and even a cook, if desired. The Vancouver base at Coal Harbour has 16 boats ranging from 33 to 50 feet (10-15 meters). Wannabe sailors can take lessons that cater to beginners up to advanced yachtmaster offshore certification. Whatever style of vacation you choose, some of the Pacific Northwest's most spectacular coastline is available: the Sunshine Coast, Gulf Islands, and Desolation Sound. You can even make up your own itinerary.

Fishing

Of course, with all that water surrounding Vancouver, it's a paradise for sailors and fishers alike, with many marinas offering boats for hire, for charter, and for fishing. For all types of fishing, whether in freshwater or the ocean, you'll need a nonresident fishing license. Tackle shops as well as fishing charters sell licenses. A five-day license is about $35; a one-day salmon license costs $14.

Bite on Salmon Charters (1601 Bayshore Dr. between Georgia and Cardero Sts.; 604-688-2483) has fully guided salmon fishing leaving from Westin Bayshore Resort and Marina Hotel. It has five- and eight-hour fully guided fishing trips on twin-engine yachts. At **Sewell's Marina** (Horseshoe Bay, North Shore; 604-921-3474), you're in the heart of fishing country, along the 25-mile-long (40 km) inlet of Howe Sound. Sewell's Marina, with its 60-plus rental and charter boats, is a local fishing institution. The company is located on the docks next to the ferry terminal.

Golf

There are 75 golf courses within an hour-and-a-half drive from downtown Vancouver, and only a few of them are private. Just south of downtown, toward the Canadian–U.S. border and accessible by BC 99, the main road south, are four of the region's most challenging and easiest to access: **Mayfair Lakes Golf and Country Club** (604-276-0585; 5460 No. 7 Rd, Richmond; www.golfbc.com/courses/mayfair_lakes), **Hazelmere Golf and Country Club** (604-538-1818; 18150 8th Avenue, Surrey; www.hazelmere.com/hazelmere), **Peace Portal Golf Course** (604-538-4818; 16900 4th Avenue, Surrey; www.peaceportalgolf.com), and **Morgan Creek** (604-531-4653; 3500 Morgan Creek Way, Surrey; www.morgancreekgolf .com). Vancouver, Burnaby, and North Vancouver all have municipal courses within their city boundaries. Others are business-run courses with a variety of prices. Virtually all have driving ranges and pro shops.

Hiking

If you have a good set of lungs and thighs of steel, try hiking straight up Grouse Mountain along the Grouse Grind trail, 1.8 miles (2.9 km) straight up to the top. You leave from the bottom of the Skyride at the end of Capilano Road just beyond the parking lot (see Capilano Suspension Bridge under Attractions). This really is quite a hike, so carry water and wear hiking boots. If you're in great shape, it'll take about an hour, but expect somewhere between 90 minutes and two hours for a comfortable pace. And be careful. Occasionally, someone thinks that nature is always docile—with tragic results.

Skiing

Vancouver's ski season is one of the city's great assets, with the three ski hills just minutes from downtown. That fact went a long way toward the city, along with Whistler/Blackcomb, being granted the 2010 Winter Olympics. Whistler is the crème de la crème of North American skiing, and there's a steady stream of traffic during the winter (November 25 through April–May) out of Vancouver to Whistler for day skiing. It's an easy but attention demanding two-hour drive. (See Whistler in chapter 4, Side Trips from Vancouver). Make certain you have good snow tires or chains before you set out. The local ski hills have areas devoted to cross-country as well as downhill.

Cypress Bowl (604-926-5612; www.cypressmountain.com) is the newest of the North Shore mountain ski centers, and it's more suited to advanced skiers than the other two. It's also the biggest of the hills, with more and longer runs. You drive to the parking lot at the base, from where you take a chair to the top. (Take BC 1/Upper Levels Hwy. toward Horseshoe Bay and take the well-marked Cypress Bowl turnoff.) Be sure you have good winter tires.

BC Place Stadium's patented fabric dome Toshi

Grouse Mountain (604 984 0661; www.grousemountain.com) is a family hill that offers facilities and instruction for skiing, snowboarding, snowshoeing, and backpacking. A variety of runs range from the gentle slopes of the Cut to the moguls and advanced runs of the Peak. Because it's the closest to downtown Vancouver, it's also the mountain that's the busiest on good skiing days and nights. Like the other two North Shore hills, it has night skiing on well-lit runs. (Take Lion's Gate Bridge to Capilano Rd., turn left, and take it to the top.)

Mount Seymour (604-986-2261; www.mountseymour.com) is an inexpensive way to try out a variety of winter sports, with lower-cost teaching schools plus an area devoted to tobogganing. There's a wide irregularity of terrain, more so than at the other two hills, and that attracts snowboarders. (Take Second Narrows Bridge and get off at the Seymour Pkwy. exit. Turn left at the well-marked exit.)

Spectator Sports

For spectator sports, the National Hockey League's Vancouver Canucks, the Canadian Football League's BC Lions, and minor-league baseball's Vancouver Canadians offer major-league entertainment. In addition, there's professional soccer, lacrosse, and horse racing to keep your interest at any point during the year. Although Simon Fraser University and the University of British Columbia have intercollegiate basketball, football, and hockey teams, they do not create the same passionate following as does, say, the University of Washington Huskies.

If you're in Vancouver during the CFL football season, the **BC Lions** (604-661-3626; www.bclions.com) play in the 60,000-seat domed BC Place Stadium (see below) in a season that runs from June to November, with the Grey Cup (Canada's Superbowl) game played in a different venue around the country each year. CFL rules differ from the NFL's, the Canadian version having 12 players instead of 11 and three downs instead of four. That makes for a wide-open passing game, especially since there is no "man in motion" rule. Backs are allowed to move at will, and the field is 20 yards longer and 10 yards wider.

The **Vancouver Canucks** hockey team (604-899-4625; www.canucks.com) came into the NHL in 1970 and since then has generally broken the hearts of hockey fans every year. The Canucks play at GM Place Stadium (see below) to enthusiastic, usually sold-out audiences between October and late May. The team surprised itself by being in the 1982 Stanley Cup finals against the New York Islanders, a then-unstoppable dynasty. A half million people lined Burrard Street for a "victory" parade when the team lost, waving white towels for what everyone knew was a moral victory for the "working-class" team. Then, in 1994 after a mediocre season, the team surprised everyone by actually winning its way to the finals once again, only to be beaten in the seventh game by the New York Rangers. Since then, as has been the case for the Seattle Mariners and Seahawks, the general attitude has been "maybe they'll do it next year."

Summer is a great time to watch minor-league baseball with the **Vancouver Canadians** (604-872-5232; www.canadiansbaseball.com), a single-A affiliate of the Oakland A's. They play at Nat Bailey Stadium (4601 Ontario St., East Vancouver), near Queen Elizabeth Park. This has been the greatest $7.50 entertainment package in the city for years. Nat Bailey Stadium was named after a restaurant entrepreneur, and it's a throwback to the time when baseball was in its infancy. The up to 6,500 spectators have some of the most gorgeous views in baseball, real grass, and one of the few manual scoreboards left in baseball.

The **Vancouver Whitecaps** (604-280-4400; www.whitecapssoccer.com) continue to enthrall fans at Swangard Stadium, named after a former newspaper executive with the *Vancouver Sun* newspaper, in Burnaby's Central Park (Kingsway and Boundary Rd.). The professional season starts in May and ends in September.

And if the nags are to your liking, you'll find thoroughbred racing at **Hastings Racecourse** (Hastings and Renfrew Sts.; 604-254-1631; www.hastingspark.com) April through October in what used to be the Pacific Exhibition grounds. With the North Shore mountains as a background, you can't find a more scenic place to bet your hard-earned cash.

BC Place Stadium

777 Pacific Blvd.
Downtown
604-669-2300
www.bcplacestadium.com

There is more to this place than just jock business, even though it is the home of the CFL's BC Lions football team. It opened in 1983 as the world's largest air-supported dome, and with 60,000 seats it also hosts major star concerts, trade shows, and other large gatherings. It was in this enormous building that Queen Elizabeth II invited the world to Expo '86. Some of the province's largest trade and consumer shows, such as the Pacific International Auto Show, B.C. Home and Garden Show, Golf Expo, Ski Show, Vancouver International RV Show, and Vancouver International Boat Show, take place under the dome each year. The design consists of a fabric outer membrane and an inner liner made of the same material, attached to a two-way steel-cable net system, which is in turn anchored to a concrete base ring. The patented technique for designing the length and direction of the cables and the shape of the ring derives from a mathematical solution formulated by David Geiger. There's enough concrete in BC Place to build a sidewalk from Vancouver to Tacoma, Washington.

GM Place Stadium
800 Griffiths Way
Downtown
604-899-7440
www.canucks.com

Nobody but nobody in town calls it General Motors Place. The corporate officials from General Motors may hate the name, but locals call it "the Garage." Get it? General Motors . . . garage? It's the newer of the two major downtown sports facilities, and it's the home of the Vancouver Canucks and was the home of the dearly departed Vancouver Grizzlies, who moved off to Memphis. GM Place hosts about 170 events each year in a 20,000-seat arena built to resemble a vertical shaft, rising sharply from ground to sky, so that even people in the last row have the impression of looking down directly over the arena floor.

Windsurfing
Sometimes it seems as though there are hundreds of tiny sailboards darting about English Bay on a windy day. And certainly there are plenty of chances for anyone to learn what it's like to ride the winds with just a thin, narrow board beneath your feet. The best known place of instruction is **Windsure Windsurfing School** (1300 Discovery St.; 604-224-0615)

Shopping in Chinatown Toshi

at the Jericho Sailing Centre at Jericho Beach. The school offers a six-hour course that guarantees results. **Pacific Boarder** (1793 W. Fourth Ave.; 604-734-7245) in Kitsilano and **Northshore Ski & Board** (1625 Lonsdale Ave.; 604-987-7245) offer wet suits and board selections.

SHOPPING

In Vancouver, shopping is about style and experiencing the wide variety of cultural realities that make up the city's mosaic. In Chinatown you can see, hear, taste, and feel a bit of Asia; along East Vancouver's Commercial Drive, you can wander in stores with labels and accents from Italy and India; in the village of Steveston, antiques stores and arts and crafts outlets abound. If you treat shopping in Vancouver not as a credit-card experience but as a cultural one, you'll soon understand the essential character of the place. There are literally hundreds of stores in the downtown area, and throughout Vancouver you'll find thousands, enough to fill a book twice this size. Generally speaking, stores in Vancouver are open daily from 9 to 6, and on Sundays many are open noon to 5.

Vancouver's Chinatown is the old-style Chinese ghetto, where things are found as they are nowhere else in the city—or the country, for that matter. Many of the stores that seem as though they've been around forever really have been, some dating to the turn of the 20th century. Although Chinatown has become a diverse Asian mix, with Vietnamese, Taiwanese, Japanese, and Filipinos adding their cultural influences, it is still predominantly Chinese in character.

If you want an experience of shopping in Hong Kong or contemporary Asia, prowl the five closely clustered shopping malls in Richmond that are under the general banner of Asia West: Aberdeen Centre, Fairchild Square, Parker Place, President Plaza, and Yaohan Centre. This is the new reality: areas of high energy where the old traditions are not entirely lost among the bright lights, chrome, and glass. The centers are an exotic tourist destination also accepted and frequented by the whole community.

In the **Kitsilano** neighborhood, when the hippies of the 1960s and '70s grew up, they opened up stores in the '80s and were bought out in the '90s, many replaced by upscale shops and restaurants. The heart of the area is along Fourth Avenue between Burrard and Balsam Streets. The old hippie atmosphere may be gone, but the shops still attract a young crowd, though with different tastes. Fourth Avenue shopping is convenient for the people living in nearby apartments.

South Granville Street and Broadway bound a widely dispersed area that includes just about everything between Granville Island and the Fraser River east of and including Granville Street, East Broadway, upper Granville Street, and Oak Street. Granville Street between 15th Avenue and Broadway is where antique shops and some of Vancouver's most sophisticated stores are located. Interior design, home furnishings, and specialty shops are spread out between the Granville Street Bridge and 16th Avenue. Along Broadway between Cambie and Granville Streets are numerous designer fashions, shoe stores, and restaurants.

But downtown, as you'd expect, is the city's primary shopping area, with many stores and boutiques throughout **Robson and Granville Streets,** the **waterfront,** Water Street in **Gastown, Granville Island,** and the **West End** offering almost limitless opportunities for those wanting to be separated from their cash. A couple of blocks north of Georgia and

A Richmond shopping center Toshi

Granville Streets are two upscale shopping areas—Sinclair Centre (see Clothing) and the Landing (see Centers and Malls)—with boutiques, restaurants, and services for those who prefer a more personal relationship with their salespeople.

What's not so apparent is the fact that the downtown core is laced with **underground shopping**, much as you'll find in Montreal. You can wander for hours among the underground corridors that link department stores and office buildings. The busiest part is at the corner of Georgia and Granville Streets, where three stores—the Bay, Sears, (see Department Stores) and Holt Renfrew (see Clothing)—are connected by the underground Pacific Centre Mall (see Centers and Malls), easily reached through the department stores or through the office towers situated on the street corners. Farther along Georgia Street, a long passageway of stores is found beneath the Royal Bank of Canada and the Hyatt Hotel in the Royal Centre Mall (see Centers and Malls) on the corner of Burrard and W. Georgia Streets. The **Bentall Centre** (1055 Dunsmuir St.; 604-681-6211) office complex is farther north along Burrard Street. Although it's not as complex as the Pacific Centre Mall, it has boutiques not found elsewhere. Bentall Centre is really a series of corridors that connect four office towers, western Canada's largest integrated office complex, occupying 5 acres (2 hectares). The 53,000-square-foot (4,924 sq. meter) retail concourse shopping area is below the office towers.

Centers and Malls

Aberdeen Centre
4151 Hazelbridge Way
Richmond
604-273-1234

Oddly, this is one of western Canada's most popular tourist destinations, with a diverse range of stores, Chinese and Japanese restaurants, a bowling alley, a movie house showing Chinese films, and a variety of fashion boutiques. A $130 million state-of-the-art shopping and entertainment complex, with 380,000 square feet, it is triple the size of the original mall that was torn down and replaced by this one, which opened on December 12, 2003.

Granville Mall
Granville St. between waterfront and Smithe St.
Downtown

This pedestrian mall, a five-block stretch of Granville Street, has been a work in progress since it was first proposed. It was once the glitziest stretch of roadway in Vancouver, with neon signs, nightclubs, and theaters—simply the place to be on a Saturday night. Then in the 1970s it was turned into a pedestrian mall, providing a fashionable place that attracted the well-to-do. To give the area to pedestrians, the only vehicles allowed access between the wide sidewalks from W. Hastings Street to Nelson Street are buses, taxis and limousines, emergency vehicles, custom transit vehicles, bicycles, and commercial vehicles with a special Granville Mall permit. Park there illegally and you'll be towed away.

Now the Granville Mall has Vancouver's major department stores along its route, and it's the location of the Orpheum, home of the Vancouver Symphony. Although the street never did become the upscale fashion and arts model it was originally designed to be, it's still an enjoyable stroll for window shoppers, especially between W. Georgia Street and the waterfront. Much of the street has been surrendered to street people, partly because beneath the pavement, people are shopping underground out of the winter rain. After dark it's both exciting and a bit seedy, attracting young street people, panhandlers, and concertgoers in a wild mix of lifestyles on the move. During the day, however, the mall is essentially a conduit for walkers and shoppers going into Sears, the Bay, the Granville Book Company near the Orpheum, and the Pacific Centre.

The Landing
375 Water St.
Gastown
604-687-1144

At the entrance to Gastown, this mall is located in another heritage building, one dating from 1905 when it was built as a warehouse. It is now a multilevel shopping and dining area. Inside are designer boutiques such as Polo, Ralph Lauren, and Fleet Street. You can get to the shopping plaza by exiting from the Steamworks Restaurant or through an elegant entrance off Water Street.

Lansdowne Park Shopping Centre
5300 No. 3 Rd.
Richmond
604-270-1344

Five minutes from the airport, this sprawling mall has 120 shops, including many specialty shops and major stores such as Future Shop, Zellers, and Winners.

Library Square
350 W. Georgia St.
Downtown
604-331-3670

It may look like the Roman Coliseum, but you won't find any gladiators here—except on the bookshelves. Completed in 1995, the postmodern seven-level library is an ambitious complex that also includes a nearby 21-story office tower. The circular, brown cement walls hide a series of retail outlets in a massive atrium that includes restaurants, bookstores, and other small shops. The trilevel parking garage offers the least expensive parking in the downtown area. The library itself is designed for the future, with computer terminals connected to the Internet spread throughout the facility.

Pacific Centre Mall
W. Georgia St.
Downtown between Dunsmuir and Georgia Streets
604-688-7236

If you're downtown at any of the central hotels, this is likely one of the first downtown shopping malls you'll encounter, and with some 200 or so stores in its underground facility, it's also the biggest, spreading over three city blocks. There's a complete range of stores—men's and women's fashions, jewelry stores, restaurants, and even a hotel (the Four Seasons). The north end of the complex is the newest section, where you'll find a three-story waterfall, a glass rotunda, and a lighted atrium that makes the place cheery and bright even on a rainy day. If you take the Sky Train in from the suburbs, get off at the Granville station under the Bay, and you can do your shopping in the mall without ever going outside.

Parker Place
4380 No. 3 Rd.
Richmond
604-273-0276

With more than 130 shops and services, this is the most consumer focused of the five centers that are part of Asia West. It has electronics and high-tech stores, European fashion boutiques, and Asian grocers. The large Asian food courts are complemented by a large water fountain and overhead skylights.

President Plaza
8181 Cambie St.
Richmond
604-270-8677

Attached to the four-star President Hotel, this is a place for the flesh—fresh meat, fish, and poultry—with one of the most exotic Asian supermarkets you'll see in the area, plus wide selections of Chinese tea and ginseng.

Richmond Centre
6551 No. 3 Rd.
Richmond
604-273-4828

Not only is there a wide selection of department stores here (the Bay, Sears, Zellers), but there's also an international mix of merchants, including Benetton, Esprit, Biana Nygard, and Jacob. There's also a Famous Players movie theater complex.

Royal Centre Mall
1055 W. Georgia St.
Downtown
604-689-1711

Located directly beneath the Royal Bank of Canada building, adjacent to the Hyatt Hotel, the Royal Centre has fewer shops than Pacific Centre does, but it nonetheless provides some unique shopping opportunities. For example, it houses Dack's Shoes, the Canadian shoe manufacturer that has produced quality men's footwear for a century. Keep walking south along the corridors and you'll link up with the extension that meanders beneath the Bentall Centre, a group of office towers along Burrard Street, before it finally empties out onto W. Hastings St.

Yaohan Centre
3700 No. 3 Rd.
Richmond
604-231-0601

You will feel as though you are walking in a mall in Asia. A block north from the President Plaza, this Japanese supermarket is one of the largest in North America, with a wide range of Japanese products and seafood at reasonable prices. After you've toured—and eaten—at the massive food fair with its Japanese, Chinese, Taiwanese, Korean, and Malaysian cuisine, take the escalator to the second level, where you'll find fashion boutiques and specialty shops.

Clothing

On Burrard and Hornby Streets between Georgia and Robson Streets, you'll find international haute couture shops that cater to tourists and locals alike, with **Chanel Boutique** (900 W. Hastings St.; 604-682-0522), **Gianni Versace Boutique** (757 W. Hastings St.; 604-683-1131), and **Salvatore Ferragamo** (918 Robson St.; 604-669-4495) among the major outlets. Salvatore Ferragamo, on the corner of Robson and Hornby Streets directly across from the Courthouse plaza, is the first outlet of the Italian shoe store in Canada. **Roots Canada** (1001 Robson St.; 604-683-4305) is totally Canadian, and here you'll find casual clothing for men and women, including leather bags, footwear, and athletic gear.

Boboli (2776 Granville St.; 604-257-2300) is a really-with-it clothing store with contemporary designers for men such as Claude Montana and Yohi Yamamoto. Women's fashion carries labels from Armani and Ferretti. **Tilley Endurables** (2401 Granville; 604-732-4287) has clothes for those going on a safari as well as elegant styles for casual and hiking wear, with shorts, shirts, safari jackets, and windbreakers all made of cotton. And be sure to buy one of those wonderful Tilley safari hats, the kind you see being worn by heroes in safari movies.

Holt Renfrew & Co.
633 Granville St.
Downtown
604-681-3121

This boutique store prides itself on selling the best-quality goods in town. Certainly it's a showcase for international fashion for men and women. The store's layout is a series of ministores within one, with clothing and accessory collections from Giorgia Armani, Donna Karan, Gucci, Prada, Louis Vuitton, Hermes, and Tiffany as well as Brown's shoes, Birger Christensen furs, cosmetics, and fine fragrances. It is located in the Pacific Centre Mall directly across the street from the Bay, and the store is as West Coast as any.

Sinclair Centre
757 W. Hastings St.
Downtown
604-666-4438

Once the site of a historic riot in 1938 when unemployed protesters clashed in a violent confrontation with the local constabulary, this old Canada Post Office building, dating from 1909, is today a collection of small and large fashion houses. Leone, an upscale women's fashion store, is the major retail outlet, a place where the most fashion-conscious women do their shopping. But there's also a wide selection of men's wear. With labels from Armani, Versace, Byblos, and others attracting the with-it crowd, don't be surprised if you see a movie or TV star looking through the racks.

Department Stores
Army & Navy Department Store
27 W. Hastings St.
Gastown
604-682-6644

Decidedly down-market, A&N is where you shop if you're looking for everyday items that are necessary to have but have no prestigious value. Spend some time in this on-the-edge-of-Gastown store and you'll likely find bargains galore in the various departments. The semiannual designer shoe sales are two of Vancouver's most semiriotous events, turning staid and proper shoppers into aggressive mobs.

The Bay (Hudson's Bay Company)
674 Granville St.
Downtown
604-681-6211

More than any other Canadian institution, this company is responsible for much of the exploration that led to Canada becoming a nation. Established in 1670 by the Royal Charter of King Charles II, the Hudson's Bay Company is one of the oldest commercial enterprises in North America. Original trading-post sites eventually became large cities, Vancouver being no exception. More than just another department store, today Vancouver's major outlet, the downtown Bay (nobody calls it the Hudson's Bay Company), is much like any other department store. Yes, you can still buy a Hudson's Bay woolen blanket, but there are also ministores such as Hilfiger, DKNY, Polo, and others within the large complex that sits on the northeast corner of Granville and Georgia Streets. Bay outlets are also found in most suburban shopping malls.

Sears
701 Granville St.
Downtown
604-685-7112

Located diagonally across the street from the Bay, Sears is housed in the Pacific Centre Mall office complex in the building that used to be the Eaton's company store before that Canadian institution went bankrupt. You can't miss the huge, white-tiled edifice that many Vancouverites have nicknamed "the Mausoleum."

Inside Granville Island Public Market

Farmers Markets

From May through September, there's a public night market at Pender and Carrall Streets near Shanghai Alley, where the original Chinese settlement developed even before the City of Vancouver was incorporated in 1886. Vendors sell everything from faux Gucci bags and Rolex watches to dried squid and imported pottery.

Granville Island Public Market
1669 Johnson St.
Granville Island
604-666-6655
www.granvilleisland.com
Open: 9–6 daily
Wheelchair accessible: Yes

The public market is the heart and soul of Granville Island and one of the city's "must-see" places. Like Seattle's Pike Place Market, it's a delicious mix of smells and character, with visitors buying fresh produce, meat, breads, seafood, and fast foods. But in Canadian fashion, it's more conservative and less boisterous. Italian, Japanese, southeast Asian, Chinese, and European homemade and homegrown products are sold at stalls in this 50,000-square-foot (4,645 sq. m) waterfront building. Vancouverites arrive early in the morning and walk among the hundreds of stalls just people watching and experiencing the moment. Outside on the northside dock are benches and tables for leisurely snacking. Try not to bring your car.

Lonsdale Quay
123 Carrie Cates Ct.
North Shore
604-985-6261
www.lonsdalequay.com
Open: 9:30–6:30 Sa–Th, 9:30–9:00 F Apr–Oct; 9:30–6:30 Sa–Th, 9:30–8 F Nov–Mar
Wheelchair accessible: Yes

In 1985–86, the City of North Vancouver decided to copy the success of the Granville Island Market and build its own, and it has been a howling success. The market's glazed and galleried interior is a throwback to 19th-century industrial architecture. Getting there is half the fun, gliding across the water on the Seabus, the ferry service that crosses Burrard Inlet from the old Canadian Pacific Railroad terminal. And once you get here, you have the choice of shopping at the market or simply sitting at one of the water-view restaurants, gazing across to the Vancouver skyline.

Gifts and Jewelry
Chinatown: Asia Imports (155 W. Hastings St.; 604-687-4912) has handmade quilts, embroidered silk blouses, exotic kimonos, jade, ivory, and other expensive items. Ask for the Battenburg-style lace and cutwork. The **Ten Ren Tea and Ginseng Co.** (550 Main St.; 604-684-1566) has the finest selection of Oriental teas in the city, some of which are as much as $150 a pound ($68 per kg). If the shop isn't busy and the owners feel up to it, they'll honor you with a Chinese tea ceremony. **Tung Fong Hung Foods Co.** (536 Main St.; 604-688-0883) has a sign that claims it is a food company, but that's simply to appease city regulations. It's really a Chinese medicine store where you'll find jars and bins of items such as dried seahorse, thinly sliced deer antler, and bird's nests. There's an on site herbalist to help you select items for your particular ailment.

Downtown: Birks (898 Hastings St.; 604-669-3333) is to Vancouver what Tiffany's is to New York—the place where Vancouverites have always done their jewelry shopping, long before competition came to the city. **Virgin Megastore** (788 Burrard St.; 604-669-2289) is located in the site that the old Vancouver library once occupied, and it has the largest collection of music and entertainment items in the country, with tapes, CDs, and multimedia for PC and Mac computers.

Kitsilano: The Flag Shop (1755 W. Fourth Ave.; 604-736-8161) has a flag for every city, country, and region in the world that has a flag to represent it.

South Vancouver: Dorothy Grant (1656 W. 75th St.; 604-681-0201) is a First Nations designer who works out of a shop that looks like a longhouse. Her fashions are uniquely Haida. Grant was married to acclaimed Native American artist Robert Davidson, so you'll find art items from him as well. **The Umbrella Shop** (1106 W. Broadway; 604-669-9444) has umbrellas with cheery prints and matching totes for shopping along fashionable Robson Street, plus versatile foldaway numbers that slip into the smallest briefcase, hand-painted originals for artistic collectors, and more conservative ones. If you thought you knew umbrellas, you'll change your mind on a rainy day when you step into this mecca of bumbershoots.

Sporting Goods
Coast Mountain Sports (2201 W. Fourth Ave., Kitsilano; 604-731-6181) is a store for the experienced mountaineer or hiker. High-end camping, hiking, and other outdoors and travel goods such as sleeping bags, water purifiers, freeze-dried foods, and even satellite tracking systems are available. **Mountain Equipment Coop** (130 W. Broadway, South Vancouver; 604-872-7858) has rack upon rack of outdoor needs—from pants to boots to rain gear for camping, biking, hiking, water skiing, snow skiing, and recreation of all kinds. You'll have to join this nonprofit cooperative to make a purchase, but it's cheap to make a purchase—lifetime memberships are $5—and you'll receive spring and fall catalogs.

EVENTS

Vancouverites like festivals and events. If there's an excuse to have one—any excuse—they will. Some of the events are small; others are grandiose, such as the Symphony of Light, which pits three or four nations against one another in a dazzling display of pyrotechnics. The Vancouver Children's Festival and the Bard on the Beach Shakespeare Festival, both located at Vanier Park in Kitsilano, are major events attracting visitors from throughout the Pacific Northwest. Some events, such as the Vancouver Fringe Festival, are leading edge and sometimes off the wall. Others, like Festival Vancouver, bring together the finest national and international performing artists. In addition to these highlights are many other smaller events listed in Vancouver's daily newspapers.

January

Polar Bear Swim (604-257-8400; www.city.vancouver.bc.ca/parks/events/polarbear) Swimmers brave the cold for a quick dip in English Bay on New Year's Day; Januray 1.

Dine Out Vancouver (604-683-2000; www.tourismvancouver.com) In late January, many of Vancouver's restaurants join with Tourism Vancouver and VISA for 14 days of eating out at special prices; late January.

Chinese New Year (604-662-3207; www.vancouverchinatown.ca) Held on the first Sunday of the Chinese (lunar) New Year, usually in late January, the parade through Chinatown celebrates the arrival of spring with thousands of marchers and floats, plus storytelling, crafts, and lucky red packets (small gifts) 10–4:30.

February

Vancouver International Boat Show (604-661-7373; www.bcplacestadium.com) Western Canada's largest and oldest boat show features the latest in power and sail vessels, accessories, electronics, fishing gear, and lodges; at BC Place Stadium; second week in February.

Outdoor Adventure Sports Show (604-661-7373; www.bcplacestadium.com) More than 200 exhibitors, free seminars, exciting sports events, and challenging interactive features attract consumers interested in active outdoor lifestyles; at BC Place Stadium; mid-February.

Golf Expo (604-661-7373; www.bcplacestadium.com) More than 100 exhibitors, new golf equipment demos, golf instruction, destination resorts, celebrity appearances, and interactive contests are featured at BC Place Stadium; mid-February.

BC Home and Garden Show (604-661-7373; www.bcplacestadium.com) Western Canada's largest indoor flower and garden show has more than 450 exhibitors at BC Place Stadium; last week in February.

March

Vancouver Celtic Festival (604-724-2670; www.celticfestvancouver.com) The Celtic community celebrates the week of St. Patrick's Day with entertainment, dancing, and a parade along Granville Street in the heart of Vancouver's entertainment district; March 11–17 .

Playhouse International Wine Festival (604-873-3311; www.playhousewinefest.com) The ultimate wine adventure features wine events for every level of wine lover, including seminars and tastings held at the Vancouver Convention and Exhibition Centre and various venues; late March.

April

Pacific International Auto Show (604-661-7373; www.bcplacestadium.com) Presented by the B.C. Auto Dealers Association, this well-attended event has cars and more cars at BC Place Stadium; first week in April.

Vancouver Sun Run (604-689-9441; www.sunrun.com) One of the world's largest 10K races; anyone can walk or run a scenic route through downtown Vancouver, finishing at BC Place Stadium for snacks, refreshments, and entertainment; mid-April.

May

Adidas Vancouver International Marathon (604-872-2928; www.vanmarathon.bc.ca) Participants come from all over the world to compete in Canada's largest marathon on a course that meanders from BC Place Stadium through False Creek to Stanley Park and the Kitsilano neighborhood; first weekend in May.

Vancouver International Children's Festival (604-708-5655; www.vancouverchildrens festival.com) This family festival features theater, music, dance, and puppetry from around the world under tents in Vanier Park; mid-May.

Cloverdale Rodeo and Exhibition (604-576-9461; www.cloverdalerodeo.com) Top cowboys and cowgirls on the professional rodeo circuit compete in traditional rodeo events including bareback, saddle, bronco, and bull riding at the Cloverdale Rodeo and Exhibition Fairgrounds in the suburb of Surrey; last week in May.

Hyack Festival (604-522-6894; www.hyack.bc.ca) One of the Lower Mainland's most popular festivals includes a family day, May Day celebrations, an anvil salute, an antiques fair, fireworks, and a parade in New Westminster; late May.

June

Bard on the Beach Shakespeare Festival (604-739-0559; www.bardonthebeach.org) This festival lasts through the end of September and features intimate stagings of Shakespeare's plays under an ingenious tent structure that allows you to look out onto English Bay while watching the action onstage at Vanier Park; early June through late September.

VanDusen Garden Show (604-687-4780; www.vandusengarden.org) This yearly event is a coming-out party for all kinds of flowers and blooming things at VanDusen Botanical Gardens on the edge of the Shaughnessy district, with exhibitors and presentations by garden gurus and some of Vancouver's top chefs in a spectacular 15-acre (6 hectare) outdoor setting; early June.

Vancouver Francophone Summer Festival (604-736-9806; www.lecentreculturel.com) This festival reflects on the multicultural character of French-speaking peoples in more than 40 countries around the world. Outdoor stages for music and theater are set up at various venues in the heart of the city; mid-June.

Dragon Boat Festival (604-688-2382; www.adbf.com) More than just a race of the multi-crewed dragon boats in False Creek, this is a weekend of racing and cultural activities, including stage entertainment for the whole family, at False Creek and the Plaza of Nations; late June.

Vancouver International Jazz Festival (604-872-5200; www.coastaljazz.ca) Some of the biggest names in jazz take the stage at various venues in the Vancouver area. In addition, a free, two-day New Orleans–style street festival is held in Gastown and at the Roundhouse Community Centre; last week in June.

July

Canada Day Celebrations (Canada Place: 604-775-8025; www.canadadayatcanadaplace .com) (Granville Island: 604-666-5784; www.granville island.com) On July 1, Canada's National Day, Vancouverites celebrate with entertainment for the whole family. At Canada Place, songs and dancing are featured. At Granville Island there's all-day family celebrations with interactive displays and games; July 1.

Dancing on the Edge Festival (604-689-0926; www.dancingontheedge.org) Professional Canadian and international dancers perform works from both established and emerging choreographers at the Firehall Arts Centre in East Vancouver; second week in July.

Vancouver Folk Music Festival (604-602-9798; www.thefestival.bc.ca) You'll hear music from local and international folk singers, songwriters, musicians, and storytellers, with daytime and evening performances and special children's programs at Jericho Beach Park and various venues; mid-July.

Vancouver Chamber Music Festival (604-602-0363; www.vanrecital.com) Some of the most talented young musicians from Canada and around the world get together at Crofton House School and the lawns of Cecil Green College, University of British Columbia; mid-July.

Vancouver International Comedy Festival (604-683-0883; www.comedyfest.com) This public celebration of comedy and laughter features an eclectic, diverse mixture of comic artists from around the world at Granville Island and various other venues; late July.

Vancouver Early Music Festival (604-732-1610; www.earlymusic.bc.ca) Presented by Early Music Vancouver, this outstanding series of early music concerts features local musicians, international guest artists, and ensembles at the University of British Columbia Recital Hall; mid-July.

Tour de Gastown (604-683-5650; www.tourdegastown.com) Canada's top cyclists take on North America's best on a thrilling 1K course in historic Gastown. Lance Armstrong is a former winner of the event; late July.

HSBC Celebration of Light (www.celebration-of-light.com) Three countries compete in a spectacular display of fireworks at English Bay; last week in July through the first week in August.

Powell Street Festival (604-739-9388; www.powellstreetfestival.com) Traditional Japanese cuisine, arts, and martial arts performances are held at Oppenheimer Park on the east side of town and at the Firehall Arts Centre; last weekend in July.

August

Vancouver Pride Week Celebration (604-687-0955; www.vanpride.bc.ca) Vancouver's gay and lesbian community celebrates with activities including the Gay Pride Parade on August 1; first week in August.

Festival Vancouver (604-688-1152; www.festivalvancouver.bc.ca) Vancouver's newest and largest summer music festival features national and international artists performing orchestral, choral, world, and chamber music as well as jazz and opera in more than 80 concerts at various venues; first two weeks in August.

Vancouver Chinatown Festival (604-632-3808; www.vancouverchinatown.ca) This mid-summer fest celebrates Chinatown's history and culture; early August.

Abbotsford International Airshow (604-852-8511; www.abbotsfordairshow.com) One of North America's biggest exhibitions of planes and demonstrations of stunt and technical flying is held at Abbotsford Airport, about 45 minutes east of Vancouver; mid-August.

Pacific National Exhibition (604-253-2311; www.pne.bc.ca) A variety of concerts, folk and country music, agricultural exhibitions, and an amusement park through Labor Day highlight the end of summer; the exhibition is held on the Pacific National Exhibition Grounds at Hastings Park; late August.

September

Vancouver Fringe Festival (604-257-0350; www.vancouverfringe.com) With more than 90 shows and about 95 theatrical groups from local, national, and international productions performing at various venues, this is one of Vancouver's most-anticipated events; mid-September.

Vancouver International Film Festival (604-685-0260; www.viff.org) One of the largest film festivals in North America has 300 films from 50 countries shown in various theaters around town; late September through early October.

October

Vancouver Home and Interior Design Show (604-661-7373; www.bcplacestadium.com) This marketplace for homeowners offers new ideas, advice, and home products for remodeling and decorating; it's held at BC Place Stadium; mid-October.

Vancouver International Writers Fest (604-681-6330; www.writersfest.bc.ca) Literary stars and promising new writers from across Canada and around the world give readings and advice on Granville Island; varies between late October and early November.

November–December

Christmas Carol Ship Parade (604-878-8999; www.carolships.org) Boat owners from around Greater Vancouver decorate their vessels and cruise around the waters of Vancouver Harbour; December 1–23.

The Fairmont Empress Hotel welcomes visitors to Victoria's Inner Harbour. Courtesy of Fairmont Hotels

4

SIDE TRIPS FROM VANCOUVER

From Skis to High Tea

CRUISES

Vancouver is the major port serving the Alaskan cruise market; 12 cruise companies totaling 30 vessels make about 300 sailings that transport almost 800,000 passengers a year. The industry brings in an estimated $200 million to the local economy. The city is home to two modern cruise terminals: **Canada Place**, which is part of the Pan Pacific Hotel/Vancouver Convention and Exhibition Centre complex, and **Ballantyne Pier**, close to the city center, which hosts the largest of the ships. There are one-way and round-trip sailings, depending on the cruise line. Taking a cruise is virtually worry free. You and your baggage are picked up at the airport and the next time you're together is in your stateroom.

FERRIES

BC Ferries (250-386-3431 (US), 1-888-223-3779 (British Columbia); www.bcferries .com) operates passenger- and vehicle-carrying vessels with service from two terminals in Greater Vancouver to Vancouver Island or other destinations. The Tsawwassen terminal, about 45 minutes south of downtown Vancouver, links the city to Victoria (at Swartz Bay) and Nanaimo (at Duke Point) on Vancouver Island as well as to the Gulf Islands. The Horseshoe Bay terminal, 25–30 minutes north of downtown Vancouver, links the city to Nanaimo on Vancouver Island, Bowen Island, and the Sunshine Coast. The new Harbour Lynx high-speed passenger ferry travels from downtown Vancouver to downtown Nanaimo. BC Ferries also offers an overnight trip from Port Hardy on northern Vancouver Island through the Inside Passage to Prince Rupert; you can also take a ferry from Prince Rupert to the Queen Charlotte Islands.

Whistler

Thirty years ago, a garbage dump occupied the area where Whistler's restaurants, hotels, and boutiques now stand. The only human inhabitants were a few cross-country skiers and tourists who came down the road from the original Whistler Mountain gondolas to watch the huge black bears rummage through hotel and restaurant leftovers. Today Whistler/Blackcomb, 75 miles (121 km) north of Vancouver and 195 miles (201 km) from Seattle, is one of the world's great ski destinations. Its village, built on the onetime garbage dump, is now a snow-draped fairyland.

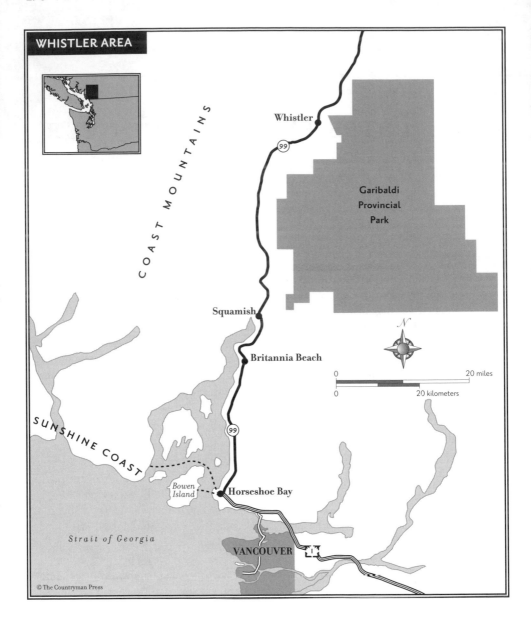

Whistler's international status was cemented when it, along with Vancouver, was awarded the 2010 Olympic Winter Games. Named the best overall ski resort by a variety of skiing magazines over the past decade, the resort caters to the first-class tastes of those who want to be seen where the very best hang out. Like most ski resorts, Whistler has also become a summertime playground, with activities such as boating, hiking, and biking throughout the region and countless minifestivals taking place on the mountainsides and in the hotels and convention center.

The village design favors pedestrian traffic, and that gives it a friendly, European feel, with all of stroll areas paved in red brick. Everything is within easy walking distance. The resort has a mix of 90-plus upscale and middle-class restaurants, snug bars, and bistros where the young go hoping to get lucky. The most popular places to hang out are what locals call the cement beaches—the massive outdoor patios of the Longhorn Saloon, Merlin's, the GLC, Monk's Grill, Citta's, and Dusty's in Whistler Creekside. Since the invention of the propane tree, quaffing a brew on a cement beach during winter is as pleasant as anything you can do in summer.

The resort has 116 hotels, condos, and B&Bs, offering more than 5,200 rooms in a mix ranging from luxurious to comfortable. Among the high-end accommodations are still rooms at reasonable prices, $75–$125 a night at many B&Bs, condos, or other accommodations.

There are 200 retail shops, as well as banking/foreign exchange machines, church services, medical and dental clinics, physiotherapy and massage therapy, office services, a public library, a museum, a movie theater and video rentals, health and fitness centers, a swimming pool, an ice rink, indoor tennis courts, and spa facilities and beauty salons. And,

The Fairmont Whistler Hotel in winter, at the foot of Whistler Mountain Courtesy of Fairmont Hotels

of course, there are myriad real estate offices flogging homes that average $1 million per. Even in Canadian bucks, that's a lot of cash.

Throughout the summer, Whistler's street scene is a beehive of jugglers, musicians, magicians, and mountain-bike stunt riders seeking your attention. And if you're looking for art, including paintings, soapstone carvings, basket weaving, pottery, traditional and modern Native American art, intricate glasswork, and amazing photography, there are galleries scattered throughout Whistler Village, including the downstairs mall in the Delta Whistler Resort.

GETTING THERE

Domestic flights from all over Canada and international flights from the United States and other parts of the world fly into Vancouver International Airport (see chapter 3, Vancouver), a 2.5-hour drive from Whistler. Choose from car, bus, van, SUV, limousine, train, floatplane, or helicopter transportation to make your way to Whistler along the spectacular Sea to Sky Corridor, BC 99, which takes you along Howe Sound and through the Coastal Mountains.

From downtown Vancouver, cross the Lion's Gate Bridge to North Vancouver, take the West Vancouver exit, and stay in the right-hand lane. At the first light, turn right and go uphill. You'll run into the freeway (BC 99) along Howe Sound, one of the most gorgeous scenic roads in the country; just follow the directions to Whistler. At Horseshoe Bay is the dock for both the ferry to Nanaimo on mid–Vancouver Island and the ferry to the Sunshine Coast (Langdale, Gibsons, Sechelt, and points north). Beyond Horseshoe Bay, you'll pass Lions Bay, Porteau Cove, the community of Brittania Beach, Shannon Falls, Squamish (a rock-climbing mecca), and Garibaldi Park.

ACCOMMODATIONS

The selections are unlimited, ranging from luxurious hotels, condominiums, and townhouses to B&Bs, with new facilities opening every year. Visit the Whistler Web site (www.mywhistler.com) to check out the individual sites. The **Fairmont Chateau Whistler** (604-938-8000; www.fairmont.com) is Whistler's landmark hotel. Located at the base of Blackcomb Mountain, the 550-room resort offers ski-in/ski-out convenience. The **Pan Pacific Mountainside** (604-905-2999; www.panpac.com), in the lower village at the base of the Whistler Mountain lift, is a full-service boutique hotel offering studio, one-, and two-bedroom suites. The **Four Seasons Whistler Resort** (604-935-3400; www.fourseasons .com/whistler) is the newest luxury property in the village, having 202 rooms and suites. The **Sundial Boutique Hotel** (604-932-2321; www.sundialhotel.com) has 49 luxurious suites with full kitchens and gas fireplaces.

RESTAURANTS

Whistler's dining choices are also unlimited, whether it's Japanese, French, Italian, Chinese, or American you want. With an Italian cuisine and an extensive wine list, **Quattro at Whistler** (604-905-4844) has two cozy fireplaces, an open kitchen, and hand-painted silk chandeliers that cast a warm glow over the restaurant's Venetian interior. Rich mahogany wood, an eclectic mix of tables, and a vibrantly designed floor complete the warm, passionate look. The **Bearfoot Bistro** (604 932 3433), with its award-winning wine list and lengthy chef's tasting menu, offers culinary classes for the discerning gourmet and budding home chefs in groups of eight to 30. Classes are offered throughout the summer and winter, by arrangement, beginning in the late morning and continuing into the afternoon.

La Rua (604-932-5011) takes its name from the Spanish term for the archway entrance to European towns, yet the cuisine is international, with the Pacific Northwest influencing the menu. **Hy's Steakhouse** (604-905-5555) is one of Whistler's oldest eateries, with a menu specializing in grilled seafood, rotisserie chicken, prime rib, and Alberta steaks. Although **Les Deux Gros** (604-932-4611), west of the village, may be a bit removed from the mainstream, its traditional French menu has been worth the trip for years. It's one of the region's ongoing treats. **Umberto's Trattoria** (604-932-5858) looks as though it came straight out of Tuscany, with burnt-umber art-adorned walls and fixtures of wicker and iron, cool tiles, rich fabrics, and light streaming in from the outside.

Light Japanese cuisine can be found at **Sushi-Ya** (604-905-0155), with a menu that features traditional favorites and specialties such as Northern Light scallops, which is a green-bean tempura in rice, wrapped with avocado and sliced salmon. The spacious 140-seat **Araxi** (604-932-4540) is a village mainstay, offering an extensive and innovative menu. A separate wine room provides a semiprivate setting for group dinners for up to 18. During the summer, the 80-seat patio is great for people watching in the hub of the village square. The **Aubergine Grill** (604-935-4338), at the Westin Resort & Spa, offers caribou strip loin harvested by Nunavut hunters from the Far North—since you're in a special place, why not try something special?

ATTRACTIONS

Museums

BC Museum of Mining National Historic Site
On BC 99 on the way to Whistler
Britannia Beach
1-800-896-4044, ext. 227
www.bcmuseumofmining.org
Open (tours): 9–4:30 daily
Admission: $12.95 adults, $10.95 students and seniors (summer); $5 everyone (winter)
Wheelchair accessible: No

If being underground doesn't bother you, then the former Britannia Copper Mine—now a National Historic Site—is a world you wouldn't want to miss seeing. This was once the largest copper mine in the British Commonwealth. A guided underground tour on electric rail carts gives you an idea of what it was like drilling and retrieving ore. You can also pan for gold and keep it.

NIGHTLIFE AND OTHER PLEASURES

Every season at Whistler brings a host of "in" spots and new meeting places. Some are meat factories, others are more intimate. There are so many places for late evening activity that the first thing you should do when you arrive is check out the listings of night-time fun, ranging from sedate to pulsating; at the **Whistler Activity and Information Centre** (4010 Whistler Way; www.tourism whistler.com).

Garibaldi Lift Company Bar and Grill (604-905-2220) in Whistler Village is the latest of the town's "in" places, and it offers great entertainment throughout the year, which is one of the reason it's an après-fun hangout. Whistler's biggest and baddest nightclub is **Garfinkle's** (604-932-2323), a Whistler landmark serving up fresh DJs and live music every week, spinning a mixed bag of rock hits, funky classics, and hot dance tracks. At the crossroads of the Main Village and Village North, the two-level **Savage Beagle** (604-938-3337) has been one of Whistler's more popular nightclubs for many years. Upstairs, the mood is relaxed, while the downstairs is usually tightly packed, with upbeat music and bass pounding on the state-of-the-art sound system.

Moe Joe's (604-935-1152), located in the heart of Whistler Village, offers a mixture of weekly live music and DJs. Locals say it's a great, casual, fun-filled atmosphere to party in.

Buffalo Bill's (604-932-6613) attracts an over-30 crowd and also spices up the scene with regular comedy nights and hypnotists.

Of course, if your idea of a wild night out on the town is relaxing with a brew, there's no shortage of spots in Whistler. The **Dubh Linn Gate Irish Pub** (604-905-4047) at the Pan Pacific Hotel has Whistler's largest draft beer and whiskey selection, along with live music every night. **B.B.K.'s Pub** (604-932-9795) is the first pub in Whistler to be smoke free, and with only 24 seats it has created its own personality. It is the quiet alternative to the loud and noisy bars in the village, and as cozy as your living room. The **Boot Pub** (604-932-3338), Whistler's original watering hole, has been serving up the fun since before Whistler was the "in" place. Recently refurbished, with the addition of such goodies as a giant-screen TV and a smoke extraction system, it has bands every Friday and Monday nights.

If you want quiet sophistication, go to the Upper Village to the **Fairmont Chateau Whistler's Mallard Lounge** (604-938-2340), where soft music in elegant surroundings is guaranteed to calm nerves.

RECREATION

Whistler options are virtually endless. In summer, every hotel has outdoor activity programs. Some soft and hard adventure possibilities are listed here, but check out what's available by contacting the **Whistler Activity & Information Centre** (4010 Whistler Way; 604-938-2769, 1-877-991-9988).

Summer activities include skateboarding, rafting, tennis, wildlife viewing, fishing, mountain biking, horseback riding, in-line skating, hiking, swimming, and canoeing. Whistler has tennis courts that are free to the public, and the **Whistler Racquet Club** (604-932-1991) offers heated indoor courts open to the public all year-round. They also offer two- and three-day tennis camps from the beginning of June to the end of September, with coaching provided by Tennis Canada and USTA-certified instructors. The Chateau Whistler Resort's adult tennis camps offer two- and three-day tennis camps from the beginning of June to the end of September, with coaching provided by Tennis Canada and USTA-certified instructors.

Golf

Golf Digest has rated the Whistler area as the number-one golf resort in Canada. And all four Whistler-area golf courses (see below)—Nicklaus North, Big Sky, Chateau Whistler, and Whistler Golf Club—are award winners. Created by great designers—Robert Trent Jones Jr., Arnold Palmer, Jack Nicklaus, and Robert Cupp—they are all within a very short distance of one another, which means very little travel time. The season begins in May and ends in October. Greens fees depend on when you play a particular course; rates are greatly reduced for the shoulder seasons of May and September, and a variety of stay-and-play packages are available through hotels and tour companies.

In addition, there are courses near or on the way to and from Whistler that also rate among the finest in British Columbia. Even if you don't play the premium resort courses, there's plenty of affordable, demanding golf awaiting you in the Whistler area. One of the best bargains in the region is at the Pemberton Valley Golf and Country Club, located next to the Big Sky layout and nestled under majestic Mount Currie. And Squamish Valley Golf and Country Club on the way to Whistler—redesigned by architect Robert Muir Graves in 1992—will test your shot-making abilities just as readily as the resort courses.

Big Sky Golf and Country Club (1690 Airport Rd., Pemberton; 604-894-6106, 1-800-668-7900; www.bigskygolf.com)

Chateau Whistler Golf Club (4612 Blackcomb Way, Whistler; 1-800-684-6344; www.chateauwhistler.com)

Furry Creek Golf and Country Club (150 Country Club Road, Furry Creek; 604-896-2224; www.golfbc.com)

Nicklaus North Golf Course (8080 Nicklaus North Blvd., Whistler; 604-938-9898, 1-800-386-9898; www.nicklausnorth.com)

Pemberton Valley Golf Club (1730 Airport Rd., Pemberton; 1-800-390-4653; www.pembertongolf.com)

Squamish Valley Golf and Country Club (2458 Mamquam Rd., Squamish; 604-898-9691; www.squamishvalleygolf.com)

Whistler Golf Club (4001 Whistler Way, Whistler; 604-932-3280, 1-800-376-1777; www.whistlergolf.com)

Hiking

Numerous hiking trails permeate the Whistler region. The easiest is the Valley Trail, which links five lakes and numerous parks in the valley bottom, taking you past golf courses, through alpine resorts, and along rivers. You can walk or bike the trail. A nearby ghost town, a former logging community called Parkhurst, can be reached with a short hike or mountain-bike ride. You'll find remnants of houses and other buildings of a once-thriving mill town.

Patience and timing will bring you sightings of deer, hoary marmots, coyotes, and even wolves as you walk along some of the hiking trails. Loggers Lake—a volcanic crater lake—is a well-kept hiking secret that offers great views of the Cheakamus Valley and Black Tusk. Do it on your own or take the four-hour hike with one of Whistler's many guided tours. Keep your eyes open for black bears that wander along the open ski trails grazing on clover, grass, and horsetail. They sleep from November to March, but each spring black bear families emerge from their dens, feed on native plant species and berries, rear their young, seek out new mates, and feed some more. Join a **bear watching tour** (Whistler Activity & Information Centre, 604-938-2769, 1-877-991-9988) with local expert Michael Allen to learn how Whistler's local black bear population and Whistler's 10,000 human residents have learned to live alongside one another.

Skiing

At Whistler, as at Vail, Colorado, or any number of European ski resorts, Hollywood stars hide behind sunglasses and goggles, and corporate execs and politicians live out their own winter fantasies far from the ordinary folk. Still, the snow is real, the mountains are spectacular, the village is fresh and contemporary, and you don't have to sell the family treasures to have a great time.

The two mountains—7,500-foot (2286 m) Blackcomb and 7,200-foot (2195 m) Whistler Blackcomb—have the two tallest vertical drops of any resort on the continent: 5,200 feet

(1585 m) and 5,180 feet (1579 m), respectively. To get from one mountain to the other, you simply ski down to the edge of the village site and hop aboard a lift up the other mountain. The runs fall into the village like a giant V, with the village sitting at the point of the V.

The season opens in mid-November, and spring skiing, with sunshine and corn snow, lasts into May. There's an average 450-inch (1143 cm) snowfall annually, with some artificial snow added at the lower level. Because of the West Coast weather patterns, you can experience widely varying snow conditions from top to bottom.

You can't get bored at Whistler. With more than 200 runs, the variety of skiing available on the two mountains is unlimited; 33 lifts transport 59,000 skiers an hour. The longest run on both mountains is 7 miles (11 k) long. There are 12 bowls, three glaciers, and more than 200 marked trails—steep powder chutes, challenging mogul fields, secluded tree skiing, and groomed-to-perfection cruising runs—that offer skiers and snowboarders endless enjoyment. And snowboarders, in addition to using the entire mountain, have seven different runs.

The terrain mix at Whistler/Blackcomb is 20 percent novice, 55 percent intermediate, and 25 percent expert. Ski programs are designed for specific age groups: Wee Scamps for three- to six-year-olds; Ski Scamps for seven- to 12-year-olds without experience; and Super Scamps for seven- to 12-year-olds with experience.

While you're on the hills, you have 17 restaurants to choose from, excluding those that are in the village itself. The roundhouse at the 6,420-foot (1957 m) level provides one of the most spectacular rest and restaurant sites anywhere; the Coast Mountain range seems to touch the horizon in all directions.And, of course, there's a lot of other winter sports, too: cat skiing, heli-skiing, heli-tours, and dogsledding on nearby glaciers and undeveloped peaks; sleigh riding, snowmobiling, snowshoeing, and cross-country skiing; tennis; or just lounging around in a spa. Cross-country trails have been cut throughout the area, most leaving from the village. Information for all of these activities is found at the **Whistler Activity and Information Centre** (604-938-2769, 1-877-991-9988).

EVENTS

Winter brings more than just skiing to Whistler. Fun events include the **Telus Winter Classic** (604-938-7321) in late January, an action-packed weekend featuring ski events, food and wine galore, auctions, and entertainment. January 26 is Australia Day, which is celebrated in Whistler since so many of the people who work there are young Aussies. June and July brings the **Whistler Jazz and Blues Festival** (604-938-2769) with jazz, blues, Latin, swing, and gospel at free and ticketed venues. The **Whistler Comedy Festival** (604-938-2769) headlines comedy talent in November. Also in November is **Cornucopia,** (604-938-2769) Whistler's five-day food and wine celebration, with 50 top wineries from around British Columbia, Washington, Oregon, and California having tastings, dinners, and seminars.

Victoria

The old description of Victoria is that it's a place where old people go—to visit their parents. Although impressions are difficult to change, the reality is that Victoria, while retaining its old-country charm and relaxed atmosphere, is a vibrant city with plenty to do and things to see. With a major university, an active night scene, and thousands of government workers, the city long ago outgrew its "retirement" image.

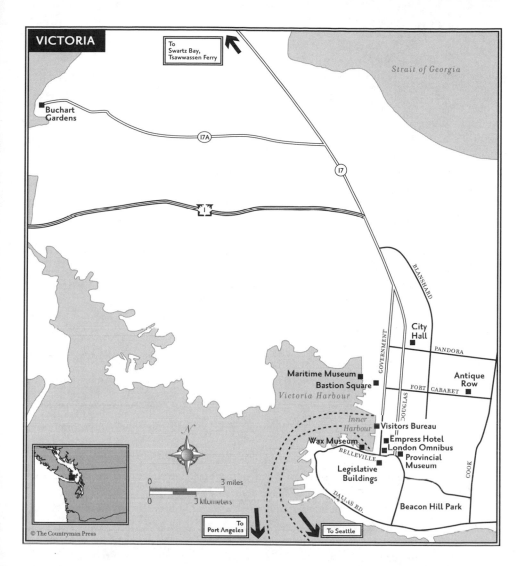

The city was founded in 1843 as a Hudson's Bay Company fort, and it has preserved its history of British customs. Victoria is British Columbia's capital, located on the Saanich Peninsula, on the southeastern tip of Vancouver Island.

Many of Victoria's major tourist attractions, such as the stately Fairmont Empress Hotel, Legislative Buildings, museums, and galleries, surround the picture-perfect Inner Harbour within a few blocks of the downtown core. In the summer, horse-drawn carriages or double-decker buses (the city is more British than Great Britain) get you around the center of town. Almost every tour begins and ends in front of either the Legislative Buildings or the Fairmont Empress Hotel, where the double-decker buses are located. If you are pressed for time, the three most important places to visit are the Royal British Columbia Museum, Butchart Gardens, and the Fairmont Empress Hotel.

GETTING THERE

Visitors from the Lower Mainland of British Columbia travel to the Saanich Peninsula by ferry from the **BC Ferries Tsawwassen terminal** in Delta (250-386-3431 (US); 1-888-223-3779 (BC); www.bcferries.com). To reach the Tsawwassen terminal, drive south on Oak Street to Hwy. 99 toward the U.S. border and exit at Hwy. 17, just past the Deeqs Island Tunnel. Drive south on Hwy. 17. to the Tsawwassen terminal. Total driving time is about 40 minutes. Sailing time is 90 minutes for the 27 miles (44 km) across the Strait of Georgia to the Swartz Bay terminal, 20 miles (32 km) north of Victoria. To get to Victoria from Swartz Bay, exit the ferry onto Hwy. 17 and keep going south 20 miles (32 km). You'll end up at downtown Victoria and the Legislative Buildings in about 25 minutes.

A more convenient way is by a round-trip bus tour with the **Maverick** (604-940-2332) or **Pacific Coach** (604-662-7575) lines, which leave from many downtown Vancouver hotels. For quicker access, take a **Helijet** (604-273-1414) or one of **Harbour Air**'s (604-688-0212) floatplanes for service from downtown Vancouver to downtown Victoria. Both Vancouver terminals are along the waterfront.

From the United States, you can get to Victoria via ferry from Seattle, Anacortes in northwest Washington, or Port Angeles on the Olympic Peninsula.

From Seattle, the **Victoria Clipper** (2701 Alaskan Way, Pier 69, Seattle waterfront; 206-448-5000, 1-800-888-2535; www.victoriaclipper.com) makes a two- to three-hour trip through spectacular inland waters past the San Juan Islands. The company operates four high-speed passenger-only catamarans from the Seattle waterfront to Victoria's Inner Harbour. The *Victoria Clipper IV*, which has gas turbines and can travel at speeds of up to 40 knots, is known as one of the fastest passenger vessels in the Western Hemisphere, making the Seattle–Victoria trip in just two hours. Fares vary depending on season and destination. Special packages and discount fares for seniors, children, and groups are available throughout the year.

From Anacortes (on Fidalgo Island near the Washington mainland, via WA 20 and I-5 about 62 miles/100 km north of Seattle), **Washington State Ferries**' (206-464-6400, 1-888-808-7977; www.wsdot.wa.gov/ferries) Anacortes–San Juan Islands–Sydney route winds through the beautiful San Juan Islands (with stops at four of the largest islands) to Sydney on Vancouver Island, just north of Victoria, April through October. The Washington State Ferries terminal in Sydney is 3 miles (5 km) south of Swartz Bay. Exit the ferry on Ocean Avenue and drive along the seashore to Lochside, where you'll turn right and proceed one block to McTavish; turn left and drive to Hwy. 17. Turn left onto the highway and follow the signs south to Victoria.

From Port Angeles on the Olympic Peninsula, two ferries travel to Victoria. **Blackball Transport Inc.** (360-457-4491, 250-386-2202) operates a car and passenger ferry, the MV *Coho*. From midspring through early fall, **Victoria Rapid Transport Inc.**, (604-361-9144, 1-800-633-1589; www.victoriaexpress.com) offers a passenger-only ferry, the *Victoria Express*, between the two cities. The Olympic and Saanich peninsulas are separated by the Strait of Juan de Fuca, a 17-mile (27 km) stretch of (almost) open ocean. The MV *Coho* and the *Victoria Express* both dock in Victoria's Inner Harbour close to the Legislative Buildings and the Empress Hotel.

Accommodations

Accommodations in Victoria span a wide range from inexpensive to very expensive. The best source for hotels and motels is the **Tourism Victoria Information Center** (812 Wharf St.; 604-382-2127; www.tourismvictoria.com). It is located at the waterfront, across from the Fairmont Empress Hotel, and is open daily from 9 a.m. to 5:30 p.m. Most Vancouver Island information is also available here.

High tea at the Butchart Gardens Tearoom Courtesy of Butchart Gardens

The Italian Garden at Butchart Gardens Courtesy of Butchart Gardens

ATTRACTIONS

Whatever you do in Victoria, set aside time for high tea. It is a set menu of honeyed crumpets, scones with cream and jam, and finger sandwiches. Reservations are usually a must, and proper dress is required, in very British style, meaning no shorts or T-shirts. Elegant-casual is the general mode of dress. High tea is served at the Fairmont Empress Hotel (see Historic Buildings and Sites) at 1 p.m., 2:30 p.m., and 4 p.m., as well as at other places in Victoria, such as the Butchart Gardens Tearoom (see Gardens and Parks).

Gardens and Parks

For spectacular views of the Olympic Mountains, go for a strol in historic **Beacon Hill Park,** (www.beaconhillpark.ca), at the foot of Douglas Street near the Legislative Buildings. It was the site of a village that had been inhabited for thousands of years. In 1956 renowned Native American artist Mungo Martin and his team raised the world's tallest free-standing totem pole, at 128 feet (38.8 m), which still stands here. **Thunderbird Park,** (675 Belleville Street) adjacent to the Royal British Columbia Museum, displays an impressive collection of totem poles of the First Nations of coastal British Columbia. With the enriched perspective that such a visit brings, you'll look at the landscape with new interest and appreciation.

Butchart Gardens
800 Benvenuto Ave.
Brentwood Bay
250-652-5256
www.butchartgardens.com

Open: 9–9 daily in summer; reduced hours in winter
Admission: $22 adults in summer, with discounts for seniors, students, children;
$5.25 for everyone in winter
Wheelchair accessible: Yes

Here is one of the great horticultural destinations in North America, with 55 acres (22 hectares) of floral displays and some 5,000 varieties of flowers. It draws thousands of visitors every year. Once a limestone quarry, it was transformed in 1904 when Canadian cement pioneer Robert Butchart began building bridges and walkways and planting shrubs and flowers within his 125-acre (50.5 hectares) estate. A perfection of detail has gone into the thematic gardens. In the Italian Garden, the Japanese Garden, and the English Rose Garden are many of the plants the Butcharts collected on their personal worldwide tours. The gardens are located 12.5 miles (20 km) north of Victoria and 4 miles (7 km) south of the Swartz Bayferry terminal.

Historic Buildings and Sites

The Inner Harbour area in front of the Fairmont Empress Hotel and the Legislative Buildings is one of the busiest places in the city. A walkway below Government Street takes you dockside for an Inner Harbour walk along Belleville Street, where you will find the **Royal London Wax Museum** (250-388-4461), with its 300 wax figures of famous people. The oldest part of Victoria is near Centennial Square between Government and Douglas Streets and Pandora and Fisgard Streets. The buildings in this area date from 1880 and 1890. **Victoria City Hall** (1 Centennial Sq., at Pandora and Douglas Sts.), originally constructed in 1878, has high, arched windows and a clock tower.

The foyer of the historic Fairmont Empress Hotel in Victoria Courtesy of Fairmont Hotels

Fairmont Empress Hotel

721 Government St.
Inner Harbour
250-384-8100

The Fairmont Empress is a symbol both of the city and of Canada's links with the Canadian Pacific Railway (CPR). Originally opened in 1908, the hotel is one of the great châteaux built by CPR (others include Château Frontenac in Quebec City, Château Laurier in Ottawa, Château Lake Louise in Banff, and the Banff Springs Hotel as the railway moved east to west). The high, beamed ceiling and wood floors lend a historic and traditional atmosphere to the Empress's high tea. In the basement is a historical collection of photos and items from the hotel's history. Try the exotic Bengal Lounge for a light lunch. At night, the Empress Hotel is floodlit.

The Legislative Buildings
501 Belleville St.
Inner Harbour
250-387-3046

The Legislative Buildings dominate the Inner Harbour. On the sides of the building that was completed in 1897 is a statue of of Sir James Douglas, who chose the location of Victoria, and one of Sir Matthew Baille Begbie, the man in charge of law and order during the gold rush era. Atop the building's dome is a gilded statue of Capt. George Vancouver, who first sailed around Vancouver Island. In front of the building is a statue of Queen Victoria. At night, the building is outlined by 3,000 lights. Tours of the Legislative Buildings (in any of six languages) are available several times during the day, but times change seasonally; call ahead.

At night, Victoria's Legislative Buildings are ablaze with 3,000 lights. Courtesy of Butchart Gardens

Museums
At the **Royal Maritime Museum** (250-385-4222), dugout canoes, model ships, Royal Navy charts, photographs, uniforms, and bells chronicle Victoria's seafaring history. The building was the city's original courthouse. A little-used 90-year-old open-cage lift, believed to be the oldest in North America, ascends to the third floor.

Royal British Columbia Museum
675 Belleville St.
Inner Harbour
250-356-7226, 1-888-447-7977
www.rbcm.gov.bc.ca
Open: 9–6:30 daily Jul–Oct; 9–5 daily rest of year
Admission: $22.50 adults; discounts for seniors and youth
Wheelchair accessible: Yes

Across the street from the Legislative Buildings, the museum chronicles the impact that nature has had on humans. It's a Disneyland of science and humanities, a place where adults and children can wander for hours in a world that appeals to each person's intellectual level. The time sequence starts in the 20th century and then you're taken back in time 12,000 years. You confront a towering woolly mammoth, walk through prehistoric forests. You explore the streets of a turn-of-the-20th-century town, and you experience the First Peoples' Gallery, the Totem Pole and Art Gallery, and the Kwakiutl Indian Bighouse. Exhibits are arranged so that you follow the ring of time through the industrial era to the early days of fur trading and exploration. Then you move forward from early examples of humans in British Columbia to the effects of modern history on the Native American cultures.

Recreation

When you're in Victoria, you're really not far from the wilderness. Vancouver Island is a wonderful place to see wildlife and to explore the ocean. Land mammals such as black bears, cougars, deer, and elk can often be seen along Vancouver Island's back roads and highways, especially in the pristine wilderness of the island's northern and Pacific Rim regions.

One of the area's biggest tourist attractions is whale watching, and you'll never forget seeing a massive orca breaching out of the deep water only 328 feet (100 m) from your boat. Tours can be taken from Victoria as well as from several other communities on the island. Several companies specialize in whale-watching tours—information is available at **Tourism Victoria** (812 Wharf Street; 250-953-2033; www.tourismvictoria.com). The office has a wide variety of tours and information about accommodations, dining, and events taking place in Victoria and throughout Vancouver Island. Tour operators strictly follow the regulations for viewing marine life, as outlined by the Department of Fisheries and Oceans. The best time to see migrating whales off Vancouver Island is in March and April, although about 50 of the gray whales don't migrate and instead spend their summers feeding in Clayquot Sound (near Tofina on Vancouver Island's west coast) and in nearby Barkley Sound. Orcas (killer whales) that live in local waters are best seen from May through December when they are at their feeding grounds in and around Johnson Strait, along the northeast side of Vancouver Island.

Golfers can combine their game with boating. Many marinas on Vancouver Island and the Gulf Islands are close to golf courses, and some clubs even provide boating golfers with free shuttle service to their courses. Vancouver Island golfing and fishing packages are also available from many fishing lodges. Check with **Tourism Victoria**, across the street from the Fairmont Empress Hotel, for information and booking.

Shopping

It's easy to shop in Victoria because virtually everything is centralized, and the city offers specialized items. Begin at the Empress Hotel and walk north along Government Street; in quick succession, you'll encounter specialty shops and quaint boutiques selling English woolens for men and women, Native American art, and foods.

One block northwest of City Hall is Chinatown. In the 1870s, Victoria's Chinatown was the largest one north of San Francisco's, with a population of nearly 10,000 people working in the coal mines, building the railway, and searching for gold. Few Chinese people now live in the area, but many quaint shops and traditional restaurants are still owned and operated by members of the Asian community.

Market Square (560 Johnson St.) is a collection of funky shops in a complex (five blocks northwest from the Empress Hotel along Wharf St.) where, in 1887, some 23 factories produced 90,000 pounds of opium a year for what was then a legal business. Be sure to walk **Fan Tan Alley** (off Fisgard St. between Government and Store Sts.), Canada's narrowest "street," which measures about three shoulder widths. South of Chinatown and north of the Empress—virtually between the two—is **Bastion Square**, with its gas lamps, restaurants, cobblestone streets, and small shops.

If you turn right at Fort Street and walk four blocks, you'll come to **Antique Row** (between Blanshard and Cook Sts.). Victoria has 60-plus antiques shops, many of them along Antique Row, specializing in coins, stamps, estate jewelry, rare books, crystal, china, furniture, paintings, and other works of art.

Events

As in Vancouver, there's hardly a month that goes by without some kind of special event. But, unlike its sister city to the east, Victoria takes a more conservative approach to its celebrations. The population is simply, well, less raucous. Information for all these events is available from **Tourism Victoria** (812 Wharf Street; 250-953-2033) www.tourismvictoria.com).

January

History at Butchart Gardens (250-652-4422; www.butchartgardens.com) Every year the gardens present a demonstration on how a rock quarry eventually became one of North America's finest flower gardens; late January through early March.

February

Victoria Independent Film and Video Festival (250-389-0444; www.vifvf.com) More than 150 screenings of indy films and videos that most theatres never see; early February.

Chinese New Year (250-920-0881; www.oldchinatown.com) Much like the Vancouver festival, though on a smaller scale, the Victoria event includes a parade, firecrackers, and music; variably in mid-February.

Victoria Festival of Wine (250-595-0277; www.bcwineguys.com) Two days of tastings pits BC wines against international competition; mid-February.

Flower Count (250-414-6985; www.tourismvictoria.com/flowercount) The residents of Victoria count all of the flowers in their gardens, report the numbers, and then Tourism Victoria sends the figure to the rest of Canada, 99 per cent of which is under a blanket of snow; last week in February.

March

Antique and Collectible Show (250-744-1807) This is the largest antique show on Vancouver Island; last week in March.

April

BCYBA Victoria Harbour Floating Show (250-245-8910; www.bcmta.com/bcyba /04shows /vicboatshow) This collection and sale of pre-owned boats brings gawkers and potential buyers of yachts and speedboats to the Victoria Inner Harbour waterfront; late April.

Victoria Hot Jazz Jubilee (250-882-5299; www.victoria-hot-jazz.com) This new music festival has a small collection of musicians, but they come from throughout North America; mid-month.

May

Fort Rod Hill Military Historic Encampment (250-478-5849; www.tourismvictoria.com) Actors and participants reenact Victoria's military past as an early-Canadian outpost; late May.

Swiftsure Race (250-592-9098; www.swiftsure.org) A Victoria Day celebration (May 24 is Queen Victoria's birthday and a national holiday) where some 90 or so sailboats compete in the annual Swiftsure Race in the Starit of Juan de Fuca (Last weekend in May).

Victoria Conservatory of Music Garden Tour (250-386-5311; www.vcm.bc.ca) Selected gardens throughout Victoria are open for tours; many feature performances by music students; early May.

June
Tall Ships Festival (250-953-2033; www.gvedcvictoria.com/TallShips/tallships/index .html) While there will be a variety of activities from concerts to sailing races, waterside barbeques, maritime-themed activities, and theater productions, the main focus will be the 30 tall ships themselves from around the world that are making Victoria their first stop in a series of ports worldwide; late June. The Tall Ships Festival is part of a summer-long series of maritime events throughout Victoria.

July
Victoria International Garden and Flower Festival (250-381-7894; www.flowerand garden.ca) Held downtown at Market Square, this festival brings exhibitors and gardeners together for a flower frenzy; late July.

August
Dragonboat Festival (250-704-2500; www.victoriadragonboat.com) These dragonboat races bring competitors from throughout the Pacific Northwest; mid-August.

Fringe Theatre Festival (250-383-2663; www.intrepidtheatre.com) Similar to Vancouver's Fringe Festival, but smaller; late August/early September.

October
Royal Victoria Marathon (250-382-0042; www.royalvictoriamarathon.com) This annual race is run through downtown and the waterfront suburb of Oak Bay; early October.

November
Fall Salmon Run (250-953-2033; www.scholefieldhouse.com/eventscalendar/salmon run.htm) Salmon return to the Goldstream River to spawn practically right in downtown Victoria; through November.

December
Christmas At Emily Carr House (250-383-5843; www.emilycarr.com) This is where artist Emily Carr was born and every Christmas she is celebrated with an arts and crafts sale of works by local artists; through December.

Index

LODGING BY PRICE

DINING BY PRICE

DINING BY CUISINE